ASIA 2030
THE UNFOLDING FUTURE

ASIA 2030
THE UNFOLDING FUTURE

Editors: Ajey Lele, Namrata Goswami, Rumel Dahiya

Lancer • New Delhi • Frankfort, IL
www.lancerpublishers.com

LANCER

Published in the United States by

The Lancer International Inc
19558 S. Harlem Ave., Suite 1,
Frankfort, IL. 60423.

First published in India by

Lancer Publishers & Distributors
2/42 (B) Sarvapriya Vihar,
New Delhi-110016

Printed and bound in India.

ISBN-13: 978-1-935501-22-0 • ISBN-10: 1-935501-22-4

Online Military Bookshop
www.lancerpublishers.com

IDR Net Edition
www.indiandefencereview.com

Contents

About the Authors

Air. Cmde (Retd). Ramesh Phadke is a retired Air Commodore and is associated with the Institute for Defence Studies and Analyses, New Delhi.

Mr. A. Vinod Kumar is an Associate Fellow at the Institute for Defence Studies and Analyses, New Delhi.

Dr. Cherian Samuel is an Associate Fellow at the Institute for Defence Studies and Analyses, New Delhi.

Mr. Avinash Godbole is a Researcher at the Institute for Defence Studies and Analyses, New Delhi.

Mr. Sanjeev Shrivastav is a Researcher at the Institute for Defence Studies and Analyses, New Delhi.

Col (Retd). Ali Ahmed is a Research Fellow at the Institute for Defence Studies and Analyses, New Delhi.

Col. Harinder Singh is a Research Fellow at the Institute for Defence Studies and Analyses, New Delhi.

Dr. Medha Bisht is an Associate Fellow at the Institute for Defence Studies and Analyses, New Delhi.

Dr. Priyanka Singh is an Associate Fellow at the Institute for Defence Studies and Analyses, New Delhi.

Dr. Nihar Nayak is an Associate Fellow at the Institute for Defence Studies and Analyses, New Delhi.

Col (Retd.) P.K. Gautam is a Research Fellow at the Institute for Defence Studies and Analyses, New Delhi.

Dr. Anand Kumar is an Associate Fellow at the Institute for Defence Studies and Analyses, New Delhi.

Mr. S. Samuel C. Rajiv is an Associate Fellow at the Institute for Defence Studies and Analyses, New Delhi.

Dr. Pankaj Jha is an Associate Fellow at the Institute for Defence Studies and Analyses, New Delhi.

Ms. Pranamita Baruah is a Researcher at the Institute for Defence Studies and Analyses, New Delhi.

Ms. Gunjan Singh is a Researcher at the Institute for Defence Studies and Analyses, New Delhi.

Dr. Ishida Yasuyuki was a Visiting Fellow at the Institute for Defence Studies and Analyses, New Delhi.

Foreword

It gives us immense pleasure to place before the strategic community, *Asia 2030: The Unfolding Future.* While it is widely agreed that the future can never be accurately predicted, it is important to work out a range of alternative future possibilities so that we are not taken by surprise when events unfold in international politics. A serious exercise on the future can therefore offer some guideposts to planners, policy makers and those interested in international politics and security. The Asian century is one such issue that requires serious future study so that we learn from history and not repeat the mistakes of the past, plagued by terrible devastation of mankind, as we move ahead.

The contemporary rise of Asia propelled by the rapid development of countries like China and India is one of the most watched phenomenons of the 21st century. Indeed, if projections by reputed organizations like the National Intelligence Council (NIC) of the US and the Development, Concepts and Doctrine Centre (DCDC) of the UK are taken into account, the global transfer of wealth from the West to the East at the scale as is happening today has never been witnessed in any earlier epoch of human history. Hence, most future analysts argue that the health and nature of the international system by 2030 will be mostly dependent on the internal health and external policies of countries like China and India on issues ranging from internal political developments, economic policies, governance issues to external issues like nuclear proliferation, arms control, space, climate change, war and peace, and international institutions.

The uniqueness of the rise of Asia is vindicated by the fact that while most systemic changes in international politics have been the consequence of either inter-state wars (the Napoleonic Wars, World

War I and II) or heightened state tensions backed by military force as was the case between the two ideological blocs (the Cold War between the US and the USSR), Asia's current rise is mostly peaceful and rather smooth without overt show of military strength or threats to subvert the international system as it exist today. However, the rise of China has been creating apprehensions amongst the strategic community especially in the West as China is an authoritarian state and has a non-transparent political system. Since the media in China is also closely monitored and controlled by the Chinese state, information on China's military modernization and intentions at the international level are suspect. India on the other hand, with its democratic political system, free media, and transparent civil society invokes much more confidence amongst the nations of the world as a country with benign intentions. Hence, India's considerable defence spending unlike China's do not create tensions at the global level as India has the reputation of being a responsible global actor and is keenly entwined with the UN system of global governance.

This book is an effort to understand how the future will unfold in Asia in 2030 keeping these sensibilities in sharp relief. It is also important to examine whether Asian states will continue with the present pace of their economic growth or lose momentum and undo the change occurring today at the regional and systemic level of international politics. Various chapters in the book have addressed issues ranging from air power, cyber security, climate change, ballistic missile defence to geo-political and regional issues pertaining to East Asia, South East Asia, West Asia and South Asia. The authors of these chapters are mostly young Indian scholars in the age group ranging from 25 to 35 and hence their views on the rise of Asia are significant since they will be living the future they have so described.

It is our hope that this modest attempt will help in generating an informed debate on issues critical to Asia and offer certain clarity about the way our own scholars view the nature and character of strategic issues in Asia in 2030.

Editors

Introduction

The rise of Asia: an inevitable consequence of history with the present powerful winds of change propelling a future that belongs to Asians.

The art of imagination and creativity are assets set aside for the human race. This power enables us not only to seriously analyze and describe what occurred in the past and give a sense of the present but also equips us with an ability to envision to an extent what the future trajectory of life as a whole will have in store for us. This future imaginative exercise is especially critical in areas of security studies and international politics given the fast paced nature of the winds of change that states have to grapple with at the systemic level.

Whatever the past history of relations between nations have been, it is one of the key requirements of policy studies to offer alternative future scenarios on issues of change in order to equip statesmen with an understanding on a range of alternative possibilities regarding the future. Once that is done and over with, the perceptive genius of the statesmanship of men and women who deal with the everyday possibilities of international politics (ruled by anarchy) and its uniquely opposite domestic variant (ruled by order) should take over and offer a guideline on human affairs in matters intrinsically political.[1] The rise of Asia is one such issue that needs special focus since it has been argued that "the international system---as constructed following the Second World War---will be almost unrecognizable by 2025 owing to the rise of emerging powers, a globalizing economy, an historic transfer of relative strength and economic power from the West to the

---

1   Isaiah Berlin, "On Political Judgment", *The New York Review of Books*, 43/5, 1996, pp. 1–28.

East".[2] Important to note is the fact that this kind of speedy transfer of power has never been witnessed before in any phase of human history. The global projections for countries like Brazil, Russia, India, and China (BRICS) forecast that they collectively will match the original G-7 combined global GDP share by 2040-2050. In 2010 China has become the second largest economy in the world surpassing Japan and a military power of global dimensions, and India will be the third largest economic power in the next two to three years.

Significantly, according to *Global Trends 2025*, China and India are not following the Western liberal model of development.[3] Instead they are following a kind of "state-capitalism" in which the state has a prominent role to play in economic management based on strict regulatory mechanisms for the market, although in India the trend has significantly changed. Interestingly, other Asian countries like South Korea, Taiwan and Singapore are also following the same economic model. This economic mechanism has stood these countries in good stead during the global financial crisis of 2008 in which the developed world faced recession like situations whereas the economies of India and China remained largely unaffected and showed robust GDP growth patterns.

Due to the enormous importance of future forecasting in world politics and especially on the rise of China and India in the 21st century, it is critical that such work is done in a systematic and serious manner. This is all the more important given that the 20th century has been largely dominated by devastating wars in its first phase, a Cold War till 1991 followed by the rise of extremism, and religious terrorism in the post cold war period. Now, one could make realistic assumptions about the future based on solid research and a good sense of reality. However, future forecasting/predictions are not always on target and hence have to be taken with healthy skepticism and not as absolute truths on a particular subject matter. The conclusions arrived at have also to be revisited from time to time and reevaluated in light of changing scenarios.

---

2   *Global Trends 2025: A Transformed World*, National Intelligence Council, Washington DC, 2008, p. vi.

3   Ibid, p. vii.

Dr. Lee DeForest (1883-1961) 'the father of radio and the grandfather of television' who had invented the vacuum tube that helped start the 'age of electronics' had once said that "man will never reach the moon regardless of all future scientific advances". History proved him wrong in 1969. But, he is not the only one to predict the future and go totally wrong. Thomas Watson, chairman of IBM, had predicted in 1943 that "there is a world market for maybe five supercomputers." In 1981, Microsoft founder Bill Gates had said that "640K ought to be enough for anybody". How wrong they proved to be given the rapid expansion of information technology and computer software. On the other hand, people like Sir Arthur Clarke (1917-2008) have been correct with most of his predictions. Almost three decades before the US Apollo moon mission, he had predicted that man would reach the moon by 1970s. He also predicted interplanetary travel many decades before the idea became germane. Andrew W. Marshall, the Pentagon's futurist-in-chief who has been the Director of the Office of Net Assessment since the time of the Nixon Administration successfully predicted the end of the Cold War and in conceptualizing Star Wars (Strategic Defence initiative, SDI) during the 1980s which is becoming a reality in the 21st century as the initiative on missile defence.

All these lead to the basic assumption that forecasting the future is difficult but not impossible. Some of the above observations made by a few great minds which do not match with existing reality should not be viewed as an attempt to portray their intellectual shallowness. Rather, they are indicative of the fact that foretelling the future is an intricate activity even for such creative thinkers. Conversely, the success achieved by few in envisaging the future indicates that it is worth an attempt to prognosticate the future. More importantly, as Andrew Marshall has once articulated that "when it comes to predicting the future, it is better to err on the side of being unimaginative".

Prognostication of the future is normally done based on present information. However, it is not necessary that the future will always evolve based on present events. This becomes more significant when one is attempting to visualize the status of social and developmental issues two or three decades into the future. It becomes even more difficult now since the challenges to humanity in the 21ˢᵗ century are far too many in comparison with the earlier periods. These challenges include both military and non-military threats. While it is critical that we find amicable solutions to these challenges to humankind, states have an unenviable task of developing a better understanding about the likely future of such challenges. In view of this it is essential to explore possible and probable futures. Such assessment in turn would help the policy makers to plan for tomorrow.

For future analysts, the biggest obstacle for any predictive exercise is to avoid getting trapped in his/her individual biases. At times, such trappings occur because the analyst either knowingly or instinctively takes into consideration various factors which he/she feels are important for assessment mostly based on past experiences. It is necessary therefore to ask correct questions particularly 'why' and 'how' past trends might change and what effect such changes will have on one's assumptions. Naturally, such assessments do bring in prejudices in the analysis. Also, predicting likely future trends cannot be accomplished by taking into account a single viewpoint. It requires an exercise which accounts for different perspectives on a single issue including the ability to anticipate future events based on structured analysis. It demands a combination of putting a wide array of expertise together. It also involves carrying out assessments based on historical facts and analysis of data by using some statistical and extrapolation techniques. While doing so, at every stage there is a need for the researcher to bring in his/her visualization capabilities into play. It is important to visualize future not only from the point of view of deriving a solitary outcome but to identify a group of likely possibilities adequately, by catering for surprises. Future studies are important for any nation-state to device a strategic planning approach. They could be of more relevance particularly in the present era of greater uncertainties. It is important to undertake such studies because there is a need to be proactive about the future and it is always better to avoid surprises as far as possible.

Even if future is forecasted correctly, many a time the prevailing circumstances can render one's judgment irrelevant. Alan Kay, an American computer scientist who had once famously said that 'the best way to predict the future is to invent it' mentions in one of his writings that "the railroads made a study after World War I which showed that for as far as they could see into the future, aircraft transportation would always be more expensive than railroad transportation. They're still right today; it's still more expensive. The problem is the railroads are almost gone because nobody cares if air travel is more expensive, they're willing to pay for it. The railroad industry missed the idea that not everything is a commodity market, and that price is important, but there are also value markets where people are willing to pay extra for extra value".[4]

This indicates the requirement of choosing correct variables for the analysis. At times slight changes in input parameters make the predictive analysis look totally different. This could happen because this form of statistical analysis relies heavily on arresting the connections between the explanatory variables and the predicted variables from past events. Predictions based on regression techniques also take into account relationships between dependent and independent variables. Such techniques play a major role towards finding solutions to scientific or economic problems. Mathematical models are even available for finding solutions to complex problems from social science sphere. But it is very difficult to quantify few variables which essentially are much more influenced by human behaviour. Hence, forecasting events related to geopolitics-wars, political power shifts, community behaviour, failing states, poverty, social unrest etc. are difficult, if not impossible, to predict entirely based on mathematical formulation. In order to make some sense of such a complex reality, the method of scenario-building is perhaps one of the best research techniques available to us to enable the crafting of plausible futures in the realm of policy making since both tangible and intangible factors can be considered in this exercise.

---

4   Alan C. Kay, "Predicting The Future", *www.ecotopia.com/webpress/futures.htm, accessed on Nov 10, 2009.*

THE METHOD OF SCENARIO-BUILDING

As a research technique, scenario building was pioneered by Herman Kahn in the 1950s while working at RAND. He was followed by Ted Newland, Pierre Wack and most importantly by Jay Ogilvy, Paul Hawken, and Peter Schwartz.[5] From a purely definitional point of view, Kahn and Weiner defined scenarios "as hypothetical sequences of events constructed for the purpose of focusing attention on causal processes and decision points".[6] Scenarios are not so much about predicting the future based on a short term analyses. Rather, they are about "perceiving" the future based on long term analyses of an issue with a particular purpose/goal in mind. According to Peter Schwartz, "Scenarios provide a context for thinking clearly about the otherwise complex array of factors that affect any decision; give a common language to decision makers for talking about these factors, and encourage them to think about a series of "what if" stories; help lift the "blinkers" that limit creativity and resourcefulness; and lead to organizations thinking strategically and continuously learning about key decisions and priorities".[7]

It must be, however, kept in mind that scenarios have a high degree of uncertainty tagged to them. Therefore, studying the future based on the scenario-building method is mostly an activity based on conjectures. With that caveat in mind, it is important to note that the method of scenario-building is one of the most accepted techniques of making some sense of an ever dynamic and complex future. It enables us to grasp a whole range of forces, factors, and possibilities that we could take note of while planning for the future.

The Importance of Scenario-Building for Policy

- Scenarios are stories or narratives that portray what

5   Peter Schwartz, *The Art of the Long View: Planning for the future in an Uncertain World*, Doubleday, New York, 1996.

6   H. Kahn and A. Weiner, *The Year 2000 A Framework for Speculation on the Next Thirty Three Years*, Macmillan, New York, 1967, p. 12.

7   Peter Schwartz as quoted in John C. Ratcliffe, "Scenario-building: A Suitable Method for Strategic Construction Industry Planning?", Dublin Institute of Technology, Ireland, 2006, p. 3.

might happen, why it might happen, and with what
consequences;

- Scenarios are powerful tools to contemplate the range of
possible futures that could develop from the influence of
key drivers, events and issues;

- Scenarios make policy makers aware of where one might be
going right or wrong;

- Scenarios face the challenges of the future;

- Scenarios stimulate critical thinking and challenges key
assumptions on the part of policy makers.

- Scenario-building equips policy/decision-makers to explore
all plausible future scenarios in order to inform their present
process of decision-making and planning. In other words,
scenarios brings to sharp relief underlying variables/drivers
which emerge as a result of interactions between the factors
that make up the reality of past and present environments;

- Scenarios help in making new decisions by fresh
considerations of a situation;

- Scenarios help reframe issues;

- Scenarios provide recommendations on how one adapts or
should do in the new emerging circumstances.

- Scenarios help in developing policy and strategy.

The key to scenario building is the ability to bring new thinking
to bear on a subject matter. As Ratcliffe argues" Good scenarios always
challenge and surprise---bad ones merely confirm current conceptions
and perpetuate personal prejudices".[8]

LIMITATIONS OF THE SCENARIO-BUILDING METHOD

Based on the above, it can be said without doubt that futuristic
scenario-building can be used to identify, test, and develop alternative

---

8   Ratcliffe, John, "Scenario Building: A Suitable Method for Strategic
Construction Industry Planning?", Dublin Institute of Technology,
Ireland, 2006, p. 3.

policy practices or strategies for Asia. This method has been used extensively in government, business and other private sectors in order to enable decision making in a risk prone environment. Since the world around us is uncertain, we assume that human beings are rational and hence will decide keeping their best interests in mind. In this context, Game Theory with its fictitious conceptual frameworks like "Prisoner's Dilemma", "Chicken Game" and "Stag Hunt" became very popular during the Cold War to understand future possibilities of a nuclear showdown between the US and the USSR.[9] The critique to the sets of games developed then was that they were mostly fictitious and abstract without any basis in the real world. This is an inherent limitation of the scenario-building method as well. Though scenario-building in the context of Asia is based on past and present empirical data, the future is imagined and fictitious. Nevertheless, scenarios help in planning for the future and enable adaptation to unfavourable circumstances, and towards implementing strategies and policies that guarantee maximum success in a politicized and conflict ridden atmosphere.

---

9   "The "dilemma" faced by the prisoners here is that, whatever the other does, each is better off confessing than remaining silent. But the outcome obtained when both confess is worse for each than the outcome they would have obtained had both remained silent. A common view is that the puzzle illustrates a conflict between individual and group rationality. A group whose members pursue rational self-interest may all end up worse off than a group whose members act contrary to rational self-interest. More generally, if the payoffs are not assumed to represent self-interest, a group whose members rationally pursue any goals may all meet less success than if they had not rationally pursued their goals individually", See "Prisoner's Dilemma", *Stanford Encyclopedia of Philosophy* at *http://plato.stanford.edu/entries/prisoner-dilemma/* (Accessed on March 20, 2009). The game of chicken implies that each player does not give in to the other and these could result in the worst outcome for both. See "Game Theory.net" at *http://www.gametheory.net/dictionary/Games/GameofChicken.html* (Accessed on March 19, 2009). Stag Hunt is a game which is a prototype of the social contract. Rousseau argues that if a group of people were assigned to hunt a deer with specific positions, it is always possible that one person gave up the fight when a hare is sighted. See Brain Skyrms and U C Irvine, "Stag Hunt", Presidential Address, Pacific Division of the American Philosophical Association, March 2001, pp. 1-20.

METHOD FOR SCENARIO BUILDING

1. Identifying key drivers/factors of the subject/issue under study;

2. The storyline/narrative of the scenarios; (critically based on review, field knowledge, discussions and expert opinions);

3. The relationship of each scenario with the key drivers must be clear;

4. Alternative scenarios (minimum of three, maximum of five);

5. Always within a time frame. It covers a minimum of three years to a maximum of 50 years: Base year.

6. Time horizon and time steps;

7. Highly flexible and adaptable;

8. The element of uncertainty factored in;

9. Implications of the scenarios (consequences);

10. Feed-back the scenarios to target audience;

11. Discuss the strategic options;

12. High degree of ownership.[10]

PROCESS UNDERTAKEN IN SCENARIO-BUILDING

Since future projections are always in the realm of high plausibility and uncertainty, there are certain recommended steps to increase the level of probability. These are:-

1) Scenario-building is a team exercise. Experts must be involved in different stages of the building process. Divergent views are the key driving factors leading to alternate futures. While encouraging wide participation, the role of each participant must be clearly defined and random anarchic thoughts discouraged.

---

10 Martin Rhisiart, "Scenario Building", Futures Workshop, Cardiff University, 2006.

2) Expectations must be realistic aimed more at understanding the future and "out of the box" thinking. The time taken for scenario-building must be stated.

3) The number of scenarios must range between two to four. Those constructing the scenarios must not strive to get the right answer in just one single scenario. Instead, scenario building exercise is mostly geared towards the unfolding of events as they occur.

4) Scenarios must be named with vivid and meaningful titles signifying the essential logic, which is driving the scenario. Vivid titles have better chances of being utilized in policy talk. All the scenarios must, however, have equally meaningful titles and attract equal creativity.

5) Scenarios must have relevance for policy. However, scenarios are neither policy nor are they implementable. Instead, scenarios offer a leaning and strategic thinking framework, whose main objective is to lay out before the policy maker, alternative scenarios, so that they are not caught by surprise by future events.

6) Scenario building must have a clear roadmap. The focus is on examining the drivers and avoiding internal inconsistencies.

7) Scenarios must be highly researched and imagined. Weak scenarios are those that rest their case too much on speculation and are poorly researched.

8) Scenarios are both an intellectual and an emotional exercise capturing the intellectual acumen and emotional thought process of those who develop it.

9) Scenarios include both advocacy and dialogue between the actors.

10) Scenarios are based on expert opinions but a healthy scepticism about commonly accepted wisdom must be always maintained.

11) Though scenarios are an imaginative exercise, empirical data is an important element of the process.

12) Scenarios start from the present date and depict a final stage at the time line fixed.

GENESIS OF THE BOOK

Based mostly on the method of scenario-building, this book is an attempt to discuss the future of critical issues related to security and the international relations of Asia in 2030. The chapters have been written with this timeframe in mind.

The first section deals with "Strategic Futures" in Asia pertaining to issues of thematic significance like the future of air power, trends in the technological development of ballistic missiles defences, the future of the internet and strategic technologies like nano, space and cyber. The second section provides a vivid future description on matters of geo-political significance like economics, demography, water-resources, nuclear issues, climate change and the environment, governance, and state relation pertaining to the regions of South Asia, South East Asia, West Asia, and East Asia. Given its wide expanse and insightful future analysis on issues of significance particularly to Asia, it fills a critical gap in the domain of future studies in India.

This book is the first attempt by a team of IDSA scholars to look at the past and present trends concerning some critical issues which will be of importance to determine the future. Scenario building exercise, within the limits of their understanding of the subject, is attempted to forecast the likely outcomes. The process will be further refined going forward and it is hoped that the studies carried out hereafter will be structured to include likely scenarios in next 20-30 years.

Ramesh Phadke discusses the Future of Air Power in Asia and that of China, India and Pakistan in particular. He is of the view that the Air forces of the future will grow in sophistication and range of platforms while simultaneously focusing on reducing the types and vendors of the aircrafts. There will be a greater focus on indigenisation or joint development and that air and space power will remain critical for fighting successful conventional war although their effectiveness in fighting sub conventional wars will be limited.

A. Vinod Kumar examines the trends in BMD technology development in the past decades and discusses latest projects under development or consideration, mainly by the US, with other powers still at a rudimentary stage of development of technologies. He argues that political drivers will remain central in the evolution of interception technologies and at least some of these technologies would have matured by 2030.

Cherian Samuel discusses the transformational impact of internet on modern society, economy and security. He believes that the true potential of internet is yet to be realised fully and that regulation of this medium will become extremely important since its disruption or misuse will affect security and freedom of individuals and nations.

Avinash Godbole discusses the likely future of the climate change debate in Asia. He is of the view that any meaningful action on this front will have to involve radical changes in the global energy policy and that nations will have to think globally to save the planet and arrive at mutually acceptable goals.

Sanjeev Kumar discusses the US's Asia policy for the next two decades. He examines various drivers that are helping shape American policy presently and will be of relevance going ahead. He asserts that the US is set to face major challenges in Asia in the near future and that it will have to make hard policy choices to remain the pre-eminent power in this region.

Ali Ahmed focuses on the progress that India has made since independence and the opportunities it has let slip while examining the current state of polity, economy and governance. He argues that it would be premature to declare that India has arrived and that much progress will be required before India's rise becomes certain.

Harinder Singh examines the key drivers of religion, politics, extra-regional interests and hostility towards India as the drivers that are propelling Pakistan towards a very uncertain future. He envisages that a stable and progressive Pakistan is unlikely to emerge in next two decades.

Medha Bisht discusses the possibilities of conflict or cooperation due to water sharing between the states in South Asia. She argues that a purely nationalistic approach while ignoring the needs and rights of other states and ignoring the consequences of climate change will not be helpful. The region is likely to see heightened tensions in the next two decades if the water issue is not resolved satisfactorily.

Priyanka Singh examines the state of affairs in Pakistani Occupied Kashmir (POK) and highlights the security threat emanating from there due to militancy and growing Chinese footprint. She argues that POK will be better of if it comes under India's control failing which it will most probably be at crossroads of conflicting interests of India, Pakistan and China.

Nihar Nayak examines the current fluid state of politics in Nepal, the respective strength and policy planks of various political parties and the future portents. In his opinion, political instability is more likely in years ahead and that no party other than the Maoists has the potential to come to power on its own. The country is likely to export instability and may become a battle ground for foreign influence.

PK Gautam discusses the issues confronting Tibet, mainly the effect of climate change on its ecology, society and way of life. He also examines the role of religion in Tibet and the policies being followed by China in the Tibetan Autonomous Region. He recommends that India should take initiative in facilitating dialogue between the Chinese government and the exiled Tibetan Administration in India.

Anand Kumar examine the scale of illegal migration into India and its likely impact on India's demography, social cohesion and security. In his view, the scale of illegal migration and the apathy of the Government will have serious repercussions and calls for immediate and strong measures to stop it.

Samuel C. Rajiv explores the drivers, issues and trends likely to impact West Asia in the next two decades. In his opinion, West Asia has the potential to become a stable, peaceful and prosperous region but has equally strong reasons for the status quo to remain with flash points emerging from time to time. It also has the potential to become a nuclear jungle.

Pankaj Jha highlights the centrality of South East Asia to the political and economic architecture of Asia. He postulates that an economically and militarily growing China will cast a large shadow over the region and its behaviour will determine the role of other players as well. In his opinion, interests of several states including the US, China, India and Japan will often overlap and clash in South East Asia.

Pranamita Baruah examines the trajectory of Japan's foreign and security policies after the Second World War and concludes that it is yet to become a normal state despite acquiring great economic power. She argues that, short of sufficiently strong external triggers, Japan is unlikely to abandon its pacifist policies and that the US-Japan security alliance will remain the linchpin for stable order in the region.

Gunjan Singh examines the developments in China and identifies economic growth, environmental degradation, ethnicity and nationalism as the drivers of change. She argues that China has to overcome formidable obstacles before it can reach anywhere close to American power but that in next two decades China's role in global affairs will be much greater.

Ishida Yasuyuki identifies the security challenges being faced by East Asia and discusses the strategic trends in the region. He argues that the regional order is in a state of flux and that great power's geo-politics, globalisation and liberalization, regionalism and regionalization, energy, resources and environment are the key drivers for East Asia that will determine the future of the region.

These essays were written independently of one another and reflect the authors' own assumptions and conclusions, and not that of IDSA. They present a wide-ranging review of the security situation in

Asia on many of the important issues. Largely untouched is the work are the issues related to armed conflict scenarios and military balances because it is that they demand an independent attention. Taken together, however, the essays reflect upon some of the important challenges that the region is bound to face by 2030 and hence, the essays as a whole are expected to offer at least some glimpses into the future of Asia.

Ajey Lele, Namrata Goswami and Rumel Dahiya

1
STRATEGIC
FUTURES

1
Future of Asian Air Power-2030
—Ramesh V Phadke

INTRODUCTION

Air power has been with us for nearly a century. Within less than a decade of the historic first flight of a 'heavier than air machine' at Kitty Hawk in the US on 17 December 1903, the Italians were bombing Turkish forces at Ainzara in Libya. On 01 November 1911, Lt. Giulio Gavotti dropped four bombs each weighing a mere two Kg. on Turkish positions at Ainzara. Subsequent bombing attacks were denounced by the Ottoman Government as contravening the Geneva Convention.[1] Air power saw rapid progress through the two World Wars and major advances in technology further accelerated the pace of modernisation of air power in the second half of the last century.

Air power is defined as 'the ability of a nation to assert its will through the medium of air.' This is usually further expanded to include 'the ability to project military force by or from a platform in the third dimension and includes a nation's total aviation activity; potential as well as existing, public and private, and civil or commercial and military'.[2] This definition clearly remains applicable and highlights the importance of forces in being as also the nation's potential to continually upgrade its forces to meet emerging challenges. Force structures are invariably constructed on the basis of affordability, access to technology and above all the current and

---

1   Bombing and the Air War on the Italian Front, 1915-1918, Journal Article by AD Harvey, Air Power History, Vol.47, 2000, accessed from www.questia.com on 15 June 2010.

2   Doctrine of the Indian air Force, Amended Reprint, 1997, p.28.

future capability of the likely adversary and not his demonstrated or perceived intent.

The likely development of aerospace power in the next two decades would depend on many of the factors cited above. Given the high costs of research its progress is likely to be incremental rather than dramatic. Some of the questions that this essay attempts to answer are: Would it become more effective in sub-conventional warfare? Are there any enduring trends in the way platforms and weapon systems are being developed? What role would the Unmanned Aerial Systems (UAS) and missiles play in the future? Would the US and its Western allies continue to dominate the air power arena? Is there a possibility of some of the developing countries of the Asian region becoming more self-reliant in this field? What role does the indigenous aviation industry play in these countries?

RECENT TRENDS

The experience of the wars of the 1960s to 1970s raised the importance of air power but it was the 1991 Gulf War that proved beyond doubt its efficacy. Operation Desert Storm saw that the USAF led Allied Air Forces mounted an air campaign against Iraqi targets for six weeks before the ground forces entered the war and successfully defeated the formidable Iraqi ground forces in a matter of days. This not only proved the thesis proposed by Col John Warden of the US that air power must target the 'centres of gravity' of the enemy but also that air power could significantiy reduce the casualties to one's ground forces.[3] This was a turning point of sorts and those countries that had not paid much attention to modernising their air power assets sat up and took notice.[4] The People's Liberation Army Air Force (PLAAF), the Indian Air Force (IAF), (Pakistan Air Force) and many

---

3   Col. John A Warden III, "The air Campaign: Planning for Combat" NDU Press Publication, 1988 electronic copy available at, http://www.au.af.mil/au/awc/awcgate/warden/ward-toc.htm, accessed on 02 Nov.2009

4   Ibid. Today, after a gap of nearly twenty years, critics feel that air power is not necessarily as effective as it is made out to be especially when the enemy does not present the classical target system as happened in the 2001 Afghanistan Air War.

other air forces in the region renewed their efforts to modernise their fleets. Iran, DPRK, Singapore, Indonesia, Malaysia, South Korea, Saudi Arabia and Israel are some of the other Asian countries that today posses sizeable air power assets.

FUTURE TRENDS

Offensive Platforms

Although the jet fighter had already crossed the sound barrier on 14 October 1947 (Chuck Yeager flying the Bell X-1)it was a decade before the supersonic aircraft became commonplace. The ever rising costs of the platform resulted in the pure fighter soon doing strike missions and later graduating to multi-role capability. With improvements in the thrust/weight ratios of the turbo-jet, turbo-fan variety of jet engines it became possible to steadily increase their capacity to carry more fuel and armament. Progress in solid state electronics resulted in microminiaturisation of avionics further improving the effectiveness of the modern platform. Increased fuel gave greater range while Inertial Navigation and later, space-based assets like the GPS further enhanced accuracy.

Improved performance of air defence radars, early warning and interception put a limit to how low a fighter could fly to avoid radar detection by the enemy and forced the manufacturers to look at ways to reduce the radar signature of the aircraft. The over-two-decade old RMA or Revolution in Military Affairs is generally accepted to include stealth, long range, and precision fire power. By the end of the 1990s the earlier platforms such as the Hawker Hunter, Folland Gnat, Dassault Mystere and Oregon, the MiG -15/17/19'21 and F-4 Phantom F-5 Freedom Fighter, the Mirage F-1, III and V were being gradually phased out. Some of the old types like the MiG-21 variants and Jaguar Deep Penetration Strike Aircraft (DPSA) and indeed the F-4 and F-5, continue to fly with many air forces. The Lockheed Martin F-16 Fighting Falcon designed in the early 1970s and comprehensively modified and upgraded throughout its long years in the service with many air forces is the sole exception to the rule and today remains a front line fighter in the US, Europe and many other countries.

One of the most noteworthy developments in the region was the relatively early introduction of the Su-27/30 class of the air superiority/multi-role fighter in China in 1992[5] followed by India in 1996 and much later in Vietnam, Indonesia and Malaysia. The end of the Cold War and the economic difficulties faced by Russia as well as the spectacular rise of the Chinese economy were the major triggers to this event. Until its entry, the F-15 and F-16, its Western peers, were available to only American friends and allies in the region such as Japan, South Korea, Singapore, Pakistan and Saudi Arabia. Having learnt its lessons from the 1991 Gulf War, China had by the early 1990s embarked on a full scale modernisation and indigenisation process. It not only inducted the Su-27 in sizeable numbers but also began to manufacture the J-11, its licensed version, in the country. Newfound access to money and technology also helped it to quickly build two of its own fighters the FC-1 or JF-17 and the J-10 in record time. The availability of the Russian RD-93 and the Saturn Lyulka AL-31F aeroengines was the key to this achievement.[6] Of the 1653 combat capable aircraft with the PLAAF some 936 comprise MiG-21 and J-8 variants that are unlikely to last more than a decade.[7] The 80 odd H-6 (Tu-16) medium bombers and air refuelling tankers would also be phased out by 2020 but it must be noted that the fifty year old Tu-95 Bison four-engined bomber/reconnaissance aircraft is still performing its Cold War task of long range surveillance in the Baltic and North Atlantic theatre. The much modified version of the H-6 bomber is thus likely to serve with the PLAAF for many years. In 2030, the PLAAF and PLAN would likely have some 800+ J-10, another 800 Su-30/J-11Bs, and many JF-17, JH-7, L-15/FTC-2000 advanced trainers and an assortment of XXJ (sometimes called JXX) and other fifth generation stealth fighters.

5   John Wilson Lewis & Xue Litai, "China's Search for a Modern Air Force", International Security, Vol 24, (Spring 1999) p. 89.

6   Jon Sigurdson, "Technological Superpower China", Edward Elgar Publishing Limited, Cheltenham, UK, 2005, pp. 191-214. Also see, Sergio Coniglio, "China's aviation- A Military and Industrial Perspective", Military Technology, MILTECH 11/2004.

7   IISS, The Military Balance 2009, Routledge, London, East Asia & Australia, pp. 386-387.

In India, the IAF had acquired a large variety of new types in the early 1980s which included the Jaguar (1979), MiG-23 (1980), Mirage-2000 (1984), MiG-29(1987) and the MiG-27 (1989). Of these the MiG-29 aircraft are being upgraded but it is unlikely that these fighters will meet India's needs for the next two decades. What, however, will continue to restrict India's options is its lacklustre record in building its own defence industry. Of the 600 combat capable aircraft of the IAF as many as 293 comprise the old and ageing MiG-21 variants leaving only a mere 48 Su-30MKI, 48 MiG-29 and 36 Mirage-2000[8] clearly highlighting its 'air defence orientation'. The 98 recently upgraded MiG-27 and the soon to be up-rated 80 Jaguar DPSA aircraft would be on their way out by 2030. Instead the Su-30MKI, Tejas LCA and later the MMRCA, 126 of which are now on order, will form the backbone of the IAF fighter fleet. The emphasis would be on long-range multi-role capability. In 2030, the IAF can hope to possess some 200 Su-30MKI, 100 Tejas LCA, 60 MiG-29 and about 36-40 Mirage-2000 and if all goes as per plan, some 200 MMRCA fighters that are currently on order. The Russian 'fifth generation fighter' deal has been signed and 100 PAK-FA Indo-Russian fighters may also form part of the IAF inventory by 2030.[9]

Pakistan has had to depend on the US and PRC for its defence needs. Despite long term sanctions the PAF has maintained its F-16 fleet and has recently added some 18 new units. The co-production/development agreement with the PRC for the JF-17 has helped it to order some 250 fighters of this type along with a smaller number (36?) of J-10 (FC-20). Later even the Super-10 an advanced version of the J-10 will most likely join the PAF. Pakistan will also gain from its collaboration with the PRC in building its aeronautical industry and in all probability, by 2030 become capable of manufacturing its own fighters. Of the 383 combat capable aircraft on the PAF inventory only the 46 F-16 and 8 JF-17 are of the third generation.[10] All its Mirage III/V variants, the Chinese Q-5 and the F-7 PG/MG would be

---

8   Ibid. Central & south Asia, pp.348
9   Air Marshal (Retd) VK Bhatia, "Forecast for 2030", SP's Aviation Issue
     9, 2009, pp. 40-41.
10   Op. Cit. IISS Military Balance, pp. 354-355.

phased out latest by 2020. It would then have some 200 JF-17, 100+ J-10 and possibly 50+ F-16.

Due to its strained relations with the West, Iran has only 25 MiG-29 fighters; all its US origin offensive platforms like the F-14, F-4, and F-5 face spares/support problems and hence their serviceability in the future is in question. Iran is, however, making up this deficiency by developing a variety of short and long range surface-to-surface missiles. The future of its air arm is thus uncertain unless China comes to its help or in a dramatic shift, its relations with the West and Russia improve. It is noteworthy that Russia has so far not delivered the S-300PMU advanced air defence missile system to Iran under a deal signed many years ago.[11]

The Saudi Air Force currently possesses about 100 Panavia Tornado, 69 Boeing F-15S and 89 MD F-15C/D fighters and a whole host of other air assets including the BAe Hawk trainers and other aircraft of US and European origin. It has recently signed a deal to buy 72+ Eurofighter Typhoon fourth generation fighters. In the future too the Saudis would depend on Western sources for its needs.[12]

Japan, South Korea and Singapore are also planning to replace their ageing F-4 and F-5 aircraft possibly with the US Boeing F-15 SE. Due to its poor proliferation record North Korea, however, has little option but to live with a nearly obsolete air force unless China, its only friend, comes to its help.

Forecast International has said that in the five years ending 2013, the major players in this field, Lockheed Martin, Boeing, Eurofighter, and Sukhoi will maintain their lead and produce about 40-50 aircraft per year but Chengdu Aircraft of China will also produce 45-50 fighters every year.[13] This trend is likely to continue for the next two decades with the Chinese fighters becoming more

---

11 JDW
12 Aviation Week & Space Technology, Aerospace Source Book, January 2009, World Military aircraft Inventory, p. 253. henceforth AWST Source Book.
13 Ibid Changing Landscape, pp. 16-20

and more sophisticated and reliable with a sizeable export market. There are reports of Egypt's interest in locally manufacturing the Sino-Pak jointly produced JF-17.

The high cost and restricted availability of the F-22 Raptor and the Joint Strike Fighter (JSF) F-35 make it difficult for these to enter the region by 2030 except possibly with a few of the US allies such as Japan, South Korea, Taiwan and Singapore. But in the mean time, "under its Next Generation Air Dominance (NGAD) programme, Boeing has unveiled its design concepts for a sixth-generation fighter to replace the US navy's F/A-18E/F Super Hornet after 2025 and to succeed the US Air Force's F-22 Raptor two or three years later. These are said to be stealthy, tailless, supercruise-capable and would include optionally manned cockpits." One of the defining characteristics of the programme is likely to be its affordability.[14] In sum the prohibitively high costs of the modern fighter platforms will compel the countries of the region to look for other options including refurbishing the old types and Unmanned Combat Aerial Vehicle (UCAV). Continuing advances in microminiaturisation and space based assets are likely to enhance the capabilities of the UCAV in the coming decades and relatively lower costs would make them more attractive the air forces of the region.

Airborne Weapon Systems

The quest for accurate delivery of bombs and munitions gained added urgency in the Vietnam War and the Laser Guided Bomb (LGB) soon became the most sought after weapon. The LGB can, however, go awry due to smoke, clouds and other atmospheric obscurities. The LGB's popularity was the simplicity with which a dumb bomb was converted into a 'smart' weapon by adding a kit that included the laser seeker and fins to guide the bomb to the target illuminated by the laser designator carried either by the fighter bomber in 'autonomous' mode or by a 'buddy' fighter, or sometimes by a Forward Air Controller (FAC) on ground. In Operation Desert Storm (1990-91), only 229 US aircraft were

---

14 Jane's Defence Weekly, Vol. 47, Issue. 20, p. 5.

capable of delivering laser-guided munitions. By 1996 the expanded installation of Low-Altitude Navigation and Targeting Infrared by Night (LANTIRN) pods on F-15Es and block 40 F-16s had increased this capability within the Air Force to approximately 500 platforms. These weapons known as Precision Guided Munitions (PGM) became increasingly popular as they promised reduced collateral damage. It is noteworthy that the IAF used its MiG-27 and Mirage-2000 fighters in 'buddy' mode to target camouflaged enemy positions with LGBs in the high mountainous terrain during the 1999 Kargil operations.

In the West the limitations of the LGB resulted in the development of Joint Direct Attack Munitions (JDAM) and later the Joint Standoff Weapon (JSOW) family of weapons that relied on the INS/GPS for guidance and made it possible to deliver these even in bad weather so long as correct geographical position of the target was available. Although countries other than the US have also produced these weapons they remain expensive and are not easily available to developing countries of the region. It is likely that these regional players will try their utmost to locally produce these and other efficient advanced PGMs. A new family of the Sensor Fused Weapons capable of firing small bomblets at specific targets such as the hot engine of tanks and vehicles, are also being used but their efficacy in operations other than conventional wars is questionable since these 'smart' weapons cannot differentiate between the engine exhaust heat of an armoured vehicle from that of a school bus.[15] A family of anti-tank weapons such as the Milan, TOW, Eryx, FGN-148 Javelin, and AGM-114R Hellfire are once again in demand and are increasingly being used in irregular warfare both from ground and airborne platforms. "Raytheon has delivered more than 30,000 Javelins and about 3,300 have been fired in combat. Production is running at between 1300 and 2000 per year.[16]

---

15 Mets David R, "Airpower and Technology: Smart & Unmanned Weapons", Praeger Security International, Westport CT., 2009, pp. 128-129.

16 Caitlin Harrington, Janes Defence Weekly, Vol. 47, 31 March, 2010, pp. 24-31

The air-to-air missile has also seen major improvements with the All-Aspect-Missile (AAM) and Beyond Visual Range (BVR) Missile entering service with most air forces of the region. India is also reportedly testing its first air-to-air missile the Astra. It is said to be a BVR with a range of 44 km that may be increased to 80 km in the future. This is another area where self reliance will become even more important for cost and access considerations. These missiles will become even more effective with the introduction of AWACS to the region.

Air Defence

The region has seen the induction of more sophisticated surface-to-air missiles (SAM) in the recent past with China receiving a large number of Russian S-300 PMU family with ranges exceeding 150-200 km. These are also effective against enemy missiles. India too has obtained these missiles while continuing to develop its own Akash SAM system.

With the gradually increasing reach of modern fighters such as the F-16, Mirage-2000, Su-27/30 and even the MiG-29K and the induction of the air-to-air-refuelling tankers and AWACS in China and India and also some other countries, the air defence envelope has expanded with the fighter/interceptor set to engage the enemy at far off ranges. This trend is likely to continue. Ranges may further increase with new BVR missiles entering service with some of these air arms. Operations with these force multipliers are however very complicated with the tanker and the AWACS platforms themselves needing protection.

Support Platforms

Fixed wing transport aircraft and helicopters have proved their usefulness in peace and war with them seeing regular employment in strategic mobility, troop lift, disaster relief, evacuation of own citizens from troubled areas, providing support to civilian authority in Counter Insurgency Operations (COIN) and, in the case of India, daily air-maintaining troops and civilians in the high altitude frontier areas. In the absence of adequate infrastructure in the mountains these aircraft of the IAF have proved to be the life line of the inhabitants of these remote regions of the country. The IAF has been using the Il-76 and An-32 as the main platforms for over two decades. The Hercules C-130J a 'Special Forces' version of the US cargo plane is soon slated to enter service with the IAF and would likely continue until at least 2030.

The PLAAF has also used its fleet of 30+ Il-76 and large numbers of An-24 for some time with the Y-8 a locally produced copy of the An-12. China and India are both trying to produce their own tactical transport aircraft and by the end of the next decade some of these may well enter service with the PLAAF, PAF and IAF.

Pakistan has ordered six SAAB Erieye AEW&C aircraft from Sweden, the first of which rolled out on 26 mar 2008.[17] These countries may add to their existing assets of tankers and AWACS. China has already inducted its locally developed AWACS, the KJ-2000. This aircraft led the fly past at the 60th Anniversary Parade in 2009.

Helicopters have proved their versatility both in war and peace and hence are likely to remain in great demand for the foreseeable future. India's Advanced Light Helicopter (ALH) 'Dhruv' is already flying with its army, navy and the air force and is also on the export market. China has produced the Z-8 support and Z-9 attack helicopter and both these are also likely to be exported in the future. India has placed an order for 197 Light Observation Helicopter (LOH) for its army and the same are likely to enter service by 2014. The Indian Navy has also placed orders for some refurbished Sea Kings and with Tata signing a JV with Eurocopter the Indian helicopter market is likely boom. Given the mountainous nature of India's Northern borders, the helicopter would continue to remain important in all its roles; armed/attack, scout/reconnaissance, support, tactical troop lift, medical casualty evacuation, combat search & rescue even if its effectiveness in the attack/combat role is restricted at heights above 10,000 feet AMSL.

---

17   Jane's Defence Weekly, 26 March 2009, p. 19.

Other Asian powers would continue to operate a variety of helicopters of Western and Russian origin but it is not clear if any of them will start their own production programmes since their needs are not large.

UAV/UCAV

The idea of using unmanned aerial vehicles has been around for a very long time but its fruition is of more recent origin. These were effective in battlefield surveillance role and gave valuable additional information to the ground forces without having to depend on dedicated reconnaissance aircraft. The wars in Afghanistan, Iraq, Lebanon (2006) and the conflict in Georgia (2008) all saw extensive use of the UAV.

The UCAV as also High/Medium Altitude Long Endurance (HALE, MALE) UAV are now fast becoming more popular with all armed forces. The success of the US in October 2001 Afghanistan Air War in the early and effective targeting of the Taliban and Al Qaeda fighters with the Predator MQ-1 launching Hellfire anti-tank missiles made this modified UAV a legend. This kindled renewed interest in the UAV with many countries developing their own. Small UAV that can be launched by an infantryman are also becoming more and more commonplace. A variety of UAV, UCAV and Man-portable and Micro UAV will see resurgence in the near future because of their low cost, relative ease of import and local manufacture. Presently the market is expanding but fully autonomous types are not being fielded for reasons of safety to other users of airspace and the need to first confirm that the target is indeed hostile before its engagement.

Some low cost UCAV designed to home on to radiations of a radar set and destroy the radar by diving into it are already in use in the region. According to the Aviation Week & Space Technology (AWST) the US remains the dominant producer and operator of the UAV and from a mere 1000 flight hours in 1987 the figure had gone up to 600,000 in 2008.[18] Northrop Grumman the manufacturer of

---

18   AWST, "New Respect for UAVs". pp. 94-97.

the famed Global Hawk HALE UAV, has recently offered for trials a UCAV, the X-45, that will display stealth characteristics, and carry PGMs such as the JDAM and the small diameter bomb. The X-47B technology demonstrator capable of carrier operations is currently undergoing trials. What with the rapidly increasing costs of manned fighters there is a strong possibility of the UAV/UCAV combination becoming more popular with the armed forces of the region.

This is one instrument of modern air power that will probably become the most sought after weapon system by all the countries of the region and its intelligent and early adoption would result in considerable cost savings. Being of a relatively short range and limited armament, access to these vehicles and associated technologies may also become easier.

Missiles

The 'aircraft versus missile' was a long enduring debate during the 1960s and 70s with the central focus on the delivery of nuclear weapons. Here we shall only consider the conventional missile in all its forms. For some years now, China has been producing conventionally armed surface-to-surface missiles of the M-9, M-11 variety. India has recently unveiled its solid fuel version of the Prithvi with a conventional warhead. In the recent past, short range missiles and rockets have caused two major conflagrations in West Asia, first the 2006 Lebanon War and later the August 2008 Gaza conflict. A variety of ship and air launched missiles for use against ships and ground targets already fill the inventories of many countries with the PRC laying considerable stress on this 'easy-to-produce' simple weapon system. Both Iran and Pakistan are also busy producing different types of missiles including the cruise missile. The reason for such interest is perhaps their relatively low cost and ease of manufacture, high accuracy and their usefulness in the initial stages of a conventional war when air superiority is not yet attained.

A recent report says that, "in 1970 there were only two countries developing cruise missiles with ranges of more than 150 km, but by 2009 this figure had increased to 17. Cruise missiles cost between 10 per cent and 25 per cent of the price of a ballistic missile; they use general aircraft technologies and they tend to be more accurate."[19] It is quite possible that the next two decades will see more and more of these missiles in the region. As seen during the 1995-96 Taiwan Straits Crisis, the missile may also become the weapon of choice in signalling the intentions of a country. Selectively targeting the enemy's military assets such as fuel dumps, ammunition storage depots, forward airfields, army/air force HQs and communication nodes can prove a very safe, cost effective and decisive option in the opening days of the war with low risk of attrition to own aircraft and to enemy civilians. This may thus become the preferred tool for the developing countries of the region. The American Stinger man-portable SAM or MANPAD has over time acquired a high reputation for accuracy and lethality. The IAF lost a helicopter and a fighter aircraft and sustained damage to one of its medium reconnaissance bomber due to Stingers during the 1999 Kargil Conflict. It must, therefore, be remembered that a low cost MANPAD SAM can be a major deterrent to offensive air operations and a force multiplier for the defender.

The Brahmos supersonic missile jointly developed by India and Russia is another example of effectively long range engagement of the enemy with relative safety. The next two decades may see a proliferation of missiles of all types as manned fighters/bombers become costlier and out-of-reach of developing countries. The aircraft and helicopter lose their overall effectiveness due to reduced lift and engine thrust at high altitudes. The ballistics of the shell and bomb also become more unpredictable at higher altitudes. Interdiction of enemy supply lines is, therefore, preferable to attacks on targets in close proximity of own troops. Future air operations in the mountains would have to allow for these limitations of the aircraft and helicopters. Man-portable anti-tank (MANPAT) and anti-aircraft missiles and Multiple Launch Rocket Systems (MLRS) may be more effective in the mountains. In fact, the intelligent use of the UCAV-missile combination might prove a winning future strategy and enhance their attractiveness in the future.

---

19 Duncan lennox, Jane's Defence Weekly, Vol. 47, issue 13, 31 March 2010, p. 22.

Training

Both flying and technical training is perhaps the most important if unglamorous activity of any air force and may also see some major changes. In the UK basic training has already been outsourced to private companies. The IAF is looking to replace its basic trainer the HPT-32 and Kiran AJT-16; the latter with an indigenously produced IJT Sitara which is now reported to be powered by a Russian engine. The HPT replacement is yet to be chosen. China has produced two jet trainers. The JL-8 or K-8 Karakoram was co-produced with Pakistan's Aeronautical Industry but only 12 of them are flying in the PAF. China unveiled its L-15 third generation advanced supersonic trainer at the Nov 2008 Zhuhai Air Show. Developed by the Hongdu Aviation Industry Group (HAIC) with inputs from Russia's Yakolev bureau', the PLAAF is likely to induct these in large numbers. China has another trainer, the Guizhou JL-9 or FTC-2000, produced by Guizhou Aircraft Industry Corporation (GAIC) for the PLAAF. China may export these in the future to friendly developing countries. Basic and advanced jet trainers will continue to be in demand and this is one area where developing countries of the region can make their mark by intelligently entering into joint ventures with the aerospace majors of the West. "The Italian Alenia Aermacchi M-346 is a case in point with the company looking for sales of a light attack version of the lead-in fighter trainer (LIFT). The company sees an international market for at least 2000 M-346 class aircraft over the next 20-25 years."[20]

GAZING AT THE FUTURE

Of late, there have been many other developments in the field of aerospace power and related technologies in the Western world. Past experience shows that sooner or later these new technologies find their way in the developing world. It would thus be axiomatic that the region would see many unexpected developments. Some of the more important of these are listed below.

Solar and Renewable Energy Platforms

Much work is under way to develop solar and hydrogen cell

---

20   Janes Defence weekly, Vol. 47, Issue 17, 28 April, 2010, p. 9.

powered aeroplanes and UAVs. Initially, difficulties in obtaining/ generating more usable power and hence limitations of all-up weight might restrict these technologies to UAVs and light reconnaissance platforms but the potential is as yet not fully realised. e. g. The solar powered Zephyr flew for 82 hours in a test flight in 2008.[21]

End of Fossil Fuel

Availability and desirability of using fossil fuel for aviation may soon become a hotly debated issue if fears of climate change attain greater salience. The military aircraft would be most vulnerable. According to one estimate the US Air Force uses 2.5 billion gallons (approx 10 billion litres) of fuel each year. In 2008 it cost the US government nearly US$ 7 billion, slightly more than half the total fuel bill of the entire US government, to fuel its air force. It is also said that aircraft release about 600 million tons of CO2 each year but have a greater impact than other sources of combustion products because the aircraft directly delivers it into the atmosphere. Thus even though aviation accounts for just 8 per cent of the total use of refined oil, and only 3 per cent of greenhouse emissions, the overall climate effect is about 13 per cent. It is thus evident that soon military aviation would have to search for alternative sources and types of fuel.[22] Many alternative fuels and even solar energy are being considered but which of these, if any, would suit the requirements of aviation is difficult to say at this time. In the near future fuel may thus become a major constraint to military aviation and may even adversely affect the production of some of the fighters and other platforms.

Use of Near Space

Officially designated to extend from 75,000 feet to 62 miles near space has been attracting the attention of aerospace research scientists for a variety of reasons. Use of airships and tethered balloons or

---

21 Hue Williams, Jane's International Defence Review, Vol. 43.June 2010, pp. 82-87.

22 Mark J. Lewis, "Military Aviation", Aerospace America, September 2009, pp. 24-31.

'aerostats' at high altitudes on the fringes of the earth's atmosphere for reconnaissance, surveillance and ELINT gathering has been considered for some time. Absence of severe weather, strong winds, and above all, the low cost of manufacture and operation of these air ships/balloons are the main points in favour of such an idea. The major advantage is that such platforms could remain on station for weeks if not months and would be much cheaper than satellites and provide a continuous picture of activities in the areas of the 'foot print' of the platform. These may prove very useful in the future.[23]

Hypersonic and Scramjets

On 26 May, 2010 the Boeing Phantom Works and engine manufacturer Pratt& Whitney made X-51A WaveRider used a rocket booster and an air breathing scramjet (supersonic ram jet) engine to reach speeds of Mach 5 and created a record for the longest flight using such an engine. Hypersonic research has been with us for many years. The USAF SR-71 black Bird strategic reconnaissance aircraft could reach speeds of M 3 plus and remained in service for nearly three decades. The current programme's fore runner was the X-43A that also used the scramjet and achieved speeds of Mach 9.6 in November 2004.

It is claimed that the WaveRider rides its own shock wave and has the potential for true hypersonic flight. The scramjet carries liquid hydrogen but scoops oxygen from the air as it travels at high speed. The engine has few or no moving parts with the compression of the oxygen being accomplished simply by passing through the engine. This frees the vehicle from the need to carry liquid oxygen which effectively reduces the pay load and hence makes it an attractive idea, e.g. the Space Shuttle needs 143,000 gallons of liquid oxygen that weighs a staggering 616,432 kg. Without this liquid oxygen the shuttle weighs a mere 74,842 kg.

The scramjet cannot work at low speeds so it is accelerated to about Mach 4 by a Pegasus booster rocket. This combination is taken

23 http://www.gaerospace.com/press-releases/pdfs/Near_Space_SpaceToys.pdf

to 20-40, 000 feet by a specially designed B-52. Once the booster rocket reaches the high speeds it falls off, the scramjet engine is lit and it then travels on its own before a splash in the ocean. The longest flight referred to earlier lasted only 200 second, giving a clear estimate of the problems ahead. By 2030, this research is likely to present more options for high speed commercial and military flight.[24]

Micro and Hand Launched UAVs

Much work has already been done in this novel field. American and NATO soldiers are already using hand launched small UAVs to get a picture of what lies 'on the other side of the hill'. Micro UAVs of the size of small birds capable of quietly sitting on a window sill have been developed to eavesdrop on the conversations inside the room. The ability to pack ever bigger data in extremely small devices (the 8-10 GB pen memory for instance) and the possibility to make micro trans-receivers would certainly transform the way militaries communicate and transfer useful data. Micro UAVs would play a major role in the near future.[25]

ENDURING PROBLEMS

Target Identification. Despite major advances in air launched weapons and attendant target designation and aiming/homing systems the problem of target identification continues to be a severe constraint on strike missions especially in sub-conventional warfare when the risk of collateral damage is high. Fighter aircraft and attack helicopters face such situations on almost daily basis when operating against terrorists, guerrillas and insurgents. Non-state actors have often used innocent civilians as human shields while launching attacks on government forces. Not a day goes by without some report of a civilian target being mistakenly destroyed in Afghanistan and elsewhere. Air operations in urban areas are even more difficult even though some very accurate attacks were indeed launched on targets in Baghdad during the Second Gulf War. In today's world of 24-hour TV news channels and the increasing role of NGOs keeping an eagle

---

24 http://www.howstuffworks.com/hypersonic-plane.htm, jane's Defence weekly, Vol. 47, Issue. 22, 02 June 2010, p. 5.
25 Refer Note 20 above

eye on all government operations, nation states find it increasingly difficult to explain and justify these mistakes. A recent such attack in North Afghanistan on an oil tanker that was thought to be surrounded by Taliban fighters but which actually turned out to be civilians collecting fuel resulted in the tragic death of some 90 innocents.[26] Afghan marriage parties where participants often fire weapons in celebration have been mistakenly targeted bringing opprobrium on air power operators. The arms manufacturers would have to work to improve the present target identification methods if indiscriminate use of fire power is to be avoided.

Air Superiority. "With it anything is possible; without it everything is at risk," said Major General (Retd) Charles Link of the USAF.[27] It is a truism that no major armour activity can be undertaken without air superiority. One of the most important tenets of air power employment, the concept of air superiority has often been mistakenly associated with air forces fighting their 'own battles' against enemy air forces and failing to come to the support of own ground forces when most needed. Nothing could be farther from the truth. No air force can mount air operations before it first effectively neutralises or at the very least reduces the ability of the opposing air force to interfere with own operations. There are many ways to achieve this basic objective; offensive counter air, airfield strike and deep interdiction including strikes on enemy's leadership are some of them. Admittedly, air superiority is not automatically achieved but has to be hard fought and sometimes may take time. The US and its allies have not fought a single war since Vietnam without first neutralising enemy air. SEAD or Suppression of Enemy Air Defence operations are, therefore, vital and have to be undertaken at the very initial stage of a conflict. The ground forces often overlook this fact and bitterly complain that the

---

26 www.longwarjournal.org/archives/.../nato_airstrike_in_ku.php *accessed on 02 Nov 2009.*

27 Link, Maj. Gen. Charles D, USAF Ret, 'The Role of the US Air Force in the Employment of Air power', in Richard H. Shultz & Robert L. Pfaltzgraf, (Ed), "The Future of Air Power", Maxwell Alabama, air University Press, 1998, p. 88. Also see Mets David R in Airpower & Technology, p. 12.

air force does not provide them 'Close or Offensive Air Support' (CAS/OAS) to first soften up the enemy before they can launch an offensive. Col. John Warden who formulated the air strategy for the 1991 Gulf War and many others are of the view that 'something has already gone drastically wrong, if the army demands immediate air support meaning thereby that joint planning should already have taken into account the needs of the surface forces. Problems of target identification, friendly fire incidents and collateral damage will in all likelihood continue to plague the modern air forces for the foreseeable future.

Missiles. As seen above, many Asian countries are rapidly building their capacity to indigenously produce short-range ballistic, anti-ship, cruise and other missiles apparently to make up for deficiencies in manned combat aircraft. The PRC has over the last two decades built up a stock of some 1500 SRBMs and a whole host of cruise and other missiles and has also exported them to Iran, Saudi Arabia, Pakistan and Syria giving these countries to deter some extent, future threats. Given the changing nature of warfare in which sub-conventional and irregular conflicts appear to predominate, building of indigenous military/defence capabilities naturally becomes inescapable. The rapidly rising prices and increasing difficulties in accessing state-of-the-art technologies together place serious strains on a country's economy. This perhaps makes the relatively cheaper and easy-to-produce missile a weapon of choice. It must be noted that missile technology has rapidly proliferated with some 40 countries pursuing some missile programmes of their own.[28] As these technologies become more diffuse and widespread with increasingly affordable missiles with high accuracy and bigger conventional warheads, it is possible that these will play a bigger role in both deterrence and Warfighting.

Conclusion

The foregoing has shown that technology has continuously shaped and sharpened the effectiveness of air power as a decisive element in conventional warfare. Air power has also been successful as a deterrent to conventional wars. It has, however, not been as

28 Janes Defence Weekly, Vol. 47 Issue 13, 31 march, 2010, p. 22

effective against insurgents, terrorists, guerrillas and those indulging in ethnic cleansing activities. Other limitations such as very high unit costs of aircraft and weapons and the inability to produce these locally place developing countries in a difficult situation when planning their force structure upgrades. Developing own military aviation industry is, therefore, inescapable if dependence on foreign suppliers is to be avoided. It is likely that the next two decades will see efforts in reducing the types and vendors of the aircraft and equipment used by the air forces in the Asian region. China, and with its help Pakistan, may become more independent in this field. Both the PLAAF and PAF are likely to consolidate their inventories greatly relying on indigenously manufactured products. India's GDP has been growing at a steady 6-7 per cent for some time and if this pace is maintained, adequate funding would be available for the IAF to also become a truly balanced and capable air arm despite its current problems of dwindling assets. Its leadership would have to focus on fewer types such as the Su-30, Mirage-2000, MiG-29 and the Tejas while simultaneously developing its capabilities to upgrade them as the need arises. India cannot, however, be counted among modern developed nations if it does not soon build a robust aviation industry. Modern air power undoubtedly will play a decisive role in national security but it cannot be viewed as a panacea for all problems. Its effectiveness would continue to depend on the freedom it gets from the political and military leadership of the country.

2
Ballistic Missile Defences in 2030: Trends in Technology Development
—A Vinod Kumar

Not only can we hit a bullet with a bullet, we can hit a spot on the bullet with a bullet.

–Lt. Gen. Henry A. Obering, Former Director,
Missile Defense Agency, USA

History has often shown that a military technological invention could be neutralized or riposted with a countervailing technology that would, if not mitigate its capability, certainly provide an alternative or response to the first technology. Only a handful of military inventions, like nuclear weapons, have escaped this trend; ballistic missiles have not. Right from the days of the German V-2 rockets, major military powers have explored defences against rocketry. Though air defence seemed an immediate answer to ballistic threats, there was always a need to construct a "shield against this sword" even if it implied a metaphorical scenario of "hitting a bullet with a bullet". A challenging technological endeavour, evolution of interception technologies has been a laborious grind since the initial efforts in the 1940s.

A host of these baseline technologies are currently under development in major military-industrial bases, notably the United States and Russia. These technologies intend to create various interception, tracking and surveillance applications on ground, sea and airborne platforms, with the space frontier extensively being explored for parking tracking and surveillance machinery. Some have matured and progressed into deployment in limited numbers, while a host of others are at various stages of development. Most of these platforms are expected to pass through greater technology augmentation and upgradation lifecycles in the coming years. In that sense, the next few decades might witness operational maturity of many systems as well as the birth of new interceptor-vehicle concepts, largely influenced by the nature of the emergent nuclear security environment and the scenarios of proliferation of weapons of mass destruction (WMD) and their delivery systems.

This chapter attempts to trace the direction of technological evolution in missile defences by the year 2030, and the factors that will shape this evolution. For this technology forecast, however, it is pertinent to analyse the past and current evolution of this technology and its strategic drivers. There are other variables also which merit attention, including the nature of the security environment in 2030, and whether it will merit the existence of ballistic missile defences (BMDs). Of equal interest will be the impact of BMDs in strategic equations, more so on nuclear deterrence.

I
Evolution of Interception Technology Development

The initial forays into interception technology started with the German *Wasserfall*, and followed by the Soviets' *Berkut* and US projects *Wizard* and *Thumper* in the 1940s. Actual work on anti-ballistic missiles (ABM) started with the US *Project Plato* and the Soviet "A" in the early 1950s.[1] Propelled by their nuclear competition, the superpowers competed to develop defences against the other's longer-range missiles, which resulted in the US' *Nike-Zeus* and *Nike-X* programmes, countered by the Soviets' A-35 armed with the thermonuclear-tipped *Galosh* A-350 interceptor.[2] Subsequently the

---

1   "Missile Defense: The First Sixty Years", Missile Defense Agency Backgrounder, 15 August 2008, at <www.mda.mil/mdalink/pdf/first60.pdf>.

2   A. Karpenko, "ABM and Space Defense", *Nevsky Bastion*, No. 4, 1999, pp. 2–47, at <http://www.fas.org/spp/starwars/program/soviet/990600-bmd-rus.htm>.

US developed the *Sentinel* and the *Safeguard* system, deployed by the late 1960s. As this race threatened to destabilize deterrence equations based on Mutual Assured Destruction (MAD), the two sides agreed on the Anti-Ballistic Missile Treaty of 1972, which banned all forms of missile defences in order to maintain mutual vulnerability.[3] However, both countries continued to pursue ABMs in their bid to gain strategic advantage.

The need to overcome the strategic stalemate created by MAD was reflected in President Ronald Reagan's March 1983 speech announcing the Strategic Defence Initiative (SDI) or Star Wars programme in which he called for ABMs that would make "nuclear weapons obsolete" and shift the balance in US favour. The SDI heralded the development of a new generation of baseline BMD technologies and architectural models, many of which are being pursued even today and are likely to be reflected even in the systems of 2030. The SDI's four-layered architecture called the Strategic Defence System (SDS) consisted of ground-, sea-, space-based and airborne components,[4] delineating interception phases of a missile, namely, boost, post-boost, midcourse and terminal – form the fulcrum of contemporary BMD architectures. A vast array of systems were planned including space-based sensors and interceptors and various kill mediums consisting of nuclear-tipped, kinetic and directed energy (laser and particle beams). Considering the possibility of collateral destruction created by nuclear warheads, focus shifted to Kinetic Kill Vehicles (KKV) - destroying the warhead through collision (hit-to-kill).

Significant part of KKV ventures revolved around two programmes: the *Smart Rocks,* which aimed at huge satellite garages to host a large number of KKVs; and the *Brilliant Pebbles*, which

---

3   Initially, two ABM deployments, one each for the capital and another site, were allowed. The ABMs had to be within a radius of 150 km over designated areas with not more than 100 launchers and six radars. The 1974 protocol to the treaty restricted ABMs to a single area. While the Soviets maintained *Galosh* coverage over Moscow, the US deployed the *Safeguard* in Grand Forks, which it closed down in February 1976.

4   For a detailed analysis of the SDS, see Sanford Lakoff, *Strategic Defense in the Nuclear Age* (Westport: Praeger Security International, 2008).

relied on "singlets" or small, self-contained kinetic interceptors orbiting the space in large numbers.[5] The *BP* was considered more feasible and was to be backed by a constellation of low-orbit satellites called *Brilliant Eyes*. However, concerns over violation of the ABM Treaty, diminished threats from ICBMs after the Cold War, among others, led to termination of the *BP* programme, though its space component survived. A series of theatre defence projects were also initiated by SDI, including the Theatre High Altitude Area Defence (THAAD), *Patriot* (Phased Array Tracking to Intercept of Target), and the *Arrow*.

The Soviets were not far behind. The Soviets had the first viable ABM system, A-35/A-350 (ABM-1), armed with the *Galosh* three-stage solid-fuelled interceptor missile, with a range of over 300 km, thus perceivably achieving exo-atmospheric capability as early as 1968.[6] After the ABM Treaty, A-35 was deployed outside Moscow consisting of 64 nuclear-tipped *Galosh* systems. The Soviets upgraded this architecture to ABM-1B and -2 in the 1970s,[7] and replaced it in the 1980s with A-135 (ABM-3) layered system with both endo- and exo-atmospheric capabilities through the long-range *Gorgon* (SH-11/ABM-4/51T6)[8] and short-range *Gazelle* (SH-08/ABM-3/53T6). An interesting twist to this competition was the technological strategy the Soviets adopted during the Star Wars years, by shifting the focus

---

5   From an initial plan for a 4000-strong constellation, the *BP* was to have over 100,000 *Pebbles* in outer space. See "Brilliant Pebbles" at <www.missilethreat. com/missiledefensesystems/id.13/system_detail.asp>, accessed 19 October 2009; also see "Missile Defense, Space Relationship, and the Twenty First Century", *Independent Working Group Report, 2009 Report*, The Institute for Foreign Policy Analysis, accessed 15 October 2009.

6   "Strategic Defense and Space Operations", *Soviet Military Power 1987*, at <http://www.fas.org/irp/dia/product/smp_87_ch3.htm>, accessed 15 October 2009.

7   ABM-2 consisted of S-225 endo-atmospheric interceptor developed during the early 1970s. See <www.fas.org/spp/starwars/program/soviet/s-225.htm>.

8   Over 32 *Gorgons* and over 68 *Gazelles* are currently deployed around Moscow. For more details on System A-135, see <www.missilethreat. com/missiledefensesystems/id.7/system_detail.asp>.

to strategic air defence systems with innate ABM capability. In the years to come, Russia thrived on this niche to develop a new generation of strategic air defence systems which, it claimed, were on par with lower-end US BMD systems.

President George Bush (Sr.) initiated the Global Protection against Limited Strikes (GPALS) in 1991 focusing on ground-based defences against limited missile threats and accidental launches.[9] President Clinton transformed it to a limited nation-wide defence (NMD) project consisting of ground- and theatre-based interceptors, along with the Airborne Laser (ABL).[10] His successor George W. Bush sustained these projects and announced a robust BMD deployment plan by 2004. After withdrawing from the ABM Treaty, he re-designated the NMD programme as Ground-Based Midcourse Defence System (GBMDS), which though could not be declared operational through 2005 owing to consecutive test failures.[11] In 2006 many programmes showed signs of optimistic progress, prompting President Bush to plan the first foreign deployment of GBMDS in East Europe.

The US BMD plans, however, hit new roadblocks with President Barack Obama, who sceptical on the technology and had vowed to deploy only proven technologies while cancelling the money guzzlers.[12] After a heightened debate, Obama withdrew from the East European BMD in September 2009 and instead backed a mobile deployment consisting of *Aegis*, THAAD and PAC-3 across Europe. Avowed to the disarmament cause, Obama perceives BMDs as destabilizing and

9   "Missile Defense Act of 1991", Part C of National Defense Authorization Act for Fiscal Years 1992 and 1993: Conference Report to Accompany H.R. 2100, Report 102-311, US Congress, House of Representatives, 102nd Congress, 1st Session.

10 See James M. Lindsay and Michael E. O'Hanlon, *Defending America* (Washington: The Brookings Institution, 2001).

11 Bradley Graham, "U.S. Missile Defense Test Fails", *Washington Post*, 16 December 2004; "US Missile Defense Test Ends in Fiasco", *AFP*, Washington, 15 February 2005.

12 See Obama for America, "A 21st Century Military for America: Barack Obama on Defence Issues," at <www.barackobama.com/pdf/Defense_ Fact_Sheet_FINAL.pdf>, accessed 20 March 2009.

could desire to curb many technological endeavours that could trigger an arms race. Nonetheless, the pursuit of baseline technologies could flourish, driven by the fact that missile technologies entwined with WMD resources continue to proliferate globally.

II
The Current Baseline Technological Spectrum

(a) American BMD Pursuits

The current phase of US BMD technology development is an assortment of baseline technologies pursued since the Clinton and Bush years. While some projects were revamped and some terminated, the key ones are at advanced stages of maturity, promising interception capabilities for layered defence. For terminal or theatre defence phase, there are three notable systems – PAC-3, *Arrow-2* and THAAD – which have moved into deployment. An improvement of the *Patriot* air defence system, PAC-3 has a 15 km-plus range at Mach-5 speed and is considered ideal for defence against slower, low-flying missiles.[13] *Arrow-2*, a US-Israeli joint venture, has a higher altitude range (90 km); the two-stage solid-fuel system could intercept at upper segments of Earth's atmosphere.[14] While PAC and *Arrow-2* operate as endo-atmospheric systems, the THAAD with a 100-plus km range has extended theatre defence capability to intercept missiles beyond the endo-atmosphere.[15] The flagship project of US BMD is GBMDS,

---

13   PAC-3 is single-stage mobile system with a hit-to-kill capability and can carry 16 missiles at a time. For more on PAC-3, see "Lockheed Martin *Patriot* PAC-3", *Directory of U.S. Military Rockets and Missiles,* at <www.designation-systems.net/dusrm/app4/pac-3.htm>.

14   With Mach-9 velocity, *Arrow* 2 is an endo-atmospheric ABM. It uses an initial burn for a vertical launch, a secondary burn to sustain its trajectory, and destroys missiles through a blast fragmentation warhead. See <www.israeli-weapons.com/weapons/missile_systems/surface_missiles/Arrow/Arrow.html>

15   THAAD entered the manufacturing phase in 2000. A single-stage rocket with thrust vectoring to boost it beyond burnout, THAAD operates in conjunction with the X-band radar. The latest operational test in July 2010 was a success. See <www.defenselink.mi/specials/missiledefense/tmd-thaad.html>.

which is being developed to protect against long-range missiles in midcourse. Its primary vehicle, the GBI,[16] relies on a variety of satellites and radars (such as Cobra Dane, X-band and AN/SPY-1) for launch warning, tracking, targeting, and discrimination. Bogged by development failures, the project sprung back to life after a successful interception in September 2006, adding to over thirty successful intercepts out of forty-two since 2001. After initial deployment in Alaska and California, the plan is to deploy over 30 GBIs by 2010, and to over 44 by 2013.

Currently, the only operational midcourse system is the *Aegis* BMD. Formerly known as Navy Theatre Wide, the BMD system integrated on *Aegis* destroyers forms the foremost sea-based component. Its main interceptor is the Standard Missile-3 (SM-3) with over 270 km range and capability to engage short- to interim-range missiles in their early ascent or descent stage. *Aegis* has dual functionality of being a first-tier mobile interceptor as well as a forward-deployed early-warning system.[17] The long-term plan is to deploy 84 *Aegis* ships with SM-3. The SM-3 Block I is redesigned to achieve a midcourse and even a boost-phase capability after upgrade to an advanced version, SM-3 Block IIA, undertaken with Japan. The successful intercept of a dysfunctional satellite by SM-3 in February 2008, while declaring its ASAT utility, also validated the interceptor's capability to engage faster targets.

Among boost-phase technologies, the most visible in terms of innovation is the ABL programme, the world's first high-energy laser weapon on an aerial platform operating inside Earth's atmosphere. The system consists of a chemical oxygen-iodine laser (COIL) mounted on

16 GBI, comprising a booster vehicle and an exo-atmospheric kill vehicle (EKV), flies to a projected intercept point upon threat identification. The EKV uses its in-built propulsion and guidance control for final-seconds decisions to acquire the target, perform identification and steer itself to the warhead. See "Testing: Building Confidence", *BMD Fact Book*, Missile Defense Agency, 2009.

17 The *Aegis* system integrates SPY-1 radar, MK41 vertical launching system and long-range surveillance and tracking system. Together with X-band radar, *Aegis* can track and engage multiple targets simultaneously.

redesigned Boeing-747 aircraft.[18] The first ABL aircraft rolled out in October 2006; the laser system has undergone a series of ground-based testing before being integrated on the test aircraft. The future of the programme will hang on the results of a crucial in-flight firing test of the laser system sometime in 2010, when the system's capability to shoot down a boosting missile during flight should be proven.

Along with these interception technologies, the United States is also deploying a layered sensor network through ground-, sea- and space-based platforms, namely the sea-based X-band radar, Upgraded Early Warning Radars (UEWRs) in California and UK, a Cobra Dane radar in Alaska, and AN/TPY-2 in Japan and Israel - together forming an integrated battle management, command and control and surveillance network. The X-band radar is conducting the world's sole naval BMD patrol in conjunction with the AN/TPY-2. For space-based sensors, NASA is working on the STSS low-orbit satellites with infrared sensors to track missile launches, midcourse flight and re-entry, and an NFIRE satellite for signature collation assistance. The space-based infrared system (SBIRS), meanwhile, had to be supplanted with the alternative infrared satellite system (AIRSS), due to cost overruns.

(b) Russian BMD Ventures

Post-Soviet Russian BMD architectures, while being as vibrant as those of the US, exhibit a different character. The primary arm of Russian BMDs is their theatre defence platforms which integrate both ABM and air defence roles as operationally compatible components in a comprehensive-tiered architecture. The chunk of Russian forays revolves around S-300, S-400 and the futuristic S-500 programmes. S-300 is developed in two variants, namely, S-300P (SA-10/PMU

---

18   The aircraft crew operates the laser at altitudes of around 12,000 metres, by flying over friendly territory and scanning the horizon for the plumes of rising missiles. For more on ABL functioning, see A. Vinod Kumar, "Airborne Laser Aircraft Rolls Out", *IDSA Strategic Comments*, 6 November 2006.

Grumble) and S-300V (SA-12A *Gladiator*, SA-12B *Giant*).[19] S-400 (SA-20 *Triumf*), Russia's new showpiece air defence system with ABM utility, is an upgrade of S-300 with over 400 km range.[20] The system is envisioned for both extended air defence as well as BMD roles with its capability to target short- and medium-range missiles, aircraft and other aerodynamic threats with effective ranges up to 3500 km.[21] S-500 is the ambitious project planned to match US midcourse interceptors with an intended exo-atmospheric range of 3500 km. In the post-S-400 phase Russia would be working on compact and manoeuvrable fifth-generation air defence/ABM systems which "combine the elements of air, missile and space defence for targeting enemy system deeper into space" – implying an intention to gain greater exo-atmospheric capabilities.[22]

(c) Other Prominent Players

A handful of other countries have made notable inroads in BMD technology development. China is known to be developing strategic air defence systems with ABM capabilities, though publicly opposing missile defences. Known Chinese projects include FT-2000 and variants of the *Hongqi* system (*Hongqi*-2, -9, -10 and -15), assumed to be based on Russian systems such as S-75 and S-300 PMU. Propelled by HQ-9 and HQ-15 missiles, FT-2000 is intended to achieve

---

19   S-300P is designed to detect, track, and destroy incoming ballistic missiles, cruise missiles, and low-flying aircraft. It has been modified several times, the recent variants being S-300PMU-1 (SA-10D) and S-300PMU-2 (SA-10E Favorit).

20   S-400 consists of an upgraded S-300 missile, multi-target radar, and observation and tracking vehicles which can simultaneously track and guide missiles to multiple targets. For more on S-400, see <www.missilethreat.com/missiledefensesystems/id.52/ system_detail.asp>.

21   On 6 August 2007, Russia deployed the S-400 *Triumf* air defence system in Elektrostal outside Moscow. See "Russia unveils air defence, eyes U.S. missile shield", 6 August 2007, at <http://in.reuters.com/article/worldNews/idINIndia-28848420070806?sp=true>

22   Statement by Russian Air Force Commander, Colonel General Alexander Zelin; see "Russia working on missile to hit targets in space", *Times of India*, 9 August 2007.

interception coverage of between 150 and 200 km. Israel also has achieved major milestones in interception technologies. Besides *Arrow 2*, it has developed a series of strategic air defence systems, namely the *Barak* anti-ship missile, *Spyder, Hawk, Shavit* and *Nimrod,* all with varying augmented air defence capabilities.[23]

India is the latest entrant with the development of two systems, *Prithvi* Air Defence Experiment (PADE) and Advanced Air Defence System (AAD) – intended to be deployed by 2015. The project was launched in 2000 to attain an indigenous BMD capability on the lines of *Arrow-2*. Though the first interception test on 27 November 2006 was achieved at 50 km range, the project aspires to attain capability for two intercept modes, to hit a target within four minutes at both exo-atmospheric and endo-atmospheric levels. With the 500-plus km *Greenpine* as its pathfinder, the PAD system is powered by a liquid-fuel first stage and a solid-fuel second stage, and carries active radars. The endo-atmospheric AAD would be a lower-tier air defence system with 15 km range. Its first two tests in December 2007 were declared successful as it managed to intercept the target on both occasions.[24]

III
BMD in 2030: Technological and Political Paradigms

The previous sections evaluated the evolution of BMD technology to impart a perspective on existing technological templates. This section moves forward to forecast the probable/possible direction of BMD technology through an assessment of hypothetical technological and political paradigms likely to develop in the next few decades that will shape the nature of BMD technologies in 2030.

(a) Technological Paradigms
The longer the period of technology forecast, the greater will

---

23 Israel is also researching a short-range interceptor called "Iron Dome" and a medium-range interceptor called "Magic Wand". See <www.israeli-weapons.com/israeli_weapons_missile_systems.html>.

24 "Advanced Air Defence Missile Test-Fired", *The Hindu*, 6 December 2007.

be the challenges to predict accurately. Technology futures have often been denoted by imaginative narratives, largely in the realm of science fiction. However, technology forecast has been undertaken through rigorous scientific methods also. Various tools for futures research have been developed by Spyros Makridakis, Bertrand de Jouvenel, T.J. Gordon, T. Modis, M. Dublin, among others.[25] They include methods such as Delphi (tacit knowledge), analogy (study of another comparable system), extrapolation (observation from the sample system), statistics (based on variables to be predicted) and causal relations (studying the phenomena). Besides, there are other analytical methods like genius forecasting, simulations, scenario building, cross-impact matrix, decision trees, etc., which are used for futures research.[26]

Though these methods have inherent limitations, adapting suitable models for specific cases or an assortment of methodologies can drastically influence and assist forecasts. For example, use of comparatively easier denominators like the study of the system/technology's evolution and position in the probable/possible "life curve" or the "road mapping" of this evolution can help in forecasting the functional or structural progress of technologies. Often, the key to such approaches towards forecasting lies in *identifying the trends, mapping the possible/probable innovations and imagining revolutions* on a particular technological construct, an approach this chapter prefers to pursue. While trend identification has been done in previous sections, the task now is to outline the possible or probable route of innovations, potentially influenced by causal relations from political and technological drivers.

---

25   Some of their noted works include: Nikita Larry and Bertrand de Jouvenel, *The Art of Conjecture* (New York: Basic Books, 1967); S. Makridakis, "The Art and Science of Forecasting", *International Journal of Forecasting*, Vol. 2, 1986; T. Modis, *Predictions: Society's Telltale Signature Reveals the Past and Forecasts the Future* (New York: Simon & Schuster, 1992); M. Dublin, *Futurehype: The Tyranny of Prophecy* (New York: Plume, 1989).

26   David S. Walonick, "An overview of forecasting methodology", 1993, at <www.satpac.com/research-papers/forecasting.htm>.

Like many military technologies, development cycles of BMD have spanned ten- to twenty-year periods. Hence, one could start with the assumption that most of the baseline technological paradigms in BMD development exist and are not expected to dramatically alter in the next two decades, but for a few systems. This could facilitate easier mapping of the probable/possible route of the technological development process currently underway and identify the potential innovations in their future evolution. As a causal relationship variable, strong political drivers could shape the progress of these developments or radically change their character. However, a focused study of this evolution could also be done in a *ceteris paribus* approach,[27] implying that technological lifecycles would move in predictable phases of conceptualization, development, maturity and consolidation, and that political drivers will not evolve in a manner that will dramatically transform the nature of technological development in a limited period of time. The causal impact of political drivers could, however, be inducted at appropriate levels to infer the possible shifts in the development lifecycles or influences on the conceputalization processes.

For example, in the US pursuits, various development periods like C1, C2 and C3 of the SDI Organization (SDIO) phase or Block I, II and III of the Missile Defense Agency (MDA) phase carried a five- to ten-year development period from conceptualization to development maturity of technology baselines. Yet, most of the matured technologies took an average of ten to fifteen years to complete the development lifecycle before moving into deployment phases. While technological templates remained constant during this period, the nature of decisions on conceputalization or development was influenced by political drivers, including change in the strategic environment and the influence of political leaderships or ideologies. The US BMD development since the SDI years embodies this phenomenon. While the Cold War dynamics influenced the nature of SDI-era technologies such as *Brilliant Pebbles* and directed energy programmes, the end of the Cold War and change in dispensation affected only the development programmes, not the

---

27 Where all other factors, including political environment, remain constant.

technological concepts, many of which continued to be pursued with new nomenclatures. Though political factors such as the ABM Treaty affected the development of space-based interceptors, the concept remained strong as the US continued to vouch for military uses of space platforms. The ABM Treaty, despite being a major political driver, could only block the deployment of BMD systems, but not its continuing research and development.

Assuming that MDA would take another ten to fifteen years to realistically deploy its contemporary technologies for a comprehensive nation-wide layered defence, the space for the next fifteen years or so after this phase could be devoted to conceptualizing revolutionary BMD models. Here too political drivers could influence and dramatically alter this process. While assuming that the BMD architectures two decades from now could inevitably be advanced manifestations or matured models of the current baselines, the revolutionary innovations expected beyond that period could be compatible with the political environment prevailing at the time. Though imaginative thinking could prevail, technological paradigm predictions of a twenty- to thirty-year period would be as challenging as forecasting political paradigms. Nonetheless, going by the evolution of BMD since the 1950s, the nature of technological progress of a twenty- to thirty-year period would very much be within the limits of realistic imagination. As some programmes described below would testify, technologies thought about in the 1960s are being revived for future development with deployment plans of ten to fifteen years from now. Many of the components of Star Wars then thought to be in the realm of science fiction, have since been pursued and achieved, though in limited terms.

Some of the contemporary baseline technologies qualify strongly to become futuristic applications because of their innovative character and creative magnificence. They include concepts such as ABL, Kinetic Energy Interceptor (KEI), and *Brilliant Pebbles*. These technologies cover a whole spectrum of directed and kinetic energy and space-based applications, which could be futuristic templates. The concept of hitting a ground-based or airborne target from a mobile aerial platform (ABL system) through a laser beam is a futuristic technology which cannot be overlooked, especially because much headway has been achieved by MDA. Going by the progress made, seemingly only a few technical challenges constrain this programme from fruition. The key challenge is to focus a high-powered beam of light on a rapidly moving target while maintaining its intensity amidst atmospheric absorption and aircraft-oriented jitters before concentrating on a small point for kill.[28] Though systems integration of ABL may be proven in upcoming tests, its capability to function under stressful battle conditions may need more strenuous conditioning. This project is, however, now sidelined because of its heavy costs. Yet the technology is futuristic and is likely to rebound into development in the near future, depending on changes in the security environment. This could be replicated in most other directed energy technologies too.

A challenging area for research and development since the 1950s has been the development of requisite kill vehicle technologies. While nuclear and explosive payloads were initially in use, most developers preferred the KKV concept. They are deemed to be more cost-effective as their power depends on the interceptor velocity and mass of the payload. Yet, some KKV projects such as KEI have not found favour. Several current systems, including GBI, SM-3, ABM-3 and THAAD use exo-atmospheric hit-to-kill vehicle (EKV). Unlike directed energy vehicles, KEI is a high-energy, three-stage interceptor that can travel at 19,000 kmph and is meant to target medium-, interim-range ballistic missiles and ICBMs in boost and midcourse phases.[29] Highly mobile and transportable in a C-135, the KEI launcher deployment comes with choices of close proximity to the target or as a midcourse interceptor. Though KEI was considered as replacement for SM-3

---

28 In July 2007, the MDA tested the ABL's ability to target a missile with tracking beams, to adjust for atmospheric disturbances and to start the high-powered destructor laser sequence. See Global Security Newswire, 31 July 2007, at <www.nti.org/d_ newswire/issues/2007_ 7_31.html#C2278269>.

29 The system had a successful flight test in September 2006, and was destined to replace SM-3 in the *Aegis* ships. For more on the KEI, see <www.military.com/soldiertech/0,14632,Soldiertech_KEI,00.html>.

in *Aegis*, huge costs, weight and size limitations led to its rejection. However, the concept of advanced KKVs still remains strong, especially with the revival of the Advanced Technology Kill Vehicle (ATKV) of SDI days. The ATKV is considered for SM-3 Block IIA and is expected to significantly improve the missile's acceleration and final velocity due to its reduced weight and provide a better suite of sensors than EKV. It can also be improvised as multiple kill vehicle (MKV) by placing a number of KVs on a single interceptor to engage several targets. In fact, MKV is being vigorously pursued as a future template by MDA. As a result, exo-atmospheric kills of the future would involve multiple (independently operating) KVs from a single interceptor that could be effective against MIRVed threats as well as countermeasures.

The spectrum which remains largely out of bounds for BMD experimentation is the space frontier, owing to the global consensus – with some exceptions – against militarization of space and initiatives like the United Nations Outer Space Treaty and PAROS.[30] Even during the Cold War, the ABM Treaty largely restricted programmes such as *Brilliant Pebbles*, as a result of which the space frontier was confined to surveillance, early warning sensors and tracking applications. While these applications would continue in the next decades, there is pressure from sections in the US scientific and military establishment to optimally exploit outer space for BMD applications.[31] In fact,

---

30 The United Nations Outer Space Treaty, effective since October 1967, provides the basic framework on international space law affirming that space should be reserved for peaceful uses. In late 2000, the UN General Assembly voted on a resolution called the "Prevention of Outer Space Arms Race." In October 2006, 166 nations voted for a resolution to prevent an arms race in outer space. Israel abstained; the US voted against.

31 Besides the Pentagon request for a billion-dollar space-based weapon programme in 2008, the US Joint Chiefs of Staff urge "full spectrum dominance" in space. The 2006 National Space Policy explains that the US will "preserve its rights, capabilities, and freedom of action in space; dissuade others from either impeding those rights; take those actions necessary to protect its space capabilities; and deny, if necessary, adversaries the use of space capabilities hostile to US national interests."

an independent group recommended the revival of space-based interceptors of the *Brilliant Pebbles*-era for layered interception along with a space test bed.[32] Though the revival of these projects in the Obama-era is unlikely, the emergent threat from ASAT capability among newer nations such as China, proliferation of long-range missile capability, slow progress in ground-based technologies, etc., could contribute to at least some elements of interception being considered from space-based platforms. That Russia is also seeking to exploit space resources in a formidable manner also reflects the new attention on outer space applications. As a result, a host of advanced tracking and sensor technologies is likely to be developed, especially in low earth orbit, with higher resolutions and tracking capabilities to assist boost and midcourse interception, while deeper-space endeavours might follow in future.

For the near future, the US Air Force has been contemplating realistic possibilities of integrating newer interceptors on airborne platforms. This proposal itself is not new as the Air Force had in the 1960s conceptualized an Airborne Ballistic Missile Intercept System (ABMIS) for protection against low-trajectory attacks, through radars and interceptors integrated on specially equipped aircraft on around-the-clock patrols.[33] Similarly, the Navy had examined the scope for a midcourse system called the Sea-Based Anti-Ballistic Missile Intercept System (SABMIS), with radars and interceptors mounted on vessels and submarines. While the Navy programme later evolved into the Navy Theatre Wide and the *Aegis* BMD, the ABMIS is seemingly reincarnated through the ABL programme, though emphasis has been on directed energy kill medium. Considering the costs of laser programmes, and assuming the ABL will be blocked by the Obama administration, the ABMIS concept with KKV interceptors could see a rebirth.

A host of other futuristic projects are also at the conceptualization stage at the MDA. They include the Early Launch Detection and Tracking (ELDT) system, meant to cover tracking gaps in the initial

---

32   "Missile Defense, Space Relationship, and the Twenty First Century", n. 6.
33   "Missile Defense: The First Sixty Years", n. 1.

launch seconds; and the Over-the-Horizon Radar (OTHR) meant to pick signals over long ranges for early launch detection.[34] Another interesting concept with shades of ABL is the High-Altitude Airship (HAA) – an unmanned airship to carry sensors and tracking systems over hostile areas to detect and monitor launch possibilities. Then there is *Project Hercules*, which intends to develop robust detection, tracking and discrimination algorithms to help quicker identification and targeting, and the MEMS (microminiaturized electro-mechanical systems) meant to assist the MKV projects are planned future missions.

The brighter side is the radical augmentations in theatre and augmented air defence systems, which in all likelihood would thrive due to their tactical nature and affordability. Driven by newer lower-tier threats especially from non-state actors, a new generation of advanced air defence systems with point and area defence capabilities is on the ascendancy. A handful of these systems are currently in operation and stand out for their technological brilliance. The most noteworthy are *Sky Shield* and *Skyguard*. *Sky Shield* uses a unique 35 mm AHEAD (Advanced Hit Efficiency and Destruction) shell that ejects sub-projectiles on the path of the incoming target, especially aircraft and short-range missiles. Derived from the Tactical High Energy Laser (THEL) programme, the *Skyguard* (*Nautilus*) is an air defence system that uses *laser cannons to create a protective shield* of over 10 km radius over strategic zones like airports, urban areas or force deployments to protect against short-range threats.[35] Another system of this variety is the *HAWK* Air Defence System[36] – supposedly the world's most advanced all-weather, medium-altitude air defence system in service

---

34 Gary Payton, "Advanced Concepts in Missile Defence", *Washington Roundtable on Science and Public Affairs* (Washington, DC: George C. Marshall Institute, 12 September 2005).

35 A product of US-Israel cooperation, the THEL was conceptualized to deal with the short-range rocket menace from Hezbollah. In July 2006, Northrop Grumman unveiled *Skyguard*; see <www.gizmag.com/go/5868/>.

36 Development details of the current upgrade, Phase III HAWK, can be accessed at <www.raytheon.com/products/hawk/>.

since the 1960s. There are other prominent ones of this genre, like the MBDA's *Aster SAMP/T* – a limited-TMD system designed to provide point and area defence against lower-tier threats, and *Spada 2000* – an all-weather air defence system with a range of up to 60 km and capable of intercepting targets at 25 km while engaging four simultaneously.

Two variables emerge from these present and futuristic concepts. First, most advanced BMD concepts in vogue are being developed in the US. After the end of the Cold War, Russia lacked the capability to invest heavily in advanced technologies and shifted the focus towards cheaper theatre and air defence systems. But for Russia, Israel and Japan, most other military powers are still working on rudimentary BMD technologies. Second, it is likely that the future course of BMD technology development will be predominantly determined by political factors. While missile and WMD proliferation scenarios will influence future technology concept, political ideologies, especially in Washington, will determine the fate of their development and deployment. Though BMD technologies will endure and might even trigger a new arms race, the momentum for disarmament could also drastically affect the pace of innovation.

(b) Political Paradigms

As mentioned earlier, Political drivers will remain central in the evolution of interception technologies though their influence would vary depending on the character of the strategic environment. Primarily, there are three political drivers that can be analysed in this context: (1) proliferation of WMD/delivery means; (2) impact of BMDs on arms race and stability; and (3) nuclear security environment and deterrence.

Proliferation of WMD/delivery means

The dominant logic of pursuing BMD programmes is the perceivable threat from increasing instances of proliferation of WMD and their delivery systems. According to various assessments, the number of countries with ballistic missile capabilities has risen from nine in 1972 to over thirty in 2008, while those with NBC (nuclear, biological, chemical) capabilities rose from fifteen in 1972 to thirty-five in 2008.[37] As the number of countries with delivery-vehicle capabilities increases, it will commensurately reflect in the number of countries pursuing BMDs, which has increased from two in 1972 to around eight in 2009. The current geo-political equations show very limited possibilities to reverse this trend despite the influence of various counter- and non-proliferation initiatives like the Missile Technology Control Regime (MTCR). Regional conflicts and security dilemmas among states have contributed to this phenomenon. Nonetheless, there is renewed movement towards strengthening non-proliferation instruments to reverse this trend. The new wave in favour of elimination of nuclear weapons and their delivery systems, though at a slow pace, is likely to derive dividends in the coming decades. The Obama administration's determination to plug holes in the non-proliferation regime could also boost these efforts. If this momentum consolidates and sustains in the next two decades, it could lead to a new security environment favouring steady decline in proliferation.

Yet this is a complex task, as the initiative has to come from nuclear weapon states to help reduce the security deficit among weaker states, which could reduce incentives for engaging in WMD proliferation. The shift from an offensive to a defensive posture through BMDs could be a catalyst, provided the emphasis on BMDs generates and projects this posture in good measure. Unfortunately, the present evolution of BMDs has produced a contrarian effect, one which postulates competition for interception capabilities that could consequently trigger arms races rather than containment of proliferation. Development of the US BMD and plans for its deployment abroad has only compounded the security dilemma, not just among states which are targeted, but also among other nuclear weapon states which feel a negation of their nuclear deterrent. States which are supposedly targeted by the US BMD have striven

---

37 Peppi DeBiaso, "Missile Defense in the Evolving Security Environment", Office of the Missile Defense Policy, Department of Defense, April 2008. Also see "World Ballistic Missile Inventories", Arms Control Association Fact Sheet, September 2007, at <www.armscontrol.org/factsheets/missiles>.

to enhance their deterrent capabilities both of ballistic missiles and nuclear programmes. As a result, there are likely to be more actors getting into missile development.

Impact of BMDs on Arms Race and Stability

A key factor that could influence the future of BMDs is their potential to trigger a new arms race, especially among the nuclear weapon states. Missile defences, with their inherent capability to negate nuclear deterrence and neutralize offensive forces, create competitions that could affect the existing strategic calculus. The race to construct and deploy BMDs could create a domino effect as states would seek to riposte consequent threats. The response envisaged by various states like China and Russia is to aggressively augment their offensive forces to overwhelm a US BMD shield. This is based on the belief that BMDs are not foolproof defences and hence could be countered through massive attacks, especially with MIRVed missiles. This drive has inspired other states to develop their own BMDs to gain similar advantage.

While Washington argues that its BMDs are an inherent part of its defensive strategy and are meant to deter "rogue states" with clandestine nuclear programmes and their ballistic missile capability, traditional rivals like Russia sees a US BMD in their neighbourhood as posing a direct threat and also negating the deterrent capability of its nuclear forces, in effect creating a Cuban missile crisis-like situation. As a result, Russia is developing new ICBMs such as Topol-M to overwhelm the US BMD, along with its plan to develop advanced interception capabilities.[38] Notwithstanding its opposition to space militarization, Russia is also preparing to augment its capabilities in space, not just to counter the US BMD but also to seek influence and dominance in outer space.[39]

The same applies to China, which perceives US BMD systems such as GBMDS as space weaponry since they can target assets in

---

38   See n. 22.
39   See Pavel Podvig and Hui Zhang, "Russia and Chinese Responses to U.S. Military Plans in Space", American Academy of Arts and Sciences, 2008, at <http://belfercenter.ksg.harvard.edu/files/militarySpace.pdf>.

outer space.[40] China believes BMDs would be a force multiplier to the US nuclear doctrine and in effect negate its nuclear deterrent. For, China believes even a limited US BMD can neutralize its twenty ICBMs capable of reaching the US shores.[41] As a result, China is also pursuing various responses which add to the competition. Apart from the primary effort of augmenting its missile inventory, including with MIRVed ICBMs, China is developing ASAT capability along with development of countermeasures. China is also known to be working on ground-launched compact kinetic-energy and high-energy laser weapons and high-powered microwave weapons for ASAT applications.[42] Finally, Beijing has belied its posture of opposing missile defences by demonstrating its BMD capability through an exo-atmospheric interception in January 2010.[43] While it was always believed that China has a rudimentary air defence programme with extended theatre defence capabilities, the January 2010 test confirmed Chinese plans to match the US BMD challenge in kind. Like the US, China too perceives the strategic benefits of having twin layers of defensive systems to complement its offensive forces.[44]

Amidst this great-power race as an inherent feature of BMDs, there are other zones where such domino effects could create instability. For example, the Indian BMD venture is seen as a means to counter Chinese IRBMs supposedly deployed in Tibet, as well as Pakistani missiles. The mere fact that India is developing BMDs could disturb the nuclear calculus in South Asia, with Pakistan worried about the tenacity of its nuclear deterrent. While not exhibiting BMD

40   Liu Huaqiu (ed.), *Arms Control and Disarmament, Handbook* (Beijing: National Defense Industry Publishing, 2000).

41   Sha Zukang, "The Impact of the US Missile Defense Programme on the Global Security Structure". Paper presented at the CPAPD/ORG Joint Seminar on Missile Defense and the Future of the ABM Treaty, Beijing, 13–15 March 2000, cited by Podvig and Hui Zhang, n. 39.

42   Ibid.

43   "With Defense Test, China Shows Displeasure of U.S.", New York Times, 12 January 2010.

44   See A. Vinod Kumar, "The Dragon's Shield: Intricacies of China's BMD Capability", IDSA Issue Brief, February 2010, http://www.idsa.in/issuebrief/IntricaciesofChinasBMDCapability_250210.

capabilities, Pakistan with its known skills for clandestine technology development is likely to pursue a counter to the Indian BMD shield, besides enhancing its missile inventory as a natural riposte to the Indian BMD. A similar picture is visualized in the Middle East where countries such as Iran are projecting medium- and longer-range missile capabilities to overwhlem Israeli and US theatre defence systems.

Nuclear Security Environment and Deterrence

Missile defences have a great impact on nuclear deterrence equations. While Russia and China fear their nuclear deterrents being neutralized by US BMDs, Washington perceives BMD as central to its nuclear deterrent strategy. In the US scheme of things, BMD advances deterrence by *dissuading* countries from pursuing ballistic missiles as it could impose costs on their missiles. It could *deter* ballistic missile use by denying benefits of an attack and in the process undermine the quantum of its threat. In a comprehensive architecture, offensive forces could increase the risks to an aggressor while defences like BMD would decrease potential gains, thus forcing aggressors to question the utility of their ballistic missiles.

Beyond these rationales, BMDs are seen as a way out of the MAD-oriented strategic equation, as referred by President Reagan. During the Cold War, US planners had devised various deterrent strategies, from assured destruction and massive retaliation to mutual vulnerability. While threats of assured destruction and massive retaliation primarily guided nuclear deterrence equations between the Cold War adversaries, the propriety of leaving space for mutual vulnerability found few takers, notwithstanding the three-decade endurance of the ABM Treaty. It was perceived that defensive systems could offset first-strike capabilities along with diminishing success of assured destruction by the enemy's second strike, thus imparting undue advantage to the nuclear weapon states armed with BMD capability. As a result, even when the ABM Treaty was in force, the superpowers purused the development of ABM systems to gain strategic advantage. While Russian ICBMs are no longer perceived as a primary threat by Washington, that may not be the case as regards China, whose ICBM and nuclear forces remain a key factor in American security planning. Added, there are new states with nuclear weapons like North Korea (and others on the threshold like Iran) which may use nuclear weapons as tools for blackmail or brinkmanship, and may not necessarily subscribe to threats of assured destruction. Instead, they may seek to deter the US through their missile capabilities and ranges to reach US soil or its foreign interests. These are threats which the US perceives can only be addressed through BMDs.

However, the possibility of an arms race and the concerns raised by China and Russia demand a new equation for a BMD-oriented security environment, if this technology has to endure in future as a contributor to deterrence stability. Though the US has withdrawn from its initial Eastern Europe plan, it is yet to devise the means to ensure that instability is not permeated by its BMD deployments. There are multiple strategies that could be explored to manage a potential arms race caused by BMDs, while formulating a new BMD-driven deterrence equation. For example, there could be stability among the nuclear weapon states if they can agree on an offensive-defensive balancing equation, as done in the case of nuclear deterrence during the Cold War. While mutual vulnerability is plugged with the deployment of BMDs, there can be a possibility of balancing BMD capabilities and inventories alongside their nuclear forces. This could lead to a zero-sum equation as BMDs would limit the scope for massive retaliation through a second strike even while checking first-use options.

If executed in a bilateral framework, this could mean a (mutual) defensive deterrence arrangement. Even in the scenario of nuclear forces reduction, as currently pursued by the US and Russia, BMDs will act as a stabilizer when such movements are executed. In the long run, balancing of missile defence capabilities might devalue the gains and utility of nuclear deterrence and encourage timely reduction of nuclear weapons, potentially leading to total elimination. However, such optimistic scenarios have limited possibilities considering that security dilemmas are dynamic, uncontrollable processes being created and influenced by offensive (or even defensive) postures of nations. The US BMD created a security dilemma for Russia and China, prompting them to beef up their offensive and defensive capabilities, thus causing a competition. The path to 2030 and beyond would be embroiled in such competitions though such heightened races might facilitate mutually agreeable stability arrangements. Considering that the ABM Treaty came about as a result of strategic instability created by the superpower arms race, there are possibilities for such new agreements and covenants shaping up when a BMD-driven arms race adds to greater strategic instability.

IV
Future Scenarios

Determining the role or relevance of missile defences for global security by 2030 could be an uphill task, with possibilities of near-certain inaccuracies. The decades from now could witness massive changes in the global security environment along with a natural progressive evolution of technological forces. There are potential for great power rivalries, peace dividends and strategic stalemates. War could also possibly move to retrograde levels involving lower levels of conflict where technology might not be a saviour or balancer. Considering these eventualities, a handful of scenarios could be envisioned for the period based on the trends derived by the above-given postulations.

Scenario I: Politically Driven Slow-paced Technological Progress

A probable scenario will be the continuation of the existing security environment, without major transformations, and a handful of technological templates being pursued in consonance with existing demands with the political drivers exercising varying influence on the nature of the technological innovations. In such a scenario, many of the projects currently envisaged might move from conceptualization or development stages to maturity and deployment. This could mean that many of the US BMD programmes currently under development might reach deployment during 2025–30. Many of the current variants could undertake natural upgrades and augmentations. While Russia would attempt to prefect its BMD planning and deploy systems such as S-400 and S-500, other nations pursuing BMD capability such as India and China could be expected to develop and deploy their new systems during this period.

The rise in instances of proliferation and concomitant challenges from a belligerent North Korea or a nuclear-armed Iran might endow further shifts in the political environment, which will be reflected in the US BMD postures through more foreign deployments and extended coverage. Countries such as Japan, Australia and Israel could host theatre-level and exo-atmospheric US BMD systems in their regions while Europe might be expected to be covered by an extended US shield. The rise of new BMD-armed nations such as India and China might complicate the nuclear deterrence equation in Asia. On the other hand, a push for space-based systems might happen, propelling increased competition in this domain. However, the momentum against space militarization might be a spoil the attempts for maximum exploitation of this domain. Thereby, the nature of BMDs by 2030 would be an imaginable extreme of the technologies envisioned today based on a hand-to-mouth requirement, and strongly driven by political push-and-pull factors.

SCENARIO II: PEACE DIVIDEND

Another possible scenario could be the dramatic change in the nature of BMD development through the benefits of a peace dividend, derived from the momentum in favour of nuclear disarmament. The Obama administration's declared intent to work towards total elimination of nuclear weapons and curb proliferation through enhanced nuclear security has raised hopes of reversing the armament drive, with lesser incentives for proliferation and arms races. This could favour a preferential leap towards defensive postures, which will be reflected in the BMD landscape, as a phased reduction of nuclear warheads and delivery systems will ultimately diminish the political utility of missile defences. However, their role as a stabilizer in the phased reduction process could also be valued if the nuclear weapon states decided on parity in BMD systems to balance the deterrence equations on the route to total elimination. If this momentum is initiated and sustained in the next two decades through a strengthened Nuclear Non-Proliferation Treaty (NPT) or a stand-alone treaty, it could lead to reversal of funding and lesser emphasis for military technological innovations, thus facilitating a decline even in BMDs. However, the risks of proliferation, especially among threshold states, which could misuse the reduction process among the nuclear weapon states, could be a spoiler. In such scenarios, BMDs might exist as a shield against limited missile and nuclear threats. If the peace dividend fructifies, the period around 2030 might see a slide towards formidable reductions both of offensive and defensive missiles. However, going by the lukewarm response to the Obama pacifism and with possibilities of security deficits likely to continue along with enhanced military competition among major powers, this scenario might not be a sustainable proposition.

Scenario III: Great-power Competition and Technological Revolutions

The third potential scenario, and a more realistic one, is the expected dynamism in BMD development that could be generated through heightened competition between the major military powers to gain strategic depth along with a double-edged deterrent capability. The mere fact that various systems are currently under development and that newer technological templates are emerging indicates the potential for a technological competition that could generate a domino impact, in the process triggering and consolidating a new arms race. This impact chain could start with the US BMD expansion that would influence the security calculus of second-tier powers like Russia and China, which in turn will flow down to the third tier of technology-developers like India, Pakistan and Iran, among others. The US would be propelled to provide missile defence umbrellas to its allies in strategic zones like East Asia and the Middle East, which would create a security deficit in these regions. A complicated nuclear equation would thus be the most potent political driver for BMD expansion. An inherent asymmetry endowed by the US technological supremacy would be a pushing factor for other countries to embark further on this technological domain.

V

Conclusion

As the scenarios show, missile defences by and large could remain an irrevocable phenomenon, even if a peace dividend gradually emerges on the scene. However, considering the contemporary and past history, such dividends might not be sustainable and could only be the beginning of a new era of power competitions, strategic rivalries and resultant instabilities. As a defensive mechanism, missile defences could have a brighter scope of endurance. Even for wild card scenarios of great wars, missile defences might be the trump card against total annihilation. Beyond all, there are not visible political contingencies expected to such potent level that can reverse this trend. Just like technologies have evolved into an infinite process, BMDs might be at the central of future burgeoning of military technologies. This is inevitable, considering the current revolution in military affairs (RMA) and the expected revolution in military and dual-use technologies. Ballistic missile defences, needless to say, will be a major component of this evolving technological paradigm. Though there would be increasing opportunities for strategic stability among BMD-armed nations, the innovations in technology could inevitably generate competition among the major powers, potentially creating a new complex strategic environment by 2030.

3
The Future of the Internet
—Cherian Samuel

The Internet has been referred to as the classic example of the proverbial "Black Swan" – an invention or an event that is rare, has extreme impact and "has retrospective (though not prospective) predictability."[1] Such inventions have led to fundamental shifts in the human condition, impacting on the societal and economic arenas in particular. Despite the incredible strides made over the last four decades, the Internet is still in its infancy, and has an infinite number of vertical and horizontal uses, still waiting to be discovered. This makes predicting the future growth of the internet and its consequent impact a well nigh impossible task. Nevertheless such an exercise needs to be attempted given the potential for its use and misuse. This paper will attempt to examine the current trends in the growth of the Internet, the various actors, their relative influence and their varied perspectives all of which have an impact in the shaping of the Internet.

The Current State of the Internet

The success of the Internet has partly been attributed to its relative openness and low barriers (including minimal security features) to entry. However, the same openness, while allowing companies to flourish, has also been responsible for those with malicious intent also to operate with relative ease.

The origins of the Internet can be traced back to the attempts

---

1   Other cited examples of the Black Swan are the invention of the telephone, 9/11 and the Global Financial Crisis of 2008.

by the DARPA (Defense Advanced Research Projects Agency) of the US Department of Defence to create a communications network that would survive a nuclear exchange between the two superpowers. It was subsequently used by academia as a means of communicating and collaborating on research projects. The rise in the popularity of the Internet and its gradual evolution into what it is today can be traced to elements of it being taken up by commercial players as well as the concomitant rise in computing power, as well as attendant technologies such as chip fabrication, optic fibre, and flash memory that kept in pace one with the other to make the internet what it is today.

The uniqueness of the Internet in being an open structure with few barriers to entry is the outcome of the circumstances in which it was conceptualized and a result of the worldview of its initial champions. Though a military project, its very nature of being a communications project plus the fact that it was quickly adopted by academicians as a means of collaboration led to a quick cross-over to the civilian domain. This same set of factors led to its quick roll-out nation-wide and subsequently worldwide. The fact that the technology did not belong to any one company saw the implementation of standards for its various protocols, which was responsible for continuing innovation and improvements of its capabilities. The success of this approach was one of the factors that led to the open source movement with its emphasis on interactive communities modifying the basic building blocks of software to fashion modified versions of software products to suit their needs. The open source approach is intrinsically linked to the free and easy flow of information over the Internet and has been successfully adopted and adapted to other areas ranging from the scientific[2] to media content.[3]

Google executive Marissa Meyers has likened current status of Google's development to that of the earliest days of Biology and Physics:

---

2   Sreelata Menon, Researchers sans borders, *Business Standard*, 1 March 2009. Available online at http://www.business-standard.com/india/news/sreelatha-menon-researchers-sans-borders/00/19/350429/

3   See *Creative Commons* licenses at http://creativecommons.org/

Search is a science that will develop and advance over hundreds of years. Think of it like biology and physics in the 1500s or 1600s: it's a new science where we make big and exciting breakthroughs all the time. However, it could be a hundred years or more before we have microscopes and an understanding of the proverbial molecules and atoms of search. Just like biology and physics several hundred years ago, the biggest advances are yet to come.[4]

This sentiment could be said to hold true for the Internet as a whole. The limits of the expansion of the Internet are set only by the imagination and technical dexterity of innovators and creators, and by certain immutable such as Moore's law, Kryder's Law, Cooper's Law and Gilder's Law.[5] As Eric Schmidt, CEO of Google noted in a recent interview, this implies that any device that has a chip, whether it be a cell-phone or a computer would be 100 times more powerful than it is today in ten years time.[6] Vint Cerf, the "father of the Internet" goes so far as to predict the introduction of internet capability to "existing neural interface technology such as cochlear implants", in other words, computer chips implanted and connected to the brain.[7]

IMPACT OF THE INTERNET REVOLUTION

The Internet Revolution has had ripple effects across the entire spectrum of human activities, particularly through the democratization

---

4   Marissa Meyers, Official Google Blog, *The Future of Search*, 10/09/2008, http://googleblog.blogspot.com/2008/09/future-of-search.html
5   Moore's law states that computing power doubles every 18 months, Kryder's law states that digital storage capacity doubles every 23 months, Gilders' law and Cooper's law, respectively state that bandwidth capacity doubles every 2 years. *Pew Internet Survey*, The Future of the Internet, June 2010, p.3
6   CNN GPS, Interview with Fareed Zakaria, 29 November 2009. Transcript available online at http://transcripts.cnn.com/TRANSCRIPTS/0911/29/fzgps.01.html
7   *Sunday Star Times,* Google 'evangelist' sees web, brain implant link, 23 August 2009. Available online at http://www.stuff.co.nz/technology/digital-living/2779006/Google-evangelist-sees-web-brain-implant-link

of information flows and decreasing transaction costs. However, this revolution has largely been confined to the developed world and is only now begun to percolate to the less developed parts of the planet. Governments in the developed world themselves have been hard put to fulfil their role of providing the appropriate environment for these technologies to flourish while putting in place the required framework to channel their correct use and to prevent any misuse. The rise in the Internet population has meant that while the threats and vulnerabilities inherent to the Internet and Cyberspace might have remained more or less the same as before, the probability of, and the damage from, disruption has grown apace with the rise in the number of users. Whilst individuals were also at risk in the early days of cyberspace, these risks were seen as an occupational hazard that went with using the Internet, and the sporadic patterns of such attacks and their targets suggested them to be largely the handiwork of hackers and low level criminal elements. The expansion of the Internet both vertically and horizontally in terms of population reach and geographical spread and the tremendous transformative potential of the Internet has given rise, inevitably, to countervailing forces that are controlled by those that see the current trends as inimical to their interests, whether it be control over information, or political power. Therefore, while the last forty years of the Internet have been largely shaped by forces and actors including technological innovation, business needs, and public consumption, the next twenty years are likely to see security needs and perceptions become an important factor in shaping the framework of and setting the rules governing the Internet. The interaction of the various forces and the extent to which they are able to make their views prevail set the stage for alternate futures for the Internet. Maintaining the equilibrium between security needs and the fundamental rights of the individual will be a major challenge in the years to come. A consequent challenge will be to frame international agreements on governing cyberpace taking into account the differing perspectives of various governments and other stakeholders.

The Coming Securitization of the Internet

As information becomes the currency of the 21st century, and computers, the banks that hold this information, albeit with very little of the security that one associates with banks, they have become irresistible targets for state and non-state entities. The nature of digital information is such that once the defences of a system or network are breached, the digital information contained therein can a) be retrieved, b) altered, or c) watched for changes. Information security is assured only when the principles of confidentiality, integrity and accessibility are maintained. This applies as much to systems and networks maintained by governments, militaries, and commercial entities as it does to individuals.

The rise in the Internet population has meant that while the threats and vulnerabilities inherent to the Internet and Cyberspace might have remained more or less the same as before, the probability of disruption has grown apace with the rise in the number of users. Similarly, the increasing complexity of computing systems that are connected to the Internet as well as those that keep it operational is one of the factors for increasing vulnerabilities. The current threats[8] take advantage of existing vulnerabilities[9], whether it be in software, networks or security architecture.

At the same time, the prevailing perception of the Internet, as a "global commons" has meant that no one country can unilaterally take on the responsibility of defending or policing networks owned

---

8   A threat was defined by the Computer Emergency Response Team (CERT) in 1993 as "Any circumstances or event that has the potential to cause harm to a system or network. That means, that even the existence of a(n unknown) vulnerability implies a threat by definition."

9   Vulnerabilities are defined as a) A feature or bug in a system or program which enables an attacker to bypass security measures. b)An aspect of a system or network that leaves it open to attack, and c) the absence or weakness of a risk-reducing safeguard which had the potential to allow a threat to occur with greater frequency, greater impact or both. Anil Sagar, *An Overview to Information Security and Security Initiatives in India*, Powerpoint Presentation, 18 January 2008. Available online at *www.elitex.in/paper2008/anilsagar.ppt*

variously by nation states, commercial companies and individuals. In fact, cyberspace is characterised by blurred boundaries, there are no clear demarcations between civilian and military, state and non-state, and foreign and domestic as in other domains. It is those same characteristics that make it an ideal medium for committing *malafide* activities which can have repercussions for national and international security.

THE STATE-CRIMINAL NETWORK-HACKER NEXUS

Criminal networks have, over the years, professionalised the business of discovering and exploiting weaknesses in software that allow them to undertake a variety of actions ranging from taking control of those computers, accessing information on those computers or rendering them unusable. Whilst hackers provide the technical expertise, existing international criminal networks have learnt how to squeeze the maximum out of these compromised computers, and have turnovers estimated in the billions of dollars. Whilst this would remain at the level of criminal activity, it has acquired dangerous proportions and impinges on national security when a state-criminal network-hacker nexus builds up. There is enough circumstantial evidence to show that some states have turned a blind eye to cyber-space centred criminal and illegal activities, perceiving certain advantages to be had from building up such a capacity.

States have the same advantages as criminal networks in undertaking actions over the Internet. These include: the ease of expanding geographic reach to cover virtually the entire world at negligible cost in terms of scaling up; the difficulties with attribution and the concomitant advantage of deniability leading to the inability of the target state to frame a suitable response; and the increasing number of "e-ready" targets, with new concepts such as "cloud computing" coming to the fore.

Recent examples include Distributed Denial of Service Attacks (DDOS) and the installation of custom built malware on targeted computers by entities that have been traced back to China, with the governments of the United Kingdom[10], the United States[11], France[12], Belgium,[13] Germany[14], and India[15] stating that their systems and networks have been infiltrated and attacked by these entities. US officials have been reported as saying that Chinese attacks against Department of Defence (DoD) had reached the level of a "campaign-style, force-on-force engagement" with actions running the "gamut of technology theft, intelligence gathering, exfiltration, research on DOD operations and the creation of dormant presences in DOD networks for future action."[16] The blurred boundaries and the anonymity provided

10   The *Times* reported that the Director General of MI5 had sent a letter to 300 chief executives and security chiefs highlighting "concerns about the possible damage to UK business resulting from electronic attack sponsored by Chinese state organisations, and the fact that the attacks are designed to defeat best-practice IT security systems." The Times, *Secrets of Shell and Rolls-Royce come under attack from China's spies*, 3 December 2007. Also see *China 'tops list' of cyber-hackers seeking UK government secrets*, Times of London, 6 September 2007. Available online at http://www.timesonline.co.uk/tol/news/world/asia/article2393979.ece

11   *Los Angeles Times,* Chinese hacking worries Pentagon, 4 March 2008. Available online at http://articles.latimes.com/2008/mar/04/world/fg-uschina4 Also see Lawmakers Say Capitol Computers Hacked By Chinese, *Huffington Post,* 11 June 2008. Available online at http://www.huffingtonpost.com/2008/06/11/lawmakers-say-capitol-com_n_106640.html

12   AFP, *La France victime de cyber-attaques avec "passage" par la Chine*, 8 September 2007. Available online at http://afp.google.com/article/ALeqM5i6dSqt39zfQcKG-I-HZUTRaN3Zvw

13   vnunet.com, *Belgium accuses China of cyber-crimes*, Available online at http://in.ibtimes.com/articles/20080520/china-hacking-computer-hacker.htm

14   *London Times,* China accused of hacking into heart of Merkel administration, 27 August 2007. Available online at http://www.timesonline.co.uk/tol/news/world/europe/article2332130.ece

15   *DNA India,* Chinese hackers penetrate crucial MEA network, 10 April 2008. Available online at http://www.dnaindia.com/report.asp?NewsID=1159279 Also see DNA India, *Cyber attack on 10 govt websites,* 7 June 2008. Available online at http://www.dnaindia.com/report.asp?newsid=1169339

16   *Federal Computer Weekly,* Cyber officials: Chinese hackers attack 'anything and everything', 13 February 2007. Available online at http://www.fcw.com/online/news/97658-1.html#

by cyber-space make it difficult to pin responsibility for such attacks, which, going by current trends, will be perpetrated by individuals, networks, communities and organisations, with the state acting as facilitator, and nationalistic fervour providing the motivation.

ALTERNATE FUTURES

No phrase is more apt for the Internet than the one that the only constant is change itself. As far as the public internet is concerned, while technological change, business decisions and societal impulses are major factors in determining the future direction of the Internet, its increasing integration into the very fabric of human existence means that the ultimate arbiter of its destiny will be the state. Policy makers will be confronted by the problem of trying to maintain a balance between societal and commercial calls to consider the Internet and cyberspace as a "global commons" which should be kept open and free like other "global commons" such as the high seas and space. On the other side will be those that will, equally rightly consider the Internet as critical infrastructure, "equally strategic to national security as its electricity grid and water supply", that would need to be protected, for its own good through restraints and barriers. At the same time, it must be kept in mind that over-regulation can have a negative impact on the Internet and even choke it.[17] The struggle to maintain the balance between openness and security is one that afflicts open societies in the physical world as well, with the important difference that physical barriers are way easier to put up than digital ones, and that the repercussions are limited.

Though cyber laws have been enacted by countries the world over, they have largely been ineffective and unable to keep pace with the changing nature of the threats. Such laws have been flayed

---

17 The impact of such actions or non-actions cannot be underestimated. Part of the reason why there is an increasing trend towards accessing the Internet on mobile devices, apart from the convenience, is that many companies are restricting the use of internet in the office either by blocking sites or ports. Similarly, the porn industry has been considered one of the most important factors for the success of the Internet, leading to advances in audio and video streaming technologies, and for popularizing electronic payments over the Internet.

by public interest groups for violating fundamental human rights, for impinging on privacy and for giving undue powers to the government.[18] The same problems hold true for a treaty approach which has been advocated by some governments. As a case in point, Russia has for long been pressing for a cyberspace treaty with the United States on the lines of the Chemical Weapons Treaty and focusing on constraining the military uses of cyberspace. The United States has been resisting this approach and instead wants to focus on the criminilisation of cyberspace, arguing that a law enforcement approach was more important considering the imminent threats.[19] Both sides are suspicious of each others intentions; while the Americans feel that a treaty approach would legitimize censorship of the Internet and increased governmental oversight would facilitate increased control by totalitarian regimes, the Russans disfavour the law and order approach since they feel that this would infringe on their sovereignty. Existing inter-governmental agreements such as the Council of Europe Convention on Cybercrime allow for cross-country investigation of cybercrimes without the necessity of first getting approval from the governments concerned.[20]

If the increasing security threats on the Internet see the balance swing overwhelmingly in favour of heavy-handed oversight over the Internet by governments and their security agencies, this might increase the security and stability of the Internet, but it could also sound the death-knell of the Internet as a harbinger of greater openness and freedom for individuals and societies around the world. Whilst so far, the open source movement has been in the vanguard of maintaining the unique nature of the Internet, it is dying a slow death as regular business enterprises have swallowed up many of the companies built on the back of this philosophy. Even as the user base grows, it is far too fragmented

18 See *Business Standard,* Amended IT Act comes into effect, 28 October 2009. Available online at http://www.business-standard.com/india/ news/amended-it-act-comes-into-effect/374538/

19 *The New York Times*, U.S. and Russia Differ on a Treaty for Cyberspace, 27 June 2009. Available online at http://www.nytimes.com/2009/06/28/ world/28cyber.html

20 Ibid.

to be an effective force guarding against the excesses of the state. Only users in the United States and Europe users have been vocal in their opposition to attempts both by business and government to restrain what has come to be seen as an extension of their fundamental rights.[21] Any further procastination would ultimately lead to the fragmentation of the Internet, across the spectrum. For instance, while the US military has only just begun to separate its military communications network from the Internet (in effect building an Internet of its own),[22] such a scenario already exists in China where the government's tight control over connectivity has resulted in a vastly different and highly sanitized internet experience for a Chinese resident.[23]

An article on the blog Google Blogscoped titled *How to Access the Internet (A Guide from 2025)* paints a worse case scenario if current trends continue.[24] "Beginning with identification requirement as a pre-requisite for accessing the Internet, other developments according to this scenario include the fragmentation of the Internet based on geography with content being provided on a similar basis as well as in keeping with restrictions imposed by national governments. An internet surfing licence, similar to a driving license would also have to

---

21 *The New York Times*, E.U. Leaders Bolster Internet Access Protections, 5 November 2009. Available online at http://www.nytimes.com/2009/11/06/technology/internet/06net.html. While there have been attempts to frame an Internet Bill of Rights, none of them have managed to gather any momentum.

22 *The Register,* DARPA, Microsoft, Lockheed team up to reinvent TCP/IP:'This time it will actually be for the military, promise' 16 October 2009. Available online at http://www.theregister.co.uk/2009/10/16/darpa_microsoft_reinvent_internet/

23 However, the Chinese government has also met with significant push-back from local internet communities and has had to roll back some of the more blatant attempts at internet censorship such as installing the "Green Dam" internet monitoring software on all computers. *Wall Street Journal*, China Pulls Back From Edict On Web-Filtering Software, 14 August 2009. Available online at http://online.wsj.com/article/SB125013563611828325.html

24 *Goolge Blogoscoped,* How to Access the Internet (A Guide from 2025), June 24, 2010. Available online at http://blogoscoped.com/archive/2010-06-24-n15.html

be obtained after passing a test including components on safe surfing, and recognizing malware filled sites. Accessing such sites would result in one's licence being cancelled." Even if such a scenario might seem farfetched now, the actions and inaction of governments, even if with the best of intentions, only serve to make this an inevitability. The complexity and multi-dimensional nature of many of these issues has led to most governments resorting to a piece-meal approach to resolving them. This is evident in actions ranging from the Indian government making it a requirement that all wi-fi connections should be registered[25] (after emails intimating such attacks were sent over un-secured connections) to the US Congress deliberating a bill that would give the President powers to virtually take over the Internet in case of a "cyber-security emergency".[26] Coupled with inevitable technological advances such as the decision by the Internet Corporation for Assigned Names and Numbers(ICANN) to approve the use of scripts other than Latin to be used in internet addresses,[27] this approach could result in unintended outcomes and presage a future in which the Internet becomes increasingly fragmented, eventually multiplying into Internets, replicating in the virtual world what currently obtains in the physical world.[28]

---

25 See *Medianama*, Indian Government Wants Telcos To Register WiFi Users Within 60 Days, 20 October 2009. Available online at http://www.medianama.com/2009/10/223-indian-government-wants-telcos-to-register-wifi-users-within-60-days/

26 *Huffington Post*, Internet 'Kill Switch' Approved By Senate Homeland Security Committee, 25 June 2010. Available online at http://www.huffingtonpost.com/2010/06/25/internet-kill-switch-appr_n_625856.html

27 *Times of India*, Now type internet URLs in your own language, 30 October 2009. Available online at http://timesofindia.indiatimes.com/city/pune/Now-type-internet-URLs-in-your-own-language/articleshow/5178055.cms

28 As another case in point, domains that are registered in the Chinese script in China can only be visited within China, or by computers using Chinese DNS (Domain Name System) servers. See *PC World*, No Rush to Adopt Domain Names Written in Chinese in China. 10 November 2009. Available online at http://www.pcworld.com/article/181802/no_rush_to_adopt_domain_names_written_in_chinese_in_china.html

In the final analysis, those who have power over the internet would do well to approach it from the perspective of it being a force for good in the world, and see what they can do to enhance rather than inhibit it. As the American computer scientist Alan Kay put it, "the best way to predict the future is to invent it".

4
Climate Change Future of Asia
—Avinash Godbole

For an exciting continent like Asia where dynamics of power and politics are changing exceedingly rapidly, the exercise of engaging in and developing a discourse over the possible course of future events becomes extremely difficult. However, the pace of this change and its implications for world order makes this exercise equally important. The Henley Centre's 2001 Report, *Benchmarking UK Strategic Futures Work*, precisely explains the purpose of the future centric work in the statement that "...the benefit of strategic futures work is not that it predicts the future, which is unpredictable, or (that it) enables organizations to control it. It is about rehearsing possibilities, so one is better able to respond if they happen".[1] This paper is based on this idea.

The Asian economies have risen by the average rates ranging between 7 and 10 percent per annum in the last one decade. This process was propelled by the increase in their interaction with the world economy and with the global financial markets. This has also created domestic economic stimulus in the large economies of India and China. Therefore, it was seen that even while the global financial meltdown has impacted projected increase in the growth rate, the

---

1   The Henley Centre (2001), *Benchmarking UK Strategic Futures Work, A report for the Performance and Innovation Unit*, Available Online at http://www.cabinetoffice.gov.uk/media/cabinetoffice/strategy/assets/ benchmarking.pdf; p. 23 cited in The DCDC Global Strategic Trends Programme 2007-2036 published by Development, Concepts and Doctrine Centre's (DCDC) p. 1.

Asian economies have generally performed above the global average of economic performance.

The pace with which Asian economies are expanding, particularly those of China and India, lends them greater voice on the debates surrounding the issues of geopolitical and strategic importance. It also means that their activities on these issue areas are being monitored by the larger world in more details than ever before, more so because Asian countries' energy requirements, their individual and collective policies on climate change and their projected demographic patterns are going to influence how the world approaches these issues. More importantly, these three drivers are important for Asia regardless of the external interest in the Asian perspectives as it will not be farfetched to argue that the nature of the often talked idea of the Asian Century will be determined by the developments in these three drivers in the next couple of decades. Another reason for the importance of the drivers of energy, climate and demography is the inevitability of their interaction. No government or non-governmental organisation can single out any of these even if they so wished. The following section studies these three drivers.

1. ENERGY SECURITY:

One major consequence of the rise of Asia has been the increase in the Asian share in the global oil demand. The report titled *International Energy Outlook 2009* published by the Energy Information Administration (EIA), of the United States Government, projects the total energy demand to rise by 44 percent by 2030 over the level of 2006, mainly led by the non-OECD countries where the projects growth will be 104 percent.[2] Given the import dependence of the major Asian economies, this projection has significant implication for Asia. These implications can be classified in two categories; the strategic implications and the implications for energy security.

---

2   The total energy demand is expected to reach about 700 quadrillion Btu from the 2006 level of 472 Quadrillion Btu. Energy Information Administration, International Energy Outlook 2009 (2009), available at http://www.eia.doe.gov/oiaf/ieo/world.html

The World Energy Outlook 2007 defines energy security as "... adequate, affordable and reliable supplies of energy".[3] This is a fairly comprehensive definition of the term. The quest for energy security is not new. Daniel Yergin famously described the history of the Twentieth Century as a quest for oil, money and power.[4] The history of the twentieth century international relations can be summed up in the three terms that Yergin uses in the subtitle of his book. The power relations of the twentieth century were based on the extent to which states could ensure their energy security. States demonstrated, enhanced and extended their military and strategic capability towards ensuring energy security and the extent of their success determined their relative position in the power hierarchy of the world.

At the core of it, the relationship between state power and energy resources is a kind of vicious circle; the more the power, more the ease to ensure energy resources, however more power makes it more likely that the state is dependent on energy resources from beyond their borders. At present China imports about 40 percent of its crude oil resources. It is projected that this will go up to 50 percent in the next 12-15 years. India will continue to import 70 to 75 percent of its oil requirements. At the same time, given the fact that the per capita energy consumption is set to rise in these countries commensurate with their economic rise, the added number will be huge. Thus for the large Asian countries, scale and magnitude of energy dependence is set to rise.

2. CLIMATE CHANGE:

It can be argued here that the issue of climate change is the unimagined and undesirable outcome of the politics which Yergin talks of in his book. In order to look at the future course of events and interactions regarding climate change, energy and development,

---

3   World Energy Outlook 2007 (2007), International Energy Agency, Paris; p. 160.

4   Daniel Yergin (1992), *The Prize: The Epic Quest for Oil, Money and Power*, New York; Touchstone, cited by Martha Harris (2003), Energy and Security in Michael E. Brown (ed.)*Grave New World; Security Challenges in the 21ˢᵗ Century*, Washington; Georgetown University Press, pp.157-177.

one needs to find out the ways in which any country would keep its energy supplies adequate, affordable and reliable and how it would be different from the way it was done in the past

Since the emergence of the realisation that human economic activity was responsible for the increasing environmental degradation, a lot of attention has been paid to the area of environmental consequences of human activity. Its long term permanent impact came to be known as climate change. It was believed that climate change was one of the drivers of change in international order. It had the potential to redefine the security framework in the post cold war era, since its nature makes the political boundaries irrelevant. However, the euphoria around the idea died soon and the debate has been caught in the North-South framework of international relations as witnessed in the latest round of UN sponsored climate talks at Copenhagen.

Despite the repeated expressions of optimism, the debate on climate change has not changed much. The reason for this has been the lack of firm commitments from the major parties to the debate on climate change. It has been observed that the climate change debate is caught between the gross versus per-capita debate and historical versus present and future carbon emissions. Given this reality, one can easily guess the state of affairs in the global initiative towards cooperation on the subject of climate change. Observers were already writing obituaries to the COP 15 Climate Change Conference in Copenhagen even while it was in progress. In general, the climate change debate suffers from the trust deficit that is experienced in the other arenas of international relations. However, leading to Copenhagen, various leaders of developing countries have made important announcements about their emissions which help assess the way in which these major developing countries would likely approach climate change in the next couple of decades. Developing countries have in principle committed that their per capita emissions will remain lower than that of the developed world even as these countries develop rapidly. Thus, one can expect the development process to be generally more sustainable than what has been seen so far.

The picture presented by developed world about the large developing countries' approach to climate change projects, advertently or inadvertently, that the large developing countries want to enjoy the power status that their development process accords them *without* taking up concomitant responsibilities that should go with the power status. In any case, the logic of developing countries sharing the burden of historical emissions of the European and American development process is absurd and unlikely to succeed. Developing countries must be allowed equivalent carbon space for their growth as was taken by developed countries. Developing countries face the questions of equality, access, participation gender associated with the process of development. Many in these countries see the attempts to enforce emission reduction targets on these countries as neo-imperialism.

In addition, actions on climate change will not succeed if the process is top down. As seen from the examples in the west itself, the move towards sustainable development will be more effective in achieving its desired outputs if the push for it comes from the society concerned itself. If it is seen to be top down or as one that is enforced by the outside powers, then it is likely to meet greater resistance and thus is less likely to be useful. The domestic push for sustainable development process will accelerate in the large developing countries if development is accompanied by enlightenment and democratisation at the grassroots level as seen in the example of mushrooming of the environmental Non Governmental Organisations in urban China. It is not just the numbers but the maturation of these green organisations has been important. The green NGOs in urban China have not only worked as watchdogs on the government activities but they have also looked to expand their sphere of influence to other aspects of governance in China.

In all likelihood, China and India will continue their independent action plans on climate change in the absence of global cooperation or assistance in therms of joint strategies. China is getting more stricter on emission norms and efficiency benchmarks. India has also announced conservancy and energy diversification strategies in the form of the National Action Plan on Climate Change (NAPCC) under which it will undertake different missions aimed at comprehensive strategies on climate change mitigation and adaptation and for designing a comprehensive sustainable development strategy.[5]

Moreover, there has been parallel development on the two contradictory trends as far as this issue is concerned; first is the securitisation of the climate change debate and the second is the trend towards bilateral cooperation.[6] The worrying factor about the securitisation of climate change is that the calls for securitisation tend to hide the responsibilities that the governments need to undertake in order to control the negative effects of climate change. Another worrying factor is that the calls for securitisation of the climate change have come less from the vulnerable sections of the world, sections that are dependent on seasonal rains for agriculture or susceptible to food shortages but more from the serious polluters, ones who need to bring about substantial changes in the organisations of economy and their lifestyles and thus domestic political scenes have been dominated by misinformed rhetoric.[7]

The problem with securitisation of climate change is that it takes the focus away from mitigation actions required from the developed economies and shifts it to the adaptive requirements. Thus, in recent times there has been an increasing focus on security implications of climate change on areas that already experience ethnic, political and

---

5   For details see http://pmindia.nic.in/Pg01-52.pdf
6   The example of the securitisation is the argument in the article in New York Times of 8 August 2009, Available Online at http://www. nytimes.com/2009/08/09/science/earth/09climate.html;   various bilateral agreements that were signed between different countries exemplify the cooperative trend for example, for a discussion on the merits and demerits of bilateral cooperation on climate issues see Avinash Godbole, Sino US Climate Pact: Context, text and subtext, IDSA Strategic Comment, 10 August 2009, available at http://www. idsa.in/publications/stratcomments/AvinashGodbole100809.htm
7   See for example Sarah Palin's rhetorical argument opposing the passing of the Climate Bill in the US Congress in Washington Post of 14 July 2009; available online at http://www.washingtonpost.com/wp-dyn/ content/article/2009/07/13/AR2009071302852_pf.html

social stresses. A large amount of research focus is on how the sea level rise of certain nature will affect low lying countries and their security while at the same time completely ignoring what needs to change in the consumption and emission patterns of the west in order to reduce the sea level rise itself! Therefore, one can argue that the solution to the environmental displacement in Bangladesh that could take place in 2030 or later is not in Bangladesh but in changing the way American SUVs consume gasoline. Even if this example is a simplification of the issue, it shows the perception gaps that exist between the developed and developing countries on the subject of climate change. Securitisation theorists find it hard to justify the gap between attempts to bring out a cooperative framework at the top and projects of conflict at the bottom as the outcome of climate change. Securitisation of climate change, rather than raising the attention paid to the subject, is more likely to exacerbate the pre-existing tensions in the developing world. Another critic of attempts towards securitisation is that examples so far do now give strong evidence of the causal link between environmental change and violent conflict. Environmental changes and resources shortages can also work as threat pacifiers, not just as threat multipliers. Just how that would happen would depend on the other associated factors; political, ethnic, linguistic and so on.

3. DEMOGRAPHY:

Asian societies have traditionally been rural societies. With rapid economic growth, this profile is bound to undergo a substantial transformation.[8] The major concern for the governments of Asia will be to ensure that this transformation is peaceful, inclusive and based on firm grounds. Large Asian states are composed of mixed ethnic profiles. When the societies transform themselves, there is bound to be intermingling of people from different identities and backgrounds. These different ethnic and linguistic identities could be strengthened or weakened in the transformative stages depending on the extent to which the transformation is just and also is seen as such. Local identity politics could exploit the cleavages that emerge during the process to

---

8   For detailed discussion see Gunjan Singh (2009), "Demography, Migration and Urbanisation: Asia in 2030", available online at http://www.idsa.in/asc/opinion8.html, accessed on 22 December 2009.

the detriment of the society. This can be aided by energy or resource stresses. We already see anti-migration politics in large developed city of Mumbai in India and elsewhere in less organised forms. There is also a trend to favour local population over the migrants. In Shanghai, for example, local administration was mulling the relaxation of the one child norm while numerous migrants lacked social security facilities.[9]

With increases in opportunities, more and more women should be able to participate in the economic activities. This process has been relatively slow in South Asia compared to East and South East Asia. Spread of education and employment opportunities for women can play a huge role in women's empowerment which will have further positive spin offs for the entire society.

Third aspect of the demographic future of Asia is about the ageing profile of the East Asian countries. Japan is already experiencing this trend. South Korea and China will start facing this problem soon. Ageing profile is the unintended consequence of the success of the East Asian population policy of the 1970s and 80s. Already there are policies in place to encourage two children in order to reduce the impact of ageing. However, the response to these policies has been slow particularly because the cost of large family is high even if both parents are working.

Scenario Building

Based on the three drivers mentioned above, one can design the future scenarios on the basis of the combination of different variables. The future of the climate change and the mitigation and adaptation action can be assessed by developing scenarios.

1) *Baseline Scenario:*

On the subject of climate change it is generally accepted that continuation of situation as it persists is undesirable. However, it

9 Mark Tran (2009), "Shanghai Couples urged to have Second Child as Chinese population ages", *Guardian*, 24 July, available online at http://www.guardian.co.uk/world/2009/jul/24/ageing-population-china-shanghai-one-child-policy, accessed on 22 December 2009.

is possible that it continues as it is if there is a failure to reach an agreement based on emission reduction commitments. In this situation in next couple of decades one could see reversal of economic growth seen around the world due to economic heating associated with the initial phase of growth. Since it is known that lack of action would lead to eventual doomsday, all the economies will try to expand their economic activities. In this process unsustainable industry like coal fired power industry will continue to get financial and political state support for business as it is. One can expect to see greening of politics without actual emission reductions. Under this scenario, there will be no lifestyle changes in the developed countries. Thus, transportation will be private and state exchequer will be used to ensure oil subsidies. Since there will not be any greater incentives as well as regulations for cleaner technologies, oil companies, automobile industry and coal industry will not find technology research viable. Thus, change to cleaner technology will be difficult and economically unsustainable. Oil producing countries will retain their pre-eminence since there will be greater competition to secure oil resources among developed and developing countries.

There will be developmental assistance to developing countries. However, due to the costs of sustainable technology and lack of subsidies on it, it will not help in reducing emission levels. Large developing countries which are dependent on oil imports will see their costs increasing and as a consequence their budgetary deficits will go up. This will lead to inflation that the government would find itself unable to manage and subsequently regional and social inequality will increase. There will be increased pressure on agriculture due to lack of ability of the industry to absorb excess rural population as industry would find it difficult to expand due to rising input costs and shrinking demands. Rural to urban migration would lead to ethnic and linguistic identification and unless there are concerted efforts towards normalisation, violent conflicts could emerge.

Sea level rise predictions due to warming and glacial meting will be seen and this will lead to mass migration and can lead to chaos in weak states. This will be evident in the economically weak states where there is high density of population, Bangladesh, for example. This will lead to mass internal migration due to failure of mitigation strategies. Variable patterns of precipitation will challenge food security and raise food prices. This will lead to extreme hunger and malnutrition especially in the already poor regions of Africa and Latin America. Smaller islands in Asia will face extinction and will seek asylum in large states, causing resource stress even in the large countries. Hardliner tendencies will find increased support if this is seen as outcome of unjust state actors. Strong state response can lead to violence or weakening of legal process.

Trans-national water courses like Brahmaputra will become causes of international conflicts. In the absence of binding water sharing agreements, national priorities will override bilateral considerations. While diversion techniques might help upper riparian countries, lower riparian countries will be at a huge loss due to loss of livelihood and sustenance. On the other hand, lower riparian countries might use the overall reduction in water resources to raise the ante against the upper riparian states in order to use its dependent position as a bargaining strategy. This might lead to armed conflicts if negotiations are not able to settle the issues.

2) *Alternate Scenario; Firm Commitments from the West of Emission Reduction with Space for Emission Increase from Developing Countries:*

This will be the best case scenario if the western countries, including the US, sign on the dotted line assuring firm and time bound emission reduction in process of climate change negotiations. By this process, the developed countries will recognise the requirement of the carbon space for the developing countries and will not transfer the burden of their historical carbon emissions. As a consequence there is a greater level of cooperation between the developed and developing countries as they are able to recognise the principle of differential responsibility in action. This will also facilitate information and data sharing. There will be greater emphasis on joint research which will lead to reduction of costs of sustainable technology making it attractive and thus economically viable. This will encourage more and more research in sustainability as it will be seen effective for environment as well as economical for producers and for consumers. This will help greater economic integration which will be environmentally sustainable and it will help the large developing countries in reducing their projected emissions from their future development process. For the effects of historical emissions, there will be better funds transfer to combat water scarcity and towards ensuring food and water security.

As a consequence of the reduction of dependence on the West Asian oil, there will be geopolitical shift in the approaches of the great powers as the large oil dependent importing countries will feel less vulnerable to oil shocks and blockades of oil routes for strategic reasons. Futility of maintaining big attack forces will lead to redefinition of great power and the great power games. This will in turn accelerate the ascendance of soft power to the position of primacy in the longer run. It will also secularise the discourse of international relations in the long run as the primacy accorded to oil will reduce. Oil rich countries will have to adapt different strategies for their relative importance, as resource rich nations and as strategic locations, will have reduced. They could move to being finance hubs or start their own soft power approach to the new International relations, based on their aid policies like Canada's Human Security approach in the last 12/15 years.

In general, this process will lead to desecuritisation of the climate change process as mitigation processes will precede aid policies for adaptation process. There will be greater focus on social, political and economic factors behind the climate change and mitigation and adaptation process.

3) *Wild Card: Continuation of the Situation as it is with limits on economic growth:* (Wild Card: Constraints on Growth Oriented Strategy)

If a large developing country in which growth is based on trade finds itself unable to grow at high rates due to economic heating due to rising costs of inputs driven by soaring energy prices as well as negative social implications of the growth process, then it will try to limit the growth rate to something which it feels it can manage politically and sustain economically. However, it will find it difficult to sustain this process from the top as well as from below. Economic forces at the top will find it difficult to digest low growth rates for its capital. And the lower strata which was hitherto out of the economic growth process, will find the voluntary curbs on growth as wall against its participation in that process. The size of these two groups, at the top and at the bottom, will determine the outcome in the end. One outcome could be the flight of capital out of that country since the returns appear to be economically unsustainable. This could also lead to closure of industry and large unemployment and political resistance from the strong middle class the support of which was the strength of the regime so far. The lower strata could be politically organised around the rallying point of exclusion if there is a leadership that emerges to guide this section of the society. State's ability in the transition period from high growth rates to slow but sustainable rates will be critical. Similarly its ability to absorb relative losses and to negotiate the relative bargain will decide the ultimate outcome in this scenario.

State apparatus can give incentives for research on alternative energy and for making available technology more affordable and effective. By this process it can mobilise its industrial resource and move gradually to more sustainable basis of economic activities. This can propel the economy from its slow pace back to more sustainable pace.

In this scenario, the relative ability of the state is critically important. If the political forces claiming to represent marginalised sections and others who lose out due to imposed slow downs become strong, then there will be internal chaos and it will have implications for domestic order. If the state finds itself unable to manage the conflict then in the worst case scenario there could be implosion of the state leading to chaos. It will have implications for other states only if there are other conflicts in the region.

The state apparatus needs to be able to reconcile the contrasting interests and manages to halt the flight of capital by ensuring its security. It should also garner greater trust from the people by canvassing the longevity of its transformative policies. In the meantime civil society and welfare policies will need to play critical roles in their respective domains.

CONCLUSION

In all the three scenarios mentioned above, cooperation or conflict would be the outcome of the presence or absence of couple of additional factors. For cooperation, state mechanism needs to be strong and political forces need to be accommodative and flexible. This could eliminate even the worst effects of climate change and violence or collapse of state machinery will be avoided. State needs to be able to reconcile the contrasting interests and manages to halt the flight of capital by ensuring its security. It should also garner greater trust from the people by canvassing the longevity of its transformative policies.

Civil Society can help in raising awareness and cooperative mechanisms. It can help the government by bringing to its knowledge the exploitative political processes and generally by encouraging internal cooperation. Civil society can take the role of welfare organisation and disseminate information and work on the areas where inequality will be most harmful hunger, gender, participation for example. Welfare State policies might look far fetched in the present era. However, since the idealism over market capitalism is far from successful and since the leadership is taking of return of welfare policies like Hu Jintao in his discourse on 'scientific development', return of states with strong welfare policies is not unimaginable. If the sound welfare policies are implemented in right measure and at right time, then they are more likely to be effective. These policies can take forms of assistance in adaptation to climate change like food security measures, educational policies, support for agriculture and farming community and so on.

From the discussion above, it is amply clear that the first and second scenarios are the most likely outcomes, the latter of which is the more desirable one. Scenario two could lead to sustainable policies. For the scenario that suits the developmental priorities of the developing countries, developed world needs to take a more holistic view of the situation.

In the wild card scenario, strong state action over a long period of time will be required if the state looks to trade the growth oriented path for a more sustainable path. Climate Change and actions to counter it could lead to quite interesting and yet unimagined outcomes for the world politics.

On the issue of climate change it is now accepted that there in no outcome of the deadlock unless all parties agree to a framework. It has also been a strategy of the developed countries to bring on board of responsibility the large developing countries. It was seen as necessary as the carbon divide has the potential create new alignments in the world order. Any action on climate change will have to involve radical changes in the global energy policy. And when energy policy is concerned, it will have implications on the economic organisation of the modern city based societies. In the situation when urbanisation is only going to rise in Asia, addressing these three drivers needs composite perspectives. Any attempt to address them individually will have counterproductive impacts in other sectors. This fact underlines their critical importance for the future of Asia and of the world as such.

5

Envisioning United States Asia Policy in 2030

—Sanjeev Kumar Shrivastav

"Asia and the United States are not separated by this great ocean; we are bound by it. We are bound by our past — by the Asian immigrants who helped build America, and the generations of Americans in uniform who served and sacrificed to keep this region secure and free. We are bound by our shared prosperity — by the trade and commerce upon which millions of jobs and families depend. And we are bound by our people — by the Asian Americans who enrich every segment of American life, and all the people whose lives, like our countries, are interwoven."[1]

–US President Barack Obama, Tokyo, November 14, 2009

INTRODUCTION

This chapter is an attempt to build scenarios for the United States (US) Asia policy in 2030. The rise of Asia is visible but this does not infer that the power of the US has diminished or is likely to diminish at least in coming two decades. The rise of Asia is probably more related to the significant growth shown by few Asian countries, particularly the India and China. According to the International Monetary Fund's projections as revealed in its World economic outlook database, the global GDP share of developing Asian economies is expected to raise from 7.1 per cent in 1980 to 22.8 per cent by end of 2010.

---

1   United States President Barack Obama while delivering Asia Policy speech at Suntory Hall, Tokyo, Japan on November 14, 2009, The White House available at http://www.whitehouse.gov/the-press-office/remarks-president-barack-obama-suntory-hall (Accessed on January 14, 2010)

Asia is the largest continent on earth which covers 29.9 per cent of the total land area and 8.6 per cent of the earth's total surface area. The region has been inhabited by more than 4 billion people which accounts for nearly 60 per cent of the total world population. In its annual report in 2007, the World Economic Forum (WEF) had recognised the growing importance of Asia, especially countries like China and India, with an expectation that it will help build the relationship and understanding between Asia and the West. [2]

Due to its vast size, varied topography, terrain and environmental conductions, diverse cultures and different historical affinities as well as different evolution of government systems, the capital concentration in Asia differs widely among and within its regions. Hence, even when the Asia is growing its growth is not found uniform and there are many 'islands' of negative growth too. The reasons for prosperity as well as poverty could be far too many but the main basis for this to happen is mostly the political.

Key Drivers Dictating Asia's Present and Future

To gauge the future of Asia one approach could be to undertake a scenario building exercise. Following paragraphs discuss few of the key drivers which may impact the future of the Asia. Such drive based scenarios may not offer the exact understanding of the future but could help to visualise policy options for the future.[3] Here three key drivers have been identified which are likely to play a critical role in the making of the US Asia policy for 2030 and beyond.

1. Security

Since 9/11 terror attacks, the US is engaged in war against Taliban and Al-Qaida elements in Afghanistan. This war has entered in its 10th year in October 2010. Post 9/11, the US is facing most

2   'World Economic Forum sees growing importance of Asia', *China Economic Net,* September 7, 2007 available at http://en.ce.cn/National/Politics/200709/07/t20070907_12827150.shtml (Accessed on January 18, 2010

3   See, Brigadier Arun Sehgal's presentation on Scenario Building, SAGARPUSP, EA 09040 available at http://www.slideshare.net/tigerzmsg/scenario-building (Accessed on January 23, 2010)

serious security threats from Afghanistan- Pakistan (Af-Pak) region as Al-Qaeda and Taliban are having strong presence in these states. The US also confronts with the challenge of saving Afghanistan and Pakistan from state-failure. The US is aware that the Al Qaeda and Taliban operate from the safe havens in the Pakistan but is unable to take a stern action against Pakistan because of strategic compulsions. Apart from Afghanistan crisis, increasing Talibanization of Pakistan also figures more menacingly in the US threat perceptions.

While announcing his Afghanistan-Pakistan (Af-Pak) strategy on March 27, 2009, President Obama has described the Pakistan-Afghanistan border as the most dangerous place in the world. Obama wishes that the Pakistan should demonstrate its commitment to rooting out Al-Qaeda and the violent extremists within its borders.[4] It is likely that the future threat to the US interests within and outside the country may originate from the Afghanistan-Pakistan region.

For the US, the threats from Asia for next two decades are not likely to emanate only from the Afghanistan-Pakistan region. East Asia is also a region of concern for the US. At the same time few states in this region and in other parts of Asia have been in the alliance with the US for many years. Hence, the Asian landscape as whole offers both, the challenges as well as opportunities for the US to decide its future policy.

US-Japan Alliance

Japan has been the priority and the keystone of US Asia policy since the signing of 'Treaty of Mutual Cooperation and Security' between both the nations in 1960. Acknowledging the significance of US-Japan alliance, then Senator Barack Obama had said during his 2008 US presidential election campaign, "The US and Japan have shared interest in promoting security and prosperity in Asia and around the world... The US-Japan alliance must remain at the core of efforts to revitalize Japan's role in ensuring stability and security in

---

4   See, Editorial, "Obama's Af-Pak strategy", *The Hindu,* March 30, 2009 available at http://www.thehindu.com/2009/03/30/ stories/2009033053091000.htm (Accessed on January 27, 2010)

the region"[5] However the United States-Japan security alliance faced major roadblock over the issue of force re-alignment since neither the Japanese politicians nor the people provided the support as expected by the United States. The stalled relocation of the US Marines' Futenma airbase is the probably the most serious political challenge which the Japan-US security alliance is facing at the end of the first decade of the 21st century.

Over the years the US-Japan alliance has witnessed many ups and downs. Few are of the opinion that the US-Japan security alliance is on the decline. According to a government survey which was conducted before the inauguration of Obama presidency pointed out that number of people who thought the relations between the two states were good, had dropped to 68.9 percent, the lowest since the survey began in 1998.[6] The Democratic Party of Japan over the years have emphasised that there is need for a 'close and equal' alliance with the US. In September 2009, Yukio Hotoyama began pushing for the formation of an East Asian Community (EAC) within the six days after coming to power. During the United Nations summit in New York on September 21, 2009, Prime Minister Hatoyama and Chinese President Hu Jintao proposed to work together to form an East Asian community.[7] This could be viewed as an attempt to sideline the US in the region with the coming together of the Japan, China and South Korea.

Turbulent Korean Peninsula

The US's Korea policy has been revolving around its concerns related to North Korean nuclear programme. The conduct of nuclear test by

---

5   Thomas Crampton, "Obama China and Japan policies", October 29, 2009, available at http://www.thomascrampton.com/china/obama-china-and-japan-policies/. (Accessed on January 31, 2010)

6   Hiroshi Nakanishi, "Will Obama's promise of change include US-Japan relations?" *The Japan Times*, January 1, 2009 available at http://search.japantimes.co.jp/cgi-bin/eo20090101a1.html (Accessed on February 4, 2010)

7   "Japan Wants East Asian Community", *The Trumpet.com,* September 29, 2009 available at http://www.thetrumpet.com/?q=6575.5057.0.0 (Accessed on February 19, 2010)

North Korea in 2006 demonstrates the failure of the US policy in the region. After these tests the US started a policy of engagement with the North Korea and initiated of a multilateral framework of the Six Party Talks. However, despite the various agreements concluded, North Korea did not fulfill its obligations toward denuclearization. The situation has become more threatening with the North Korea's withdrawal from Six Party Talks and the conduct its second nuclear test in May 2009.

On the other hand the US is in a close alliance with South Korea. US President Barack Obama during the 2008 presidential election campaign had described the bilateral alliance between the US and South Korea as a "remarkably strong and successful one that remains central to US security policy in East Asia."[8] The US administration is advocated for strong alliances with both South Korea and Japan in maintaining peace and security in the northeast Asia for many years.

The situation in the Korean Peninsula had remained unstable during the Bush era and not much of the change is visible even during the Obama period. South Korean news agencies had reported on March 26, 2010 that a 1,500-ton naval vessel Cheonan in the Yellow Sea with a crew of 104, was attacked by North Korean torpedoes which resulted into sinking of the ship as well as killing 46 persons on board.[9] This claim was corroborated by an international investigation which involved experts from South Korea, US, Australia, United Kingdom and Sweden.[10] A belligerent nuclear capable North Korea

8   Bruce Klinger, "Policy on Korea under Obama administration", *The Heritage Foundation,* December 11, 2008, available at http://www.heritage.org/press/commentary/ed121108a.cfm?RenderforPrint=1 (Accessed on February 12, 2010)

9   "South Korean navy ship sinks, North link played down", *Reuters,* March 26, 2010 available at http://www.reuters.com/article/idUSTRE62P30E20100326 (Accessed on June 20, 2010)

10   Letter dated 4 June 2010 from the Permanent Representative of the Republic of Korea to the United Nations addressed to thePresident of the Security Council, United Nations Security Council, June 4, 2010 available at http://www.securitycouncilreport.org/atf/cf/%7B65BFCF9B-6D27-4E9C-8CD3-CF6E4FF96FF9%7D/DPRK%20S%202010%20281%20SKorea%20Letter%20and%20Cheonan%20Report.pdf (Accessed on June 20, 2010)

with its close proximity with the Chinese regime is an issue of concern for the US.

2. POLITICS AND ECONOMICS

China and India are emerging fast to become major global powers and poised to determine the course of future events in Asia and the world. China and India together account for more than a third of the world's population. Both the nations are continuously moving towards the higher economic growth, and have significant say in major international negotiations on critically significant issues ranging from economy, security, climate change and strengthening international institutions etc. According to some projections, if China could maintain current trends in its economic growth, it will replace the US at number one position around 2035. Similarly India's economy has been performing very well and has maintained more than 7% growth despite the global economic crisis which shows India's strong economic fundamentals. Although, India's GDP is just a third of China's, but it's upwards growth rate has lifted average incomes over $1,000 for the first time.[11]

The trade between the United States and China has been growing over the years. The total trade between the two countries crossed $ 400 billion mark in 2008. Due to global economic crisis, the trade figures in 2009 have indicated at negative growth. However, with the revival of economy the treat is expected to grow in coming years.

India-US trade has also taken upwards trajectory over the years. In 2008, it reached at US $ 43 billion mark. However, in 2009, India-US trade has also seen negative trend. Again the trade surplus is expected with the 'correction' is the global economy.

The improvement in the global economy is the 2010 and the positive trend expected for the future indicates that the Indian and Chinese markets are going to play a major role towards the economic health of the world in the coming decades. In August 2010, China has

---

11   Jonathan Watts "The rise of China and India", *The Guardian,* October 17, 2009 available at http://www.guardian.co.uk/world/2009/oct/17/china-india-decade-jonathan-watts (Accessed on March 4, 2010)

replaced Japan as second largest economy in the world.[12] Following China, India is the second fastest growing economy. Under these circumstances the US and Japan need to look at the economic powers i.e. India and China not as potential competitors but more as partners. The US and Japan need to strengthen their economic engagement with China and India to create long-term partnerships for growth and prosperity which is likely to benefit the international business community.[13]

In terms of military power, the US continues to be an unparalleled super power. As per the SIPRI military expenditure database, military expenditure of the US in 2009 was $ 663.3 billion where as military expenditures figures for China and India in 2009 were $ 98.8 and $36.6 billion respectively. Similarly, according to same SIPRI database, in 2008 the United States had spent 4.3% of its GDP on military requirements as compare to 2.0% and 2.6% of China and India respectively. Given the vast difference military expenditure and advanced research and development (R&D) techniques as well as innovative abilities of the US in military technology, it is unlikely that China or India will be able to match the military might of the US in foreseeable future.

The defence cooperation between India and the US is on upswing. Since 2002 to 2009, India has signed 3.49 billion worth of defence contract with the US which includes the contract for 8, Boeing P-8I long-range maritime reconnaissance (LRMR) aircraft for 2.1 billion US $ alone. In 2010, India is expected to sign a defence contract for C-17 Globemaster III strategic lift aircraft having maximum package value of US$ 5.8 billion. If this deal is signed in its present

---

12 "China replaces Japan as second-largest economy", *Asia Times,* August 18, 2010 at http://www.atimes.com/atimes/China_Business/LH18Cb01. html

13 Responding to the Economic Rise of China and India, key Findings from binational Study Group Report Engaging China and India: An Economic Agenda for Japan and the United States, Pacific Council on International Policy

form, the amount of total defence equipment import from US since 2008 in term of contract signed would be US$ 8.9 billion making at unprecedented growth level in defence trade between the two states. Similarly, the US has conducted more joint military exercises with the India than with any other country since their resumption in 2002. Given the shared values of democracy, individual liberty, and rule of law, freedom of expression and practice of religion, multicultural society, protection to minorities etc. as well as strong substance and fundamentals in both nations, the Indo-US strategic partnership have been gaining momentum and set to attain higher trajectory. However, such momentum is visibly missing in the US relations with China except in their economic ties.

Iran's nuclear ambitions

Iran's nuclear programme is a major challenge to the US position in the West Asian Region. Iran has been pursuing its nuclear weapons programme and claims it to be a civil nuclear power energy programme. However the US maintains that Iran's nuclear program will result in developing nuclear weapon which will have dangerous consequences for peace and stability in West Asian region.

Non-proliferation experts believe that Iran is continuing its efforts to produce enriched uranium but they have diverse opinion on how close Iran is to weaponize its nuclear programe. As the case with the North Korea the US has also failed to engage Iran. The issue is Iran is both apolitical as well as security challenge to the US and is likely to remain in the near future.

Israeli-Palestinian conflict

On the issue of Israeli-Palestinian conflict, during the 2008 presidential election campaign, then Senator Obama had pointed out that "The Israeli-Palestinian conflict has been very long and complicated which undermines the US diplomatic goals in the West Asia and beyond. With roots going back thousands of years, the conflict's emotionally charged claims fuel religious, ideological, and proxy violence around the world".[14] The US policy towards this conflict has been to stressing upon their commitment to defending Israel's right to exist and calling on the Palestinian leadership and extra governmental factions to renounce terrorism. But beyond rhetoric, every US administration faces a similar dilemma and challenge for crafting a position which balances the historic US alliance with Israel against the widely recognized need to press Israel to agree an equitable peace with the Palestinians.[15]

The US has the largest Jewish population outside of Israel and also has a growing Arab-American population. Historically, the US has viewed Israel as a crucial political and economic ally in the oil-rich West Asia, and has provided Israel with the highest amount of financial and military assistance of any other foreign country. This has provided the US a significant space to use its leverage in urging Israel to resolve Palestinian conflict and take steps on the plans to establish an autonomous Palestinian state.[16] This continued conflict will remain as a major driver of US policy in West Asia in upcoming future as well.

3. CLIMATE CHANGE

Climate change is both about the sustenance and security. Asian countries being the late starters in the process of industrialisation have major energy demands. As per few estimates three major Asian nations i.e. China, India and Japan are among the top emitters of greenhouse gases. In fact, China has now replaced the US as number

---

14   "The Candidates on the Israeli-Palestinian Conflict", *Council on Foreign Relations,* September 19, 2009 available at http://www.cfr.org/publication/14756/candidates_on_the_israelipalestinian_conflict.html (Accessed on April 20, 2010)

15   Barack Obama's comments, "The Candidates on the Israeli-Palestinian Conflict" *Council on Foreign Relations,* September 19, 2009 available at http://www.cfr.org/publication/14756/candidates_on_the_israelipalestinian_conflict.html (Accessed on May 19, 2010)

16   "Israeli-Palestinian Conflict", *PBS News hour,* May 11, 2006 available at http://www.pbs.org/newshour/indepth_coverage/middle_east/conflict/keyplayers/keyplayer2.html (Accessed on May 27, 2010)

one emitter of green house gases in the world.[17] Since the signing of Kyoto Protocol in 1997, the role and responsibilities of Asian nations in global climate change dialogue have greatly enhanced. Due to massive population growth and industrialization in last two decades in Asia, greenhouse gases emissions particularly carbon dioxide (CO2) has increased considerably.[18] The United States has taken few initiatives to address the issue of climate change.[19] However, at the United Nations Climate Change Conference in Copenhagen which concluded in December 2009, has highlighted the differences in the opinion between the US and Asian countries particularly with China and India on the issues related to climate change. The energy requirement in China and India has been increasing substantially due to the population growth and industrialization in last two decades in these countries. The real challenge for the US would be to manage the growth aspirations of these countries against the likely damage to the climate. Under this backdrop the issue of climate change is likely to remain as contesting issue between the US and Asian nations and policy options for region for the coming two decades.

KEY ASSUMPTIONS

Amongst the three drivers discussed above there are some about of overlaps amongst themselves. The complexities involved in clearly identified the exact nature of the likely future of US-Asia relations involves making certain postulations.

---

17   "China overtakes US as world's biggest CO2 emitter", *The Guardian,* June 19, 2007 available at http://www.guardian.co.uk/environment/2007/jun/19/china.usnews, Also see, "TABLE-China top carbon emitter for second year running", *Alertnet,* June 9, 2010 available at http://www.alertnet.org/thenews/newsdesk/LDE6580Y1.htm (Accessed on May 1, 2010)

18   Toufiq A. Siddiqi, "The Evolving Role of Asia in Global Climate Change", *East West Center,* January 2008 available at http://www.eastwestcenter.org/news-center/east-west-wire/the-evolving-role-of-asia-in-global-climate-change/ (Accessed on May 3, 2010)

19   "Climate Change", US Department of State, Bureau of Oceans and International Environmental and Scientific Affairs available at http://www.state.gov/g/oes/climate/ (Accessed on May 15, 2010)

- The Afghanistan-Pakistan situation is likely to remain volatile for sometime. This capricious situation would be exploited by Al-Qaida and Taliban for their terror operations which will continue posing serious threats to US mainland and its interests elsewhere.

- The US super power status may be challenged by the rise of China. The US is likely to seek more economic cooperation from China and India to deal with its economic condition. There could be a relative decline in US power. India is likely to be a closer partner to the US in Asia. The US may also view India as counter balancing power to China. In terms of military capability, the US will maintain its super power status. The military power of China, India, Japan, Korea, and Pakistan is likely to rise substantially in coming few decades.

- North Korea and Iran are likely to pose major challenges for the US and its allies i.e. Japan and South Korea and Israel. It will also be a major challenge for US non-proliferation efforts.

- The identity centric Israel-Palestine conflict is not likely to be resolved though there will be various attempts from the US and other powers from time to time.

- The debate related to climate change between developed and developing world will intensify. Climate change also highlights the issue of difference in equity in world economy and its development pattern. In this contested arena, the US will face major challenge from rising Asian economies mainly China and India.

Three Scenarios: US Asia Policy 2030

1. BASELINE SCENARIO

The US super power status will relatively diminish because of the rise of China and India. The global economic crisis has provided China and India an opportunity to enhance their own growth and economic power projection as economies of India and China are least affected from the economic crisis compare to the western nations. This would mean that China, India and other emerging market powers will overtake developed world economies even more quickly. China's economy is likely to overtake the US economy around 2030 if it continues upgrading its annual growth rate. Similarly India will also become one of the leading economies of the world. There are certain risks involved for the developing Asian economies such as domestic political concerns, the maintenance of international financial stability and environmental constraints including the impact of global climate change.[20]

2. Plausible Scenario

India and China would emerge as major contesting powers. However, the rise of China would threaten the US power. India's rise will be welcomed by the US. Indo-US strategic partnership will continue to attain higher trajectory. India's rise would be 'used' by the US to counter balance to China. India would have its own concerns in regard to rise of China because of associated strategic angle.

3. Wildcard Scenario

Another 9/11 type of attack on US soil or a nuclear attacks carried out by Al-Qaeda will lower American power and prestige to far below the expected level. This will lead to a harsher American reaction in order to restore its power and dominance thus leading to chaotic developments in Asia. The US may be forced to depend more on India to address the issue related to South Asia and West Asia.

---

20   Lauren M. Phillip, "International Relations in 2030: The Transformative Power of Large Developing Countries", Discussion Paper, 3/2008, German Development Institute available at http://www.isn.ethz.ch/isn/Digital-Library/Publications/Detail/?ots591=0C54E3B3-1E9C-BE1E-2C24-A6A8C7060233&lng=en&id=54542 (Accessed on July 3, 2010)

2
GEO-POLITICAL FUTURES

SOUTH ASIA

6
India 2030: With History as Guide
—Ali Ahmed

INTRODUCTION

It is rightly said that a 'week is a long time in politics'.[1] Given this, it can reasonably be imagined what twenty years in the life of a nation imply. Twenty years are only seemingly a short period, particularly since history has itself accelerated of late. A score number of years are enough to change the trajectory of a nation. Take the changes in France between 1789 and 1809; Germany between 1848 and 1871 and Tsarist Russia between 1905 and 1925. Note the change in the US between 1939 and 1959 and the contrast between Russia and China between 1979 and 1999. Closer home, the India of 2010 is considerably different from that of 1990.

The pace and content of change depends on whether the nation is living through - as the Chinese would have it - 'interesting times'. However, twenty years is not necessarily long, when juxtaposed against a civilization dating back five thousand years, a nation going back two and a half a millennia and a state a little more than half a century. Not much can really happen in a mere two decades, particularly since India's gait is likened to a pachyderm. Uneventful back-to-back decades have also been witnessed in history.[2] Take the

1   A quote attributed to former British Prime Minister, Harold Wilson.
2   Absence of war, usually taken as stability, equally implies a period of preparation for war. In history, there are fewer periods of war than of 'peace', defined as preparation for war. See Michael Gelven, *War and Existence: A Philosophical Enquiry,* Pennsylvania: Pennsylvania State University, 1994, p. 248.

'stability' behind the Great Wall in China; the Victorian period in England or the period of the Concert of Europe. This is true of India too.

Reflection on how the next twenty years are likely to pan out would require to be driven by a judgment on dynamism of the drivers, tumult in salient forces in their inter-play, and consequent shaping of the period. Also required to be factored into any such consideration would be the unpredictable: the human agency subject to little outside control, but itself a function of internal 'demons'. Added is the impact of aspects that earlier could be taken as constants - not the least of which is climate change. Globalisation and the resulting global village; supra-national identities and ideologies; connectivity and media magnification all conspire to make comment on the future hazardous for academic reputations. It's an exercise that requires body-armour of a formally trained futurist, or more realistically in the Age of Technology, imagination of a sci-fi writer. That the Cold War ended in the manner it did and the promise of the new millennium was waylaid by Al-Qaeda, are reminders that it is best in any such exercise to err on the side of prudence and moderation.

This paper avoids the formal format of 'projections', in which inter-connection of the 'drivers' that will drive India in the next 20 years and 'uncertainties' these will encounter. Instead, the approach is to draw on India's history in three eras: medieval and modern history, post-Independence record and contemporary history. The attempt here is to highlight that reality is easier comprehended in hindsight, especially in a complex subject as 'India'. Contemporary history writing itself being so fraught an exercise, dilating on the future is considerably more so. Here, post-Independence history is accessed in twenty-year slices to demonstrate the impact and potential of such durations.[3] Thereafter, a survey of the forces currently operating in their inter-connectedness and relative salience is undertaken. Lastly,

---

3   India's sense of history, or absence of which, is best encapsulated by the ditty, *'Sikander ne Porus se ki thi ladai, to main kya karun?'* ('If Sikander messed with Porus, what's that to do with me?'). This makes recourse to history, even in a forward looking exercise, necessary.

the article takes a look at the manner the future could play itself out in the near term as also the possibilities - some undesirable - over a longer time horizon.

TWENTY YEAR SLICES IN HISTORY

Any twenty-year slice of history can be momentous, and where less so, is pregnant with forces that define the times down the line. Only hindsight makes forces at play discernible in their working and impact, and even then subjectivity is inescapable. At the beginning of a twenty year period, while it is possible to appreciate its possible course, turning points lend uncertainty. For instance, had Jayapala defeated Subuktigan of Ghazni; had Changez Khan not sacked Khwarizm; had Babur regained Ferghana; had Dara Shikoh over-powered Aurangzeb, had the INA liberated India etc, history could well have been very different. Allowance needs to be made for cataclysmic events. For instance, the upswing of the Moghul Empire in the sixteenth century, and a downswing in the seventeenth century, could have been foreseen. Likewise, a redefinition of the British Empire in India could have been expected, once the freedom movement caught steam. How both empires finally ended was a surprise. In the former case it was in defeat in the First War of Independence; while in the latter case, in Partition. From about 1930, with Muslim League championing the 'two nation' theory and the resulting communally charged atmosphere by mid-decade, the outcome that freedom would be heavily compromised, could be apprehended. Nevertheless, Mountbatten's self-indulgent decision to advance the departure of the British to coincide with a date he had accepted the surrender of the Japanese was the last imperial act.[4]

Earlier Centuries

1510-1530 AD - The turn of the second millennium is an era-transcending period, with Mahmud of Ghazni's seventeen invasions culminating in the sacking of Somnath in 1025 AD.[5] The next

---

4   For a useful biography see, Philip Zeigler's *Mountbatten: The Official Biography,* London: Weidenfeld & Nicolson, 2001.

5   Rizvi, SAA, *The Wonder that was India: Volume II*, London: Sidgwick & Jackson, 1987, p. 13. The reverberations of this event are felt a millennium later, not least due to the period of British 'divide and rule' and Orientalism that helped deepen the impact. For instance, in Agra

period of twenty years of significance is two centuries later between 1190 and 1210 beginning with the invasions of Ghori resulting in the establishment of the Delhi Sultanat.[6] The Delhi Sultanat (1206-1526) comprising five dynasties brought about a certain degree of centralization reminiscent of the Guptas (320-540 AD) and Harsha (606-647 AD) of earlier centuries.[7] Finally, an equivalent slice of history witnessed the advent of the Moghul empire (1526-1707), more appropriately comparable in extent to the Mauryan empire (325-231 BC). Babur began his invasions of India from his capital in Kabul in 1519 and by 1526 displaced the Sultanat with the Moghul empire.[8] As with earlier campaigns, the reliance of Indian armies on the ponderous elephant was over whelmed by the mobility offered by the horse, and in the case of Babur's triumph, the introduction of artillery at the battle of Panipat. The climatic battle of Khanwa that subordinated the Rajputs to the Moghuls followed a like pattern soon thereafter in 1527.[9] Babur was dead by the end of the period. Less visible, but of equal significance was the seizure of Goa from the Bijapur Sultan by the the Portuguese in 1510.[10]

1610-1630 AD – Jehangir inherited the Moghul empire in 1605 from Akbar the Great. The empire was now a reality, with legitimacy, power, unity, stability and size accruing to it through the wise and inclusive policies of Akbar. Akbar's reorganization of the administration to include central and provincial governance, fiscal system, introduction of the mansabdari system as part of army reform, judicial reforms and an enlightened religious policy, in his half

---

fort is a wooden gate from Samarkand, was brought by the British in the nineteenth century and advertised as the gate carried away from Somnath as booty by the iconoclast invader. However, the gate is said to have been returned by Afghanistan minus its gold after 1947 (South Asia: A Historical Narrative, p. 88).

6   Ibid. pp. 19-20.

7   Mohammad Yunus and Aradhana Parmar, *South Asia: A Historical Narrative*, Oxford: OUP, 2003, pp. 85-113.

8   Ibid, pp. 126-29,

9   'India', *The New Encyclopedia Brittanica: Macropedia*, Chicago: University of Chicago, 1987, p. 63.

10   *Enclyclopedia Brittanica*, p. 77.

century long reign outlasted both him and his dynasty, to be in turn inherited by the British two centuries later.[11] The period in question witnessed rule by proxy of Jehangir's wife, Nur Jahan. This led to the weathering of the Moghul-Rajput alliance built assiduously by Akbar. Jehangir's punishment with death for the Sikh Guru Arjun siding with his son and contender for the throne, Khusraw, led to long lasting disaffection between Muslims and Sikhs.[12] Of long term import was the letter presented by Thomas Roe from James I to Jehangir and receipt of a decree to open a factory at Surat in 1619.[13] Lastly, the importance of legitimate succession in India is underlined by the manner of take over of Shah Jahan from Jehangir through violence, just as Jehangir before him and Aurangzeb from him later.

1710-1730 AD – To this period is dated the decline of the Moghul empire, though the seeds were laid in the preceding half-century of Aurangzeb's rule (1658-1707). His religious policy reversed that of Akbar and his predecessors, thereby alienating the Sikhs, Jats and Rajputs.[14] His two decade long campaign in the Deccan against the rise of Maratha power, catalysed by his mishandling of the warrior king Shivaji at Agra, finally exhausted the empire and led to his death. Four rulers succeeded him in the period, with predictable consequences for the empire that had by then reached the zenith of its spatial spread that eclipsed even that of Asoka of over a thousand five hundred years earlier. It was later beset by the Marathas from the south beginning in 1731 and by adventurers Nadir Shah 1739 and Abdali later in 1761. The weakening of the Moghul empire laid the foundations for an eventual take over by the Company Bahadur beginning with the battle of Plassey of 1757. Muslim fundamentalism made its appearance with Shah Waliullah believing that a return to Islamic ways would avert the decline of Muslim glory in India. His

---

11 *The Cambridge Enclyclopedia of India, Pakistan, Bangladesh and Sri Lanka,* Cambridge: Cambridge University Press, 1989, p. 103.
12 Mohammad Yunus and Aradhana Parmar, *South Asia: A Historical Narrative,* p. 140.
13 Ibid, p. 145.
14 Stanley Wolpert, India, Berkeley: University of California, 1991, p.43.

preachings led to the first jihad in South Asia under Sayyid Ahmed of Rae Barielly in 1831.[15]

1810-1830 AD – The period witnessed the final act in the British conquest of India. Having tamed Tipu in the deep south (1799) and wrested power from the Marathas through the second Anglo-Maratha war (1803), the British reached the completed their conquest by defeating the Gorkhas to the north by 1814-16 and finally the Marathas in the third Anglo-Maratha war (1816-18). This took them right up to the Sutlej, beyond which the Sikh kingdom of Maharaja Ranjit was preserved by a preexisting treaty of 'perpetual amity' dating to 1809. To the east the British took Assam from Burma through the Treaty of Yandaboo in 1826 after the first Anlgo-Burmese war (1824-26). By 1818, the British were in control, having used the Indians recruited and trained into their army to subjugate their less able countrymen of the regional satraps they met in battle. The British system of ruling India through their subsidiaries was set. With the appointment of Bentinck in 1828 as governor general, administrative, judicial, educational and social reforms were instituted that have largely given India its modern character.[16]

1910-1930 AD – This was the formative period for the run up to independence, despite the British beginning to build a new capital at New Delhi. It began with the revocation in 1911 of Curzon's partition of Bengal of 1905, forced on the British by Bengali 'terrorism' that culminated in a bomb injuring Viceroy Hardinge.[17] Congress came into its own as a national party, even as Muslim separatism began with the Aga Khan led delegation of 36 Muslim leaders to Simla in 1906. The Congress-Muslim League rapprochement of 1916, the Lucknow pact, brokered by none other than Jinnah, was short-

---

15   Ayesha Jalal's *The Partisans of Allah* () describes the ideological linkage of Jihadi thought through history to modern times.

16   For a narrative of the rise and consolidation of the British, see C.A. Bayly, *The New Cambridge History of India: India Society and the Making of the British Empire*, Cambridge: Cambridge University Press, 1988, pp. 79-135.

17   *Encyclopedia Britannica*, p. 100.

lived with a telling long term consequence.[18] The age of competitive communalisms, whose impact has yet to run its course, was at hand.[19] The Jallianwala Bagh massacre in 1919 spurred the nationalist struggle, with *satyagraha* adopted as a strategy by Mahatma Gandhi the following year to dislodge the British through peoples participation and ownership of the freedom struggle. Despite contribution of over a million men for service overseas and over 377 million pounds to the war effort, their was little movement towards self rule post the Great War.[20] As a prelude to a dominion status for India, the first of the Round Table conferences was convened in 1930. However, it was at the end of another portentous twenty year period that India could become a Republic in 1950.

Post-Independence Slices

Though 'predicting' the future is not what is required, 'forecasting' is. The foregoing proves that India requires more than a 'technical' look for comprehension. The following can help with forecasting though not serve as substitute for it.

1950-1970 AD. To realize its potential, India set its course by socialism and non-alignment under the leadership of Nehru. The prescient creation of linguistic states belied the expectation of the likes of Churchill that India was merely a 'geographical expression'.[21]

---

18 *South Asia: A Historical Narrative*, p. 244. Interestingly, Jinnah's actions have found favourable, if controversial, mention in a statement by LK Advani and in a recent book by Jaswant Singh (*Jinnah: India, Pratition, Independence*, New Delhi: Rupa, 2009). Advani was forced to step aside from BJP's leadership in 2005, while Jaswant Singh was expelled from the party in Aug 2009.

19 Ayesha Jalal writes: 'Though the years 1919 to 1921 saw unprecedented displays of Hindu-Muslim goodwill, the experience of the first mass-based anti-imperialist struggle had done much to sharpen animosities both between and within the two communities...strident assertions of cultural difference had begun muffling the pleas for accommodation' (*Self and Sovereignty*, New Delhi: OUP, p. 237).

20 *Enclyclopedia Brittanica*, p. 101.

21 Quoted by Shashi Tharoor in his review, 'E Pluribus, India: Is Indian Modernity Working?' of Sunil Khilnani's *The Idea of India* in *Foreign Affairs*, Jan/Feb 1998.

Its progress and sense of self-regard was rudely shaken up by the 1962 Sino-Indian War. Even though India retrieved its martial and regional status through the subsequent the 1965 War thrust on it, the sixties were seen as among the 'dangerous decades'.[22] The major question then was: 'After Nehru, Who?'[23] In the event, his daughter decisively put an end to speculation,[24] but India's 'Hindu rate of growth'[25] and the PL 480 were reminders of its underdeveloped status befitting a nation-state on-the-make.[26] The manner of succession demonstrated the fragility of India's democracy. The lasting legacy of the period has been outbreak of insurgency and the twin pronged Indian counter - of political accommodation and military containment. Of long term consequence, was direction of Kashmiri politics by the Center.

1970-1990 AD. The decade began with Indian orchestration of the strategic instruments of foreign policy and military might. This was later characterized as the 'Indira doctrine', meant to carve out regional primacy for India.[27] Indira Gandhi – and India – went on to reassert power credentials through the 'peaceful nuclear experiment'

22 Title of a book by Selig Harrison, *India: The Most Dangerous Decades,* Princeton: Princeton University Press, 1960.

23 Title of a book by Welles Hangen (New York: Harcourt, Brace & World, Inc, 1963).

24 For an evaluation of the Indira personality and period, see Bipan Chandra, Mridula Mukherjee and Aditya Mukherjee, *India After Independence: 1947-2000,* pp. 268-72.

25 Gurcharan Das says of this phrase: 'There is no more defeatist expression in the dictionary than this fatalistic phrase' (*India Unbound,* New Delhi: Viking, p. xiii).

26 Gurcharan Das, *India Unbound,* p. 139.

27 See JFR Jacob's *Surrender at Dacca: The Birth of a Nation* (New Delhi: Manohar, 2001) for a military perspective of the campaign. It is interesting that DK Palit, writing about India's policy states: 'Although in the end a major decision was enforced in the east with the use of maximum force, the Indian policy till the very eve of war and even beyond it, was basically one of containment of conflict rather than gaining a decision by use of force....It was only on the third or fourth day of the war that Eastern Command was given the aim of making for Dacca as quickly as possible ('Strategy of Force: A historical survey and future concepts', *Combat Journal,* May 1980, pp. 14-15).'

in 1974; codenamed ironically, 'Smiling Buddha'. Within a few years
of its strategic zenith, however, India was at its internal political
nadir with the Emergency.[28] The Indian reality of contradictions is
seen in the perception of insecurity in the elite, despite the preceding
triumph of arms. A higher regional profile was once again sought
through the eighties.[29] India's strategic posture in the period was
energized by a self-belief in itself as a regional power. It embarked
on a strategic missile program in the early part of the decade and by
the end of the decade had proceeded with nuclearisation in wake of
the Pakistani revelations on its lead. In mid decade it had through
Exercises Brasstacks and Chequerboard honed its conventional
capability against both its putative adversaries. The major strategic
turning point in the period was the Soviet invasion of Afghanistan,
with Pakistan's elevation as a 'frontline' state. Internal and external
balancing resorted to by Pakistan, beginning with US help to the
Mujahedeen, continues to have effect. In the melee, Pakistan attained
nuclear capability. Having blunted India's conventional edge, it
proceeded with 'proxy war' first in Punjab and later in Kashmir.
Consequently, the end of the decade witnessed the Indian Army in
overstretch, in part brought on by the peacekeeping sojourn in Sri
Lanka. Economically, portentous beginnings of liberalization had
been made. On the societal front, social cohesion was impacted by the
contest between casteism and 'hindutva' ideology. This culminated
in the climatic Babri Masjid demolition of end 1992, releasing forces
operative to this day.[30]

1990-2010 AD. The key features of this period were coincidental
in timing. Internally it was adjustment compelled by liberalization,[31]
and, externally, by the end of the Cold War. On both counts, India's
rise by end of the period has belied the manifold and justifiable
apprehensions prevalent then. It has managed to degrade Pakistan's

28 *The Cambridge Enclyclopedia of India, Pakistan, Bangladesh and Sri Lanka,*
    pp. 174-75.
29 Sandy Gordon, *India's Rise to Power in the Twentieth Century and Beyond,*
    London: St Martins Press, p. 123.
30 *India After Independence,* p. 442.
31 Gurcharan Das, 'Introduction', *India Unbound,* p. xi.

challenge; though not without a little help from the constellation of international forces in wake of 9/11. This was achieved despite tightened military budgets through the nineties resulting in India being forced on the back-foot. Emboldened by incorrectly anticipating political incapacity of coalition governments, Pakistan went overly venturesome at Kargil.[32] This occasioned Indian reappraisal of the implication of nuclearisation of the preceding year. Militarily, the pendulum of opinion swung back towards the continuing applicability of force, even in a nuclear backdrop. Pakistan, under a military regime later, tested Indian restraint once again in the Parliament attack. In the event, the response – Operation Parakram[33] – was determined by the aftermath of 9/11, unfolding in close vicinity. Intervention of the international context into the regional milieu required deft management by India in order to contain Pakistan. Results on the ground have been evident in Kashmir. Nevertheless, Mumbai 26/11 indicates that the shadow of instability in Pakistan spreads over the region. The realignment of significance for the future is India's proximity with the US, the Indo-US nuclear deal being hallmark. The context of this 'strategic partnership' is US containment of rising China. This triangular relationship would no doubt resonate through the coming decades in tomorrow's Asia. Gains made by the economic trajectory and their strategic fallout, have positioned India favourably for joining the great power league.[34] On the internal front, challenges from both the extreme right and left wings remain.

That within sixty years of becoming a Republic, India awaits a place at the global high table is an index of its success. There was no certainty to this when India embarked on the journey. While placed behind China on most counts though both started at equivalent

---

32 See 'The Kargil Conflict' in P.R. Chari, P.I Cheema and Stephen Cohen, *Four Crisis and a Peace Process: American Engagement in South Asia,* New Delhi: Harper Collins, 2008, pp. 118-47.

33 For a study of the operation, see Pravin Swahney and VK Sood, *Operation Parakram: The War Unfinished,* New Delhi: Sage Publications, 2003.

34 Sanjay Baru, *The Strategic Consequences of India's Economic Performance: Essays and Columns* (Routledge, London, 2007).

levels,[35] this shortfall is compensated by democratic freedoms and that the journey has not been as tumultuous. Its performance compares favourably with most other post-colonial states and must be seen in light of the fact that it is a continent-sized country. The pertinent question at the beginning of the next score of years in India's history is, 'What does its past tell us about its future?' The answer can only be with multiple caveats.

SPILLOVERS

India's political confidence to invest in undiluted adult franchise right from the beginning, to economically readying to displace Italy, France and UK this decade, and Germany and Japan in the next has been recounted so far.[36] Movement ahead requires jettisoning 'baggage'. Identifying what qualifies as baggage of the pervious century, if not millennium, needs being done carefully. Jettisoning is another fraught exercise, involving as it would changes in power equations. This section first takes stock of positive factors and then takes 'a warts and all' look. The aim is to assess whether the onrushing twenty years will materialize the promise of India's 'tryst with destiny'. If India - younger, less powerful and relatively unsure - managed adequately thus far; pessimism on this score would be unwarranted.

Ever since the advent of 'Manmohanomics' under Narasimha Rao, any discussion on India's power trajectory must begin with the state of its economy. Though the outlook on this was bleak in the nineties, it is not so now. The economy though hit first by recession and later by the draught, has displayed a capacity for resilience. It is set to grow at 7.2 per cent.[37] Certain sectors, such as IT[38] and service sector[39] are at its core, but have a limited society-wide impact.

---

35 For a comparison with China, along with Japan, see Bill Emmott, *Rivals: How the Power Struggle Between China, India and Japan will Shape Our Next Decade,* London: Allen Lane.

36 Bill Emmott, *Rivals,* p. 133.

37 'Indian growth set to hit 7.2 per cent', *Financial Times,* 8 February 2010.

38 Nandan Nilekeni, *Imagining India: Ideas for the New Century*, New Delhi: Penguin, pp. 108-121.

39 Gurcharan Das, 'Introduction', *India Unbound,* pp. xv-xvii.

Liberalisation has led to emergence of islands of prosperity country wide, especially in the south and west. But crucially for the future, the aspect of distribution has been privileged over continued opening up of the economy.[40] This owes to the democratic constraint in place since the 'India Shining' slogan of 2004 of the NDA government did not find favour with the electorate. The impact of schemes such as the NREGA (renamed 'Mahatma Gandhi' National Rural Employment Guarantee Act) on poverty levels may be debatable,[41] but not so their electoral impact. A democratic state must be cognizant of this voice, one expressed periodically, as against that of competing elites willing India to go farther, faster.

Consequent to its rising economy, India's 'hard power' credentials are more in evidence. These include expanded defence budgets;[42] a nuclear program on course as exemplified by the launch of INS Arihant, precursor of its triad capability;[43] modernization of the military platforms of the three services;[44] and raisings of additional formations for coping with the uncertain China factor.[45] Buoyed by higher budgets, India's strategic trajectory is only superficially comfortable. For instance, acquisition bottlenecks remain[46], and 'soft power' is found wanting.[47]

---

40   P Sainath, 'Drought of justice, flood of funds', http://www.indiatogether. org/2009/aug/psa-funds.htm

41   Nilekeni is skeptical of the project, see *Imagining India*, pp. 311, 327, 330.

42   While India has maintained a defence budget of about 2 per cent of its GDP, owing to an 8 per cent growth rate, a considerable increase in the budget has resulted. For an analysis, see Laxamn Behera, 'India's Defence Budget 2009-10: An Assessment', *IDSA Strategic Comments*, http://www.idsa.in/publications/stratcomments/LaxmanBehera180209. htm

43   'PM launches INS Arihant in Visakhapatnam', *TOI*, 26 July 2009.

44   'State of the Indian Armed Forces', *Indian Military Review*, Jan 2010.

45   For a review of military capabilities and direction of developments in security in Asia, see Bill Emmott, *Rivals*, pp. 216-219.

46   Raj Shukla, 'Acquisition Reform - Lessons from Bernard Gray', Strategic Comments, IDSA, (www.idsa.in).

47   Daniel Markey, 'Developing India's Foreign Policy Software', *Asia Policy* 8, July 2009.

On the external security front, China has displaced Pakistan at the focus of the strategic community.[48] A persisting border problem with China acts as a 'fuse'. The India-US link in any future US-China face-off over hegemon status forms the 'keg'. The more immediate challenge, however, is that of the Al Qaeda-Taliban combine in 'Af-Pak' region.[49] India has been unable to fully cash in on its 'carrot and stick' policy towards Pakistan. The dialogue between the two is set to remain, but subject to continued buffeting from Af-Pak. At the level of international security, US preservation of authoritarian regimes in the Middle East by taking the fight to those opposing them - the Al-Qaeda - has set back, but not quite extinguished the Islamist agenda. This factor will remain among the consequential determinants how the future will play out at the global level. At the regional level, Pakistan has been contained for the moment.[50] Left-overs from history and balance of power maneuvering can be expected to persist.

Though the unipolar moment in global politics has ended ignominiously in Iraq and Afghanistan, a quasi multi-polar one has yet to unambiguously emerge. India sees itself as a responsible power and a candidate 'pole' in the emerging global order. Its position on several fronts such as climate change, managing global economic recovery, the shape of the emerging non-proliferation regime and on multilateral trade talks is consequential to the global outcome. It remains a

---

48   Bharat Verma, Editor, *Indian Defence Review*, opined in his editorial that another war with China is possible in 2012. Adm. Sureesh Mehta, prior to retirement as Chairman, COSC, maintained that China was a challenge (K. Subrahmanyam, 'Coping with China', *Dainik Jagran* (English), 16 Aug 2009). The previous and present Air Chiefs have also referred to China in their remarks to the press ('China now bigger threat than Pak: IAF chief', *Hindustan Times*, 23 May 2009; 'IAF strength no match to China's: Air chief', *The Tribune*, 24 Sep 2009). The NSA, Narayanan, has in an interview with Karan Thapar clarified India's position ('Media hype could create problems with China: NSA', *The Hindu*, 29 Sep 2009).

49   See Department of State briefing on the Af-Pak strategy at http://fpc. state.gov/120965.htm.

50   Pakistan constantly complains of Indian interests in Afghanistan and of Indian interference in Baluchistan. Its discomfort with the latter even found controversial mention in the Sharm es Sheikh Joint Statement.

leading contender for inclusion among permanent members in any reorganization of the UN system. In the region, the instability of the past decade among its neighbours has largely subsided.[51] However, coining of the term, 'AfPak', signifies that Pakistan and Afghanistan would remain at the center stage for some time. Though not party to the NPT, it stands along side others in disarmament initiatives that returned to center stage with Obama's Nobel prize winning initiatives. It has begun the process of resuming the peace process with Pakistan. In keeping with its increasing power indices, India is projecting itself as a mature power to deserve and demand the mantle of great power.

Despite the region being at the vortex of global politics, the major sores instead are on the internal security front. Kashmir has receded from the national consciousness. Any return to the fore would be predicated on the developments to its west. The North East continues to interminably await 'trickle down' and benefits of India's 'Look East' policy. However, of greater consequence even though less visible and remarked, is the threat from the extreme right wing. Forces espousing majoritarian nationalism complete a century of autonomous political existence fifteen years ahead. Their political project has not received much attention in the security discourse. The seemingly positive connection of nationalism and security keeps them off security radar screens. Under cover of threat of minority extremism and LWE, these forces could present themselves as 'saviors', particularly in case of any economic down turn.

While growth rates are impressive, so are indices of India's underbelly; principally its population figures.[52] This is especially so because India has not concentrated on developing these as quality

51 While Nepal and Sri Lanka have escaped from the period of violence, coping with its consequences is ongoing in both states. Bangladesh's return to democracy and Pakistan's inching towards it with the passage of the Eighteenth Amendment are positive trends in the region.

52 For an analysis on population, see National Population Commission, 'Population and Human & Social Development', http://populationcommission.nic.in/facts1.htm

human resources, unlike for instance East Asian states.[53] Economic growth rates are unlikely to translate easily into jobs. Both left and right wing ideologies are on hand to exploit problems that may result. With institutions of state such as civil administration and police constrained by legacy systems, political interference, vested corporate interest and corruption, ability of the state to cope is suspect. This could imply an increasing reliance on armed policing, currently under raising to tackle LWE.[54] Governance predicated on a responsive political system and sound political leadership is absent. By this yardstick, attention of peoples' representatives to their responsibilities leaves much to be desired.[55]

To the Future

Three scenarios are disposed off in this section in an impressionist take on the future: favourable; unfavourable; and mixed. Sketching the possibilities is to bring out the direction India needs taking.

Benevolent

At the global level over the long term, interdependence between the US and a democratizing China lends stability to the world order. The two in concert are being referred to as the 'G2'.[56] A global consensus spearheaded by the G2, however has proved elusive on climate change, disarmament and non-proliferation. This indicates that incipient to their relationship is a contest for power and primacy. Getting China into an interdependent relationship has been the US strategy for co-opting it. Success of this novel form of power shift keeps the global order on even keel.

In the short term, the Obama presidency bests the Al Qaeda's terrorist challenge. Deft of shifting emphasis onto the political prong

---

53 Meghnad Desai, 'Twin Troubles', pp. 100-03, in Ira Pande (ed.), *The Great Divide: India and Pakistan*, New Delhi: Harper Collins, 2009.

54 For instance 10 COBRA (Commando Battalion for Resolute Action) and 32 IRBs (India Reserve Battalions) are to be raised according to MHA *Annual Report, 2008-09*, p. 18. Incidentally, that COBRA battalions have been renamed indicates learning in the organisation.

55 'Vital Stats: Parliament in Winter Session 2009', PRS Legislative Research.

56 'A wary respect: A special report on China and America', *The Economist*, 22 October 2009.

as against privileging the military prong of strategy so far brings this about. This can be discerned from its amenability to 'talk' to the Taliban. Displacement of reactionary regimes in oil rich states by incorporation of democratic forces in power structures softens the terror threat. India emerges as a self-regarding state in a multi-polar order. The US-India strategic partnership yields dividend in high-end technology transfer and a reining in of China on the Asian stage. At the regional level, the China-India relationship turns its back on differences to focus on trade. The border problem is addressed without nationalist passions being played up and media hype by either side. India's stake in Afghanistan is preserved in exchange for permitting Pakistan greater strategic space there. Pakistan is set on the democratic path, a process begun by the shedding of power by President Zardari. India's smaller neighbours move away from the violence in their respective past. The still born regional organization SAARC acquires promising contours. Borders are made irrelevant through operationalisation of the SAARC program for economic integration, envisaged to culminate in a South Asian Union by 2020 after transiting the stages of SAFTA and Customs Union in the interim.[57] The North East is opened up through Myanmar to both South East Asia and to southern China. In tandem, Tibet is opened up culturally and economically by China and Pakistan opens up the trading routes connecting to the Silk Routes and Afghanistan.

A moderate leadership steers India through extremist minefields at both ends of the political spectrum. A people-centric economic paradigm with distribution paralleling growth marginalizes left wing extremists. Focus on upgrading human resources and bringing about equity in regional, community, caste and class terms, leads to defusing the right wing threat. Greater external security and self-confidence embolden India to roll back separatist insurgencies through political innovativeness, devolution of power and greater accommodation. In managing internal security, India succeeds in ensuring that the LWE problem is not aggravated by ham-handed policing action. Instead the untested developmental prong of strategy is progressed. This implies

---

57 'SAFTA', http://www.saarc-sec.org/main.php?t=2.1.6

keeping the seeming necessity to access mineral resources in tribal lands at bay for a generation. This would gain time for the inhabitants to be masters of their lands.

Armed forces undergo a 'Transformation'. Impetus for a draw-down in the military size so as to shift from a 'threat based' to a 'capability based' military gathers momentum. This is enabled by strategic dialogues with both China and Pakistan separately on doctrinal balancing. Mutual and balanced forces reduction embracing both the conventional and nuclear realms is in striking distance. The military moves from a 'war-readiness' and 'mass' military to a 'war-deterrent', and possibly, a 'warless' one.[58] Technology denial regimes having receded, the degree of self-reliance reaches desired levels.

Malevolent

The Al Qaeda-Taliban combine wrests the initiative from an exhausted NATO and isolationist US. US, scalded by heightened threat from Islamists, withdraws; as does a relieved Europe. Al Qaeda inspired Islamists move for control over respective oil producing states in wake of isolationism in the US. Pakistan is destabilised in the international community's bid to get it to 'do more' to avert the circumstance. The resulting vacuum is taken advantage of by Islamists to expand in society, polity and the Army. India gets co-opted to contain Pakistan. The 'balance of power' game intensifies, with the nuclear card seemingly in irrational hands. This stays India's conventional option; but has the advantage of preserving India from launching into an unnecessary war. In effect, the eight year war launched by Saddam's Iraq against Iran in wake of the Iranian revolution is averted. On the China front, 'splittist' turmoil in China results in its muscle-flexing along the border. Pakistan lends itself strategic location on the far side of India to Chinese geopolitical aims. Smaller regional neighbours return to turmoil, brought on by fallout of an unmanaged regional situation.

---

58 Terms used by military sociologist, Charles C. Moskos in his *The Postmodern Military: Armed Forces after the Cold War*, Oxford University Press, USA, 1999.

Inadequate leadership, training and cohesion in the newly raised counter Naxal forces results in a worsening of the situation. External interests abate it. The usual suppression-alienation-intervention cycle catches up. The left wing threat and 'Islamists-at-the-Indus' discourse is taken advantage of by right wing forces to compel a right wing lurch in the polity. Regionalism raises its head in the relatively forward states, such as in India's south and west. Institutional incapacity of policing and administrative resources leads to reliance on the Army. The military grows to mirror the Army in Pakistan.

'In between'

Managing the situation to yield a benign outcome is a tall order. It would require a departure from India's traditional comfort levels with ambiguity. It also requires a reasonable constellation of external forces. Absence of a cataclysmic event is prerequisite. At the global level this could be nuclear terrorism; and at the regional level it could be of assassination of key political players. Since surprises and shocks happen - particularly in a world of diffusion of technology empowering all actors - the future may fall short of the benign outcome. The dire outcome above is also remote since 'positives' also have a momentum ruling out the 'worst case'. Therefore, as with most crystal-ball gazing, for any analysis – such as this – to tread the middle path is unexceptionable.

In this scenario, at the global level, there is a level of uncertainty in which the US is challenged by both China and Islamists. At the regional level, the significant aspect is contention within Pakistan between the secular-rational element and Islamists in society, polity and the Army. The former manage to stay afloat and in control of the nuclear arsenal, with tacit support from India. Further evolution of SAARC remains an aspiration. China, skeptical of India's US connection, is less amenable to friendly overtures; though not hostile. Internally, India's growth trajectory continues; with lip service to the distribution imperative continuing. This accentuates the internal security problematic. Internal security forces - higher on their learning curve - are on hand to manage the unrest. As the right wing marches towards the centenary of its movement, they constrict political space for liberals and the minority. Militarily, India modernizes and deepens its nuclearisation. This increases its reliance on power balancing and on deterrence. The risks are apparent.

THROUGH THE PRESENT

How India traverses the next two decades depends on how the past will influence the future, through the present. In this section, two factors are reflected on – factors privileged on account of their inter-relatedness. The attempt will be to bring out that the choices India makes will be crucial to how much it approximates the 'benevolent' scenario above.

Power transition for an Asian century can be said to be well underway.[59] Economically China and India have helped conserve the global economy from extremes of recession. Politically and militarily, the US and NATO have been exhausted by Iraq and Afghanistan. India is therefore set to take up its place in the world. Self-congratulations on this is warranted. However, it bears recall that the decade's principal drivers are as yet unfolding. This section attempts to build in caution as balance.

Two features still spooling out of the last decade, respectively in the external and internal domains, are taken here as the defining ones: 9/11 and the communal episode in Gujarat. The former is self-evident. The latter would likely face competition in selection from issues as the rise of Naxalism and 26/11. Since selection is a subjective exercise, here the latter is privileged over the others though it is conceded there would be a strong case for others.[60] The logic in favour of the choice is that turning the spot light on this, less remarked, internal security issue would usefully alert India. The others in any case find sufficient and increasing mention in the discourse and rightly so.

Looking at the external plane first, it is now a 'given' that had

---

59 Bill Emmott, *Rivals*, pp. 8-9.
60 See GD Bakshi, 'Left Wing Extremism in India: Context, Implications and Response Options', CLAWS Manekshaw Paper 9, 2009; and, Ashley Tellis et al. 'The lessons of Mumbai', RAND Corporation, http://www. rand.org/pubs/occasional_papers/2009/RAND_OP249.pdf

the 'eye' not been taken off the 'ball' in play in Afghanistan in favour of a detour in Iraq, the world would by now have transited out of the aftermath of 9/11. This is a contestable assumption. It is quite likely that the challenge to the US would have engulfed Pakistan more speedily in early 2002. The Parliament attack indicates the potentiality of destabilisation then. In the event, the present can be reckoned as 'destabilisation in slow motion'. At this juncture, the MacChrystal proposals for a further 'surge' are in implementation stage. Operation Moshtarak over, the US is set to retake the locus of Taliban power, Kandahar. Obama's considered decisions on Af-Pak at the turn of the decade, reflected in his West Point speech, will prove consequential for the rest of the decade.

In the internal domain, the communal episode in Gujarat is coming to a closure. Just as the killings of Sikhs in New Delhi on the assassination of Indira Gandhi twenty five years ago cast a pall over the following decade, shadows of the Gujarat episode fell over the internal security situation over the last decade. That Pakistan profited from India's predicament is of a piece with its earlier interference in Kashmir. The clichéd lesson is 'prevention is better than cure'. This needs progressing. Tackling terror, irrespective of origin, needs be done with equal alacrity. On this score, majoritarian nationalism requires the scrutiny it is currently receiving.[61]

A shortcoming of strategic analysis is the studiedly external focus. This keeps it oblivious to internal implications of the external. The external and internal are seldom insulated, particularly in democratic and open societies as India's. Motivated identification of terrorism and Islam in the post 9/11 discourse has had a moulding influence

---

61 Secular activist Asghar Ali Engineer writes: '...they do not think on other lines at all despite many obvious indicators and despite repeated attempts to draw their attention to these other indications by human rights activists and others. I think some powerful sources and organizations are behind all these terrorist activities and it requires great ingeniousness, political will and unbiased approach to solve this mystery...The police investigation must change its direction, if they want to succeed in curbing terror ('And they struck again', countercurrents.org, 22 Sep 2008).

internally. Likewise, Pakistani 'need' is to offset India's power. This it does through sustaining internal strife. The implication is that both the external and internal need working on conjointly. For instance, a mellowing of the India-Pakistan relationship externally would have positive implications for the internal. This would have positive implications on how the future shapes up in Af-Pak and at one remove in West Asia. An approach cognisant of the internal-external link provides the rationale and action agenda for the future.

But equally importantly, potentiality of conflict between the two nuclear powers should act as spur.[62] There is an element of scepticism on the escalatory potential of a low level India-Pakistan conflict, justifiable on the basis of past record of restraint of both sides. However, nuclear weapons acquisition implies a change of era: one in which war avoidance is the primary rationale for militaries.[63] India could instead to proactively shape the coming decade by reaching out to Pakistan.[64] The traditional balance of power game can only help India in conflict management, but not with conflict resolution. The connotations of an eased Pakistan relationship for the northern front against China are obvious.[65]

CONCLUSION

India's very destination is contested and so is the route and intended pace.[66] While many may wish India to be potentially

---

62 The Home Minister has administered a warning to Pakistan in which he has indicated India has reached its level of tolerance to jihadi terror and could retaliate with military force at the next provocation ('Chidambaram's final warning to Pakistan', *The Economic Times*, 2 November 2009).

63 Bernard Brodie, said 'Thus far the chief purpose of our military establishment has been to win wars. From now on its chief purpose must be to avert them (*The Absolute Weapon*, Harcourt Brace, New York, 1946, p. 76).'

64 'PM extends 'hand of friendship' to Pak', TOI, 29 October 2009.

65 Note the attention paid to the China front, Gurmeet Kanwal, 'Red Dragon Rising: China's White Paper Emphasises Offensive Defence', CLAWS Issue Brief; and his, 'Breathing Fire: China's Aggressive Tactical Posturing', CLAWS Issue Brief.

66 Nilekeni writes: 'Our coalition governments at the center often give themselves labels that reiterate unity and common purpose...But

counted among the developed states by 2030, it is also seen as a case of a 'bridge too far' by those privileging indices of poverty and inequality in the reckoning. The political tussle between the three positions[67] – realist, liberal and radical - would continue and would in turn impact the route and pace. India, therefore, would likely exhibit some schizophrenia in its strategic policy. One end of the spectrum would prefer a 'hands on' engagement with strategic issues such as the rise of China, the nature of the strategic partnership with the US, and the contours of India's regional power status. The logic advanced is that India must play up to its weight. It must learn to navigate with strategic finesse since it cannot escape the additional responsibilities that come with ascending the global power hierarchy.

The other perspective would prefer a period of introspection, gaining India time to contend with internal political, social and economic problems. Premature 'arrival' at the world stage could result in a setback reminiscent of '1962' and the late eighties. This perspective would prefer nurturing of the indices of power, prior to venturing into exercising power. Time gained is also necessary to arrive at an amicable *modus vivendi* within the region. To expect India to transcend the region is unrealistic. Regional rivals function as Trojan horses and would continue to 'box' India in. Incentivising their concord needs a degree of accommodation. It bears mention, India stands to gain asymmetrically.

Driving on Delhi's roads has much to commend it in terms of analogy for making projections. The destination is clear. That one would reach is also assured. However, in what shape and how one

in reality they represent fiercely sparring ideals, and reflect an India that is intensely fractured, its divisions sharply defined not so much by ideology as by religion, caste, class and region' (*Imagining India*, p. 11). Though he refers to internal divisions in these coalitions, the three grand coalitions of Indian politics (NDA, Left (Third Front) and UPA) represent diverse strands in the central debate.

67   See Kanti Bajpai, 'Indian Strategic Culture' in Michael R. Chambers (ed.), *South Asia in 2020: Future Strategic Balances and Alliances*, Strategic Studies Institute, November 2002, P. 245 – 305; available at http://www.stramod.ru/SP_004.html.

gets there is debatable. If the monsoon rains have a lesson, there is the weather to be factored in. Traffic jams need be catered for. Unexpected VIP movement may hold up a smooth ride. Kamikaze motorcyclists, drunken truck drivers and hell-raising Muruti owners constitute the unpredictable. Drawing analogy from this, that India would traverse the interim to 2030 in reasonable shape is certain. That the 'idea of India'[68] would undergo buffeting by forces within and outside is a reasonable expectation. That some or other cataclysmic events would require coping with, is a given. These have potential to deflect India from the intended destination and also its balance. The survey of history instills confidence that the journey would comprise of both consistency and novelty.

Of consequence to the destination and the ride is how India sets the sights and thereafter remains steady. It requires a vision of an equivalent order as the Nehruvian one earlier to decide on the destination and set the sails. Those wishing to broadcast India's 'arrival' as a player at the Asian, if not global stage, comprise a formidable constituency. Therefore, the debate would continue and the manner it shapes up would determine India's final positioning at the end of the next two decades.

---

68   Sunil Khilnani, *The Idea of India,* New York: Farrar, Straus and Giroux, 1999.

7
Pakistan 2030: Possible Scenarios and Options
—Harinder Singh

INTRODUCTION

George Friedman once said that the first line of defence against Islamic radicals would be the Muslim states themselves. It could be believed that Pakistan quite accurately represents this fault line. As the second largest Muslim state, it is difficult to imagine how an acutely divisive and terror afflicted state can sustain itself in the long term. Given the continuing instability, internal unrest and political turmoil, it is imperative to determine as to where the state of Pakistan is headed in the foreseeable future. While it may not be possible to precisely predict the future, but one can surely visualize the uncertainties and strategic discontinuities emerging in Pakistan. An exercise of this nature could be fraught with risk, especially when there are doubts already expressed on the viability of state. This chapter attempts to analyse some of the key uncertainties faced by Pakistan and the likely scenarios that may unfold over the next two decades or so.

A STATE IN FLUX

In the current strategic discourse, the state of Pakistan is often referred to as the pendulum state, where the political reins of the country consistently change hands between the powerful army generals and the well heeled politicians. In recent times and especially ever since dismissal of General Mushraf's regime, the domestic politics seems to have become even more fragile and unpredictable. The assassination of PPP leader Benazir Bhutto particularly plunged the country into one of the worst political crises in recent decades. Consequently, the federal elections which had raised high hopes of a vibrant democracy were soon belied by the irreconcilable differences between mainstream political parties. The balance of power it seems is again tilting in favour of the Pakistan military and their leadership.

The future of Pakistan hinges on several critical questions. Where is the state of domestic politics in Pakistan headed? Would religion and radicalism continue to dominate the future of Pakistan? What are the key strategic uncertainties that lie ahead? Can the Pakistani establishment hold out against these fears and uncertainties in the long term? Is the revival of a viable democratic culture ever feasible in Pakistan?

In this context, one can arrive at a purposeful appreciation of the country's future by constructing alternate scenarios based on a socio-politico and military understanding of the Pakistani state.

THE STRATEGIC DRIVERS

The key drivers which could play an important role in shaping the future of Pakistan are discussed at six broad levels:

Political Turbulence: In the post Musharaf period, there has been some revival of political activity in Pakistan. Though much was expected from the Zardari-Sharif duo, the strong mutual antagonism has led to a drift in domestic affairs of the state. It comes as no surprise that Pakistan's polity and politics continue to be fragile. Some even apprehend that if the political establishment fails to deliver the mandate, the Pakistan army could soon step in. It therefore becomes important to examine if there are any indications that the pendulum may swing again. If yes, then how would the new dispensation contain the raging radicalism and fissiparous tendencies in the state. And what if it fails? The key issue here is that how long will these power swings between the political and military establishment continue. In the ensuing political and dissonance could the disparate radical groups emerge as new power centres, and in turn lead to greater radicalisation of the polity and political institutions in the country.

Religion and Radicalism: It is a matter of concern that religious fundamentalism rages unabatedly across the length and breadth of the country. Unprecedented acts of terror signal a sharp rise in radicalisation of the civil society. An array of radical groups rules the roost and their ability to strike at will clearly threatens the very foundation of the Pakistani state. The state's political institutions seem to have corroded irreversibly and are under severe stress. And lately, its adverse impact has become a matter of concern for the Pakistani armed forces as well. The key aspect being that religious fundamentalism is impacting the pillars of the state – the political leadership, the civil society and the armed forces. It would have to be carefully watched if the Pakistani state ever succeeds in containing the tribulations of rampant religious radicalism within the country.

Cracks in Federalism: Ever since its independence in 1947, Pakistan has been characterised by a weak federal structure. The turbulent peripheries i.e. the NWFP, FATA, Balochistan and Balawaristan today pose a serious challenge to the unity of the state. Sindh suffers from serious ethnic divide with Karachi being the hotbed of sectarian strife. In the west, the Durand line conundrum could intensify the demand for an independent Pashtun homeland. The Afghans in any case disregard the sanctity of any international boundary and have for several years demanded the right for free access and trade in the frontier provinces. Punjab too seems to be an emerging hotbed of radical Islam. The Seraiki influence in the South Punjab, and the demand to trifurcate the province into North, Central and South Punjab has been gradually gaining salience. Is the Pakistani state capable of holding out against these divisive tendencies will have to be carefully analysed. Is it possible for the Pakistani establishment to satisfy demands of greater federal autonomy in the provinces of Balochistan and Balawaristan. Some experts even argue that the instability and chaos prevailing among the peripheral provinces could lead to the fragmentation of the Pakistani state.

Economic Revival: The current economic situation within the country looks grim. High dependence on foreign aid, a burgeoning fiscal deficit, sluggish economic activity and increased military spending seem to be exacerbating the economic distress. The social indices seem to be under severe stress with education and health being the prime areas of concern. Unemployment is rising, inflation is soaring, and lower agricultural production is creating food shortages - the fall out of which is being seen at several levels. The mushrooming of local madrassas as a consequence of poor social indices in Pakistan is a fact well known. How will these economic imbalances be corrected and can the economy simply sustain itself on foreign aid. Is radicalism impinging upon the country's economic health and would an equitable management of resources lead to a favourable business environment are questions that need to be addressed.

Relations with Neighbours: India, Iran and Afghanistan make up the immediate neighbourhood. And the antagonism between neighbours seems to have been cast in stone. The long standing dispute in the state of Jammu and Kashmir, the deep sectarian animosity with Shiite Iran, and the search for strategic depth in Afghanistan show hardly any signs of improvement or reconciliation. The caustic relationship with India surfaces every now and then and, in fact has adversely affected its ability to concentrate on the counterinsurgency campaign in the frontier provinces. Its inimitable obsession of strategic competition with India for influence in Afghanistan affects the probability of improved relations in the neighbourhood. How does Pakistan reconcile its differences with its neighbours will be an important driver for lasting peace in the region.

Extra-regional Interests: Global strategic focus is gradually shifting from Afghanistan to Pakistan. Leading nations of the world are worried about the evolving internal security situation in the country. United States and China, its key allies are earnestly looking to contain the situation lest it implodes and affects their geo-strategic interests. Pakistan is crucial to the United States, for securing its energy interests in the Middle East. Also Iran's intransigence and unpredictable behaviour can partly be countervailed by United States' continued presence and relationship with Pakistan. China too seeks to secure its interests in Pakistan through strategic infrastructure development ventures, military cooperation and commercial investments. Both countries could be expected to play a key role, if the situation deteriorates beyond the control of the state in Pakistan.

At yet another level, Saudi Arabia's interference in the political and religious context could become an area of serious concern. Japan and France too have long term developmental and commercial interests within the country and therefore could be expected to play an important role in times of crisis.

THE KEY UNCERTAINTIES

Some of the aforementioned drivers carry a high element of embedded uncertainty. These factors consequentially can cause the future to be much different from today. The trajectories could even go off course and thus be highly uncertain. Four drivers which would make the most crucial difference are discussed:

- **Radicalism:** The key issue is to ascertain whether or not religious radicalism is the most dominant threat to Pakistani state. Would Pakistan be able to contain the spread of religious fundamentalism within the state? If not, then how far could the political and social landscape of the country worsen? Could it lead to conception of a theocratic state or could it end up in some form of Islamic socialism in Pakistan? Would the state be able to sustain this extremely charged religious environment or do we see the emergence of a revolutionary situation - a la Iran - in Pakistan? The resulting environment shall surely carry severe consequences for countries in the neighbourhood.

- **Provincialism:** Whether or not the growing demand for provincial autonomy is a threat to Pakistan's unity and cohesion? Can the Pakistani establishment fulfil the compelling aspirations of the individual provinces within constitutional confines of the federal structure? If not, then could it lead to further turbulence and instability within the Pakistani society? Can these fissiparous tendencies over time lead to 'Balkan-isation' or 'Lebanon-isation' of Pakistani state? The issue is gathering import and could be expected to carry serious consequences in the future. The promulgation of the 18ᵗʰ Constitutional amendment is perhaps an important step towards partial mitigation of the federal differences. It however remains to be seen whether this amendment would produce sound political dividends in the future.

- **Democracy and Politics:** Whether or not the current political dispensation in Pakistan be able to weather the gathering storms of 'radicalism' and 'provincialism'? Would the political climate deteriorate to hasten the return of military rule? If yes, then when could the Pakistani state swing in favour of the military rule? Would the country witness yet another two to three bouts of civil-military rule before it fully reconciles to merits of a constitutional democracy? However, the continued importance being accorded to the military hierarchy by extra-regional powers does not seem to suggest so. General Ashfaq Kayani's silent rise and lately the accorded of three year long extension in service and so for pointers in this direction.

- **Current Economic Crises:** Whether or not one would see the revival of the country's economy? The Pakistani economy is sustained largely by foreign aid and loans. The social sector indicators such as health and education too paint a not so good picture. As long as the West shows interest in Pakistan, it may be in a position to finance its failing economy. But their disengagement from the region could surely spell doom for Pakistan's economy. The unprecedented floods in Pakistan that have caused much damage and devastation further aggravate the economic health of the country.

The foregoing uncertainties could be the prime drivers in shaping the future scenarios in Pakistan. In the following section, these have been inter-woven to evolve the generic trend lines in conjunction with other less consequential drivers. The conceptualisation of trend lines has been confined to the discussion of key uncertainties.

The Decadal Trend Lines

Each strategic uncertainty has been analysed to outline the trajectories i.e. the current situation and decades till 2020 and 2030.

These trend lines then form the basis of postulating plausible scenarios for 2030.

Key Uncertainties	Current Situation	Trend line 2020	Trend line 2030
Radicalism	Radical forces on the rise; increased unrest and instability; and visible signs of degradation of the state's political institutions.		
	Increased Islamic radicalism gives rise to religious agendas among the political parties; polity and politics reflect strong religious overtones in Pakistan.		
	Islamic character of Pakistani society reflects strongly in all aspects of public life; a mercurial cleric like Ayatollah Khomeini may emerge in Pakistan; though it is less likely that it could revolutionise Pakistani society.		

	Current Situation	2020	2030
Provincialism	Growing chorus for greater federal autonomy in Pakistan; Baloch insurgency builds up to a point of secession; FATA and NWFP come under serious distress.		
	Baloch insurgency now transcends the insurgency in FATA; call for Pakhtunva gains support in NWFP; Northern Areas too show signs of unrest; Karachi becomes a hub of political dissent; Sindh begins to politically countervail the province of Punjab; the Pakistani state seems to be headed for Lebanon-isation.		

	Balochistan secedes; call for Pashtun-istan hots up; the Durand line is no longer relevant; Sindh becomes turbulent resulting in widespread clashes between Mohajirs and Sindhis; Karachi becomes the hotbed of ethnic and sectarian violence; the insurgency in Northern Areas become an issue of concern; the Pakistani state seems to be headed for Balkan-isation.		
Politics	**Current Situation**	**2020**	**2030**
	Political climate turns fragile; struggle for political leadership builds up; Pakistan army closely watches the evolving situation.		
	The political power swings again; Pakistan army assumes power; attempts to reign in the raging radicalism and provincialism with force; does not appear to be very successful; and it continues to struggle to ensure unity of the state against strong fissiparous forces.		
	The state ceases to exercise control over the provinces; few provinces succeed in seceding; The Pakistan military however continues to hold power; demands for return of the civilian rule hot up again; the shrinking Pakistani state becomes even more volatile and unpredictable.		
Economy	**Current Situation**	**2020**	**2030**
	The economy continues to survive on external aid. United States continues to bear the cost of conflict. FoDP too pitches in with liberal doses of financial and material aid.		

| | The economy becomes addicted to aid infusions. The economic indicators reflect the poor state of financial health. The fiscal deficit grows beyond state's control. The Pakistani state is no longer able to bear the cost of conflict with the radical forces. | |
| | The economy is in tatters. The donors too shy away from their earlier commitments. The economic distress levels sound alarm bells across the world. There emerges a severe contest amongst the great powers to exploit the state's abundant mineral resources. | |

PLAUSIBLE SCENARIOS 2030

Four broad visualisations denoted as the `4F Scenarios` emerge – functional, fragile, failing and fragmented Pakistan. Each scenario is based on a mix of trend lines drawn from the key uncertainties discussed above. There could be a few intermediate scenarios; however these are not discussed. Notwithstanding the negativities observed in the trend lines, the probability of the Pakistani state pulling itself out from the current mess cannot be ruled out.

Scenario I: Functional Pakistan. It is quite possible that state of Pakistan is able to drive itself out of its current internal problems. The Pakistan army sensing the security implications comes down heavily against the radical elements. The Taliban momentum is eventually rolled back and the al-Qaida is denied safe havens. The success of allied operations in Afghanistan facilitates in calming down the frontier provinces. The rival political groups and parties begin to cooperate with the military in order to bring some sense of order within the country. The civil administration recognises the criticality of the situation and begins to perform. The social sector indicators such as health, education and law and order start looking up as a result of sound economic policies. The diplomatic relations with its immediate neighbours show a marked improvement. The country in general shows an uptrend in all spheres of public life but the army continues to be in control.

Scenario II: Fragile Pakistan. The power struggle continues and the cyclical civilian – military rule repeats itself every four to five years. Here, the politicians get lucky in ridding Pakistan of some radical and military influences. But the age old animosity between the PPP and PML(N), and other regional political parties does not end so soon. Settling of the personal scores between the principal power centres i.e. the military and nationalist parties will continue. And just as the Pakistani state recovers from one situation, another crisis may arise. The Pakistan civil society could be expected to rally behind these power centres, but if there is no change, it could well become despondent. The politics of 'power swings' is likely to be the norm for a generation or more, till the people of Pakistan realise the futility of this brand of politics, or a charismatic figure emerges, whose vision and aura over shadows the current crop of politicians and generals.

Scenario III: Failing Pakistan. Growing radicalism and demand for provincial autonomy would be the key uncertainties driving this condition. A civil war may possibly erupt in the state of Pakistan wherein the peripheral provinces go their own way, radicalism rules and al-Qaida operatives come close to laying their hands on some nukes. The internal fault lines are accentuated by issues of food shortages, climate change and water security, and the sharing of natural resources and minerals. And even if, the existential threat from the Pakistani Taliban is somewhat reduced, this protracted conflict with the Taliban would eventually weaken the state. The Pakistani populace becomes increasingly vulnerable to the battle between the religious forces and secularists, capital investment flees, economic development slows down and Pakistan becomes a nation of conflicting interests. In the process, chaos and anarchy sets in. Pakistan looks to be headed for 'Lebanon-isation' and even possible 'Balkan-isation'.

Scenario IV: Fragmented Pakistan. Pakistan's several power centres such as the military, political and religious parties and radical elements become pawns to extra-regional players – with the US, Russia and China being the lead contenders. Pushed around for strategic and ideological gains, Pakistan's capacity to influence its future is reduced or simply non-existent. At best, it can rent out its territory for others' games or power play. This would affect the state's cohesion and development, and enrich only those actors, who conspire to be part of this great game. The resulting power politics would focus on simply getting a piece of the cake - legitimately or illegitimately. Certainly the Pakistanis can be expected to favour their trusted ally China - because of its strategic importance, economic clout and geographical proximity. China could easily outsmart others in furthering their strategic and commercial interests. China successfully creates several trans-national corporations to check mate the western powers in Pakistan. Giligit-Baltistan shows signs of amalgamating with China. The United States may retain some control over certain political constituencies in Pakistan. India too may vie for re-claiming some of its territory in Jammu and Kashmir. A resurgent Russia and the Shiite Iran would also not like to be left out of the resulting imbroglio.

WILD CARD SCENARIOS

Several wild card situations are possible and those remotely likely are discussed. First, the take over of the Pakistani state by a radical Taliban regime could portend grave challenges. Taliban led by a messianic leader and supported by a few political parties initially assume power at the provincial level and gradually emerges as a powerful political force in the centre. An Afghanistan like situation of mid 1990s emerges which blatantly tramples all democratic values and institutions across the length and breadth of the country. Second, the country's nuclear assets despite best attempts of the military leadership and the United States pass in part or whole into the hands of radical elements. Such a situation engineered by the al-Qaida could force the United States to launch a counter strike to wrest back the nuclear assets. This could generate an intense internal backlash eventually resulting in a civil war. And thirdly, increased attempts by the United States to unilaterally strike at some of the al-Qaida strongholds within the frontier provinces leads to a political backlash within the country, and the radical elements seize the opportunity and rise to force a regime change.

The massive floods in Pakistan surely proved to be a disastrous wild card. With more than 20 million people displaced; 1.8 million houses damaged; 1.2 million cattle heads lost; a fifth of the cotton crop wiped out; and vast tracts of the most fertile arable land along the Indus River deluged, this tragedy surpasses any other disaster witnessed recently. The magnitude of the devastation and damage caused has been colossal and some experts argue that Pakistan may take years before its fully recovers.

Conclusion

In absence of clear alternative futures, the pendulum of power will continue to swing, with the possibility of a collapse always looming in the background. But then a weak Pakistan threatens everyone in the region. Pakistan's future scenarios are linked to the regional future which all must work to transform. Given the current political and religious drift, it is unlikely that these ideal conditions can ever be achieved. This process will have to be multi-faceted and anticipatory rather than reactive. And if it does not happen, then like all else it will be subsumed in due course. And then there would be far too much at stake for all stakeholders, and especially the lead countries to allow the current downward trajectory to continue. Could Pakistan draw itself out from the scenarios – fragile, failed and fragmented - and become a functional state is the big question. No wonder betting on plausible politico-military alternatives in Pakistan by 2030 can be inherently risky and fickle.

8
Scenarios 2030: A Long Term View of Hydro Politics of South Asia

—Medha Bisht

Negotiating water sharing agreements on South Asian rivers have often proved to be tenuous, arduous and full of interstate misgivings. While much sweat, intellect and polemical debate has gone into these negotiated agreements, most of the water sharing settlements between countries rest on suspicious and guarded grounds. Some perennial questions which have occupied the minds of the policy makers and experts are: would shared transboundary rivers induce cooperation or would they trigger conflicts/war in the subcontinent. What could be the major trends and patterns of change in the years to come? A pertinent response to these questions would be to focus on the long view of hydropolitics by 2030. It would perhaps be therefore interesting to analyse whether shared water resources would trigger a path dependent behaviour reflecting a continuation of current policy trends or whether the environmental, technological, social, economic or political changes in the South Asian region induce states to opt for different policy responses, than the ones they currently follow?

Benefits -perceived and actual have been the main driving force for cooperation. These perceived benefits have ranged from generation of extra revenues, access to navigational facilities, optimal utilisation of waters, flood control or other foreign policy goals which might not have direct linkages with water issues, but can be path breaking in inducing states to cooperate on the same. The hydrology of an international river basin links all the riparian states, requiring them to share complex network of environmental, economic, political and security interdependencies.[1] Riparian fears (upstream-downstream), geographical regime of the river (is it a border creator or a through border river), asymmetry of power, reciprocity of benefits, side payments, issue linkages are some factors which have played an important role in facilitating cooperation or inducing defection amongst states. Some of the best case examples amongst others at the international level where countries have successfully cooperated on sharing transboundary rivers are Brazil and Paraguay - the Parana River, United States and Mexico - the Colorado river, Turkey and Syria --the Euphrates river and Egypt and Sudan - the Nile river. Though scholars have attributed various reasons for cooperation, lessons from these transboundary rivers can indeed contribute some insights on transboundary cooperation between countries in South Asia.

A Primer on South Asian Rivers

The water agreements between India and its neighbours are governed by various bilateral treaties and frameworks. While the region can be distinctly divided into two basins—the Indus Water Basin and the Ganga-Brahmaputra-Meghna Basin, all the South Asian countries have adopted a bilateral understanding on water issues rather than undertaking a regional or basin-wide approach. For instance:

- The Indus River which flows through India and Pakistan is divided between the two countries, whereby the Western Rivers i.e. Indus, Jhelum, Chenab have been given to Pakistan and the Eastern Rivers i.e. Sutlej, Beas, Rabi have been given to India. The terms of river sharing arrangements have been made under the Indus Water Treaty signed between both countries.

- The Ganges River flows through India and Bangladesh. Sharing of river waters is the major thrust of the Ganges Water Treaty signed by both countries in 1997. Teesta Water Sharing Agreement, which would divide the waters

1   Dinar Shlomi, *International Water Treaties: Negotiation and Cooperation Along Transboundary Rivers*, London & New York: Routledge, 2008.

of the Teesta river between both countries might be signed soon.

- Indo-Nepal relations are governed by various agreements aimed at harnessing river waters through the construction of dams and barrages. The hydropower projects serve twin purpose of energy generation and enhancing irrigation potential. Most of these dams serve to benefit the border areas of Bihar and Uttar Pradesh in Northern and Eastern India and the districts in the Terai region of Nepal. The four rivers which have occupied much attention of both countries are Mahakali, Kosi, Gandak and Karnali.

- There are four major rivers in Bhutan: the Torsa (Ammochu), Sankosh (Punatsangchu), Wangchu (Raidak) and the Manas. As all these rivers have a total generation capacity of 30,000 MW, they have been considered as a suitable site for building run of the river projects, as all of them are perennial rivers. Apart from having institutional framework to support flood forecasting method, India and Bhutan share a progressive bilateral cooperation on hydel projects. Both countries signed MoUs on December 2009, to develop 10,000 MW of power. The electricity generated would be exported to India.

- China does not have a water sharing agreement with any of the South Asian countries. However in 2002, India and China had entered into a MoU for provision of hydrological information on Brahmaputra river from 1st June to 15th October every year, which is utilized in the formulation of flood forecasts by the Central Water Commission. Another Memorandum of Understanding was signed in 2005 for supply of hydrological information on Sutlej. In 2006 both countries agreed to set up an expert level mechanism to discuss interaction and co-operation on hydrological data, emergency management and other issues regarding transborder rivers.

Given the nature of these rivers and the issues governing them, there are three areas which are often negotiated between South Asian countries. These are: (a) water rights and allocation, (b) water resource projects (dams/barrages/run on the river projects etc.), and (c) perceived and actual benefits accruing from water cooperation. Some discussion on these key focal issues is imperative because most of them would in essence remain the decision-makers dilemma in 2030 and beyond.

Map of South Asian Rivers

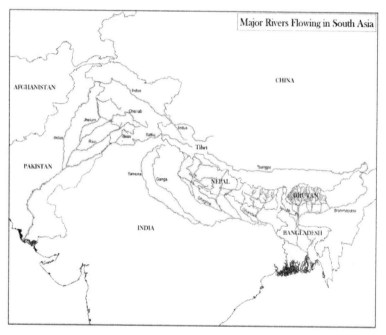

The factors which might shape some of these key issues by 2030 and therefore could trigger a different policy response are: climate change, political developments both internal and external, economic growth, technological developments and population growth. However before one delves into the critical 2030 projections key issues that have impacted or shaped water negotiations in the past merit some attention. Thus while *section one* would look into these focal areas of negotiations, *section two* will primarily focus on key drivers which would impact these focal issues by 2030, *section three* would focus on scenarios and trend variations as they appear by 2030.

Section One

WATER RIGHTS AND ALLOCATION

Water rights and allocations are two issue areas which are embedded in the discourse of water negotiations. While water rights implies the down stream-upstream rights which riparian states are entitled to, water allocation has been defined as the process through which an available water resource is distributed (or redistributed) to legitimate claimants. In other words it can be said that water allocation processes generate a series of water rights governing the use of water within a catchment.[2]

The issue of water rights and allocations in the South Asian context can be divided into two broad strands. The first strand refers to formal (technical) allocation of waters which the state is entitled to (as negotiated between countries). The second strand refers to rights which a downstream or an upstream country can claim on the river flowing through its territory. These rights can emanate from competing claims often stemming from diversion of the river for irrigation and other domestic needs, construction of barrages and dams and unfair compensation packages amongst others. While water allocation has been the main theme between India-Pakistan and India-Bangladesh water negotiations, water rights has emerged as one of the main contentious point between India-Pakistan, India-Nepal and India-Bangladesh. It also needs to be mentioned that water needs of upper-riparians can sometimes unduly affect the defined water allocations made to the downstream states. The main actors which can influence the discourse on water allocation and water rights are states, international organisations, domestic lobbies –the main water users like provinces/states, farmers, shipping industry (as in the case of Farakkha barrage), technocrats/water bureaucracy and the affected population representative of environmentalists and social groups.

2   Bird, Arriens and Custodio, *Water Rights and Water Allocation: Issues and Challenges for Asia*, Philippines: Asian Development Bank, 2009. p 13.

INDIA-BANGLADESH

In the South Asian context water allocation has often been perceived as a zero-sum game, where the benefit of one actor is considered as the loss of the other. For instance a major part of the controversy relating to Ganges Water Treaty between Bangladesh and India revolves around augmenting flows during the dry season (1st January- 31st May). While the Bangladesh position underlines the need to utilise the waters of the Ganges either through the construction of dams in Nepal and India, which could release the water to Bangladesh in the lean season, or through construction of link canals in West Bengal, which could also link Nepal rivers with Bangladesh rivers, thus providing Nepal an inadvertent access to the sea; India on its part has rejected these propositions and instead suggested diversion of Brahmaputra waters to the Ganges River by construction of a barrage across the Brahmaputra upstream of Bangladesh to divert waters into the canal. Bangladesh has however has refused India's proposal.

INDIA-PAKISTAN

Water rights and allocation between India and Pakistan over the Indus river water have been defined by the Indus Water Treaty signed in 1960. Though the allocation of water was an equally irresolvable issue between Pakistan and India, the negotiations were primarily shaped by the World Bank mediation, which amongst many things suggested a trade off between Eastern Rivers (Sutlej, Beas Rabi) to India and Western rivers (Indus, Chenab, Jhelum) to Pakistan. In return Pakistan was compensated in material terms by both India, World Bank U.S., France, Canada, Italy amongst others, to build canals in order to compensate for the loss of water from Eastern rivers. However the issue of water allocation has re-emerged as a significant political issue between both countries as Pakistan in last some years has been upset over the construction of Baglihar and other projects on the Western rivers. Pakistan points out the reduced water flows with respect to the allocation rights which were defined by the Indus Water Treaty in 1960. India, which has a right to construct "run-of-the-river" projects on Western rivers has however rejected Pakistan's contention of reduced river water stating that the project is crucial for the power-starved Kashmir. Another dimension which has emerged on the issue of rights is the domestic opposition of Kashmir over the Indus Water Treaty. Motions for instance have been moved in the state assembly of Jammu and Kashmir on various occasions by the legislators asking the central government in India to review the treaty and pay compensation to the state.[3]

INDIA-NEPAL

Meanwhile, though Indo-Nepal relations have not been much concerned about water allocations, they have been engaged over the issue of inadequate financial compensation over water resource projects, which in turn have given rise to the issue of water rights. The four rivers which have occupied much attention of both countries are Mahakali, Kosi, Gandak and Karnali. Water rights between the two countries revolve around the construction of dams and barrages which go towards the generation of hydro-power and catering to the irrigation needs of the border areas of Bihar and Uttar Pradesh in Northern and Eastern India and the districts in the Terai region of Nepal. The Nepalese argument is that India has built projects for its own benefits without giving adequate compensation to Nepal. Compensation it argues is an essential right of Nepal as much of its territory is submerged due to dam construction. Nepal also argues that benefits from irrigation and hydropower are not benefiting Nepal as much they benefits India. Nepali contention is that as India is the only state which is most feasible buyer of Nepalese electricity and that India often exploits this geographical factor. They contend that had Nepal been economically strong, the same benefits would be sold to India at a much higher cost that Nepal currently gets. India on the other hand considers unstable politics in Nepal as the main reason for the dysfunctional agreement and argues that agreements were negotiated with sovereign consent and not imposed on Nepal. Due to pressures from the Nepalese side, two water sharing agreements viz. the Kosi and the Gandak have been amended but grievances still remain the same with allegations and counter allegations continuing on both sides.

---

3   Athar Parvaiz, "India/Pakistan: Indus Water Treaty Agitates Kashmiris"IPS News, October 15, 2008, at http://ipsnews.net/news.asp?idnews=44268

WATER RESOURCE PROJECTS

Water resource projects are often defended and opposed on account of the benefits and costs they provide/impose on a country's resources. Therefore it is one of key issues while negotiating water sharing agreements. There are generally two views (often diametrically opposite) on the use of water resource projects. The technocentric view argues for economic and direct/visible benefits and proposes that upper riparian could benefit from surplus energy and storage facility that is produced and lower riparian could benefit from flood mitigating mechanisms due to excessive water that is stored during rainy seasons and the excess water which is released during the lean season. The socio-environmental view on the other hand highlights issues in context to risks vis a vis benefits and responsibility vis a vis rights. The socio-environmental view draws attention to the likelihood of increasing water logging, sedimentation and salinity problems and loss of biodiversity and vegetation cover due to loss and diversion of the river water upstream. The proponents of this view argue that though dams are built to store waters, often displacement at a massive scale takes place, without adequate rehabilitation and resettlement schemes in place. They also point out the environmental hazards dams pose to seismic zones. This view emphasises the interconnected hydrological cycle and point out that man-made interventions often lead to high social and environmental costs.

Some of these issues can be clearly seen in the existing discourses on dams in Pakistan, India, Bangladesh, Bhutan and Nepal.

INDIA-PAKISTAN

The technocrats in India and Pakistan look at exclusive engineering solutions. This approach treats water as a raw material and attempts to use technical and scientific knowledge to harness water in its full capacity. India's relations with Nepal, Bhutan and Bangladesh have often been shaped with this approach. Though this approach has been able to accrue material benefits, in some cases its limitations has given rise to problems of water logging and salinity. Pakistan's Mangla and Tarbela dam is the most appropriate example on this front.

India-Bangladesh

A controversy pertaining to the impact of dams has also been a major bone of contention between India-Bangladesh relations. Opponents and proponents of dams in both countries are at loggerheads over the issue of Tipaimukh dam which is proposed to be built in the state of Manipur in order to generate hydropower worth 1500MW. A storage site it is argued would also enhance flood control and would inturn benefit Bangladesh. Section of Bangladesh population argues that the construction would lead to the drying of two main rivers the Surma and the Kusiyara, which provide much of irrigation needs of Northeastern Bangladesh. Meanwhile in India also Tipaimukh is being opposed as experts have suggested that apart from displacing the population, the dam would have an adverse seismic impact in the region. These controversies for long have deferred any decision on the subject and the construction of the work has stalled since March 2007 due to protests.

India-Nepal

Meanwhile India-Nepal relations though are most keen to construction of dams, both countries are often at loggerheads on account of financial compensation, and politicisation of water sharing agreements. Irrigation benefits which are harnessed from the rivers of Nepal have been an issue of debate and discussion between both countries, whereby Nepal feels that the location of dams are often built in India's favour so that maximum water goes to India. The Gandak and the Kosi projects have been criticised on these grounds. In 1996, the two countries signed the Mahakali treaty which includes the construction of Tanakpur Barrage, Sarada Barrage and Pancheshwar project. Though the Mahakali treaty is regarded by experts as the most fair and equitable arrangement with regards to benefit sharing, not much action on this front has stagnated progressive cooperation on this front.

India-Bhutan

Hydro-power cooperation between India and Bhutan on the contrary have benefited both countries. As the residential sector in

Bhutan consumes about 48.7 percent of the total energy[4] with the maximum domestic demand of 130 MW[5], Bhutan exports most of the electricity. It is precisely for this reason that cross-border, hydro-power projects are a classic example of win-win situation for both India and Bhutan. Also in Bhutan unlike Nepal, most of the dams are single purpose projects where the cooperative agreements between both countries are on turn key basis whereby sixty percent of the investment for any hydro project is provided as a grant, and the rest is loan. As a result the project's total cost is slashed by 60 percent and therefore the cost of generation also goes down by roughly half. For instance Bhutan consumers pay the cheapest rate in the world for electricity i.e. Nu 0.70 per unit in urban areas and Nu 0.50 in rural areas. This benefit has made Bhutan sign more agreements with India.[6]

PERCEIVED AND ACTUAL BENEFITS

Perceived and actual benefits is the third issue and a critical factor in bringing states to a common table. For instance it was the utilisation of the Indus river which brought Pakistan and India to negotiate with each other. Nepal and Bhutan meanwhile also perceive cooperation as a profitable venture because it would enable them to utilise water resources for revenue generation. Meanwhile access to Indian and Bangladeshi territory for navigation facilities to the Bay of Bengal is another area on which the two countries are increasingly interested. Bangladesh on the other hand due to its excessive dependence on

---

4   "Energy data directory released," *Kuensel*, August 1, 2007.

5   "Vibrant trade marks India, Bhutan ties", *Financial Express,* March 30, 2009, at: 2009,at http://www.financialexpress.com/news/vibrant-trade-marks-india-bhutan-ties/350823/0

6   The Chukha Hydro-power Corporation Ltd contributes 336 MW to the installed capacity (71.69 percent); Kurichu hydro project offers 60 MW while the Tala has added another 1020 MW to the existing capacity. Some of the other projects envisaged between the two countries are: Punatsangchhu H.E. Project Stage-I (1095 MW), Punatsangchu H.E. Project-II (992/1000 MW), Mangdechu H.E. Project (360/600 MW), Manas Multipurpose Project (2800 MW), Wangchu Reservoir Scheme (4X225 MW), Bunakha H.E. Project (3X60 MW), Sankosh Multi-purpose project (4060 MW).

transboundary rivers (fifty-four rivers) has no option but to negotiate with India on water allocation issues. It is also interested in proposing water storage sites in Nepal and India, so that floods can be prevented from devastating its Northern areas.

FLOOD CONTROL AND MANAGEMENT

Flood control and forecasting is another area of potential cooperation between India and its eastern neighbours. However these arrangements have triggered a different response from different countries. Though flood forecasting mechanisms exist between Nepal and India in various treaties, due to poor progress on water relations between both countries and poor maintenance little effort has been undertaken to make it operational in substantive terms. The Kosi floods which often revisit Bihar and Southern Nepal is a stark example of this.

INDIA-BHUTAN

On the contrary flood control is an area where India and Bhutan have made systematic plans to contain future eventualities. A Joint Group of Experts (JGE) on Flood Management has been constituted between India and Bhutan to discuss and assess the probable causes and effects of the recurring floods. Recently the Union minister has also announced a scheme called "Comprehensive Scheme for Establishment of Hydro-Meteorological and Flood Forecasting Network" on rivers common to India and Bhutan in order to prevent threats of floods in near future.[7] This network consists of 44 hydrometeorological/meteorological stations located in Bhutan and is being maintained by Bhutan with funding from India. The data received from these stations is utilised in India by Central Water Commission for formulating flood forecasts. Cooperation on this front is in progress[8].

---

7   "Bhutan hydro projects not responsible for Assam floods", Times of India, March 2, 2009, at: http://timesofindia.indiatimes.com/ Guwahati/Bhutan-hydro-projects-not-responsible-for-Assam-floods- /articleshow/4209437.cms

8   India-Bhutan Cooperation, at: http://india.gov.in/sectors/water_ resources/international_corp.php

INDO-BANGLADESH

As far as Indo-Bangladesh relations are concerned cooperation on flood management has made substantive progress. A meeting of Indo-Bangladesh Experts on Flood Forecasting and Warning System took place in August, 2000 in which the two countries discussed the issues of strengthening and expanding the existing co-operation for improving the Flood Forecasting and Warning System.[9] Oflate India is providing flood data of Farakkha for Ganga regarding flood forecasting methods, Bangladesh has also given consent towards joint dredging by the two countries to facilitate river navigation along the Calcutta-Haldia and Karimganj river routes.

Mutual reciprocity through issue linkages can enable countries to cooperate and help them create an enabling atmostphere. This would not only help them manage perceptions and misperceptions but also enable them to come together to solve trans-national threats such as disaster risk management, illicit drug trafficking, trans-national illegal migration, fighting terrorism and non-state armed groups. Cooperation on water resources can also improve economic prosperity—a much needed element in the South Asian region. However political will to negotiate such issues and an atmosphere of mutual trust and cooperation along with a mindset of positive sum game is essential for reaching such agreements. Perhaps such benefits can be possible by changing the framework of water agreements, including more stakeholders and issue areas, which could potentially and positively shape the processes of negotiations and hence the negotiation outcome. It needs to be noted however that in the South Asian context though these benefits are well known, not much has been achieved on the functional plane. Thus a critical question that arises at this juncture is that would such responses be different by 2030 and if so then what factors do we keep in mind to achieve the best case scenario which could benefit all South Asian countries. The following pages would delve in length on this issue. However as there would be a number of intervening factor

---

9   Indo-Bangladesh Cooperation, Ministry of Water Resources, at http://wrmin.nic.in/writereaddata/linkimages/CHAPTER%20-%2071809012297.pdf

between 2009 to 2030, the next section would focus on the key drivers which will potentially influence South Asian environment in the next twenty years. These are climate change, technological development, industrialisation and growing urbanisation, domestic and external politics and population growth.

Section Two

CLIMATE CHANGE

In global-scale assessments, basins are defined as being water stressed if they have per capita water availability below 1,000 m^{3}per year. With the present water availability amounting to 1,330 m^3 per person per year in the Indus water basin, North-Western India and Pakistan would be the most stressed water deficit countries by 2030. It is also estimated that melting of Himalayan glaciers could lead to disastrous consequences on the Ganges and the Brahmaputra dependent areas.[10] It needs to be noted that nearly 70 percent of the Ganges water comes from Nepal which is fed by glaciers. If the Himalayan glaciers recede, rivers at lower altitude will also dry up leading to the occurrence of frequent droughts in the region. As the vegetation coverage in the Ganga Brahmaputra –Meghna basin is just 20 percent and 39 percent in the Indus water Basin, with climate change the existing eco-system and maintenance of the soil balance would deteriorate further. Also reduced flow of water would increase soil salinity thus leaving large tracts of land uncultivable in Nepal, India, Bangladesh and Pakistan. Based on climate models, the area flooded in Bangladesh is projected to increase by at least 23–29 percent with a global temperature rise of 2°C by 2030.[11] In addition, sea-level rise is projected which would extend areas of salinisation of groundwater and estuaries which could result in a decrease of freshwater availability for humans and ecosystems in coastal areas. Environment refugees therefore could increase and migration into

---

10 Babel and Wahid, "Fresh Water under threat in South Asia," UNEP & Asian Institute of Technology, 2008,at http://www.unep.org/pdf/southasia_report.pdf

11 IPCC, Climate Change and Water, Technical Paper VI, June 2008, at http://www.ipcc.ch/pdf/technical-papers/climate-change-water-en.pdf

cities in search of alternative livelihoods-might result in conflicts and sharpening of regional affiliations.

Meanwhile population pressures would exercise increasing demand on resources and it is likely that water and food insecurity in consistence with the projected climate change realities are going to be critical domestic issues in all countries by 2030. Water allocation not only between states at the regional level but also between states at the domestic leval would be critical area of concern. Also higher water temperatures and changes in extremes, including floods and droughts, are projected to affect water quality and induce many forms of water pollution–sediments, nutrients, dissolved organic carbon, pathogens, pesticides and salt, which will have negative impacts on ecosystems, human health, and water system reliability.[12] In some regions of India and Bangladesh people would suffer from arsenic poisoning and fluorosis (a disease of the teeth or bones caused by excessive consumption of fluoride in drinking water)- this can result in an even worse situation if people are forced to use more water from groundwater as a result of the lack of reliable surface water sources. The presence of arsenic could also reduced crop productivity, contributing to food shortages. Meanwhile in Pakistan further ground water extraction could lead to excessive water logging and salinity. Increased demand of water in different provinces in Pakistan could lead to disequilibrium in the society between the haves and the haves not thus leading to social anarchy, which could be capitalised by fundamentalist groups.

Changes in snow fall patterns and glacier melt will affect seasonal variation in runoff, inducing water shortages during dry summer months, an issue which would adversely impact interstate relations between India - Bangladesh and India –Pakistan. Wetlands and forests in Bangladesh would disappear due to population settlement. With increasing demand and a corresponding shortfall of supply access to drinking water and energy will become major constraints giving rise of food imports and loss of foreign exchange in Pakistan and Bangladesh.

---

12 Ibid

Impact of Climate Change on Water Sharing Issues between States.

- Water Allocation would become a key issue, with downstream riparian accusing the upper riparian of stealing water.

- Due to Climate Change leading to reduced water flows, salinity would increase - diversion of rivers by upper riparian is quite a possibility Water rights are going to become sharper in inter-state water negotiations.

- As climate change affects the water flow, opposition to dam building or storage sites would increase. The primary opposition would come from environmentalists and lower riparian. Negotiations on dam building would be increasingly hijacked by domestic and translational opposition. Environmental and social issues could be the difficult areas of negotiations on water resource projects. Meanwhile electricity and water prices for the export of electricity and consumption at the domestic level would rise due to increasing demand at home.

- Linking rivers- Ganges to Brahmaputra is quite a possibility by 2030. Its is possible that Bangladesh is able to deal on bilateral terms with Nepal and Bhutan in exchange of transit facilities to India via the Bangladeshi territory.

- The Indus Water Treaty would be under increasing criticism. While Pakistan could want more share from the Eastern rivers, dissent voices over water rights in Kashmir over the Western rivers would grow. The water politics over the Kashmir issue is likely to grow and would shape the position of both India and Pakistan. It is unlikely that the Kashmir issue is resolved under these circumstances.

TECHNOLOGICAL DEVELOPMENT

Technological development is going to be one of the major areas which could minimise water stress and enhance water availability and quality. Development of inland water structure and management of water projects for effective use could be major issues by 2030. However given its limitations due to finance and other practical constraints, indigenous methods like water management, rainwater harvesting, could be some major areas of interest and concern. Technology which can use less water but effectively increase yield per hectare would grow in importance. The effective use of water rather than fixed allocation of water could be emphasised as an effective problem solving mechanism in order to lead to integrative rather than divisive solutions.

Also due to primary threat of sea level rise, coastal and flood defence infrastructure in coastal areas of India and Bangladesh could become important part of security considerations. Focus of technology would also be on preventing glacial lake outburst flooding Nepal, Bhutan and North-East India through building barrages and storage dams. However the downstream riparian fears of India over Nepal are likely to influence state behaviour. A similar fear of any attempt to build dams or storage sites in North India would increase anxiety levels in Pakistan. This scenario is likely if bilateral relations between India and its neighbours lacks trust and is governed by mutual suspicion.

With flood defences concentrated on the cities, it is estimated that over 80 million people in Bangladesh would live in urban settings. Dhaka would therefore become one of the world's largest mega cities, with 30 million residents.[13] Though embankments and dams/barrages have their own set of problems both ecologically and socially, their demand is going to increase due to the visible perceived effects they have on flow regulation, flood control, and availability of water for irrigation during dry seasons. Design of dams to prevent flood outbursts would be improved upon and detailed project reports on the feasibility of projects would have to go through rigorous processes, due to pressure form environmental and advocacy groups. There could be debates on the use and effect of technology and social and environmental costs would be highlighted and become a critical area of concern in domestic debates. However small and medium hydro-power projects could get increased preference. With Nepal and

---

13 DFID, *Bangladesh* in *2030, A DFID* Horizon Scan, DFID, Bangladesh, 2007, at http://www.dfid.gov.uk/Documents/publications/ Horizon%20Scan%20final.pdf

Bhutan having projects on run-of-river schemes, such projects and sites would be exploited to the fullest due to the rise in population and increasing energy demands. Riparian rights therefore could emerge as an area of concern.

Countries and corporations which have an edge over water technology like Israel, Japan and the European Union could become important players in South Asia. Technology could also be employed towards repowering existing plants with more powerful and efficient turbine designs, which would be cost-effective.

In densely populated coastal area especially Bangladesh and some parts of India desalination costs may be exorbitant and research in new desalination technology would be required to reduce the costs. Desalination technology would also become important in Pakistan which at present is suffering from salinisation problems.

Technology for preventing and managing flood control would be on demand to combat the adverse impact on population living in coastal areas and downstream locations. Inter state information on water flows and forecasting would be important to address these needs. Though water managers in Bangladesh, have begun to address directly the implications of climate change as part of their standard flood and water supply management practices, such initiatives would be receiving encouragement from the governments. It needs to be noted however that examples of 'concrete' actions in the water sector to adapt specifically and solely to a changing climate are very rare. This is partly because climate change may be only one of many drivers affecting strategies and investment plans due to uncertainty in projections of future hydrological changes,

Meanwhile the development and application of technological advances could change many people's lives for the better. For example, a simple, effective and affordable arsenic removal technology could help protect the health of millions of people. However as no such single technological solution currently exists, and it remains to be seen whether science will provide an answer. This would be particularly valuable for Bangladesh and India.

Due to change in climate patters, agriculture efficient technologies would be needs. The kinds of Sprinklers Irrigation System would get an added push and according to some estimates the rural sector in Bangladesh could be increasingly dominated by large agri-business companies and contract farming, with small holders pushed off the land and increased landlessness.[14] The crop sector will reach saturation point, with no room for further improvement. Bangladesh will depend heavily on food imports and will be more integrated into regional food markets.[15]

IMPACT OF TECHNOLOGICAL DEVELOPMENT ON WATER SHARING ISSUES BETWEEN STATES

- Water management practices would be popular and due to the lack of bilateral cooperation on issues, countries could look inwards in order to solve the impending water crises and water deficit situation. This could mark a shift from water allocation debates to transfer of technology as a coping factor in water negotiations. This issue would be full of complexities given the nature of asymmetric relations (economic) in South Asia.

- Given the financial difficulties relating to water technology, indigenous solutions or best practices on water management would grow in popularity giving rise to community based solutions to water management. Civil-society interaction across borders would grow. One could also witness the entry of various donor agencies funding shared practices in water management in South Asia.

- Technical solutions would be received well due to the need of building effective barrages and coastal defences. It could be possible that inter-state cooperation on technological issues could provide a functional rather than a political approach while dealing with water issues.

- The dams lobby and water bureaucracy in respective countries would play a significant role by highlighting the

14   Ibid
15   Ibid

techno-economic feasibility of dam projects. The engineer-
bureaucrat nexus could play an important role in proposing
projects such as inter-linking of rivers and dam/barrage
construction to augment water flows. The environmentalist
and social groups are however going to grow in numbers
asking for more accountability, technical feasibility and
good governance from governments. Between these two
debates the water issue would become highly politicised
with downstream-upstream issues coming to the fore.

- Mutual vulnerabilities could lead to exchange of information
  and data in order to effectively control floods/natural disasters.
  Strategic partnerships could be formed with countries which
  have edge over water saving technology. How such issues
  are played out at the regional and international plane could
  influence the role of external powers in South Asia.

- Domestically the governments could subsidise crops which
  consume less water in relation to the ones which consume
  more in order to deal with water stress.

INDUSTRIALISATION AND POPULATION GROWTH

Rapid industrialisation and population growth could lead to an
adverse impact on food and water demand and water quality. The
projected decrease in winter precipitation over the Indian subcontinent
would imply less storage and greater water stress during the lean
monsoon period. This would inevitably affect India's relations with
Pakistan and Bangladesh, where population growth would be putting
its own pressures. Water stress therefore would be one of the most
predominant phenomenon as the number of people living under
severe water stress increase. It is estimated that from 120 million to
1.2 billion and from 185 million to 981 million people will experience
increased water stress by the 2020s and the 2050s respectively.[16]
Increased water stress could also lead to conflicts and disputes over
water within states/provinces creating strained relation between the
centre and state governments. Due to water stress suicide rates of

---

16 IPCC, Climate Change and Water, Technical Paper VI, June 2008, at
    http://www.ipcc.ch/pdf/technical-papers/climate-change-water-en.pdf

farmers would be frequent, as agriculture dependent population in South Asian countries is high. Dissent will grow and these grievances could be capitalised by non-armed state groups for cadre recruitment further weakening the writ of the state.

Due to increased industrialisation by 2030 two-third of the people would live in cities and this factor could potentially shape the food habits. The change in diet pattern would reveal a high correspondence with incomes in particular products. Such changes would also influence future agricultural water demands because diets based on livestock, sugar and oil require more water. Food production requires a lot of water as on average one kilogram of grain requires 1,000 litres of water.[17] Climate change and mode of cultivation would therefore greatly influence food production. Water rights and allocation between states would be constant issue of tussle between states, as domestic demands increase and the issue of water would be highly politicised with each state accusing the other of unfair treatment. Nepal's increased demands on water needs for irrigation and energy consumption would impact the water agreements signed between India and Nepal. Likely a similar fate would be witnessed by bilateral agreements between Pakistan and Bangladesh.

As cotton requires only small part of cultivated area, demand for cotton is expected to double by 2050 and could be grown in most parts of South Asia. Over all crop water consumption is expected to grow by 70- 80 percent by 2050.[18] For South Asia it means that crop water requirements would reach to 2860 km^3. Agriculture would be the largest sector consuming water supply. Food imports could be a major feature by 2030 in water deficit countries like Pakistan, Bangladesh and Nepal thus eating away most of the foreign exchange reserves. According to the Asia Pacific Human Development Report, 2006, food imports by developing countries would grow two to three times, from US$ 18 billion in 2004 to around US$ 50 billion by 2030.

---

17   Scenarios on Water and Food In Asia, ADB Background Paper, 2008, at   http://waterknowledgehub.iwmi.org/PDF/Scenarios_Water_Food_Asia.pdf

18   Ibid

The report notes that "considering the fact that farming supports half of Asia's workforce, growing reliance on cheap food imports could wipe out rural livelihoods.[19]

As population to land ratio would increase dams building industry could receive a major jolt as opposition to displacement would increase. Rehabilitation of project affected people would also be a highly political issue, with several activist groups raising awareness and expressing resistance to such issues at an international scale.

The population in Bangladesh is now 153 million. By 2035 there will be about 200 million and in 2050 almost 222 million people living in Bangladesh. Similarly the population of Nepal would rise to 42 million by 2030 and 46 million by 2050 and the population of Pakistan and India and Bhutan would increase by thirty three billion, one seventy four billion and one million respectively by 2050. With population pressure consumptive practices would increase and this would impose a severe stress on the demand supply equation in South Asia.

IMPACT OF INDUSTRIALISATION AND URBANISATION ON WATER SHARING ISSUES BETWEEN STATES

- Positional stand of various countries on water allocation issues would become more rigid. Countries would be on a look out for a framework in order to deal with allocation issues. Water rights vis a vis the proportion of population and total land to be irrigated could be the defining and controversial features of this framework.

- Food security and water security would be important agendas for the government at the domestic level. These national policies would greatly impact foreign policy goals of the respective states.

- Availability of land for building barrage/dam sites would be a difficult issue to negotiate as the population would have to be rehabilitated to other areas. Due to increase

---

19   **Sherna Gandhy,** Trade on Human Terms, *InfoChange*, December 2006, at   http://infochangeindia.org/200703096082/Trade-Development/ Backgrounder/Trade-on-human-terms.html

of population density per square km land availability for construction sites would be a major impediment and could be an area of prolonged negotiations between states.

- Financial compensation packages and side benefits could pay a reconciliatory role in bringing states to a common table.

DOMESTIC POLITICS AND POLICIES AND EXTERNAL PLAYERS

Due to growing consumption of food and energy demands, domestic policies will greatly be shaped by water politics. The key drivers in shaping these could be corporations, inter-state relations, domestic pressure groups like farmers, engineers/technocrats, external players (China in context to GBM basin) and (China, United States in context to Indus Water Basin). Resurrection of India's river linking projects could also be plausibility; however this could have an adverse impact on its diplomatic relations with Nepal and Bangladesh.

As food and energy consumption grows, foreign policy issues could be driven by more non-traditional security issues. Regional cooperation on translational issues would become an important driver for SAARC and BIMSTEC Summits. Food imports would increase specially in Bangladesh and Pakistan which is largely dependent on transboundary rivers. However increased water and energy demands might even change the contours of diplomatic interaction at bilateral level, whereby technological cooperation on water issues is likely get much weightage. Thus multilateral rather than bilateral options would be explored and a focus on benefit sharing on waters to satisfy the needs of states could be an important driver.

The process of democratic evolution of South Asian countries would also be a critical factor in shaping water politics. Coalition politics in most countries would hold sway and consensus would be hard to achieve due to the growing constituency demands of respective parties. However unless countries move out of ideological issues cooperation on socio-economic grounds is unlikely to reach fruition.

Bangladesh would be dominated by two party politics, though minority parties would play a role in stabilising the centre. Stable politics is also quintessential to sustain a growth rate of 6 percent per annum. Trade routes for sourcing electricity from countries like Bhutan and Nepal would be the most desired option for availing hydro-electric power and a trilateral relationship between India, Bhutan and Nepal would emerge on this front considering that Bangladesh can benefit from rivers flowing through Nepal. Nepal would witness a system of coalition politics, where smaller parties of the Terai region would be critically important for stable numbers. Terai region would also assume importance in the coming years due to its significance as Nepal's tread basket. With recent GDP growth rate of 3 percent, Nepal's focus on revenue generation through hydro power would increase in coming years. Perhaps it is for this reason that Nepal's Water Resource Strategy states that by 2027, Nepal would be exporting substantial amounts of electricity to earn national revenues. In Bhutan, a two party system would dominate but with a stronger opposition party. Glacial bursts and displaced people due to dam building and manifest effects of rehabilitation programmes is going to be critical on deciding policies. Meanwhile resource stress could increase domestic demands in Bhutan as Bhutan though receives a high amount of precipitation; it varies significantly inside the country.[20] Water policies therefore might give a priority to domestic demands rather an overt focus on exports. Rapid industrialisation which could result in contaminating water could increase disputes between Bhutan and with lower riparian states in the North East. Meanwhile North Eastern conflicts would be exacerbated due to sharpening of ethnic tendencies and property rights over water resources could be a major issue within the region North East being present in a seismic zone would witness frequent land slides and earthquakes due to the increasing pressure due to dams and resource pressures. Oppositon to dam building would be more sharp. In Pakistan domestic politics would be increasingly linked with the importance of Kashmir for a sustainable supply of river water. Perhaps food/water insecurity in Pakistan would lead to the internationalisation of Kashmir issue.

---

20   Babel and Wahid, "Fresh Water under threat in South Asia," UNEP & Asian Institute of Technology, 2008,at http://www.unep.org/pdf/southasia_report.pdf

Centre-state/provincial divide is going to increase further, with the centre largely constrained to make independent deals at bilateral and multilateral level. National policies would therefore be dictated by various pulls and pressures and it could be likely that opportunistic politics comes to play. Political leadership is therefore going to be extremely important in balancing domestic dissent. In the absence of political leadership national issues could be outweighed by myopic politics at the detriment of the people at large.

Role of external players in bilateral interaction between India and its neighbours would be critically important. One could witness improved Nepal-China, Bhutan-China, Bangladesh-China and Pakistan –China relations in the sub-continent. China being an upper riparian would lead to an increased anxiety in India. China's influence in Kashmir dispute is likely to increase. United States could emerge as a neutral player in the region. However Pakistan could use its strategic leverage to link Kashmir with most of its diplomatic interaction with the United States. United States involvement would however be contingent on the presence of terrorist groups in the region. Developing sustainable supplies of cleaner energy would be essential in terms of both the economy and the environment. Options for Bangladesh could include natural gas, solar power, clean coal technology or buying energy from regional grids fed by hydropower produced in Nepal and Bhutan. Bhutan and Nepal would play an important role in India-Bangladesh relations and there would be mounting pressures to adopt a trilateral approach while dealing with water issues. China would play an important role in Indo-Bhutan and Indo-Nepal relations in terms of its location as an upper riparian state.

IMPACT OF DOMESTIC POLITICS AND EXTERNAL PLAYERS ON WATER SHARING ISSUES BETWEEN STATES

- Domestic politics would increasingly shape issues like water-allocation, optimal utilisation of river waters, concessions and side payments. Political leadership in framing the context of negotiations on the basis of mutual payoffs would therefore be critical in avoiding conflict and inducing cooperation on water issues.

- There is a likelihood of expanding the zone of agreement on water issues from navigation rights, to trade and transit routes, to satisfactory compensatory measures and mutually acceptable financial models.

- Ownership of cost of investments would be a critical factor in negotiating water resource projects. International financial institutions, international organisations, donor states, China and United States could be potential players on this front.

- Incase there is domestic political instability water cooperation between states is less likely and water could be an important issue in national debates creating confrontation rather cooperation. Mutual interest and shared benefits would be outweighed in this scenario.

- In the absence of clear framework on water and riparian rights issues are likely to be inflated with less likelihood of a solution.

Section Three

SCENARIOS 2030

Given that all these factors can have potential impact in South Asian politics, their interaction with each other can give rise to various plausible scenarios.

WIN-WIN MIND SETS BENEFIT ALL

South Asia 2030 represents a different picture as it existed in 2010 and cooperation on water issues has emerged as the main driving force for bringing states to a common table. The political leadership has realised that prospects of mutual payoffs through cooperation is higher than confrontation. A key driver for this changed behaviour is the water stress which the countries are facing and the increasing food and energy demands being felt at the domestic level, which has made democratic governments more concerned about these impending issues. A changed approach and perhaps some out of the box thinking has enabled states to breakthrough from key positions, which earlier had impeded cooperation. Emphasis on an internal approach to have effective water policies at the national level with a long term vision has been the key driver in shaping cooperative processes. Informal discussions and generating a national consensus provided the necessary mass for taking up issues further at the bilateral level. India's role in dealing with water issues with her neighbours is also the main reason for this change. Basing her policy on the tenets of reciprocal bilateralism, India renewed its focus on water cooperation amongst South Asian neighbours. Unlike earlier, the policy is not shaped by Chinese threat perceptions but is based on mutual interest and benefit. China has signed a bilateral understanding with India on Brahmaputra river, keeping in mind the interest of lower riparians India and Bangladesh. On Ganga Brahmaputra and Meghna Basin, some of the key issues which placated its smaller neighbours were the concessions given by India to Bangladesh to access electricity from Nepal and Bhutan. Nepal and Bhutan meanwhile has gained access to the sea through the Indian territory via Bangladesh. Link canals along the trijunction of Nepal, Bangladesh and West Bengal have been built. Nepal and Bhutan through the generation of revenues have become an export hub and a South Asian tourist destination for many which is beneficial to their foreign exchange reserves. The indirect benefits can be seen through the rising inputs made by the service sector in both countries. Due to improved interaction, cooperation on other transnational issues has become more coherent and cooperative.

As domestic politics in most countries is now focused on involving stakeholders at different levels, national vision reflects an inclusive approach even bypassing the state–centre tensions, which would have otherwise impeded effective action. Multi-stakeholder engagement have also helped overcoming technical roadblocks which could have stymied cooperation. Countries due to this fresh initiative at domestic level are looking towards an integrated benefit of the basin, which inturn has served shared national interests. Data sharing and information gathering therefore is being promoted and is an ongoing process. While Bangladesh has benefitted immensely from flood mitigation measures, Nepal has been able to tap water and sell it to India towards generation of revenues. Hydro-power diplomacy in Bhutan has taken a fresh direction with partnership with

Bangladesh. Bhutan and Nepal are developing projects on lines of Clean Development Mechanism, which is helping them to sell carbon credits to developed countries. Meanwhile relations with Pakistan are being managed through a functional approach as both states have made it a policy that functional cooperation is important in order to serve public interest. A primary reason for this is the internal management of water resources, which has improved in Pakistan. Due to domestic initiatives at water management, Pakistan has been able to control much of its water salinisation and water logging problems. Thus domestic initiatives at home have been the main driver for changing perceptions and behaviour of state actors. India and Pakistan are contemplating an Indus Water Treaty-II, due to increased opposition from Kashmir on its share over Western waters. A basin wide approach is being contemplated.

People to people and civil society interaction between countries has improved and best practices over community based water management is a regional theme. Such interactions are often shared in SAARC and BIMSTEC summits. This scenario is marked by three parallel process (a) domestic initiatives (b) bilateral initiatives and (c) Regional/multilateral initiatives.

It needs to be pointed out that though this scenario would have high impact on the overall health of the subcontinent; there are key uncertainties which need to mitigated or allayed. These are:

Political compulsions do not respond to the needs of benefit sharing mechanisms as coalition politics continues to be a struggle of power, whereby socio-economic issues become a political tool to oppose the incumbent government in power. The political parties are divided into ideological basis over the approaches that should be undertaken; moreover state-centre tensions and provincial politics in South Asian states have impeded the operation of a functional framework. States are also not ready to commit to sharing information due to mistrust and suspicion between countries. Movement for independence in Kashmir has strengthened with the internationalisation of the issue whereby water politics and Kashmir is played out as an important tool to forward interests over territorial control. Bhutan though continues to be India's reliable partner, domestic needs are compelling Bhutan to lesson electricity exports to India. A trilateral framework between Nepal, Bangladesh and Bhutan is not seen as an appropriate solution in India, which continues to harp on linking Brahmaputra waters with Ganga. Due to an excessive focus on external solutions countries fail to undertake systematic domestic initiatives, which are further hampered by state-centre/inter/intra provincial tensions. Consequently, intra-state water allocation disputes have become sharper over time and these grievances are often manifested in deteriorating inter-state relations.

DIPLOMACY HAS LIMITED IMPACT-COUNTRIES LOOK INWARDS

South Asia in 2030 is vulnerable to climate change and population demands are adding increasing pressures on the available water resources. Due to the already existing scarcity negotiating positions of the respective states have become more rigid. Issue of fixed water allocation has exacerbated bilateral relations between India-Bangladesh and India-Pakistan. Both Pakistan and Bangladesh have taken the issue at various international fora, consensus and solution on it however remains a distant dream. India as an upper riparian has constantly been stating in various forums that water scarcity has been due to climate change and receding glaciers, however the situation on water allocation and rights continues to deteriorate and diversion of waters through Farrakha barrage remains a contentious issue. In the absence of any diplomatic breakthrough countries have looked inwards for technical solutions.

Inland water infrastructure is being strengthened and water diversion from Brahmaputra to the Ganges is being debated at the national level in India. This has however triggered strong responses from Bangladesh and Nepal. Meanwhile water saving technology has become one of the key priorities for various states. While technology is being imported which is taking a toll on the already stressed foreign exchange reserves, states are looking for indigenous and community based solutions for water management. Unfortunately ineffective cooperation on water issues has had spill over effect on other foreign policy engagements between India and its neighbours perpetuating a climate of mistrust and suspicion. China's relations with Bangladesh, Nepal and Pakistan have prospered with economic ties strengthened. There are great fears regarding the intentions of China regarding diversion of Brahmaputra waters in India under the South-to-North Water Diversion project as China unlike its earlier official stand has made public its intentions to divert Brahmaputra water to the North. India on its part has reversed its Tibet policy and is mobilising support amongst South Asian neighbours and international opinion to consider Tibet as global common.

Meanwhile engineering solutions towards construction of water barrages and dams are widely debated at the national level and dam lobbies (industry and commercial interests) are playing a significant role in policy making circles. Too much of focus on technical details/ambiguity over optimally utilising waters has made negotiations between countries a protracted, time consuming affair. A major fallout of this process is lack of data and information sharing institutions, which is a great impediment to effective flood mitigation efforts and benefit sharing processes on optimal utilisation of river waters.

Joint cooperation on technological issues, rather than contemplating a more dynamic water diplomacy is more diplomatic cards. Relations between India and Bangladesh, Nepal and Bhutan are growing on this front. Though limited initiatives like scholarships for South Asian students are provided by leading universities in India, the political processes on the core issues remain stymied due to lack of consensus and uncertainty on data and information sharing.

Countries which have a strategic edge over water saving technologies, especially the E.U, Israel, China, Japan, and Australia have an increased engagement in the region. The rise of donor agencies has increased multi-fold thus encouraging such initiatives. Another key issue area which has emerged is the increase of loans to South Asian countries by international financial institutions in order to support/finance water technology needs. Desalinisation technology and extraction of ground and surface water to meet water needs of states are important areas in which states are seeking cooperation. Flood defence structures have also been erected in coastal areas, which have lead to influx of population to cities. Increase of population density per square km has lead to increasing pressures on states giving rise to provincial and regional politics.

A new security risk which has emerged in 2030 is the deteriorating health conditions of the people due to groundwater contamination. Vector borne diseases is a major phenomenon across India, Bangladesh and Pakistan and upper riparian states are being called to share burden of increasing health costs. Technical solutions are being explored to combat the growing threat.

At the domestic level in Pakistan, India, Bhutan and Bangladesh subsidies are given to crops which consume less water. Water pricing is a major issue and water is no longer subsidised commodity. While rich farmers have been able to access water saving mechanisms the poor feel excluded and frustrated. The gap between the haves and haves not has increased.

This scenario is therefore marked by varying degrees of confrontation and cooperation. Though countries are engaging on water issues, not much progress can be seen in the functional plane. However technology is the main driver behind inter-state cooperation. A flip side of an over emphasis on technology driven cooperation is an overwhelming focus on technical details, which often is debated by different interest and pressure groups present in the individual countries.

KEY UNCERTAINTIES OF THIS SCENARIO HOWEVER ARE:

Due to growing poverty and inadequate economic development, countries are unable to invest in water saving technology. Due to rise of increase in food and water prices, domestic discontent is increasing. Also due to the absence of adequate coping strategies at home, unilateral policies on water diversion are being carried out. Water treatment plants are limited and an expensive investment. Water bureaucracy is increasing its hold and corruption level in the South Asian countries is high. As climate change projections rest on uncertainty little investment has been made in these sectors, due to which there is a great deal of dependence on external powers for solutions. Water sharing arrangements have been internationalised and third power mediation is a high probability.

DEMOCRACY BECOMES A BANE FOR WATER ISSUES

South Asia in 2030 constitutes a major part world population. With rising population pressures demand for food and water has increased. Meanwhile with an increase in consumption, South Asian countries like Nepal, Bhutan, Pakistan, India and Bangladesh have to import food grains in order to meet the demands of the increasing population. There has been a sharp increase in food, water and energy prices, which is leading discontent within. The incumbent governments are being increasingly criticised in all countries for their ineffective political leadership and national policies on core livelihood issues. Political stability is in constant jeopardy with the states vying for an increase in material help and resources from the states.

Meanwhile fragmegrative tendencies can be witnessed in most South Asian countries through a tussle between Centre-State relations. These tendencies are manifested in the growing demands by the states asking the centre for more responsible and accountable behaviour. Due to growing demands within states, disputes between the upper and the lower riparian have sharpened both within and outside. In Pakistan while Sind has been demanding more water from Punjab, India has been trying to negotiate deals with Nepal for import of electricity to its Northern and Eastern states. However availability of land for dam construction is a contentious issue and there is no domestic consensus within Nepal on it, primary reason being the increase of population density per square km. For hydro-power, India has been relying on Bhutan for exports, which itself is facing energy shortages due to the modernisation and investment in heavy industries which it too since 2010. Nepal to meet it own needs has built small and medium sized dams, however this is creating discontent in lower riparian India. Meanwhile on the other hand Bangladesh in order to meet its growing domestic demands has been pressurising India to release more water and stop diverting water to the Calcutta port. A combined impact of climate change with increasing domestic demand and pressures from the industry has minimised any possibilities of India making further concessions.

Meanwhile rising population pressures and increasing domestic discontent over government policies has given rise to domestic debate. There is lack of consensus on appropriate solutions, which is impeding any political solution on water disputes. The political parties are more concerned about protecting their constituency demands and likewise are pressurising incumbent government to address livelihood issues on urgent basis, state-centre/provinces drift is increasing, which is leading to disputes between upper riparian and lower riparian disputes within countries. With the failure of political leadership, water issues are tremendously politicised. The non-state armed groups in Nepal and Islamic groups in Bangladesh and Pakistan have as a result increased their recruitment base by mobilising support around these issues. Political parties in Nepal, Pakistan and Bangladesh are using the India card to divert attention from core governance issues. In order to stay in power anti-India feelings are being propagated whereby India's behaviour as a hegemon is being held responsible for the problems in Nepal, Bangladesh and Pakistan.

In this scenario thus domestic pandemonium prevails with no solution in sight. Allegation and counter allegations continue as political leadership fails to solve the crises. Also political parties are divided and due to these endogenous divisions no coherent policy on water issues with neighbours is being crafted. Meanwhile number of internally displaced people due to manmade and natural disasters have grown in number, and states are exploring solutions for rehabilitation and exploring alternative livelihoods. Damage to property and lack of government capacity to accommodate and address disasters is further leading to chaos, which has become a serious law and order problem. This has given adequate raw material to terrorists and insurgent groups for mobilising cadres into their ranks.

KEY UNCERTAINTIES IN THIS SCENARIO ARE:

Political parties have become mature and South Asia has passed its transitional phase of democratisation. Water is being purely dealt in functional terms with politics deliberately kept out of it. This has purely been possible due to the realisation that cooperation on shared water resources is in the interest of all countries. Due to demographic policies undertaken by the countries and a good deal of preventive measurers on climate sensitive crops, much of the situation is under control. Countries like Pakistan and India have adopted state water dispute settlement mechanisms, whereby disputes are solved by international precedents on river water disputes. Civil-society-state interaction has increased within and across borders on water sharing frameworks. Measures and efforts are being undertaken to provide a holistic assessment of cost- benefit analyses through social, economic and environmental indicators.

RISK FACTORS

The most important factor which could influence relations on water sector is the intervention by China and its intent on diverting Brahmaputra river through the Yarlung Tsangpo (Brahmaputra River) plan. This would affect water availability in India and Bangladesh and would have a powerful impact on India-China relations increasing threat perceptions on China as the upper riparian. This action is more likely given the perceived food and energy shortages which China would face in near future.

It could be possible that China funds dams in Nepal and trade relations between Bangladesh and China improve. It is quite possible that in the absence of effective leadership by India in the region, China fills in the vacuum as an economic power. Territorial dispute over Arunachal Pradesh is likely to be played around water issues and China's weight at the international level would make it a strategic ally of Pakistan, Bangladesh and Nepal. Probabilities of war between Pakistan and India could be played around water issues, which would be the next driving factor in India-Pakistan relations, making the Kashmir dispute irresolvable. The water discource in Pakistan might get increasingly politicised given the linkages of water with Kashmir.

POLICY LESSONS

Thus from the above arguments many policy suggestions can be drawn.

- As water resources are most prone to climatic and non climatic interventions both in terms of quality and quantity, it is important that negotiations be undertaken keeping the long term impact in mind. Benefit sharing on shared resources where the agreement is perceived as fair by South Asian neighbours is important. Side payments and increasing the zone of agreement by highlighting benefits vis a vis costs is important. A basin wide management of water resources with polluters pay principle and shared responsibility should be undertaken for effective accountability.

- Agreements on water resource projects should undertake a holistic assessment of environmental and social impact. This is important considering the sustainability of water agreements in long term.

- Domestic initiatives/investments on water saving solutions/ technology are the best coping strategy for managing water crises. Joint initiatives should be undertaken to include solutions for water logging, proper drainage, salinisation, dredging of rivers. Also addressing issues relating to ground water contamination is important.

- Investment in water management technology and water effective irrigation system could be effective in mitigating adverse impact of food and energy shortages. These sectors should be explored and encouraged to increase national preparedness.

- Community management through rain water harvesting and watershed management should be encouraged at local level and infact should become an important agenda of local governance in all the concerned states.

- Stable politics is in the national interest of all countries. The transition phase to democracy in Nepal, Bhutan and Bangladesh, Pakistan should be handled with political responsibility. Consensual politics and national debate on water issues at domestic level is the pre-requisite for successful foreign policy outcome in coming years. Sectarian politics, fanning ethnic aspirations can be increasingly detrimental to the political health of all South Asian countries.

- Coordination, collaboration and consensus between centre and states on transboundary rivers should increase and policy coordination between different ministries-health, agriculture, rural development etc. for maximum water optimization be adopted.

- Scenario building exercises on different issue areas which impact water negotiations should be undertaken, so that policy decisions are informed by the projected changes in the coming years.

- Domestic initiatives, reform and remedial measures should be undertaken by all countries and centre-state consensus on transboundary rivers should be dealt with utmost priority. The process of data sharing and information gathering should be an ongoing mechanism of cooperation between the two countries in order to manage threat misperceptions.

- Civil Society contacts between border states should increase and groups that focus on flood warning and forecasting should be supported by respective governments.

9
Pakistan-Occupied Kashmir: The Future Trajectory
—Priyanka Singh

BACKGROUND

Pakistan-occupied Kashmir (POK)[1] historically belonged to the erstwhile princely state of Jammu and Kashmir. Soon after the partition of India in 1947, Maharaja Hari Singh of Jammu and Kashmir signed the Instrument of Accession, thereby acceding to the Indian Union.[2] Hence, POK is legitimately an inherent part of India. This territory has been under Pakistan's unlawful control ever since the Pakistan Army orchestrated the tribal invasion of the territory in October 1947.[3] POK comprises the so-called Azad Kashmir and Gilgit-Baltistan (earlier named as Northern Areas) and has remained an amorphous entity for six decades now. The Trans Karakoram Tract, comprising Shaksgam from Baltistan and Raskam from Gilgit, which Pakistan ceded to China in 1963, is also a part of POK. China promised to assist Pakistan in building the Karakoram Highway as a payoff.

The so called Azad Kashmir (AJK) is governed under the Azad

---

1   Pakistan occupied Kashmir(PoK) is referred as Azad Kashmir and Gilgit Baltistan by the Government of Pakistan.

2   P.N.K. Bamzai, *A History of Kashmir* (New Delhi: Metropolitan, 1973), p. 798.

3   S. Kalyanaraman, "Dawn of Independence and the Tribal Raid" in Virendra Gupta and Alok Bansal (eds.), *Pakistan Occupied Kashmir: The Untold Story* (New Delhi: Manas, 2007), pp. 70–5.

Kashmir Interim Constitution Act passed in 1974.[4] Even though AJK has a President, Prime minister, and a council, the governing structure is totally powerless and dependent on the Pakistani establishment for the smallest issue at hand. Very often AJK is described as a "constitutional enigma" with "trappings of a country". The Karachi Agreement, which governs the rule of Pakistan over Gilgit-Baltistan, was signed between the President of Azad Kashmir, the Muslim Conference and a minister without portfolio from Pakistan, Mushtaq Ahmed Gurmani. Even though there was no formal merger between AJK and Gilgit-Baltistan, the fate of the latter was decided by Prime Minister AJK and Pakistan with no local representative participating in the matter.[5]

The Government of Pakistan announced the Gilgit-Baltistan Empowerment and Self Governance Order on 29 August 2009, which reversed the nomenclature of the Northern Areas to the original Gilgit-Baltistan.[6] The order has been widely criticized as it failed to address the basic questions of the rights of the people and the critical issue of provincial autonomy. The order introduced elements that brought Gilgit-Baltistan closer to the structure in AJK in spirit and form but with no impact, as the strings of power were placed with the Government of Pakistan.[7] The order was rejected by the political groups in Gilgit-Baltistan, the pro-independence groups, and the pro-Indian groups. There have been allegations that the order was designed to secure increasing Chinese interest in POK.

---

4   For details, see text of the Azad Jammu and Kashmir Interim Constitution Act, 1974.

5   Text of the Karachi Agreement, signed in April 1949, at <http://www. kashmir.ahrchk.net/mainfile.php/after1947/43/>, accessed 6 January 2009.

6   Ismail Khan, "Gilgit Baltistan autonomy", *Dawn* (Karachi), 9 September 2009, at <http://www.dawn.com/wps/wcm/connect/dawn-content-library/dawn/news/pakistan/04-gilgit>, accessed 9 September 2009.

7   Bhim Singh, "Pakistan Gilgit Package: Self Rule or Annexation", *Kashmir Watch*, 17 September 2009, at <http://kashmirwatch.com/showexclusives.php?subaction=showfull&id=1253210337&archive=&start_from=&ucat=15&var1news=value1news>, accessed 13 November 2009.

The development works in POK are heavily dependent on Chinese investments.[8]

POK has been in the news during this decade for wrong reasons. In the wake of the events of 11 September 2001, when the United States launched a massive hunt for the Al-Qaeda chief Osama bin Laden, there were reports that he was in Muzaffarabad, the capital of AJK.[9] On 8 October 2005, a devastating earthquake measuring 7.6 on the Richter scale hit the region; AJK is yet to emerge from the colossal damage.[10] The region also harbours militant training camps.[11] The terrorist attack in Mumbai on 26 November 2008 added a new dimension to the existing discourse on the training camps in POK. The terrorists travelled from Bait-ul-Mujahideen, the operational headquarters of Lashkar-e-Toyyaba (LeT) in Muzaffarabad, via Karachi to Mumbai.[12] The chief of LeT, Zaki ur-Rehman, the nodal person in the Mumbai conspiracy, was arrested by Pakistani authorities from Muzaffarabad.[13]

8 "The Northern Areas Reforms undertaken Due to Chinese Pressure", 4 September 2009, at <http://alaiwah.wordpress.com/2009/09/04/the-northern-areas-reforms-undertaken-due-to-chinese-pressure/>, accessed 25 October 2009. Also, "Empowering Gilgit-Baltistan or the Chinese Bulwark", *The South Asian*, 26 October 2009, at <http://www.thesouthasian.org/archives/2009/empowering_gilgitbaltistan_or.html>, accessed 30 October 2009.

9 "Osama in PoK: US may give Pak proof", *Hindustan Times*, 1 February 2002, at <http://www.hvk.org/articles/0202/9.html>, accessed 20 November 2009.

10 "Muzaffarabad Earthquake – 8 Oct, 2005", Muzaffarabad Online, at <http://www.muzaffarabadonline.com/showpage.aspx?pageid=earthquake>, accessed 14 November 2009.

11 Rajat Pandit, "42 operational terror camps in Pak, PoK", *Times of India*, 19 June 2009, at <http://timesofindia.indiatimes.com/india/42-operational-terror-camps-in-Pak-PoK/articleshow/4673319.cms>, accessed 20 June 2009.

12 Praveen Swami, "Lashkar tested sea route to Mumbai in 2007 dry run", *The Hindu*, 28 November 2008, at <http://www.thehindu.com/2008/11/28/stories/2008112861921200.htm>, accessed 30 November 2008.

13 "Mumbai terror mastermind held in PoK", 9 December 2008, at <http://www.rediff.com/news/2008/dec/08mumterror-mumbai-terror-mastermind-held-in-pok.htm>, accessed 30 December 2008.

WHY POK's FUTURE?

As a case for future scenario building, POK is immensely significant. POK's strategic geographic location has consistently been "leveraged" by Pakistan to fulfil its "strategic and economic objectives".[14] POK shares its borders with several countries – the Punjab and NWFP provinces in Pakistan to the west, the Wakhan Corridor of Afghanistan in the north-west, Xinjiang province of the People's Republic of China to the north and India's Jammu and Kashmir to the east. It is situated in the vicinity of the two fastest growing economies of the world, but remains extremely backward. The key actors in POK are India, Pakistan and China, which during the last few years has developed considerable stakes in the region. This paper, attempting to draw future projections for POK, is divided into four sections: (I) identifying and describing the key drivers; (II) envisaging future trends in the key drivers; (III) determining alternative scenarios; and (IV) Prognosis.

I

Key Drivers in POK

THE TALIBAN THREAT

Over the past few years, the Taliban have seized power in some parts of Pakistan. Few reports hinted at the possibility of Shariat law being imposed in POK; it has already been implemented in Swat in the heartland of Pakistan.[15] The Taliban would attempt to gain strategic depth in this strategically located region. The presence of Afghans in POK would further facilitate the Taliban interests,[16] enabling the

---

14   Luv Puri, "The complex reality of Northern Areas", *Dawn*, 24 September 2009, at <http://www.dawn.com/wps/wcm/connect/dawn-contentlibrary/dawn/news/pakistan/02-the-complex-reality-ofthe-northern-areas-02>, accessed 25 September 2009.

15   "Shariat Law may soon be implemented in POK", 19 April 2009, at <http://kashmirihindu.wordpress.com/2009/04/19/shariatlaw-may-soon-implemented-in-pok/>, accessed 1 May 2009.

16   Asif Shahzad, "Afghans in Pakistan: documenting a population on move", UNHCR, 31 October 2009, at <http://www.unhcr.org/print/4547518b2.html>, accessed 15 October 2009.

militants to amalgamate with the local Afghans and carry on dubious activities under a suitable camouflage. The Government of Pakistan would find an outsourced option to contrive cross-border terrorism in India, particularly in Jammu and Kashmir. Recently, the Pakistani authorities arrested and deported from Bagh and Muzaffarabad at least 200 Afghans who were living there illegally.[17] Developments such as the suicide bomb attack in Muzaffarabad on 26 June 2009 have strengthened claims of Taliban presence in POK; the Tehrik-e-Taliban (TTP) was eventually implicated in the incident.[18] Two soldiers of the AJK regiment were reportedly killed and three others injured in the attack.[19]

MILITANT TRAINING CAMPS

POK has for long provided safe haven to home-grown terrorists of Pakistan – both those operating in Kashmir Valley and those having close links with al-Qaeda and Taliban. The LeT operates freely in the area as Jamaat ud-Dawa (JuD).[20] People in POK have faced neglect from the Pakistan government for decades and they look up to these groups for help. JuD played a significant role in the relief and rehabilitation work after the October 2005 earthquake when the state machinery expressed inability in carrying out the same. The increasing number of these training camps could be attributed to

17 "Police arrest 200 Afghan nationals from Bagh", at <http://www.onlinenews.com.pk/details.php?id=154204>, accessed 31 October 2009.

18 B. Raman, "Why Suicide Attacks on Pakistan Army in PoK?", International Terrorism Monitor, Paper no. 538, June 27, 2009 at <http://www.southasiaanalysis.org/papers33/paper3278.html>, accessed 24 December 2009.

19 Tariq Naqash, "Two soldiers killed: Baitullah's suicide foray into AJK", Dawn, 27 June 2009, at <http://www.dawn.com/wps/wcm/connect/dawn-content-library/dawn/the-newspaper/front-page/two-soldiers-killed-baitullahs-suicide-foray-into-ajk-769>, accessed 20 December 2009

20 Steve Coll, "Lashkar-e-Taiba", The New Yorker, 1 December 2008, at <http://www.newyorker.com/online/blogs/stevecoll/2008/12/lashkaretaiba.html>.

foreign mercenaries present in Pakistan.[21] Due to the US-led War on Terror, the Afghan youth were pushed into these camps by the ISI, which was facing dearth of mercenaries after American pressure compelled men from Sudan, Kuwait and Lebanon to leave Pakistan. A report by India's Home Ministry in 2004, prepared on the basis of interrogation of militants and interception of wireless messages, came to this conclusion.[22] In March 2008, a status report on India's internal security by the Home Ministry reiterated that the operation of militant camps in POK was unabated.[23]

SECTARIAN DIVIDE

The demography in Gilgit Baltistan in POK has changed so much that the Shia, the original inhabitants of the land, have become a minority. Sunnis from Pakistan were given lucrative job offers and other incentives to settle in POK. President Zia intended to shift the demographic balance of POK in favour of Pakistan, primarily a Sunni state, and the orders to this effect were carried out by Pervez Musharraf in the late 1980s.[24] Similarly, the Northern Light Infantry, which mainly comprised men from POK (it was deployed in the Kargil War) is increasingly manned by non-locals as the local people are no longer trusted.[25] The ICG report on the State of Sectarianism states,

---

21 "Jehad Spillover", *Outlook*, 7 September 1998, at <http://www.outlookindia.com/article.aspx?206123>, accessed 24 September 2009.

22 "Militant training camps revived in PoK: MHA", *Indian Express*, 21 June 2004, at <http://www.indianexpress.com/oldStory/49420/>, accessed 22 October 2009.

23 "Pakistan continues to train terror outfits in PoK", CNN-IBN, 31 March 2008, at <http://ibnlive.in.com/news/pakistan-continues-to-train-terror-outfits-in-pok/62351-3.html?from=search-relatedstories>, accessed 20 December 2009.

24 B. Raman, "Gilgit & Baltistan, China & North Korea", South Asia Analysis Group, Paper no. 289, 7 August 2001, at <http://www.southasiaanalysis.org/papers3/paper289.html>, accessed 23 October 2009.

25 For details on the role of Northern Light Infantry (NLI) in the Kargil War refer to "Discord in Pakistan's Northern Areas", Crisis Group Asia Report No. 131, 2 April 2007, at <http://www.ciaonet.org/wps/icg449/icg449.pdf>, accessed 14 June 2008.

"Since 2001, Shia resentment over the inclusion of Sunni religious rituals and a perceived anti-Shia bias in textbooks for public schools has resulted in school boycotts and occasional clashes and curfews."[26]

CHINA'S GROWING INFLUENCE

The Chinese interest in POK dates back to the construction of Karakoram Highway, the highest road in the world, built at a height of 4665 metres (15,397 feet). The highway has yielded tremendous trading opportunities for both countries.[27] It has also been used extensively to transfer arms and ammunition from China to Pakistan, and fissile nuclear and missile material from China. The highway was opened to the public only in 1986 even though it was completed in 1978 and was inaugurated in 1982.[28] In November 2003, former Pakistani President Pervez Musharraf signed a Border Trade Agreement with the Chinese government to "strengthen transport cooperation and promote interflow of personnel and commodities through the Karakoram Highway".[29] The two countries signed an MoU on 30 June 2006 to widen the highway from 10 metres to 30 metres; the upgradation process was formally inaugurated in February 2008.[30]

---

26 "The State of Sectarianism In Pakistan", ICG Asia Report No. 95, 18 April 2005, at <http://www.crisisgroup.org/library/documents/asia/ south_asia/095_the_state_of_sectarianism_in_pakistan.pdf>, accessed 5 October 2009.

27 Hermann Kreutzmann, "The Karakoram Highway: The Impact of Road Construction on Mountain Societies", *Modern Asian Studies*, Great Britain, 1991, p. 725, at <http://www.mtnforum.org/oldocs/836. pdf>, accessed 27 October 2009.

28 "Karakoram Highway in China", at <http://factsanddetails.com/china. php?itemid=441&catid=15&subcatid=104>, accessed 5 November 2009.

29 Zaid Haider, "Clearing Clouds over Karakorum", *Daily Times*, 4 April 2004, at <http://www.dailytimes.com.pk/default.asp?page=story_4-4-2004_pg3_3>, accessed 5 November 2009.

30 "Address on the Inauguration of Upgradation of the Karakoram Highway", Official website of the Embassy of China in Pakistan, 16 February 2008, at <http://pk.china-embassy.org/eng/zbgx/t414855. htm>, accessed 30 October 2009.

China has made substantial investments in POK especially after the earthquake of 2005. Early in 2009, it proffered $300 million for development projects in Muzaffarabad, Rawalkot and Bagh.[31] The agreement to this effect was signed in Islamabad between the Earthquake Reconstruction Rehabilitation Authority (ERRA) of Pakistan and the Chinese Ambassador Luo Zhaohui.[32]

Pakistan and China have also signed several agreements for building dams in POK, the latest being the MoU for building a dam in Bunji in Astore district. India, which views such agreements between China and Pakistan as adverse to India–China relations, has sharply criticized this move.[33]

WATER RESOURCES

POK is rich in water resources. The Indus and its tributaries render bright opportunities for hydropower generation.[34] Recently, however, in the overall context of water scarcity in Pakistan, President AJK, Raja Zulqarnain Khan, stressed the need for water conservation. Speaking in Muzaffarabad, Khan "urged people to store rainwater and protect existing sources of water in AJK".[35] He acknowledged

---

31 "China to provide Pakistan ERRA $300 million", Official website of the Office of Economic and Commercial Counsellor's office of the People's Republic of China in the Islamic Republic of Pakistan, 3 June 2008, at <http://pk2.mofcom.gov.cn/aarticle/chinanews/200806/20080605579739.html>, accessed 5 October 2009.

32 Khalid Amin, "Chinese firms to undertake urban development project", *Daily Mail*, 15 February 2009, at <http://dailymailnews.com/200902/15/news/dmcitypage01.html>, accessed 20 February 2009.

33 Amulya Ganguli, "Behind China's sabre-rattling", *Asian Age*, 21 October 2009, at <http://www.asianage.com/presentation/leftnavigation/opinion/op-ed/behind-china%E2%80%99s-sabre-rattling.aspx>, accessed 20 December 2009.

34 "Gilgit Baltistan has potential to produce 40,000 MW electricity", *Daily Times*, 22 October 2009, at <http://www.dailytimes.com.pk/default.asp?page=2009%5C10%5C22%5Cstory_22-10-2009_pg5_4>, accessed 25 October 2009.

35 "Water conservation", *Dawn* Editorial, 8 October 2009, at <http://www.dawn.com/wps/wcm/connect/dawn-contentlibrary/dawn/news/pakistan/14-water-conservation-zj-02>, accessed 1 November 2009.

that "roughly half the population of AJK still did not have access to potable water, adding that water sources have all but dried up in some areas".[36]

A highly controversial hydropower project in POK, because of its ecological implications, is the Diamer Bhasha Dam.[37] It will inundate large tracts of land in the vicinity, rendering thousands of people homeless. According to a report, at least "31 villages will be flooded, 3,115 houses destroyed and 1,500 acres of agricultural land inundated by the reservoir".[38] The area has very little in terms of fertile agricultural land, which if absorbed by the construction of the dam could result in serious food deficit in the region.[39] POK has been facing food shortage in the past; only when the federal government issues directives the other provinces supply the required food material.[40] Also, the dam is located in a seismically sensitive zone.[41]

POLITICAL UNREST

Political unrest in POK is based on a range of issues, primarily being the denial of basic rights, constitutional and political. People from PoK have migrated to countries like US, Canada and gulf looking for greener pastures as education and job opportunities are not available and political freedom is non existent. There is also a

36 Ibid.
37 Zulfiqar Halepoto, "Bhasha Dam: Socio-Economic and Environmental Impacts", *Dawn*, 17 November 2008, at <http://www.dawn.com/2008/11/17/ebr6.htm>, accessed 14 October 2009.
38 "Diamer-Bhasha Dam in Pakistan: Report from a Field Trip", October 2008 (report prepared by the Sustainable Development Policy Institute, Islamabad, Pakistan for International, Rivers), at <http://www.internationalrivers.org/files/Bhasha_Fact_Finding_October%202008_final.pdf>.
39 "GoP to acquire over 37 thousand acres for Diamer-Bhasha Dam", South Asian News Agency (SANA), 8 October 2009, at <http://www.sananews.com.pk/english/2009/10/08/gop-to-acquire-over-37-thousand-acres-for-diamer-bhasha-dam/>, accessed 4 November 2009.
40 "Wheat for Azad Kashmir ordered", 7 March 2009, at <http://www.geo.tv/3-7-2009/36764.htm>, accessed 10 March 2009.
41 Seema Sridhar, "Dam Controversial", *Indian Express*, 8 June 2007, at <http://www.indianexpress.com/story_print.php?storyId=32956>, accessed 6 November 2009.

sectarian divide as a result of Sunni ingress in the region. The region has also been linguistically and culturally marginalized.[42] POK does not have a provincial status even though Pakistan has controlled it for nearly six decades. After a great deal of protests, recently the Government of Pakistan announced the Self-Governance Package for Gilgit-Baltistan, which provided the trappings of an AJK-like structure. Ironically, even after the new order, POK does not count as a province of Pakistan. Many in Pakistan view this development as a compromise by Pakistan on the issue of Kashmir.[43]

Reports such as the Human Rights Violation in Azad Kashmir and Baroness Emma Nicholson's *Kashmir Report* for the EU depict a distressing picture of the state of human rights in POK.[44] The *Human Rights Watch Report* opens with a statement from a resident of Muzaffarabad: "Pakistan says they are our friends and India is our enemy. I agree India is our enemy, but with friends like these, who needs enemies?"[45]

Pakistan's approach to POK has baffled many as this area is of immense strategic significance. Some have alleged that Pakistan has refrained from granting it legislative autonomy because of this strategic significance, fearing consequences. The establishment has brutally crushed political unrest in POK in the past. None the less, this movement could acquire a violent shape due to continuing impoverishment and lack of hope for betterment. Resort to violence is ingrained in the Pakistani state and society since long: recall the tribal

---

42 Alok Bansal, "Gilgit–Baltistan: The Roots of Political Alienation", *Strategic Analysis*, 32(1), January 2008, p. 81.

43 "Kashmir stance not to be affected by Gilgit-Baltistan autonomy: Gilani", Associated Press of Pakistan, 16 September 2009, at <http://www.app.com.pk/en_/index.php?option=com_content&task=view&id=86068&Itemid=2>, accessed 30 September 2009.

44 Refer "With Friends Like These ... Human Rights Violations in Azad Kashmir", *Human Rights Watch Report*, 1812(C), September 2006;. Emma Nicholson, "Report on Kashmir: present situation and future prospects", Committee of Foreign Affairs, European Union, 25 April 2007.

45 "With Friends Like These…", ibid., p. 4.

invasions of 1947 and the Mujahideen involved in the Kargil conflict of 1999; according to Pakistan they were freedom fighters well versed in guerrilla warfare.[46]

II

Envisaging Future Trends in the Crucial Drivers

Most of the drivers in isolation or in combination could be critical in the course of the next two decades in POK.

LARGER THREAT OF TALIBAN MILITANTS

The War on Terror shoved the Afghan Taliban into Pakistan. The Taliban since then has gained ground in Pakistan. In Afghanistan, the outfit is fighting a bitter battle with the US-led NATO forces, and would benefit greatly by gaining a stronghold in POK. The Pakistani state would rather close its eyes on any such development. In POK, the Pakistani authorities would not even bother to launch a superficial battle. This is because POK is away from the media glare. The region is already deluged with clandestine activities of this nature.

The United States is fighting Al-Qaeda and Taliban on Pakistani soil in several ways – providing military aid, drone attacks, and the like. If these groups spread bases in POK, the US would be compelled to expand its target areas and this could lead to a substantial US military presence in POK. China is intently strengthening its ground in POK, especially in Gilgit-Baltistan with pools of capital. This immense economic presence in the region could probably be followed by some sort of Chinese military presence in the region. In this scenario, POK could become a battleground of the Great Empires similar to Afghanistan.

In the event that the Taliban gets a stronghold in POK, it would open the gates for proliferation of extremist activities in the regions bordering POK besides Central Asia and India – the Chinese

---

46 "PML-N issues 'white paper' on Kargil war", *Dawn*, 6 August 2009, at <http://www.dawn.com/2006/08/06/nat1.htm>, accessed 11 November 2009.

province of Xinjiang, including Aksai Chin (claimed by India) which is already facing ethnic strife.[47] In Xinjiang, at least 200 people were killed and 1600 injured in ethnic riots in July 2009.[48] Afghanistan has repeatedly urged China to open the borders at Wakhan Corridor, which separates Afghanistan from Xinjiang, so that it could find alternate supply routes in fighting the Taliban effectively.[49] The Sino-Afghan border corridor is 76 km long. It has been closed for more than a hundred years. The United States supports Afghanistan's plea to open the corridor,[50] but China has declined due its vulnerabilities in Xinjiang province and "fiercely resists any move to open up its Islamic provinces".[51]

Uighur Muslims are of Turkic origin and developed ties with Pakistan with the opening of Karakoram Highway, which made people-to-people contact viable between the two countries. A large number of Uighurs have enrolled themselves in the Pakistani Madrassas and are training in jihadi ideology.[52] Even though Pakistan does not support the Uighur secessionist movement in principle, there are close chances that rampant radicalism may penetrate Xinjiang in the years to come. The possibility has compelled the Chinese to keep a strict check on the developments in Xinjiang and the adjoining areas. China

47   Howard W. French, "China confirms Protests by Uighur Muslims", *New York Times*, 3 April 2008, at <http://www.nytimes.com/2008/04/03/world/asia/03china.html>, accessed 13 October 2009.

48   "Ethnic unrest in Xinjiang – Quo Vadis?", 22 July 2007, at <http://www.dw-world.de/dw/article/0,,4510566,00.html>, accessed 14 October 2009.

49   "Fact Box – Key facts about the Wakhan Corridor", Reuters, 12 June 2009, at <http://www.reuters.com/articlePrint?articleId+USSP38950 7>, accessed 13 November 2009; Anthony Kuhn, "China becomes a player in Afghanistan's Future", 21 October 2009, at <http://www.npr.org/templates/story/story.php?storyId=113967842>, accessed 13 November 2009; "China mulls Afghan border request", BBC, 12 June 2009, at <http://news.bbc.co.uk/2/hi/south_asia/8097933.stm>.

50   "Afghanistan tells China to open Wakhan Corridor route", *The Hindu*, 11 June 2009, at <http://www.hindu.com/thehindu/holnus/003200906111512.htm>, accessed 13 November 2009.

51   Ibid.

52   "The State of Sectarianism in Pakistan", n. 25.

is giving incentives to the rebels in the form of job opportunities and by making substantial investments in the development of the region while using heavy hand to crush any sign of rebellion.[53]

Varying Number of Militant Camps

There could be three scenarios regarding militant camps – either they grow in numbers or decline or are wiped out. For instance, after the 2005 earthquake there were reports that the militant camps had vanished from the region.[54] Later on, it came to be known that these camps were closed temporarily since militants were co-opted in relief work. The drivers for each scenario intersect – if the situation in Pakistan is unaltered in the next decade or so, the number of militant camps in the region will rise, with the Army and the ISI encouraging their proliferation. However, if the situation improves with international intervention, these camps could cease to operate. In addition, China's growing interest in POK could induce China to urge Pakistan to rid the area of militant camps to ensure the security of Chinese nationals involved in several construction works. There were reports about Chinese concerns about the security of its nationals in Pakistan and in POK in the aftermath of the Lal Masjid ambush in 2007.[55] China's resistance to Taliban presence in POK is confined to securing its own interests and not the overall security of region.

Recent intelligence reports in India have disclosed that eight new militant training camps have come up in POK. The local administration has been directed by the Government of Pakistan to "accommodate the Pakistani and other jihadis by all means possible", a Kashmiri leader based in UK is reported to have said.[56] At least

53 Ibid.

54 Sumita Kumar, "Earthquake in Kashmir", *Strategic Analysis*, 29(3), July 2005, at <http://www.idsa.in/system/files/strategicanalysis_skumar_0905.pdf>.

55 B. Raman, "The Chinese under Fire", *Outlook*, 5 September 2008, at <http://www.outlookindia.com/article.aspx?238314>, accessed 30 October 2009.

56 "LeT and Pak Jihadi Groups Entrenching in PoK: UKPNP", *Outlook*, 20 October 2009, at <http://news.outlookindia.com/item.aspx?668042>, accessed 30 October 2009.

300 militants are reported to be attempting to infiltrate into Indian territory from POK to conduct Mumbai-like attacks in different parts of the country.[57] Pakistan Army has reportedly given these militants, who are reportedly Taliban, two options: either to infiltrate into India or stay in Pakistani jails.[58]

ENTRENCHED CHINESE CONTROL

Pakistan supports Chinese involvement in POK for upgradation of infrastructure and development in the region. It seeks to capitalize on Chinese presence in POK to counterbalance India in a warlike situation with India. The Chinese role in the Kargil crisis is a matter of debate even though in the later stages of the conflict China urged Pakistan to withdraw forces to the pre-conflict situation. More than a decade thereafter, the geo-strategic priorities have altered and are likely to change much more before 2030.

China has no qualms about its expansionist goals, as has been the case in claiming territories under India's sovereign control. Its inroads in POK are part of a larger game plan to expand its influence spanning almost entire South Asia encircling India – Nepal, Sri Lanka, Myanmar and Pakistan.

MISUSE OF NATURAL RESOURCES RESULTING IN ANOTHER CALAMITY

Despite protests from all quarters and most of all from the residents of the adjoining areas, the Government of Pakistan has relentlessly carried on construction work in POK. In the years to come, the region could witness another natural calamity of the kind

---

57 "Infiltration attempts across LoC increasing", *The Hindu*, 24 September 2009, at <http://www.thehindu.com/2009/09/24/stories/2009092455461000.htm>, accessed 25 September 2009.

58 "ISI pushing Taliban militants into India: Report", *Deccan Chronicle*, 6 October 2009, at <http://www.deccanchronicle.com/latest-news/isi-pushing-taliban-militants-india-report-315>, accessed 24 December 2009; Talat Masood, "Pakistan's Future: Three Possible Scenarios", *Pakistan Analysis*, 20 July 2009, at <http://www.pakistananalysis.com/index.php?option=com_content&view=article&id=185:threepossible scenariostalat&catid=28:general&Itemid=43>, accessed 20 October 2009

of earthquake witnessed in 2005. A huge water reservoir in the event of an earthquake would inundate almost all the adjoining areas.

VIOLENT POLITICAL UNREST

The possibility remains that the oppressed population in POK takes up arms against Pakistan. The Pakistan establishment would then have to open another front in POK, which otherwise is a peaceful area despite the presence of innumerable terrorist camps and other clandestine activities. The violence in Kashmir Valley would then abate, since Pakistan is likely to be caught up in a civil warlike situation in POK, with inadequate resources and time to manage cross-border militancy.

III

POK 2030: Three Alternative Scenarios

In the light of the various drivers studied, it is inevitable to assume that the situation in the region will not improve as long as it is controlled by Pakistan. The first scenario revolves around the restoration of POK to the Indian state of Jammu and Kashmir; the second, it remains with the usurper Pakistan. In case of status quo, the region will be subject to geo-political quest between the adjoining states seeking their own strategic priorities and objectives.

POK UNDER INDIA'S CONTROL

Since the region legitimately belongs to India, taking this case first is justified. The case of POK's reunion with India is argued on the basis of close cultural ties that people in this region share with the people in India. The Shias and Ismailis of Gilgit-Baltistan have close bonds with the Ladhakhis on the Indian side of the Line of Control (LoC).[59] Pakistan's lack of faith in the local population strengthens India's case for reclaiming the occupied territory.

---

59 "Treated by Pakistan as Virtual Slaves", Interview with Abdul Hamid Khan taken by Yoginder Sikand for *Outlook*, 28 June 2002, at <http://www.outlookindia.com/article.aspx?216236>, accessed 27 October 2009.

If POK is restored, it would be amalgamated into the state of Jammu and Kashmir and subjected to a similar status, which defines autonomy and equal treatment that the state of Jammu and Kashmir has been accorded over the years. In this scenario, it would no longer be possible for Pakistan to misuse the territory for clandestine activities and raising militant training camps there. The entity would largely be free of violence. Assistance from the Union budget for the state of Jammu and Kashmir is usually the highest amongst the states in India on a per capita basis and this gives a fair chance to POK to gradually overcome decades of underdevelopment and miserable conditions of living.[60] POK would be well integrated in the process of the economic development in India, which is expected to maintain at least 7 per cent growth rate even against the global recession.

India would in that case share the border with Khyber Pakhtunkhwa of Pakistan on one side and the Wakhan Corridor with Afghanistan. POK would prove India's gateway to Central Asian markets, which could provide new vistas for the growing Indian economy. The Chinese aspire to access Gwadar port in Balochistan province as a bulwark against India. Gwadar port would also provide China opportunities to harness benefits of the sea-lanes there. China plans to build a railway line from Kashgar to Gwadar as a part of this strategy. These designs to besiege India would be automatically shelved once POK comes under India's control.

STATUS QUO

POK's future association with the state of Pakistan, on the other hand, would be no good especially for the local population with the abysmal sense of deprivation continuing in the years to come. Pakistan's security situation is grave even under a civilian government and is worsening. Pakistan's control of POK would continue the era of deprivation and duality on a false pretext of UN Security Council resolutions. In fact, Pakistan has never adhered to Resolution 47 of 21 April 1948, which called for "the withdrawal from the State

---

60 Arvind Lavakare, "Deliver the truth, not poetry", *Outlook*, 29 April 2003, at <http://www.rediff.com/cms/print.jsp?docpath=//news/2003/apr/29arvind.htm>, accessed 14 November 2009.

of Jammu and Kashmir of tribesmen and Pakistani nationals not normally resident therein".[61]

Senator John McCain has lately suggested that Pakistan should move the "significant numbers" of troops from POK to the areas threatened by Taliban militants inside Pakistan.[62] McCain lost the presidential polls to Barack Obama but this statement substantially hints at a plausible course of US foreign policy towards Pakistan in future: to urge Pakistan to withdraw its forces from POK in large numbers and concentrate them on the restive belts of Swat and Waziristan and the western border.

POK AT THE CROSSROADS OF CONFLICTING INTERESTS OF INDIA, CHINA AND PAKISTAN

This scenario flows directly from status quo in POK. Viewed from the regional spectrum, POK is likely to become the geo-strategic chessboard between India, China and Pakistan. Recent exchange of diplomatic statements amongst the three states strongly indicates such a possibility, where each is vying to promote its own political, economic and strategic pursuits.

A report published in Xinhua described China's plan to undertake infrastructure projects with Pakistan in POK. India has reacted sharply, with the Ministry of External Affairs making it clear that the future of Sino-Indian relations could be held hostage to China's intervention in POK.[63] The ministry stated:

---

61 "Kashmir in United Nations", Official Website of the Government of AJK, at <http://www.ajk.gov.pk/site/index.php?option=com_con tent&task=view&id=2276&Itemid=135>, accessed 11 November 2009.

62 "John McCain wants troops from PoK to be shifted to Waziristan", *DNA*, 16 December 2009, at <http://www.dnaindia.com/world/report_ john-mccain-wants-troops-from-pok-to-be-shifted-to-waziristan_ 1324332>, accessed 20 December 2009.

63 "Hands off Pakistan-occupied Kashmir", *The Statesman*, 16 October 2009, at <http://www.asianewsnet/print.php?id=8252>, accessed 13 November 2009.

We have seen the Xinhua report quoting the President of China as stating that China will continue to engage in projects with Pakistan inside Pakistan Occupied Kashmir. Pakistan has been in illegal occupation of parts of the Indian State of Jammu & Kashmir since 1947. The Chinese side is fully aware of India's position and our concerns about Chinese activities in Pakistan Occupied Kashmir. We hope that the Chinese side will take a long term view of the India-China relations, and cease such activities in areas illegally occupied by Pakistan.[64]

The Chinese government in response said that "it was a matter for India and Pakistan to resolve and that China had no reason to change its policies on Kashmir."[65] Similarly, India registered a protest in the wake of the Gilgit-Baltistan Self-Governance Package 2009, stating that Pakistan has no right to legislate on Gilgit-Baltistan as it is a part of the Indian state of Jammu and Kashmir. Rejecting the demarche of protest that India handed over to the Pakistani High Commissioner in New Delhi, Pakistan stated that India has no locus standi on POK.[66] Regarding the elections in Gilgit-Baltistan, India's Ministry of External Affairs has categorically rejected their validity stating, "The elections in Gilgit-Baltistan are just another cosmetic exercise intended to camouflage the fact of Pakistan's illegal occupation of areas of the state of Jammu and Kashmir."[67]

---

64   "Response of Official Spokesperson to a question on Pakistan China projects in POK", 14 October 2009, at <http://meaindia.nic.in/>, accessed 15 October 2009.

65   Ananth Krishnan, "It's for India, Pakistan to solve: China", *The Hindu*, 16 October 2009, at <http://www.hinduonnet.com/2009/10/16/stories/2009101654921000.htm>, accessed 30 October 2009.

66   "Pakistan rejects Indian protest on Gilgit-Baltistan, Bunji dam", *The News* (Karachi), 12 September 2009, at <http://www.thenews.com.pk/updates.asp?id=86825>, accessed 14 September 2009.

67   "Official Spokesperson on elections in Gilgit-Baltistan", Ministry of External Affairs, 13 November 2009, at <http://meaindia.nic.in/>, 13 accessed November 2009.

IV

Prognosis

The next twenty years in all probability will see India playing a much larger role vis-à-vis POK. This is evident not only from several statements of the Ministry of External Affairs of late but also the developments with respect to China. China is playing a larger role in India's neighbourhood and the next few years would compel India in all likelihood to revitalize its claims over its lost territory.

India and Pakistan last fought in the Kargil War in 1999, which was Pakistan's futile attempt to establish control on Kashmir. The terrorist attack in Mumbai on 26 November 2008 was a high point, with an impending warlike situation. However, India exercised restraint and concentrated on strengthening its internal anti-terror structure. An incident like this if repeated could lead to retaliation from the Indian side. The repeated failure of diplomatic exercises with respect to Pakistan has aroused anti-Pakistan sentiments amongst Indians. If public opinion begins to support some sort of military offensive against Pakistan, there would be few options left before the government.

Militancy in Kashmir Valley is on the downtrend (with a few exceptions) and as a result the Indian government is expected to engage in a meaningful and consistent diplomatic manoeuvre to reclaim POK. Pakistan is losing trust with the international community, including its major ally the US. This would give India leverage to put its case more forcefully.

The premise of Taliban presence in POK provides an indication to initiate a policy debate on how to tackle the situation in case the Taliban reaches the threshold limits of India. Even though the percolation of Taliban in India is not going to be easy in view of the openness and plurality of Indian society, these militants could successfully stage terror and violence inside the country.

Pakistan is fighting a bitter battle against its own home-grown terror network. The present situation is serious and is likely to worsen in times to come. If so, the secessionists in China would find a suitable ground to gratify their extremist intents and methods. This possibility could adversely impact the otherwise smooth and friendly relations between Pakistan and China. The geo-strategy of South Asia would undergo a sea-change if there is a shift in the existing equation of China-Pakistan relations. With the increasing realization in the US about the terror network in Pakistan and a slightly stern approach in its dealings with Pakistan, it is probable that Pakistan may be isolated from both its closest allies, with them turning hostile to Pakistan's policy of nurturing militancy inside its territory, even though it would be for varying interests.

10
Nepal 2030

—Nihar Nayak

INTRODUCTION

Nepal, which has been facing political instability since 1950, became a democratic republic in May 2008 after a prolonged movement for democracy. Political uncertainties still remain, however, and the present century is likely to be eventful for Nepal considering the high expectation of its citizens from the new political system. The scenario in the next decade could range anywhere between political peace and instability.

PRESENT SITUATION

Despite the three point agreement between the major political parties on May 28, 2010, to extend the tenure of the Constituent Assembly (CA), Nepal is currently in a serious political deadlock due to differences between the major political parties on certain contentious issues such as form of government, nature of federalism, rehabilitation of Maoist combatants and competition between the major political parties to lead the national unit government. Instead of a "national consensus" government, without which a post-conflict society is bound to hobble, Nepal is currently ruled by a coalition government of twenty-two political parties. Even with this large gaggle of political parties, the ruling coalition lacks the requisite number of seats in Parliament to pass the constitution-making bills by a two-thirds majority.

The political instability has led to high inflation (14 per cent) and energy and food crisis. The Maoists' protest in Parliament has affected the presentation of the national budget. Also, the CA could not function for months towards the constitution-making process. Nepal's economy is on the verge of a big crisis due to dwindling export, shirking of remittance flow and depletion in foreign exchange reserves.

Insecurity is widespread, with frequent strikes by various ethnic groups and the UCPN-Maoists, extortion, atrocities by political party-affiliated youth groups and the criminal activities of the illegal armed groups, numbering more than 109, in the country.

POSSIBLE SCENARIOS AND KEY DRIVERS

An attempt has been made in this paper to identify some high-impact, high-uncertainty drivers – such as political, economic, security, external and internal factors – which would shape the future of Nepal.

1. Fragmented Politics and New Constitution

The largest political party in Nepal, the United Communist Party of Nepal-Maoist (UCPN-Maoist), has remained out of the government for 18 months after the Maoist lead government resigned last year. The party argue that the Constitution should be written under a Maoist led government-preferably national unity government. Therefore, they have been demanding resignation of Prime Minister, Madhav Kumar Nepal as agreed in the three-point agreement.

On the other hand, the government and its coalition partners have been asking the Maoists to transform themselves into a Civilian Party by dismantling of the Young Communist League (YCL) and Maoists cantonment, management of Maoists combatants and returning of private properties and respecting to all previous agreements as mentioned in the three point agreements. For all, they are suggesting the Maoist to come up with a time-bound plan along with combatant's number for integration into security agencies. The UCPN-Maoist leaders also argue that the present government is not legitimate because it is formed by going against the spirit of "civilian supremacy". Also they argue the government as illegitimate referring a fact that many ministers, including the Prime Minister Madhav Kumar Nepal, lost the Constituent Assembly election.

Amidst these rigid positions from both the sides, an intra-party conflict in the three major political parties on the Prime Ministerial candidate has delayed the formation of a national unity government. As a result, uncertainty looms large over the completion of the constitution-making process by May 2011. The country may face anarchy in case the political leaders fail to write the constitution in the stipulated time.

There is also a serious trust deficit between major stake holders in Nepal. The Nepali Congress (NC) and Communist Party of Nepal-United Marxist Leninist (CPN-UML) suspect that the Maoists have a long-term agenda of capture of state power by infiltrating their cadres into the Army, bureaucracy and other institutions. The Maoists on the other hand suspect that the NC along with the Army and India are trying to suppress them. Table 1 indicates serious differences between the major political parties on some contentious issues. While the Maoists have proposed fourteen federal units, the NC and the UML are not sure about their numbers. On the other hand, the Madhesi parties, representing the aspirations of the people of the Terai for autonomy, argue for only three states based on geographic zones. Similarly, only a few major political parties have chosen a presidential form of government. Even if the parties manage to resolve the integration issue, their differences such as on the form of government, electoral system, federalism and economic policy may delay the constitution-making process.

Table 1. Major Political Parties' Position on Contentious Issues

Note: CPA=Comprehensive Peace Agreement. UCPN-M= United Communist Party of Nepal-Maoist; NC=Nepali Congress, CPN-UML=Communist Party of Nepal-United Marxist Leninist, MJF=Madhesh Janadhikar Forum, TMLP=Terai Madhes Loktantrik Party.

Major Parties	Seats in Parliament	Maoist combatants' rehabilitation	Form of government	Electoral system	Federalism	Basis of federal unit	Economic policy
UCPN-M	232	Mass integration/ 5000 to 6000	President to be elected directly by the people	Proportional representation on the basis of caste and ethnicity	14 federal units and three sub-provinces in the Terai	Ethnic	New transitional economic policy
NC	116	No integration/ suggested in CPA	Parliamentary system, President elected indirectly	Majoritarian	7 federal units	Geographic, cultural, social, economic	Open market
CPN-UML	109	As suggested in CPA, no integration	Prime Minister elected directly by the people	Mixed	15 federal units	Geographic, economic and natural resources	Mixed economy
MJF (Yadav)	55	No integration	President to be elected directly by the people	Proportional representation	One Madhesh One Pradesh	Ethnic and geographic	Not clear
TMLP	21	As suggested in CPA	Prime Minister to be elected by the Lower House	Proportional representation	One Madhesh One Pradesh	Ethnic and geographic	Not clear

Source: Compiled from reports of Nepal-based English media.

Also, while the political parties are divided among themselves on ideological lines and are struggling to find a common ground to forge consensus, wide-ranging discord within the major political parties has affected the present peace process. This dissonance has emerged on account of divergent individual interests and socio-political issues.

Thus, the ruling CPN-UML has three fronts. There are personal differences between Chairman Jhalanath Khanal and senior leader K.P. Sharma Oli. The Khanal faction describes the Oli faction as being anarchists, insubordinate and pro-India. Prime Minister Madhav Kumar Nepal's faction has been trying to maintain balance between these two groups.

In the Nepali Congress there are two groups, though many leaders have coloured the internal rift as a manifestation of inner-party democracy and a transitional phase for the party. The resentment in the NC has become more pronounced after G.P. Koirala's attempt to promote his daughter Sujata – who has no political knack, experience or following – to the position of Deputy Prime Minister. The majority of the senior NC leaders have protested in the past against Koirala's efforts to anoint his daughter as his political successor. After the death of K.P Koilala few months back, NC seems to have at least three factions lead by Sher Bahadur Deuba, Sushil Koirala and Ram Chandra Paudel. Recently, the party is divided into two factions-Sher Bahadur Deuba and Ram Chandra Paudel-on Prime Ministerial candidate from NC side.

Although the cleavage in the CPN-Maoist is not clear yet, sometimes Mohan Vaidya "Kiran", the party ideologue, and others have been taking hard-line views. Deepening ideological differences apart, serious rift has surfaced in the selection of the leadership. As a palliative, the party decided to introduce multiple party positions. There is no immediate threat to Prachanda, the CPN-Maoist supremo. Mohan Vaidya is the number two in the party. But given that he lacks the charisma to lead the party. The real fight is between Baburam Bhattarai and Prachanda. They are vying for the senior position as vice chairman.[1]

---

1   Saroj Dahal, "Maoist Party", *Spotlight,* Kathmandu, 3(05) (1 August 2009), at <http://www.nepalnews.com/contents/2009/englishweekly/spotlight/aug/aug01/national2.php>.

Terai-based regional parties have also been experiencing internal rift. The turmoil of Terai politics has become complex, with two factions of the MJF acquiring formal status. The members of Parliament from the Madhesi parties are of the view that the divisions among their political leaders have weakened the movement for Madhesi autonomy.

2. Abysmal Internal Security

Despite the Comprehensive Peace Agreement (CPA), since November 2006 Nepal has witnessed a total of 1284 crime-related deaths, 2100 abductions and mushrooming of over 109 underground armed outfits. Around one-third of the violent incidents are attributed to the armed groups. While the Maoists and the state allegedly killed a total of 31 and 112 people, 1141 people were killed by new armed groups with a criminal orientation.[2] Government efforts at holding talks with the Terai outfits ended inconclusively. The announcement of the new security policy, coupled with a spate of fake encounter killings by the security forces, has reduced the possibility of talks with any of these groups.

3. Looming Ethnic Politics

The 2001 census of Nepal has recorded 103 caste/ethnic groups (including two unidentified groups), 93 languages and dialects and 9 religious groups. Among the ethnic groups 59 have been identified as indigenous peoples or indigenous nationalities.[3] These ethnic groups have been demanding to maintain their identity through inclusion and representation in the state mechanism and have formed a Joint Struggle Committee. These groups have also demanded caste-based proportional representation in all government agencies at all levels and the implementation of the ILO 169 declaration.[4]

2 "Nepal still a killing field", *Kantipuronline*, 21 September 2009. Accessed on July 5, 2010, http://www.ekantipur.com/news/news-detail. php?news_id=300587

3 Krishna Hachhetu, The Agenda of transformation: Inclusion in Nepali democracy, conferee paper organised by Social Service Baha in 24-26 April, 2003, Kathmandu.

4 "Strike by ethnic communities cripples life across the country," *Nepalnews. com*, 03 September 2009. Accessed 28 October 2009, at <http://www.

Federalism is one reliable mechanism to ensure inclusion of ethnic aspirations in the national body politic. The major political parties and civil society groups have, however, widely divergent opinions regarding the nature of the federal structure for the country. There are mainly two schools of thought. One favours boundaries drawn on the basis of geographic features, capacity, resources, the potential for development, and equal rights of all persons and communities living in a sub-national unit. Most of the Madhesi parties favour this model. The other model of the federation is based on "self–determination with the right to autonomy". This view is related to the historical territory. Most ethnic groups and the UCPN-Maoist favour this model. The UCPN (Maoist) submitted its position on federalism to the State Restructuring Committee under the Constituent Assembly proposing thirteen states.[5] According to the NC, territory and feasibility, population, natural resources and economic possibility, linguistic/ethnic and cultural majority, and political/administrative possibility should constitute a federal unit. CPN-(UML) supports a province based on ethnicity, language, culture and region. The UML has proposed to divide the country into thirteen provinces on the basis of ethnicity, language, culture and natural resources. It has stressed developing three tiers of government and constitutional bodies so that the country's natural resources are used proportionately.[6]

4. Economic Growth

The Nepalese economy has been doing well despite the ten years of civil war and the global economic crisis, for two reasons. First, the

---

nepalnews.com/main/index.php/news-archive/1-top-story/1250-strike-by-ethnic-communities-cripples-life-across-the-country-.html>.

5   "Maoists propose dividing country into 13 states; UML, NC yet to table proposal", *Nepalnews.com*, 4 September 2009. Accessed 28 October 2009, at <http://www.nepalnews.com/main/index.php/news-archive/1-top-story/1262-maoists-propose-dividing-country-into-13-states-uml-nc-yet-to-propose.html>.

6   "UML proposes 13 provinces", *The Rising Nepal*, 15 September 2009. Accessed 28 October 2009, at <http://www.gorkhapatra.org.np/rising.detail.php?article_id=24445&cat_id=4>.

economy is heavily dependent on remittances. According to Keshar Kumar Lamgade,

> The remittance money has a profound and growing impact on poverty and resource distribution in the country. At micro level, remittances shore up household income and buying capacity, while also contributing to savings; at macro level, remittance inflow is helping generate local commodity markets and local employment opportunities.[7]

According to the Nepal Rastra Bank, the country's economy in 2004/05 earned over US\$922 million in remittances from overseas workers and accounted for 12.4 per cent of national GDP. The second factor explaining the resilience of the economy is that Nepalese banking and economy are less dependent on the international monetary system and are more linked with the Indian market.

These two factors may partly explain the paradox that despite the protracted civil war and political instability, the living standard of the people has improved over the years. According to the *Nepal Labour Survey 2008* by the Central Bureau of Statistics, there has been a phenomenal change in the living standard of the people in the past five years (see Table 2). There is also positive improvement in the overall human development index (see Table 3). The literacy rate has increased to 55.2 per cent and poverty gap has been reduced to 7.5 per cent from the earlier 11.7 per cent.

Table 2. Household Indicators, 2003-2008

Sector	2003/4 (%)	2008 (%)
Electricity per household	37.2	56
Telecommunication (Land Lines) Mobile	6.1 –	9.8 28.3

---

7   Keshar Kumar Lamgade, "Nepal's Exodus for Foreign Employment", *Nepal Monitor*, 13 February 2008, at <http://www.nepalmonitor. com/2008/02/nepals_exodus_for_foreign_employment_.html>.

Household-used toilets	38.7	48.7
LPG	8.2	12.3
Tapped drinking water	43.9	45
Drinking water from well	46.1	39.1
People live in own house	91.6	89.2
Rent house	7.9	9.2
Literacy	–	63 (14% more than a decade ago)
Persons working abroad per family	–	29.1

Source: Nepal Labour Survey 2008, Central Bureau of Statistics, Nepal.

Table 3. Social Indicators

Item	1985	1990	Latest Year
Total Fertility Rate (births/ woman)	5.9	5.3	3.1 (2006)
Maternal Mortality Ratio (per 100,000 live births)	–	515.0	281.0 (2006)
Infant Mortality Rate (below 1 year/1,000 live Births)	115.4	97.0	48.0 (2006)
Life Expectancy at Birth (years)	50.9	53.6	63.2
Adult literacy (%)	26.5	48.6 (1995-2005)	55.2 (2006)
Primary school net enrolment (%)	–	64.0	86.6 (2006)
Lower secondary school gross enrolment (%)	–	63.2 (2001)	71.5 (2006)

Child malnutrition (% below age 5)	69.1 (1975)	57.0	38.6 (2006)
Population below poverty line (international, %)	–	–	55.1 (2003)
Population with access to improved water sources (%)	–	45.9	81.8 (2006)
Population with access to improved sanitation facilities (%)	–	22.0 (1995)	46.0 (2006)
Public education expenditure (% DGP)	2.7	2.0	3.8
Human Development Index	0.378	0.42	0.534 (2005)
Poverty incidence	–	42.0 (1996)	31.0 (2004)
Poverty gap	–	11.7 (1996)	7.5 (2004)

Source: Nepal Quarterly Economic Update June 2009, ADB.

Population growth rate, however, virtually remains stagnant at around 2.1 per cent. There is no impressive growth in GDP either, despite aggressive projections made in the Tenth Five Year Plan (7.0 per cent). As indicated in Table 4, while 80 per cent of the population is dependent on agriculture, the contribution of this sector to GDP is around 4.7 per cent against 8.9 per cent from the non-agricultural sector. More troubling is the fact that the growth rate keeps fluctuating wildly: there are no instances of sustained growth rate of over 5 per cent for three consecutive years. The average GDP growth rate in the past five decades was 3.57 per cent[8]. According to Labour Survey 2008, 73.9 per cent of the people worked in the agricultural sector, while only 26.1 were employed in the non-agricultural sector.

---

8   Chandan Sapkota, "Reality about Nepal's GDP growth rate", Republica, March 24, 2009.

Table 4. Economic Indicators

Item	2004	2005	2006	2007	2008
GDP growth (% in constant prices)	4.7	3.5	3.4	3.3	5.3
GDP Agriculture	4.8	3.5	1.8	1.0	4.7
GDP Industry	1.4	3.0	4.5	3.9	1.9
GDP Services	6.8	3.3	5.6	4.5	7.0
Total External Debt (% of GDP)	43.2	37.3	35.8	29.7	26.8
Population (millions)	24.7	25.3	25.9	26.4	27.0

Source: Nepal Quarterly Economic Update June 2009, ADB.

5. Demography

According to the census 2007, Nepal is one of the most densely populated mountain regions of the world with population density of 150 people per sq km. The estimate for Nepal's present population is around 27 million and that will reach 34 million by 2021 (see Table 5). According to the *ADB Nepal Quarterly Economic Update June 2009*, the annual population growth rate has been 2.1 (1985), 2.1 (1990) and 2.2 (2008). Present estimates show that the country's fertility rate (the average number of children per couple) is 4.45, a big drop from 6.3 in 1970. Infant mortality rate, a key factor in inducing couples to have fewer children if it is low, has declined sharply from 115.4 per 1000 live births in 1985 to 48.0 in 2006.[9] Migration to the Terai and the cities counts towards an alarming urbanization rate of 6.5 per cent, which means the population of the cities and towns is growing at nearly three times the national average.

---

9   Hemlata Rai, Census 2007, Nepali Times, issue 18, November 24-30, 2001.

Table 5. Projected Population of Nepal, 2001-2021

Year	Population
2001	23,151,423
2006	25,886,736
2011	28,584,975
2016	31,327,341
2021	34,172,444

Source: Central Bureau of Statistics, Nepal.

6. Food Crisis

There is a chronic food crisis in Nepal, especially in west and midwest. The adverse impact of global climate change has translated into long spells of drought. According to the Ministry of Agriculture and Cooperatives (MoAC), scarce rainfall in the five months in 2009 has led to a 60 per cent drop in the yield of winter crops as compared to 2008.

One recent report indicated that despite increase in paddy production in the last four decades, Nepal is fast sliding into a food deficit. The country is facing a food deficit of 316,465 tons in 2009/10, which is double the deficit figure of 132,914 tons recorded last year, due to 11 percent decline in paddy production. The report said the rise in population disproportional to the total production volume, conversion of agricultural land for human settlements, delayed or low plantation in major producing districts due to erratic rain fall, etc, are responsible for low production.[10]

The mountainous districts Siraha, Dhanusha, Mahottari, Sarlaihi and Kailali, Mugu, and Dhading are bearing the bulk of the brunt.[11] Food prices have risen exorbitantly. Many essentials need to be flown

---

10 "Nepal sliding to food deficit situation", *The Republica*, 28 June 2010. http://www.myrepublica.com/portal/index.php?action=news_details&news_id=20450

11 "Nepal faces food crisis amid global climate change", *China View*, 25 March 2009. Accessed 28 October 2009, at <http://news.xinhuanet.com/english/2009-03/25/content_11069727.htm>.

into Mugu by air, increasing the cost of food. Poor connectivity is another factor causing chronic food shortage in these remote districts.

7. Energy Crisis

Nepal has huge potential for hydropower development. Unfortunately, it is experiencing a serious energy crisis. Power breakdowns of forty hours a week have been the norm. To meet the deficit, the government has decided to produce 10,000 MW of hydropower in another ten years. The World Bank has approved $89.2 million to support the Energy Crisis Management Action Plan, including rehabilitation of a hydropower project and expansion of existing hydropower plants.

Table-6, Major Operational Hydropower Plants with their Capacity in Nepal:

S.N.	Power Plant	Capacity (MW)	Annual Energy (GWh)
1	Trishuli	24	292
2	Sunkoshi	10	66
3	Gandak	15	53
4	Kulekhani I	60	164
5	Devighat	14	13
6	Kulekhani II	32	96
7	Marshyangdi	69	519
8	Puwa	6	41
9	Modi	15	87
10	Kaligandaki	144	791
11	Andhikhola	5	38
12	Jhimruk	12	81
13	Khimti	60	353
14	Bhotekoshi	36	246
15	Indrawati	7.5	51
16	Syange	.2	1.2
17	Chilime	20	101

18	Piluwa	3	18
19	Sunkoshi	2.6	14.5
20	Chaku Khola	1.5	–
21	Small hydro	12.5	26
22	Small hydro (Isolated)	6.4	–
23	Microhydro	14.5	–
	Total	=SUM(ABOVE) 568.7	

Sources: Independent Power Producers' Association, (IPPAN),
http://www.ippan.org.np/HPinNepal.html

While Nepal produces around 600 MW hydropower (Table-6), its peak power demand reached to 812.50 MW in the year 2008/2009 registering 12.58 per cent increase over peak demand of the pervious year 721.73 MW.[12] Nepal's domestic power consumption may increase up to 1,742 MW by 2020. During this period Nepal's electricity demand may increase between 8 to 12 percent. [13] Despite having tremendous hydro potential, the country may plunge into serious electricity crisis if the sector is not managed properly.

8. Climate Change

Climate Change is a gobal phenomenon. Each county may face brunt of that. However, countries located at the high altitude and Islands may be affected more than others. Therefore, the adverse impact of climate change is a major concern for Nepal due to its dependence on agriculture and poor irrigation facilities. There are studies and reports studies reflected that the county is already witnessing an increase in temperature, erratic rainfall and increased unpredictability in weather patterns, including drier winters and delays in the summer monsoons, etc. The changes are presumed to be due to the impact of global warming and the melting Himalayan glaciers.

---

12 Nepal Electricity Authority, Annual Report 2009, pg. 09.

13 Upendra Gautam and Ajoyb Karki, ed. "Hydropower Pricing in Nepal: Developing A Persepctive", Kathmandu: Jalsrot Vikas Sanstha, 2004, pg.

The Oxfam study on 'climate change, poverty and adaptation in Nepal' indicated that average annual mean temperatures have been increasing in Nepal by 0.06°C between 1977 and 2000 and these increases are more pronounced at higher altitudes and in winter. As a consequence, Nepal's high-altitude glaciers are retreating at an alarming rate, resulting in the creation of glacial lakes and the threat of catastrophic Glacial Lake Outburst Floods (GLOFs). The study also observed that Changing weather patterns have adversely affected crop production, getting the farmers into debt for mere survival. More than 3.4 million Nepalese are estimated to require food assistance, due to a combination of natural disasters, including the winter drought of 2008/9 – one of the worst in the country's history.[14]

Recently, some presentation in the Singapore International Water Week (SIWW) in Singapore predicated that due to natural causes like glacial melting, four countries including Nepal would lose almost 275 billion cubic meters of annual renewable water by 2030.[15] Interestingly, the National Water Plan (2002-2027) of Nepal has not indicated such alarming situation in future. The government is certainly concern about the possible impacts of greenhouse gas emission by developed countries on climate.

9. External Powers

Nepal's geo-strategic location, sandwiched between China and India, has drawn the attention of both regional and extra regional forces. These forces have interfered directly or indirectly with the political processes of the country. Such external influence did exist earlier, but the emergence of the Maoists as a major political force and the declaration of Nepal as a republic have led to increasing engagement of USA, EU members and China in that country. Increasingly external

---

14 "Even the Himalayas have stopped smiling: Climate Change, Poverty and Adaptation in Nepal", *Oxfam International Report*, August 2009. Also see "Vanishing Himalayan Smiles: Climate Change in Nepal", *Nepal Monitor*, 31 August 2009. Accessed 28 October 2009, at <http://www.nepalmonitor.com/2009/08/vanishing_himalayan.html>.

15 'Serious water woes' in 20 yrs,' *The Kathmandupost*, 04 July, 2010. http://www.ekantipur.com/the-kathmandu-post/2010/07/03/nation/serious-water-woes-in-20-yrs/210077/

interventions and their conflicting political interests may push Nepal into a perpetual political instability. Continuous engagements of USA, EU members and their support to revival of the Tibetan movement would virtually convert Nepal from a peaceful region to conflict turn region.

CONCLUSION

As said earlier, the key drivers for this analysis, numbering nine, were chosen on the basis of high impact and high uncertainty. To sum up the discussion, they can be ranked on the impact-uncertainty matrix as given in Table 7.

On the basis of the potential impact of these drivers, the following possible two main types of scenarios may be foreseen for Nepal in the ensuing decade, in basic terms of win-lose or win-win.

Table 7. Impact of matrixes driving the future of Nepal

Driver	Impact	Uncertainty
New Constitution	High	High
Federalism	High	High
Demography	Low	High
Climate change	Low	High
Food Shortage	Low	High
Energy Crisis	Low	High
External powers	High	High

SCENARIOS

I. WIN-LOSE: POLITICAL INSTABILITY

- Although the major political parties manage to write the constitution by the end of 2011, the new constitution may fail to address the demands of the ethnic groups. That leads to ethnic tension in the Terai and elsewhere. Terai could be a flash point of violence in Nepal. India will be blamed for the Terai unrest. India's relationship with Nepal Army may be affected due to Madhesis' demand for a separate

autonomous region and subsequently a separate state. As
the Nepali polity changes and with political instability,
there will also be the likelihood of more anti-Indian
feeling, both artificially generated by some sections of the
polity as well as India's own erroneous handling of the
relations. Frequent ethnic tension and political instability
may give an opportunity to the Army to maintain itself
as an important institution. Initially, the Maoists remain
the largest political party but seek the support of smaller
parties to form the government. Gradually, the party will
consolidate. By 2030 there will be a Maoist government
with a clear majority. The party will adopt a multi-post
system with the chairperson followed by other positions to
keep the party united. They will indulge in massive political
patronage with some kind of changes in their radical views.
It will be like communist rule in West Bengal, eastern
state of India. The NC remains the second-largest political
party. But if NC could not mobilize it to the grassroots,
it will be vanished from the seen and a new modest party
with the support of the Royalists and upper class would be
emerged as like as BJP in India.

- There will be at least three big parties in existence including
the Maoists. The ex-Monarch Gyanendra will join the politics
and become the leader of all three pro-Royalist parties by
merging them into one. In the given situation the UML will
continue to be weak. The CPN-UML's traditional vote bank
will be shared with Maoists. Protracted instability induces
China to support the Maoists as a factor for stability. This
provokes India to neutralize the Chinese influence. Political
instability leads to further deterioration of law and order
and the economic condition.

- The UCPN-Maoist consolidates gradually with the
support of smaller parties and creates more divisions in the
major political parties. Political and Cultural Revolution
intensifies. Anti-India feeling is sharpened to neutralize

India's influence. Maoist-indoctrinated cadres are infiltrated in the Army. The Maoists adopt tactics to consolidate their position in the rural and urban areas. Some hardliner UCPN-Maoist leaders and lower-level workers join splinter groups for people's revolution against revisionism in the party.

• Distrust between the major political parties continues. Political parties and civil society are divided on ethnic issues. The NC's popularity wanes. It would be difficult for the NC to maintain its influence in the Terai. Its vote bank in that region will be divided with Terai based regional parties. The regional parties may get stronger and local government will have more rights. Divide-and-rule will remain the main tactic of the Maoist party both at the political and the provincial level to maintain their status quo. Nepal may lead to territorial division after entering into federalism due to a weak centre. There are a series of coalition governments headed either by the Maoists or UML. The Upendra Yadav faction of the MJF supports the Maoist-led government. This becomes manifest in the standoff between UCPN-Maoist and other political parties. The other political parties obstruct government functioning. The Maoists revive their armed young cadres, the Young Communist League (YCL) and begin to use the YCL cadres and eventually the People's Liberation Army (PLA) in armed clashes with political rivals. External forces are indirectly involved in support of the groups supporting their own agenda. The economic condition becomes precarious. There is large-scale labour migration abroad.

II. Win-Win: The Maoist government consolidates

The constitution is accepted by all the political parties and ethnic groups. The Maoist party gradually transforms into a moderate one. The Maoist party manages to convince the other parties to cooperate with it by accepting some of their demands. The moderate Maoist government also seeks India's support and keeps an arm's-length distance with China. The UCPN-Maoist adopts "national unity government" as party policy and supports the government, remaining out of the government on selected issues. The Maoists adopt political non-violent tactics to consolidate their position in the rural and urban areas.

III. Oxygen Government: Role of External Forces

In an effort to secure its southern border, China will increase its influence and greater say in the political and economic matters. China will look for a stable and favourable government in Kathmandu to serve its strategic interest. China will continue spending more and more money and time during these days to make Nepali politics more complex. However, China's role will continue to be in margin till 2030 as it has to go a long way to be influential in Nepal by building a people to people relation as it is with India. That may discomfort India. Chinese presence would lead to breach of India's security concerns in Nepal. That would lead to political instability in Nepal. Further, Western forces will take advantage of that situation to pursue their strategic interests in the region.

11
Tibet 2030

—PK Gautam

Drivers and Assumptions

Economic Tibet. China's aim is to have an economic Tibet. Urbanisation, infrastructure building, extension of rail, roads and airports, converting grasslands to farmland will continue

Demographic Changes. Demographic Changes continue by way of settlement of Hans in Tibet. Like in the case of Inner Mongolia or Xingjian, the local become minorities.

The Status and Role of the Dalai Lama. By having government's role in incarnation, the selection of the future Dalai Lama is with the state (like done in case of Panchen Lama). No one born out side China can lay claim for reincarnation. This makes the government in theory more powerful than the spiritual leadership in exile.

Ecology and Climate Change. Due to global warming brought about by anthropogenic reasons, "the glaciers in the Qinghai-Tibetan Plateau and the Tianshan Mountains would retreat at an accelerated rate, and some smaller glaciers would disappear".[1] "In particular, accelerated melting of glaciers in western China due to climate warming will further reduce the area of glaciers and glacier ice reserves, thus having significant impacts on rivers and run-offs with sources in glacier melt water. Future climate change will further increase the vulnerability of ecological systems, diminish the geographical distribution areas of main tree species for afforestation

---

1   *China's National Climate Change Programme*, National Development and Reform Commission, PRC, June 2007, p 6.

and rare tree species, enlarge the outbreak scope of forest diseases and insect, and increase the frequency of forest fires and burnt-over areas, shrink inland lakes and cause the decrease and functional degradation of wetland resources, speed up the reduction of the area of glaciers and permafrost, and significantly alter the spatial distribution pattern of permanent permafrost of highland ecological system on the Qinghai-Tibet Plateau, and damage bio-diversity. Climate warming would possibly reinforce the drought trend in northern China, and intensify water scarcity and imbalance between water supply and demand."[2] Environmental degradation due to climate change is also considered a threat by the Environment and Development Desk of Department of Information and International Relations, Central Tibetan Administration(CTA), Dharamshala. This driver is common is both PRC and CTA. Both admit that there is an onset of an ecological crisis in Tibetan plateau and adjoining areas due to climate change.

Attitudes of the Tibetan People. Tibetans in exile may continue with their ideas of greater autonomy. Inside Tibet things are still opaque. However taking queue from spontaneous demonstration in March 2008 across TAR and also other provinces of China having Tibetan in majority or in sizeable numbers this driver is important.

Scenario 1: Hanised and Degraded Tibet

With Hanisation and Demographic Changes. Tibetan Buddhism is likely to be at cross road. The Chinese would have their own 15th Dalai Lama by then. While the CAT has not expressed openly many options may happen. Scenarios could be end of the Dalai Lama process with a democratic system, or a parallel Dalai Lama in exile. Due to internationalization of Tibetan Buddhism and culture, the humanitarian and cultural responsibility to preserve Buddhist culture will not only be shared by India but also the international community.

---

2   *China's Policies and Actions for Addressing Climate Change*, Information Office of the State Council of the PRC, October 2008, Beijing. p. 9. Ibid, p 9.

Division Between Traditions of Tibetan Buddhism. It is possible that attempts of 14th Dalai Lama to unify traditions would have borne fruit. Although the division of Panchan Lama of Gelugpa tradition is well known (one selected by China and one selected by Dalai Lama who is missing in China) the exiled government under its Prime Minister may be the temporal head. For spiritual head, Tibetans will be spilt and under a great transitional struggle. If they follow old traditions then they will be split between spiritual heads of their traditions, who may well now be in PRC. The present 14th Dalai Lama due to his charismatic personality is unlikely to be replaced with a similar lama. The 17th Karmapa who in his teen fled to India in 2000 would have come of age, but it is doubtful if he will be able to command spiritual and religious power as the 14th Dalai Lama. The fallout of the struggle is hazy and complex.

ECOLOGY

Environmental degradation of Tibet will continue. By the time the second commitment period of the Kyoto Protocol begins in 2013, business as usual emission worldwide would have added to the existing stocks of excess green house gases in the atmosphere. The trees, soil and oceans will not be able to sequester them. Scientists are worried that a warming Tibetan plateau will change the dynamics of the Asian monsoons.[3] Glaciers that feed rivers like Yellow, Yangtze, Mekong, Salween, Indus, Ganges and Brahmaputra which are shrinking by an average rate of 7% annually will impact on water, food, energy and biodiversity security.[4] About 60 to 190 billion tons of carbon locked up in permafrost may begin to release accelerating global warming.[5] Extreme weather events then will be a norm.

Pastures. The Russian Tibetonist Roerich has mentioned that deprive Tibet of its cattle breeding region and the country would

---

3   Michael Zhao and Orville Schell, "Tibet: Plateau in Peril", *World Policy Journal*, Vol. XXV. No.3, Fall 2008, pp. 171-180.
4   Ibid.
5   Ibid

starve.[6] Nomads positive relationship with ecology will end. Animal products like skins, meat, milk and butter rather than being produced though nomad may be factory produced. Use of pack animals such as yaks, dzos (cross breeds), goats and sheep for trade will declines. Health of glaciers, grasslands and the nomadic life are very delicately balanced with the ecology.[7]

In Sino-Tibetan relations, the different perspectives on the economic path of PRC and CTA is unlikely to get resolved as Hanisation, urbanization, infrastructure building, extension of railway network and roads will increase.

SCENARIO 2 – RESPONSIBLE CHINA

A clear vision of China's own identity and what type of society it wants emerges.[8] Unlike the expectations of realists, China promotes a peaceful international society based on its domestic foundation. China's peaceful rise of the last 30 years is carried forward even more peacefully in harmony. Compelled to be an important world power, China carries out reforms to cater for autonomy of Tibet. It encourages greater religious freedom and some democratic freedom in China. In Tibet it controls Hanisation and agrees to change a capitalistic mode of growth and development by taking the people's traditional preferences. Tibetan is made the official language with priority over Mandarin to help the people. With open policies it permits return of Tibetan in exile and allows the Dalai Lama to be a spiritual leader. It accommodates the Tibetan Government in Exile in its political structure. In some way it follows the Hong Kong model for Tibet. This results in manifold increase in international tourism with care of ecology. These policies also permit China to have the

6   As quoted by Wim van Spengen, *Tibetan Borders: A Geohistoric Analysis of Trade and Traders*, London and New York, Keegan Paul International, 2000, pp. 98-102.

7   Michael Zhao and Orville Schell, "Tibet: Plateau in Peril", *World Policy Journal*, Vol. XXV. No.3, Fall 2008, pp. 171-180

8   Barry Buzan, "China in International Society: Is 'Peaceful Rise Possible'?", *The Chinese Journal of International Politics*, Vol.3. No.1, Spring 2010, pp.5-36.

worlds' leadership role in Buddhism. It improves foreign relations with Buddhist countries of East and South East.

In ecological matters traditional practices of nomads are revived to sustain healthy grasslands. Ecological concerns top the policies as by 2030 adverse impact of climate change would be peaking. A realisation would have dawned on public and political leadership that solution lies in cooperation with neighbours and respecting traditional ecological knowledge.

Wild Card Scenario

Internal forces make China implode. With capitalistic policies the society becomes brittle. Societal and cultural moorings get uprooted. Restrictions and rigid state high- handedness by the state, expectations for freedom of speech and choice which is denied creates tensions in Chinese society. Disparity between rich and poor increases. Economic growth bubble based on GDP bursts with chronic and irreversible environmental degradation and pollution of rivers and cities. Climate Change exacerbates the situation with negative impact on snow and glaciers of Tibet. Water and soil stress lead to massive shortages in food. China loses its manufacturing advantage and joblessness grows. Reforms in China reach their limit. This to revival of Maoism (like Naxalism in India) with Chinese characteristics of the Great Leap forward and the Cultural Revolution. Mainland China sees shades of Warring Period remerge.

People of the regions in the periphery like Tibet and Xingjian who for long felt suppressed on top down economic policies and demographic change assert themselves. Scenario could replicate fragmentation of former Soviet Union. TAR demands Greater Tibet and turmoil takes place in China and its regions.

International community comes to help China with proviso to grant autonomy to Tibet in accordance of the desire of Tibetans as a tool of conflict termination over civil conflict and separatism.

Policies for India

POLICIES TO CATER FOR SCENARIO OR HELP SHAPE SCENARIOS?

One question that must be asked is are the policies meant for the scenario which unfolds or are the policies the one that help shape or facilitate scenario? If we continue to base our behaviour on the Cold War and pre-Cold war thinking, then it appears that a realist model based on fear and greed will dominate the thinking.[9] The ideal may be if scenarios are conceptualized and efforts applied to achieve them with a liberal view. However, it needs to be noted that "how little we understand, and how we control even less".[10]

With having written scenarios based on imagination and literature survey it is hoped that these policies may be acceptable to the Chinese, Tibetans and Indians. Rather, it may motivate both China and India to address the question of Tibet.

Tibetan Buddhism

The first policy suggestion is on Tibetans and Buddhism. India needs to take initiative to facilitate dialogue between CTA in exile in India and the Chinese. Misperceptions leading to 1962 border war need to be removed. India is a plural society and Tibetans have been given shelter for religious, cultural and humanitarian reasons. Real Tibetan Autonomy does not mean break up of China. It means religious and cultural rights and growth and development on Buddhist values and not ruthless capitalistic modes which attempt to dominate or rule nature. It is unlikely that in Scenario 1 the Tibetans will give up their external struggle even in post 14th Dalai Lama scenario. Rather post 14th Dalai Lama their may be no leader of stature for China to engage. The situation may become worst with young Tibetans shunning the

---

9   With hindsight as wisdom some scholars mention that break up of Soviet Union was planned when Star war initiative was launched in 1980s. This led to the Soviets imploding due to unsustainable high defence expenditure

10 Thomas Homer Dixon, *The Upside of Down: Catastrophe, Creativity, and the Renewal of Civilization*, Washington, Island Press, 2006, p.29.

path of non- violence. Ideal is scenario 2 though India will need to work hard to retain its top position in Buddhism. Scenario 3 will test India's foreign policy and diplomacy. It is unlikely that India will act like a predator, rather India will need to further cooperate over the water resources emanating from Tibet. India as a responsible power with regional and global influence will be pivotal in conflict resolution.

Ecology of Tibet

Tibet is a global ecosystem and a climate crankshaft similar to Amazon rain forests. It has the source of all major rivers to South and South East Asia. Narrow sovereign thinking on Tibet will do more harm than good. It is linked to the Indian Himalayas. Thus it is ripe time for the countries of the region to conduct, consolidate and record scientific studies on the degradation of the ecosystem both due to man made economic policies and due to climate change. Countries of the region must reach conclusion and understanding of both adaptations and mitigation. This is the first step on hard facts and scientific evidence. India's National Action Plan on Climate Change (NAPCC), mentions two things. It says that available monitoring data on Himalayan glaciers indicates that while recession of some glaciers has occurred in some Himalayan regions in recent past, the trend in not consistent across the entire the entire mountain chain. In its National Mission for Sustaining the Himalayan Ecosystem it "seeks to understand whether and the extent to which, the Himalayan glaciers are in recession and how the problem would be addressed. This will require the joint effort of climatologists, glaciologists, and other experts. India will need to exchange information with South Asian countries and countries sharing the Himalayan ecology". [11] For 2030 studies such initiatives must now be implemented including joint deliberations on the common rivers according to international norms of water sharing.

---

11   NAPCC, p.15 and 5.

NOMADS

The third policy suggestion is on a relook on the nomads. The time to call then primitive is now over. Traditional ecological knowledge has been their basic tool. That must be preserved. Pastures and grasslands must be allowed to flourish.

MITIGATION OF CLIMATE CHANGE BY DEVELOPED COUNTRIES

The fourth policy suggestion is mitigation of climate change. Both the Himalayas and Qinghai-Tibet plateau are unique ecosystems. They need unique global help. Here India, China and countries dependent on Tibet ecosystem must argue for the developed countries to limit emission to avoid tipping events.

12
Illegal Migration into India: Problem and Prospects

—Anand Kumar

Human population has been moving from one place to another on occasions since ancient times. This trend has got only intensified in recent times because of the ease of the movement made possible by the development of technology. The migration of population has been seen as a win-win proposition in many cases where it is controlled and legal. But problem arises in those cases where movement of population becomes uncontrolled and takes the shape of illegal migration. India has also been facing this problem despite being part of impoverished south Asia.

Globally, migration has been taking place at different levels. People move from one continent to another and from one country to another. People move even within a country from one part to another which is called internal migration. Besides, every country also has migration from rural to urban areas. It is expected that soon more than half of the world population would be living in urban areas. Generally attempt is made to control international migration. Even when migration takes place from one country to another legal migration is not a problem. The problem arises when population starts moving illegally.

In south Asia, India has been facing problem of illegal immigration for a long time. In pre-independence days India, Bangladesh and Pakistan formed part of one country. In post-independence era India and Pakistan emerged as successor states of British India. Bangladesh also became independent after its liberation from Pakistan. Though illegal migrants have been coming to India from both Bangladesh and Pakistan, the problem is much more acute from the side of the former.

There is also a large Nepali population in India. But the presence of Nepalis can not be seen as illegal migration as both countries share open border. Besides, people have also been coming from Afghanistan, though Afghans are not in such large number in India, possibly because India and Afghanistan do not share a common border. Otherwise given the unsettled conditions in Afghanistan a large population from that country would have flowed in. This has happened actually in the case of Pakistan, where because of the sharing of the common border a large Afghan population has spilled into Pakistan. But that population is in the nature of refugees.

India has however faced similar situation on its southern border, where a large Tamil population facing problems due to ethnic conflict in Sri Lanka have moved to Indian province of Tamil Nadu. The Indian Ocean archipelago, Maldives has not sent migrants to India, but it is feared that the country itself might face threat due to environmental reasons. The country might actually disappear from the face of the earth because of global warming, but all Maldivians may not be coming necessarily to India.

India has been a destination for the migrants coming from various south Asian countries. But the problem is really acute from the side of Bangladesh. This illegal Bangladeshi migration has caused demographic change in some parts of the country which has multiple implications for the country.

BASIC REASONS

Generally, international migration has been explained on the basis of economic conditions prevailing in different countries. This approach sees differentials in wages and employment opportunities as prime factors. According to economic theories of migration, individuals will emigrate if the expected benefits exceed the costs. In this approach the propensity to migrate is determined by average wages, the cost of travel and labour market conditions.

This has also been largely true for India where a majority of migrants coming are economic migrants. Most of these illegal migrants are from Bangladesh. Though they have now spread all over India their major presence is in Assam and West Bengal. Besides, most metropolitan cities have their large population.

Bangladesh in the most crowded place on the earth. It has got largest population density in the world. The growing population pressure in Bangladesh acts as a push factor whereas growing Indian economy, relatively less pressure on land and weak state resistance acts as a pull factor. It is also difficult to identify Bangladeshi nationals. Its result has been an increase in the Muslim population in the border districts of Assam and West Bengal. Reports have also indicated that in the bordering districts of west Bengal rural areas are dominated by the migrants. In fact, this has often forced the original residents to move to urban areas in search of safety.

OTHER FACTORS ABETTING MIGRATION

Though economic reasons are main driving factors behind illegal migration, there are a number of other factors which abet migration. The ability of states to control entry of migrants varies. Many states who are militarily very powerful often feel helpless against the stream of migrants flowing in. India is also reasonably militarily powerful but it has not been able to control illegal Bangladeshi migration.

India's border management on the Indo-Bangladesh border has been weak. There are several reasons for this. India shares 4096 km border with Bangladesh. Out of this about a thousand kilometer of border is riverine and in many places population lives up to very close to the border. Besides, this border was not clearly demarcated in many places. This kind of situation makes management of this border very difficult.[1] Though in recent times government has made attempt to fence the border, still it remains a porous border. Moreover, the illegal migrants are now taking even sea route to reach India. The border management is further weakened by corruption among the border guards on both sides of the border.

---

1   N.S. Jamwal, Border Management: Dilemma of Guarding the India-Bangladesh Border, Strategic Analysis, Jan-March 2004, pp. 5-36

A major role in abetting illegal migration has been played by the civil administration. The civil administration which is supposed to help border guards in checking illegal migration has actually helped to worsen the problem. The civilian authorities in states bordering Bangladesh help illegal migrants by preparing fake documents for pecuniary benefits which helps to legitimize their stay in India. In fact, it has been found that fake documents are often prepared in advance while the person is still in Bangladesh.[2] As a result, the moment that person enters India, he becomes a legal Indian citizen. Most of these illegal migrants are armed with fake voter identity cards and ration cards. Many of them have now started taking Indian passports to further strengthen their claim on Indian citizenship.[3] The Supreme Court of India has tried to intervene in this. It has ruled that by mere possession of voter identity cards and ration cards no one would automatically become Indian citizen. Despite this, identification and deportation of illegal migrants remains a problem.

The people living in bordering states have faced a dilemma. In the case of West Bengal, people have ethnic, linguistic and cultural similarity with the migrants coming from across the border. In some cases, Hindu population has moved after facing persecution. In these circumstances, it becomes difficult for people to oppose illegal migrants. But even in West Bengal, people have been forced to take a stand after large number of Muslim migrants started coming to the state, who were mostly economic migrants. This dramatically changed the demographic situation in the bordering districts. In fact, this led to a decline in law and order situation, thereby forcing natives to migrate to urban areas in search of safety and security.

The opposition to migrants has been clearer in states like Assam, where migrants face resistance as they are of different ethnic and linguistic origin. Assamese see them as threat to their culture. The migration to Assam from East Bengal has been taking place since pre-independence days. Even at that time, it was resented by the Assamese nationalists, but little could be done as it was considered

2   Revealed to author during an interaction with Indian border guards.
3   This information was collected from field visit to Dhubri.

internal migration and political parties like Muslim League were actively encouraging it.

In post-independence period Assamese resistance to illegal migration has built up. It led to a massive agitation in 1979, finally leading to Assam Accord in 1985. Though Assam accord managed to weaken the protest movement, it has not been able to solve the issue. The people of Assam are still resenting the presence of Bangladeshis among their midst.

The role of civil society becomes important in highlighting the problems like illegal migration. But unfortunately civil society has not been able to take a united stand over the issue, while groups like All Assam Students Union (AASU) or other similar society groups have opposed migration, many minority organizations have sought to defend them by making it a larger issue of security of all minorities. They argue that any action against illegal migrants often leads to harassment of genuine Muslim citizens of India. This has only complicated the whole issue.

The role played by various political parties has also not led to improvement of situation. The political parties have tried to present the issue according to their own political agenda. Interestingly, even parties like Asom Gana Parishad (AGP) who fought election on the issue of illegal migration, did little to ameliorate the situation while in power. The main opposition Bharatiya Janta Party (BJP) differentiated illegal migrants and considered Hindu migrants as refugees and Muslim migrants as illegal. This approach helped parties to create a base among the migrants and caste Assamese Hindus, but it also gave communal overtone to the whole problem. Similarly, many top Congress leaders when out of power wrote against illegal migration, but once in power retracted all they had said earlier.

As the number of migrants increase especially in states like Assam and West Bengal, the ability of political parties to even talk about this issue has started dipping. Sometime back AGP wanted to conduct a survey to check whether its association with the BJP had led to decline in its support base among the minorities. The illegal migrants who initially looked to Congress to seek protection are now not averse to form their own political organization. Extremist organizations like SIMI, Tablighi Jamaat and Jamiat-ul-Ulema Hind are active among them. In fact, fourteen similar organizations supported Assam United Democratic Front (AUDF) an exclusivist Muslim formation which contested both national as well as state assembly elections.

Though formed just a few months before the assembly election, AUDF bagged third largest number of votes capturing 10 assembly seats. The lesson from Assam seems to be that despite a fragmented polity, there was sufficient consolidation of Muslim votes behind an upapologetically Muslim Political Outfit to ensure electoral victory despite very high overall voter turnouts.[4] In their private confabulations, the party envisions itself as the political rallying point for Bangladeshi Muslims.[5] Security implications of emergence of political Islam in a region with over 30 per cent Muslim population, with portents of becoming a Muslim majority state in future, presence of nearly a dozen jehadi groups and over 1,500 km long border with a potentially radicalized Bangladesh can well be imagined. The ISI, DGFI and the Islamists are bound to exploit this in the days to come. This party has already emerged as a major political force and it is feared that in the coming elections now Congress would be forced to tie up with them to remain in power. This has caused further unease among the natives, who see political power slipping from their hand through this development.

The illegal migrants causing demographic change and thereby causing change in poltical agenda of political parties is not limited to West Bengal and Assam. Even in states like Bihar certain districts have been swamped by Bangladeshis. This has made parties like Lok Janshakti Party (LJP), to talk of legitimizing the status of

---

4   Islamic Vote Bank Politics - Ominous Portents for India Monday, June 12, 2006 http://o3.indiatimes.com/yossarin/archive/2006/06/12/776699. aspx

5   Ajit Doval, Impending storm, The Times of India, 25 Jan 2007, http:// timesofindia.indiatimes.com/articleshow/1435136.cms

Bangladeshis.[6] The Bangladeshi migrants have entered into even those states which are restricted for even Indians. They have gone into large numbers in Nagaland, a tribal state protected by inner line permit. To penetrate into Nagaland, they first settled in Dimapur, an area free from restriction. They have also now married a large number of local women, and given rise to new community known as Sumiyas. This has facilitated their entry deep into the state.[7]

Use of this method has ensured that along with Indian state even the terror outfits are helpless. Though Naga terror groups tried to restrict the number of Bangladeshi migrants by putting a quota on illegal migrants, the reluctance of locals for manual work has ensured that Bangladeshis enter in the state in large numbers. This kind of infiltration would have serious implications for small states like Nagaland, who have a small population. Bangladeshis in the state are now no longer limited to manual work. Like in Assam, they are also businessmen and landowners. The political impact of this kind of demographic change would be seen in not too distant future.

The cumulative effect of all these factors has been that unabated illegal migration has been taking place from Bangladesh and the Indian state despite its intention to stop migration has been able to do almost nothing.

IMPLICATIONS

The illegal migration to India will have serious implications for the country in the days to come. At present there is no large scale migration to India from Pakistan and Afghanistan, but it is alarming from the side of Bangladesh. This will have various implications for the country.

---

6   Paswan wants Indian citizenship for Bangladeshis, Merinews, 7 September 2008 at http://www.merinews.com/article/paswan-wants-indian-citizenship-for-bangladeshis/140674.shtml

7   M. Amarjeet Singh, A Study on Illegal Immigration into North-east India: The Case of Nagaland,"IDSA occasional paper No. 8, November 2009 p.23 at http://www.idsa.in/system/files/OccasionalPaper8_NagalandIllegalImmigrationl.pdf

SOCIAL

The increasing number of migrants has started creating social tension in many Indian states. This situation could be seen especially in northeastern states and West Bengal. In metropolitan cities where there is large congregation of Bangladeshi population, there is no organized protest from the public because generally people do not oppose such things till the time it starts directly hurting them. In Assam, this social tension is because natives feel that their language and culture would be threatened by the increasing presence of Bangladeshi population. In West Bengal too people in bordering districts are concerned as large number of Bangladeshis come from across the border endangering their safety and security.

ECONOMIC

The social tension is also increasing because of the economic reasons. Initially, Bangladeshis fulfilled the need of cheap labour. But over a period of time they have themselves become landowners and businessmen. In fact, in Assam Bodos claim that 37 percent of tribal land has got transferred into hands of Bangladeshi population. This led to a series of clashes between Bodos and Bangladeshis in lower Assam districts.[8] In these clashes lakhs of people were displaced and had to live in refugees camps. This tension is likely to further increase as pressure on land increases and per capita land holdings comes down.

It has been often argued that Bangladeshis fulfill the need of cheap labour. By this probably it is implied that India should adopt a softer approach towards illegal migration. Here it would be useful to remember that India itself is a developing country. It also has a large 'below poverty line' population that subsists on less than a dollar. There is no doubt that Indian economy has been expanding in recent years, but its benefits should first flow to poor population of India. The poverty of people and backwardness of certain regions has allowed Maoists to take root. A red corridor supposedly exist in India.

---

8   Kishalay Bhatacharjee, Communal tension brewing in Assam, August 19, 2008, at http://www.ndtv.com/convergence/ndtv/story. aspx?id=NEWEN20080062143&ch=8/19/2008%201:12:00%20PM

Clearly, any newly created job should go to Indian poor, before it is grabbed by an illegal Bangladeshi migrant. Any tolerance to illegal migration would further complicate the already existing cacophonous situation.

POLITICAL

In a democracy where every vote counts, the presence of large Bangladeshi population is bound to have serious political implications. It is alleged that states like West Bengal, initially encouraged illegal migration from Bangladesh hoping to use illegal migrants as vote banks. This strategy was adopted especially by the left parties. Few decades later, however these parties have realized to their chagrin that the political affiliation of these illegal migrants have changed and under the influence of growing extremism in Bangladesh they have even become a security threat to the state.

In Assam, initially illegal Bangladeshi migrants sided with Congress, but as their number swells many political outfits are coming up which are exclusively talking of their interests. This had also started political consolidation on communal lines. A manifestation of this is Assam United Democratic Front (AUDF) which is supported by Jamiat-ul-Ulema Hind and 14 other similar organizations. At least, five constituencies in the state have now become minority dominated and the other five are on the verge of becoming so. Religious and linguistic minorities in Assam hold the key to winning elections in at least 40 of the 126 assembly constituencies.[9] Some even say that now the situation has reached such a stage where no party can think of winning the election without the help of minorities in the state. It is feared that balance would further tilt in their favour and major political parties like Congress would have no option but to ally with AUDF if they want to remain in power. But even this strategy would work for a short period before political power shifts decisively in the hands of political outfits supported by illegal migrants.

9　　Anand Kumar, Assam: Illegal Immigration and IMDT Act, South Asia Analysis Group, Paper No. 1484, 3 August 2005 at http://www.saag. org/common/uploaded_files/paper1484.html

It may also lead to Assam type agitation in other states. Chances of this are great in Manipur where an influential civil society organization, the United Committee Manipur (UCM), published a 231-page report, 'Influx of Migrants into Manipur: A Threat to the Indigenous Ethnic People' in December 2005, indicating that migrants from Myanmar, Bangladesh and Nepal would, in 30 years' time, "either marginalise or wipe out all the ethnic groups" in the State.[10]

SECURITY IMPLICATIONS

The Indian government has recently started looking closely at the problem of illegal migration because of the suspected involvement of Bangladeshis in several terror incidents. A Bangladeshi national was found involved in suicide blast that took place at STF camp in Hyderabad.[11] Bangladeshi nationals were also suspected to be involved in serial blast that took place in many Indian cities in the year 2008. In Jaipur serial blasts bombs were tied on a bicycle which is hallmark of HUJI. Reports have also indicated that Bangladeshi terror outfit HUJI is trying to establish camps in districts of lower Assam where a large Bangladeshi population illegally lives.

HUJI and groups allied to Jamaat-e-Islami Bangladesh are active in West Bengal. The intelligence report of West Bengal Home Ministry has noted seven such outfits of which four are especially important. They are Jamait-e-Islami-e-Hind, Jamait-Ahle-Hadis, Students Islamic Organisation (sio) and Students Islamic Movement of India (simi).[12]

The illegal migration has changed demography around the Siliguri

10 Bibhu Prasad Routray, Sandipani Dash, The Northeast: Infiltration Woes, Volume 4, No. 46, May 29, 2006 at http://www.satp.org/ satporgtp/sair/Archives/4_46.htm

11 SUHRID SANKAR CHATTOPADHYAY, HAROON HABIB, Challenges in the East, Frontline, Volume 23 - Issue 01, Jan. 14 - 27, 2006 at http://www.flonnet.com/fl2301/stories/20060127006201100. htm

12 Soutik Biswas, Unease In The East: Has the ISI found a haven along the porous Indo-Bangla border? http://www.outlookindia.com/printarticle. aspx?207852

Corridor. In Siliguri corridor demographic profile within a 5-kilometre belt of the international border with Bangladesh has undergone rapid changes. This has happened primarily due to illegal immigration from Bangladesh. Bangladeshis have been encouraged to settle in this area because of thin policing. Though subsequently effort has been made to secure greater co-ordination in operations of the security forces the population complexion has already changed significantly.

In this area there is Mushrooming growth of mosques and madrassas. The dreaded Harkat-ul-Mujahiddeen (HuM) has spread its tentacles in the region.[13] Tabligh-e-Jamaat is also reportedly active around the Shiliguri Corridor and has close links with HUM.[14] The general activity of the organisation is discreet but it includes anti-India propaganda. Islami NGOs and trusts are also active with Islamist agenda. Besides, gunrunning is a key security concern of the area. The increased activity of the ISI has endangered the security of the Siliguri corridor. ISI attempted sabotage in 1999 following a bomb blast at New Jalpaiguri Station.

It is feared that increasing Bangladeshi population in Assam and West Bengal might lead to demand for greater Bangladesh. In many places, it has been found that illegal Bangladeshi population residing in bordering areas is using Bangladeshi SIM cards because most of their relatives are still in Bangladesh and calling through Bangladeshi SIM cards makes them pay less.[15] This does not only indicate erosion of state authority on Indian side of the border but is also a security threat.

IMPACT ON INTER-STATE RELATIONS

The problem of illegal migration is also causing problem in inter-state relations. When a train full of Bangladeshi migrants was

---

13   Pinaki Bhattacharya, The Shiliguri Corridor – Question Mark on Security, South Asia Terrorism Portal, at http://www.satp.org/satporgtp/publication/faultlines/volume10/Article7.htm

14   Ibid

15   Ravik Bhattacharya, Bangla SIMs in Bengal areas ring alarm bells in Delhi, The Indian Express, 25 May 2010 at http://www.indianexpress.com/news/bangla-sims-in-bengal-areas-ring-alarm-bells-in-delhi/623191/2

sent from Maharashtra for deportation to Bangladesh, the left front government of West Bengal claimed that they were legitimate citizens of the state. Similarly, People in Assam feel that illegal Bangladeshi migrants coming through West Bengal are simply sent to Assam. In northeast, all other states blame Assam of sending illegal migrants after these migrants procure fake documents in the state. In fact, Assam has often been a gateway for illegal migrants.[16] Bangladeshi migrants have even got settled in territory that is disputed between Assam and Nagaland.

IMPACT ON INDO-BANGLADESH RELATIONS

The illegal migration from Bangladesh has been a thorny issue in Indo-Bangladesh relations. India has been pointing to this problem but Bangladesh has steadfastly refused to accept that any Bangladeshi is illegally staying in India. Though privately all top Bangladeshi political leaders and bureaucrats acknowledge that a large number of their citizens are illegally staying in India, but officially Bangladesh has not accepted illegal migration. What is worse, whenever India tries to deport illegal Bangladeshi, it leads to a stand off on the border.

POSSIBLE SCENARIOS

The phenomenon of illegal migration might see four different trends depending upon how situation pans out in next twenty years in Bangladesh as well as India. The possible outcomes on the basis of certain drivers (factors that would lead to this change) are discussed below.

1. Rate of illegal migration would remain constant

The rate of illegal migration would remain constant, if the present situation continues for next twenty years. The present situation have been caused by successive democratic and military governments who failed to improve the economic situation in Bangladesh. The increasing pressure on land, few economic opportunities, frequent

---

16 Anand Kumar, Bangladesh: Assam as Gateway for Illegal Immigrants, South Asia Analysis Group, Paper No. 1444, 7 July 2005 at http://www.saag.org/common/uploaded_files/paper1444.html

natural calamities have prompted Bangladeshi people to move across the border. They were helped in this exercise by poor border management on Indian side (of course, little border management exists on Bangladeshi side, but since India is facing the brunt of this problem, it has to pull up its socks). The weak resistance offered by democratic governments in India who are always looking for vote banks and corrupt civil administration has only encouraged them. India will also have to create a system whereby new jobs created by economic growth go to Indian poor. On the other hand, if Bangladeshis manage to sell this idea that they offer cheap labour for which India has no alternative then the migration would continue unabated.

2. Migration would rise

The illegal migration from Bangladesh would rise if political and economic situation worsens in that country. A further rise in religious extremism would lead to exodus of minorities. If poor economic conditions continue or situation worsens then it would result in large number of economic migrants. It is also feared that Bangladesh would be one of the worst sufferer of climate change. A large scale climate change would lead to submergence of vast tracts of lands in Bangladesh. Bangladesh is prone to natural disasters. If these natural disasters become more frequent and deadly in their impact, then it would also result in increased migration from that country.

3. Migration would come down

The illegal migration from Bangladesh would come down if political and economic situation improves in that country. An improved political situation would instill confidence in people in the government of the day. At present, Shaikh Hasina led Awami League government is in power in Bangladesh. This government enjoys the image of being non-communal and pro-people. After coming to power, Shaikh Hasina also talked about creating a digital Bangladesh. No doubt, this would be a very difficult task, but if the government continues to work purposely, and gets elected couple of times of more in succession then it is possible that things might change in Bangladesh. This government is already working to check extremism and terrorism in the country. In this effort, it has been reasonably successful. If future governments of Bangladesh manage to successfully improve the economic conditions in the country, then Bangladeshi population would have less urge to migrate to a foreign country. Along with this, the quantum of illegal migration would also depend on how India manages its border. An effective border management might discourage migrants from coming to India.

4. Illegal migration from Bangladesh stops completely

At present this appears to be a wild card and highly unlikely to happen in near future. However, this can happen if there is a dramatic change in political and economic conditions of Bangladesh. If the Bangladesh prospers economically and becomes politically stable then there would be little reason for its population to move to some other country. The political leaders of Bangladesh and its bureaucrats to deny the phenomenon of illegal migration claim that economic situation is far better in Bangladesh. At present however this may not be the reality, but it is possible that if political stability comes to country and it grows at a fast pace then the local population would be averse to migrate. This is also possible if a relative decline takes place in India or social conditions become less secure either under the threat of Maoists or other terrorists.

CONCLUDING OBSERVATIONS

The illegal migration to India, especially from Bangladesh is a serious issue, which is highly unlikely to be checked on its own. If this phenomenon continues unabated then it would have social, political, economic and security implications for India. It has already widened social cleavages in many parts of the country. If India tries to absorb inceasing number of Bangladeshis it would make the social and economic situation further volatile. It is often argued that illegal migrants serve an economic purpose as they provide cheap labour, but on closer observation we would find that they are actually economic burden for the country. They consume a significant part of social welfare schemes carried out by the government of India. The country spends large sums of money on their identification but their deportation rarely takes place because the Bangladesh government refuses to accept them as their citizens. Though most illegal migrants originate from Bangladesh, that country would do little to prevent them from spilling over into India. In such a situation, it is advisable for India to take necessary steps, as it is this country which is at the receiving end.

13
West Asia 2030: Drivers and Scenarios
—S. Samuel C. Rajiv

West Asia[1] is one of the world's largest energy suppliers. It is also home to many kingdoms and sheikdoms, which are inherently non-democratic regimes. Security deficits exist between the countries of the region, exacerbated by extra-regional influences and interventions. The Iranian nuclear issue has brought to the forefront concerns regarding the possible nuclearisation of the region and its strategic consequences.

The following sections identify and delineate seven high-impact strategic drivers of change – energy; freedom and democracy; Israel-Palestine issue; socio-economic situation; Iraqi stability; external relations; and nuclear concerns. These drivers are will play a crucial role in shaping West Asia in 2030. While there is greater certainty about certain drivers viz., the region retaining its position as an important energy powerhouse, uncertainties surround developments regarding the other drivers. After an examination of current trends and available indicators related to the above drivers, three plausible scenarios are intended to be presented.

---

1 For purposes of this article, West Asia is defined to include Syria, Lebanon, Israel, Palestinian Territories, Jordan, Iran, Iraq, Kuwait, Saudi Arabia, United Arab Emirates, Oman, and Yemen. Turkey straddles the line between West Asia and Europe. For purposes of consistency, only its role relative to the delineated drivers is examined.

I. Drivers: Issues and Trends

A. The Energy Card

West Asia has more than 60 per cent of the world's proven oil reserve of 75.325 billion barrels, as well as 2,585.351 trillion cubic feet of natural gas reserves.[2] Saudi Arabia, the region's biggest producer, has proven gas reserves of 263 trillion cubic feet and is currently producing about 9 million cubic feet a day. Its current petrochemical production of 60 million tonnes is about 8 per cent of global production and over 60 per cent of GCC production.[3]

West Asia continues to feed the world's insatiable energy demands, which is expected to rise by more than 40 percent by 2030. The US Energy Information Administration's Annual International Energy Outlook 2009 states that world oil consumption will rise to 678 quadrillion Btu in 2030, from 472 quadrillion Btu in 2006. India and China are expected to be responsible for over 50 per cent of the rise in this demand.[4] OECD countries which currently consume over 50 per cent of the total energy produced are expected to consume about 40 per cent of the world's total by 2030.[5] The share of the Organisation of Petroleum Exporting Countries (OPEC) in world oil production is expected to remain at the current levels of over 40 per cent of the world total in 2030. Of this, the share of Persian Gulf states will be close to 30 per cent - 30 million barrels per day as against OPEC's 44 million barrels per day.[6]

However, as countries like the United States follow through on measures to become energy independent and as new sources of energy like tar sands are discovered, as in Canada, the primacy

2   http://www.eia.doe.gov/emeu/international/reserves.html

3   'Saudi Oil Min: Saudi to boost gas output significantly by 2015', Dec 2009, at http://online.wsj.com/article/BT-CO-20091209-700122.html

4   'India, China will increasingly rely on oil imports', November 19, 2008, at http://www.thaindian.com/newsportal/india-news/india-china-will-increasingly-rely-on-oil-imports-by-2030_100120991.html

5   International Energy Outlook, 2009, at http://www.eia.doe.gov/oiaf/ieo/

6   Ibid.

of the region as the world's energy power house could be under threat. The United States for instance imports around 17 per cent of its energy requirements from the region currently, as compared to 28 per cent in 1975. President Obama has termed 'dependence' on foreign oil one of the "most serious threats" to America, which "bankrolls dictators, pays for nuclear proliferation, and funds both sides of our struggle against terrorism."[7] Since taking over the presidency, Mr. Obama has initiated a series of executive and policy measures designed to ensure American energy independence. His comprehensive energy plan, 'New Energy for America,' envisages securing over a quarter of America's energy from renewable sources by 2025. New automobile emissions standards to be effective from 2011 envisage saving over 2 million barrels of oil per day.[8] Mr. Obama's first budget had significant provisions for domestic energy efficiency programmes, measures to increase America's renewable energy capacities, substantial funds to conduct research into low-carbon technologies – all efforts geared towards creating a 'clean energy economy' and increase its energy independence. Addressing Americans on June 15, 2010 in the aftermath of the British Petroleum-owned oil rig explosion off the Gulf Coast, Obama reiterated the imperative need to "end America's century-long addiction to fossil fuels". He pointed out that "each day, we send nearly $1 billion of our wealth to foreign countries for their oil." Obama added that "the tragedy unfolding on our coast is the most painful and powerful reminder yet that the time to embrace a clean energy future is now."[9]

7   'Remarks by the President on Jobs, Energy Independence, and Climate Change', East Room of the White House, January 26, 2009, at http://www.whitehouse.gov/blog_post/Fromperiltoprogress/, accessed December 8, 2009

8   The White House, "Remarks by the President on Jobs, Energy Independence, and Climate Change," January 26, 2009, at http://www.whitehouse.gov/blog_post/Fromperiltoprogress/

9   See 'Remarks by the President to the Nation on the BP Oil Spill', June 15, 2010, at http://www.whitehouse.gov/the-press-office/remarks-president-nation-bp-oil-spill

Despite the Obama administration's 'clean energy activism', and analysts like Edward Luttwak insisting that the West Asia/Middle East is 'The Middle of Nowhere'[10] despite its oil, it is a fact that coal, oil and natural gas will still account for nearly 80 per cent of US energy mix in 2030.[11] America's share in world energy consumption though is expected to decrease from the current levels of about 22 per cent to 17 per cent by 2030. Another possible spoke in Obama's energy plans could be the difficulties in realising the promise of alternative fuels. For instance, Obama envisaged an increase of the use of bio-fuels to 60 billion gallons by 2030. However, the high price of corn from which most of the ethanol is currently produced has ensured that plans to build new factories producing ethanol have become non-economical.[12]

Given the above indicators, the pivotal position of West Asia in supplying world energy needs is expected to continue, despite the promise of alternative fuels (bio-fuels), nuclear energy, or renewable energy sources like wind and solar power.

THE INTERNAL DYNAMICS

Drivers from B-E relate to internal dynamics of the countries of the region.

B. Freedom and Democracy

Liberal democracy as it is understood and exercised in other parts of the world does not exist in the Middle East. The region is full of hereditary kingdoms, sheikdoms, and religious theocracies.

---

10   Luttwak also notes that the Jewish-Palestine conflict since 1921 has resulted in fewer than 100,000 deaths, a large number but which is equivalent to the number of people who get killed in "a season of conflict in Darfur." See Edward Luttwak, 'The Middle of Nowhere', *Prospect Magazine*, Issue 134, May 2007, at http://www.prospect-magazine. co.uk/article_details.php?id=9302, accessed April 28, 2007.

11   EIA Annual Energy Outlook 2009, Early Release Review, at http://www.eia.doe.gov/oiaf/aeo/overview.html

12   See Clifford Krauss, "Ethanol, Just Recently a Savior, Is Struggling," *New York Times*, February 12, 2009, at http://www.nytimes.com/2009/02/12/business/12ethanol.html?ref=todayspaper

According to Freedom House 2009 rankings, no single country of the region is 'free'. Turkey, Kuwait, Bahrain and Jordan are ranked as 'partly free' while Qatar, Iran, Iraq, Saudi Arabia and Syria are ranked as 'not free'.[13]

While countries like Iran conduct elections for the post of president, the *'Velayat-e-Faqih'* (Rule of Jurisprudence) in vogue since the Islamic Revolution of 1979 entails that final decision-making powers remain vested in the authority of the clerics like Ayatollah Ali Khamenei, who is currently the Supreme National Leader. The controversy surrounding the June 2009 presidential elections revealed the deep divisions and discontent in urban areas against the ruling dispensation. Religious opposition to the rule of the Ayatollahs is also growing, as is evident from the charges made by one of the 'fathers' of the Islamic Revolution, Ali Montazeri, who has stated that a "political system based on force, oppression, changing people's votes ... is condemned and illegitimate."[14]

C. The Turkish Question

Turkey's 'slow and steady embrace' of radical Islam domestically since the coming to power of Recep Tayyip Erdogan to further its geo-political ambitions meanwhile is being seen with concern by its Western (and NATO) supporters and erstwhile allies like Israel. For instance, Turkish support for the Hamas dispensation in Gaza as well as its role in the floating aid incident is a case is point. The Iran-Turkey-Brazil nuclear swap deal of May 17, 2010 under the terms of which Iran agreed to send 1,200 tonnes of low-enriched uranium to Turkey and from then on Russia for enrichment is another case.[15] Both cases illustrate a Turkish desire

---

13   See   http://www.freedomhouse.org/uploads/fiw09/FIW09_Tables&
      GraphsForWeb.pdf, accessed December 8, 2009

14   Michael Slackman, 'Cleric Wields Religion to Challenge Iran's Theocracy',
      November 22, 2009, at http://www.nytimes.com/2009/11/22/world/
      middleeast/22ayatollah.html?ref=todayspaper, accessed November 23,
      2009.

15   For an early assessment, see S. Samuel C. Rajiv, 'Iran-Turkey Nuclear
      Swap Deal', May 19, 2010, at http://www.idsa.in/idsacomments/
      IranTurkeyNuclearSwapDeal_sscrajiv_190510

to expand its role in an area where it was a colonial power in the not too distant past. They also point to Turkish frustrations at continued European intransigence in not taking their candidature to become part of the European Union seriously.

D. Israel-Palestine Issue

Israel's military offensive against persistent Palestinian rocket attacks which began in late December 2008 was wound down after 22 days in January 2009. The action generated lot of controversy as it resulted in the death of over a thousand Palestinians. A UN fact-finding mission headed by South African prosecutor Richard Goldstone found fault with both the Israeli government and Palestinian militant groups for undertaking actions which amounted to "crimes against humanity."[16] The UN Human Rights Council endorsed the conclusions of the Goldstone Report in October 2009. UN Security Council censuring Israel for its actions or referring the case to the International Criminal Court was however slim.

The Palestinian issue continues to fester with all sides to the conflict as well as key interlocutors seemingly agreeing on the goal of establishing a Palestinian state but not able to agree on the contours of the process to achieve that 'elusive' goal. Intra-Palestinian conflict (Fatah and Hamas) as well as Israeli intransigence (on settlements issues or on removal of the checkpoints which it contends are essential for its security) further complicates the situation. The US under the Obama administration has remained engaged at a high-level, with President Obama and Secretary Clinton vowing to help establish a Palestinian state sooner than later. The administration also appointed George Mitchell as Special Envoy, almost as soon as it took over to impart greater dynamism into its peace-making efforts. Former British Prime

---

16 The report is available at http://www2.ohchr.org/english/bodies/hrcouncil/specialsession/9/docs/UNFFMGC_Report.pdf; See also Neil MacFarquhar, 'Inquiry Finds Gaza War Crimes From Both Sides', September 16, 2009, at http://www.nytimes.com/2009/09/16/world/middleeast/16gaza.html?fta=y, accessed September 17, 2009.

Minister Tony Blair is also playing a key role as the Special Envoy of the Quartet (US, Russia, EU, UN).

As noted above, the incident involving the Mavi Marmara and the Turkish aid flotilla on May 30, 2010 has further complicated the situation. Nine 'aid workers' died when Israeli commandoes stormed the ship in international waters on the charges that the ship could be a conduit for arms and ammunition for the Hamas. In the aftermath of the international outcry, Israel has established a commission of enquiry to look into the issue. It has also lifted some of the restrictions imposed as part of the embargo.

F. The Socio-Economic Driver

Difficult socio-economic conditions are also fuelling discontent in these countries. Four rounds of UN-imposed economic and trade sanctions in Iran on account of its nuclear programme have compounded the country's problems, along with high inflation rates of nearly 20 per cent, according to some sources. Lack of crude oil refining facilities within the country, despite being OPEC's second biggest oil producer and the fourth largest exporter in the world, imply that Tehran still imports petroleum products worth more than $5 billion annually. Lack of money to pay for these imports forced the government to go in for rationing of petroleum products which have led to discontent (riots in June 2007 for instance).

The Dubai debt crisis, which according to some estimates is worth $60-100 billion, had the potential to hurt the economic dynamism of the United Arab Emirates (UAE), which is an important player in the Gulf Cooperation Council (GCC), apart from Saudi Arabia, Bahrain, Kuwait, Oman, and Qatar. However, its impact was minimised when Abu Dhabi stepped in to salvage the situation to some extent. For instance, reports noted that Abu Dhabi heavily invested in Dubai debt bonds to the extent of over $15 billion.[17]

---

17 James Ashton, 'Abu Dhabi rides in to rescue Dubai', November 29, 2009, http://business.timesonline.co.uk/tol/business/markets/the_gulf/article6936251.ece

More pertinently, over 200,000 Indians working in the construction sector were expected to be hit as a result of the economic slowdown caused by the debt crisis. More than 5 million Indians live and work in the GCC states, as well as other migrant labour. Nearly 40 per cent of the population of these GCC countries is made up of foreigners.[18] These people are not only an essential part of the economy of the country they work in but also of their country of origin as they send back substantial sums of money. India for instance received $52 billion in remittances in 2008, over 25 per cent of it from the Gulf States. China was in the second position having received $49 billion. The GCC countries also account for nearly 25 percent of India's total trade and over two-thirds of its energy requirements.[19]

Despite the Dubai crisis, the GCC states have laid out big plans for the future. The capital of UAE, Abu Dhabi for instance has put in place an ambitious agenda for 2030 to comprehensively develop its infrastructure and tourism facilities among other assets to transform itself into a global hub of business.[20]

G. Iraqi Stability

Iraq has begun to crawl back from the sectarian mayhem witnessed in recent past. Over 100,000 civilians lost their lives as well as more than 4,600 coalition soldiers.[21] Nearly 3 million people have been internally displaced since 2003. US combat forces are set to withdraw completely from the country in tune with the

---

18 The figure is over 80 per cent in UAE. See Andres Kapiszewski, 'Arab versus Asian migrant workers in the GC Countries', May 2006, at http://www.un.org/esa/population/meetings/EGM_Ittmig_Arab/P02_Kapiszewski.pdf, accessed December 9, 2009.

19 P.R. Kumaraswamy, 'India should focus on the Middle East', *Express Buzz*, November 26, 2009, at http://www.expressbuzz.com/edition/story.aspx?Title=India+should+focus+on+the+Middle+East&artid=m0zHC3kOW6M=&SectionID=d16Fdk4iJhE=&MainSectionID=HuSUEmcGnyc=&SectionName=aVlZZy44Xq0bJKAA84nwcg==&SEO=, accessed December 9, 2009.

20 See http://www.ameinfo.com/abu_dhabi_2030/, accessed October 30, 2009

21 http://www.icasualties.org/, accessed December 8, 2009.

provisions of the Status of Forces agreement by August 2010 and all US forces are set to exit by December 2011. US forces are currently not involved in security duties within the confines of Iraqi cities, unless explicitly required and authorised by Iraqi authorities. A landmark electoral law increasing the number of constituencies to better represent the Iraqi population was finally passed in December 2009 ahead of national elections scheduled for January 2010. According to this law, the number of seats in parliament will be expanded to 325, from the present 275.

Issues of contention still remain, including the distribution of oil revenue, specifically the exploration and production of oil and natural gas in Kurdish regions, sectarian tensions, suicide attacks like those at the Iraqi Justice Ministry offices on October 25 that killed nearly 150 people and the coordinated car bomb attacks in Baghdad in early December 2009 that killed more than 120. However, bright spots included Sunni-Shia political alignments formed ahead of parliamentary elections that have the potential to heal sectarian wounds. These elections were scheduled to be held in January 2010 but were eventually held in March. Both the rival blocks claimed victory and eventually, former Prime Minister Ayad Allawi was declared a narrow winner, defeating incumbent Nouri al-Maliki after a period of political vacuum that saw a dangerous rise of suicide bombings and civilian casualties.

H. External Relations

In the aftermath of the Israel-Lebanon war of 2006, Lebanon has stabilised with a pro-Western government led by Saad Hariri being formed after it defeated a Hezbollah-led coalition in parliamentary elections held in June 2009. But the difficulties encountered by Mr. Hariri over cabinet formation indicate the existence of deep divisions. A tentative peace still holds at the Lebanese-Israel border, buttressed by the presence of international peacekeepers and at the Israel-Syria border.

Despite occasional threats to Saudi leadership from elements like the al-Qaeda which have vowed to overthrow the al-Sauds, the Custodian of the Holy Mosques remains firmly in control.

Tensions across its border with Yemen on account of the rebellion of the Houthis have flared up in recent times and Riyadh has undertaken cross-border missions in pursuit. The Houthis belonging to a Shiite branch of Islam and allegedly receiving support from Iran has added to geo-political complications.

The 2003 US invasion of Iraq has made Iran the sole contender for the crown of regional hegemon, apart from Saudi Arabia. With the Iraqi threat removed, Iran has begun to acquire greater stature in tune with its historical and geographical advantages.[22] The growth of Shiite Iran as the pre-dominant power in the Persian Gulf, buttressed by its nuclear power and long-range missile capabilities, continues to unsettle the Sunni-majority Arab States. Jordan's King Abdullah has warned of a 'Shiite crescent' of power stretching from Iran to Lebanon via Iraq and Syria.[23]

I. Nuclear Concerns[24]

Iran's nuclear pursuit has brought into sharp focus the vulnerabilities of its immediate and extended neighbours to the fore. Uncertainties regarding the Iranian nuclear programme have been cited as a possible reason behind the Arab states pursuit of nuclear power.[25] The March 2007 GCC Summit for instance warned of "a dangerous and destructive nuclear arms

22 Robert Kaplan for instance notes that geographical determinism – Iran being "the greater Middle East's universal joint" - ensured that it was "the ancient world's first superpower." See 'The Revenge of Geography', *Foreign Policy*, May/June 2009, at http://www.foreignpolicy.com/story/cms.php?story_id=4862

23 Noah Feldman, 'Islam, Terror and the Second Nuclear Age', *The New York Times*, October 29, 2006, at http://www.nytimes.com/2006/10/29/magazine/29islam.html?ex=1183176000&en=553a128f6cd9cad0&ei=5070

24 Parts of this section draw from S. Samuel C. Rajiv, 'Global 'Renaissance' of Nuclear Power: Drivers, Issues, Prospects', in Arvind Gupta (ed.), *India in a Changing Global Nuclear Order* (New Delhi: Academic Foundation, 2009), pp. 63-76.

25 IISS, 'Arab nuke ambitions stir arms race jitters', February 11, 2007, at http://www.iiss.org/whats-new/iiss-in-the-press/february-2007/arab-nuclear-ambitions-stir-arms-race-jitters

race in the region" and reiterated its support for a nuclear-weapons free zone.[26] Though Saudi Foreign Minister Prince Saud al-Faisal denied that the grouping's nuclear power plans were in reaction to the Iranian crisis, he however noted the nuclear issue was an "extra-burden" to the problems already facing the region. In reaction to the Iranian moves, UAE among GCC states has signed a 123 agreement with the US in January 2009, and the process was finally concluded in October 2009.[27] UAE intends to build 8 nuclear power plants at a cost of over $40 billions. Its first contract to build four reactors was won by a South Korean consortium in December 2009. The UAE will however not have any enrichment facilities on its soil and countries like France will most probably help enrich the UAE's uranium.

While Iran insists that its nuclear programme is purely meant for peaceful purposes and in tune with its rights as a signatory to the nuclear non-proliferation treaty (NPT), it has been under series of sanctions mandated by the UN Security Council. A stronger set of sanctions were imposed in June 2010 expanding their scope and severity. Tehran has also been censured by the IAEA for non-cooperation and for continued intransigence regarding its nuclear programme.

Israel on its part has been quite vociferous in advocating more robust action to prevent Iran from acquiring the expertise to produce a nuclear bomb. While US administrations, both under President Bush and President Obama, have not ruled out any option to deal with Tehran's nuclear ambitions, Washington has however proved to be a less than interested party in actively pursuing a military solution. President Obama, during his campaign speeches and in his public pronouncements after taking over, has acknowledged the 'dangers' of a nuclear Iran and his intent to prevent such an eventuality. Obama has called for

---

26 See 'At summit, Arabs warn of possible nuclear race in Middle East', *International Herald Tribune*, March 28, 2007, at http://www.iht.com/articles/ap/2007/03/29/africa/ME-GEN-Arab-Summit.php

27 Andrew Bast, 'Yes Virginia, There is a Mideast Nuke Deal', *Newsweek*, October 23, 2009, at http://www.newsweek.com/id/219233

"tough but direct diplomacy" to convince Iran to forgo its nuclear option. His "carrot and stick" approach holds the possibility of economic incentives and closer cooperation with the United States if it relents and the threat of even tougher economic sanctions if it does not. The breakdown of the agreement reached at Geneva in early October 2009 under which Iran would have transferred uranium to be enriched in Russia and France, and Iran's intention to construct 10 more nuclear reactors, have injected greater uncertainties into the situation.

Among the countries of the region, analysts believe that the state most likely to proliferate in response to the Iranian nuclear capability is Saudi Arabia. While latent nuclear capacities would give it the wherewithal to pursue weapons development in the future, Riyadh could also collaborate with China or Pakistan to achieve a nuclear deterrent.[28] Analysts speculate that the Israeli experience could be a model for the Saudi development of a nuclear deterrent, and that a policy of opacity offered the best chance for Riyadh to ensure its near and long-term survival in the Gulf balance of power.[29]

The Saudi-Pakistani nuclear connection is also worth pointing out. Suspicions abound that Riyadh has funded the Pakistani nuclear programme. The visit of Saudi Defence Minister Prince Sultan bin Abdulaziz Al Saud to the Kahuta facility in 1999 is cited as an indication of the closeness of the nuclear ties and the possibility that the Kingdom could acquire Pakistani nuclear warheads to be deployed on Chinese-made missiles like the CSS-2.[30] Former

28 For a study that shows that latent nuclear capacities led to decisions to pursue nuclear weapons development, see Stephen M. Meyer, *The Dynamics of Nuclear Proliferation* (Chicago: The University of Chicago Press, 1984)

29 See Richard L. Russell, 'A Saudi Nuclear Option?' *Survival*, 43(2), Summer 2001, pp. 69-79.

30 See Michael A. Levi, 'Would the Saudis go Nuclear?' *The New Republic*, 2003, at http://www.brookings.edu/views/articles/fellows/levi20030602. htm); Simon Henderson, 'Towards a Saudi Nuclear Option: The Saudi-Pakistani Summit', *The Washington Institute for Near East Policy*, Policy Watch 793, 2003, at http://www.washingtoninstitute.org/templateC05.

US President George W. Bush had expressed concerns about the dangers of a 'Sunni bomb,' and the possibility that countries of the region could seek the help of the only nuclear-armed Sunni state, Pakistan.[31] Riyadh's seeking nuclear weapons capability is however heavily dependent on the status of its relationship with Washington, which is currently strong. The GCC states have also called on Israel to renounce its nuclear weapons, noting that the IAEA standards and measures "should apply to all countries in the region without exceptions, including Israel."[32]

II. Plausible Scenarios

A. *Baseline Scenario 2030: 'The Show Goes On but gets amplified'*
West Asia in 2030 will continue to exhibit similar but amplified characteristics across the seven main drivers enumerated above. It will remain a vital energy hub, producing close to 30 per cent of world energy demand.

The various sheikhdoms and theocratic governments will continue to resist pressures to make their respective political systems more inclusive, though they will be less prone to undertake autocratic measures, for instance while suppressing disgruntled sections of foreigners living within their borders.

The number of foreigners living in GCC countries will rise to over 60 per cent of their overall population, from the current levels of 40 per cent. These will include over 15 million Indians. The increased percentage of these diaspora populations will bring greater pressures on the regimes to cater to their needs

php?CID=1671); Akaki Dvali, 'Will Saudi Arabia Acquire Nuclear Weapons?' NTI Issue Brief, Monterrey Institute of International Studies, March 2004, at http://www.nti.org/e_research/e3_40a.html

31   William J. Broad and David Sanger, 'With Eye on Iran, Rivals Also Want Nuclear Power', *The New York Times*, April 15, 2007, at http://www.nytimes.com/2007/04/15/world/middleeast/15sunnis.html?_r=1&ref=todayspaper&oref=login

32   'Saudi defends Gulf Arab atom plans, criticizes Iran', *Iranfocus.com*, March 5, 2007, at http://www.iranfocus.com/modules/news/article.php?storyid=10369

ASSUMPTIONS MATRIX

Baseline 'THE SHOW GOES ON BUT GETS AMPLIFIED'	Plausible Alternative 'RAPPROCHEMENT AND ENGAGEMENT'	Wildcard 'NUCLEAR JUNGLE'
West Asia remains a key global energy supplier	Palestinian state will have been formed; Hamas-Fatah join, recognised by Israel after Hamas changes its charter	Iranian radicals in power follow rabid anti-US policy, test a nuclear weapon; Israel, Saudi Arabia, Egypt and Turkey follow
West Asian regimes remain undemocratic and repressive	Stable Iraq will be one of the top 5 producers of oil in world; Oil wealth diminishes demands for Kurdish separatism	
Israel-Palestine imbroglio continues		
Current Turkish Islamist tendencies will increase marginally	Turkey goes back to its secular roots	
Region continues to attract Diaspora populations from South Asia		
Sectarian chasms exist and deepen in Iraq, including between Arab's and Kurds	US engages positively with Iran	
US remains hostile to Iran	'UAE Way' of nuclear power generation, with enrichment facilities abroad	
Iran fails to develop a nuclear weapon		

more effectively. Certain kind of labour reforms will be initiated, including health and education needs of children of workers, better oversight and thorough scrutiny of recruiting agencies to ensure greater accountability of work and living conditions, a degree of job security for specific categories of workers, like software programmers, medical personnel, and construction engineers among others.

Sectarian clashes will continue to occur in Iraq, and the Kurdish-

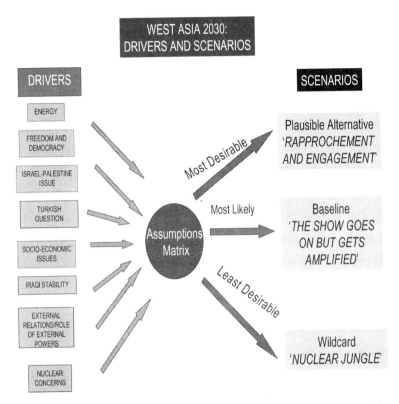

Arab chasm will widen. Despite increased oil wealth, the Kurdish imbroglio will continue to fester. Turkish Islamic tendencies will get amplified though it will not become too radical in its outlook.

Iran will find it difficult to develop a nuclear weapon, on account of technological and other difficulties. It will establish more nuclear power reactors, though under IAEA safeguards. Other countries of the region will also build nuclear power plants. There will be about 25 such plants operating, including in Iran, UAE, Saudi Arabia, and Jordan, for reasons of electricity generation, water desalination, and the prestige associated with running high-technology enterprises that can boost the region's self-confidence.

B. *Plausible Alternative Scenario: 'Rapprochement and Engagement'*
    This scenario considers the effect on West Asia of a move towards
    rapprochement and engagement by key interlocutors on some of
    the current contentious issues.

US-Iran rapprochement will have positively altered regional
conflict dynamics. Iranian nuclear bomb aspirations will have
been curtailed on account of the success of efforts of the P-5,
the IAEA and other key interlocutors. Trade and other sanctions
will have become too much of a burden to bear for the Iranian
population and the economic misery will eventually lead to the
overthrow of the radical elements. Moderates gain the upper
hand domestically and they calculate that a confrontationist
attitude with the West and US in particular is hurting Iran's
standing regionally. While they do not adopt an explicit pro-
West stance, a stable relationship will develop which will however
occasionally encounter occasional roadblocks, on issues like Iraq
and Lebanon.

A Palestinian state will have been formed after the Palestinians
rescind their claims on 'right of return.' Intra-Palestinian
differences, including between factions operating out of West
Bank and Gaza respectively, will still allow Israel to re-impose
periodic control by force. The Hamas and Fatah will have merged
into a pan-Palestinian organisation, a move supported by Israel
after Hamas modifies its charter to remove references to the
destruction of the Israel. Some of the major ministries of the
Palestinians dealing with West Bank issues will function out of
East Jerusalem but Israel will continue to exercise oversight on
external security and defence functions. The Palestinian state will
have internal security forces but will still lack a standing army
and a border force.

A relatively stable Iraq will have become one of the top 5 producers
of oil in the world, though the country occasionally experiences
sectarian spasms. Increased prosperity in the Iraqi Kurdish areas
on account of oil wealth will enable them to pressurise Baghdad
to bring to the attention of the authorities in Ankara the need to

improve the socio-economic conditions of their ethnic brethren across Iraq's border. Demands for a separate homeland for the Kurds will recede. Turkey meanwhile will have gone back to its secular roots and the Islamists will continue to suffer recurring defeats in national elections.

Most of the countries of the region allied with the West (like those of the GCC) will go the 'UAE way' in the nuclear power sector i.e., they will not have enrichment facilities on their soil but countries like France and Russia will do it for them at more economical rates than if they had to build the facilities themselves. More importantly, it will eliminate concerns about their nuclear intentions.

C.   *Wildcard Scenario: 'Nuclear Jungle*

Radicals continue to hold sway in Iran and it has enriched uranium sufficient for 25 bombs. It will also have tested a crude nuclear device near the mountains of Qom on November 4, 2024, the 45th anniversary of the storming of the US Embassy in 1979. Along with its formidable missile force, Tehran's nuclear capability makes it the undisputed regional hegemon, though it will find some difficulties in manufacturing warheads for missile cones.

Israel detonates a nuclear device in the Sinai desert a day after Iran tests its device, on November 5, 2024. It also fires a cruise missile from its latest Dolphin submarine to unequivocally convey to Tehran that it possesses robust nuclear deterrence capabilities.

Saudi Arabia will undertake urgent measures to gain a nuclear capability. It will have sufficiently enriched uranium from their nuclear power reactors to be able to afford 5-10 low grade bombs. Riyadh will detonate a nuclear device on September 23, 2027, its 95th foundation day. It is however not clear if it is an indigenous device or it is loaned from Islamabad. Saudi Arabia will also request and secure the services of Pakistani Air Force pilots to man its latest Tornado and Rafale fighter jets which will be modified to carry nuclear weapons.

Turkey and Egypt will also undertake measures to obtain independent nuclear capability but will be persuaded by Washington to accept an American nuclear umbrella. The 'nuclear jungle' in a region with serious security deficits presents clear and present dangers and challenges for countries like US, China, Russia and India.

POSTSCRIPT

Clearly, Scenario II is the most optimum while Scenario III will present the worst nightmares for policy makers. Efforts towards rapprochement need to be encouraged and pursued with greater vigour. A mutual give-and-take and strategic acuity is the need of the hour. Regional leaderships will also need to understand that rising economic stakes and closed political systems are an anathema, especially when means of communication explode and information dissemination can occur creatively, despite government clampdowns. The violence in Iran after the June 2009 elections and the use of blogs and phone cameras to disseminate information is a case in point. The dangers of non-engagement across a wide range of issues will need to be clearly delineated and impressed upon policy makers so that measured compromises can be reached.

14
Southeast Asia-2030

—Pankaj Jha

Within Asia, the economic growth as well as changing military capabilities has redefined perceptions about threats. Defence planning and modernization has been directly proportional to the threat perceptions well as alliance relationship of that particular country with the major powers in the region. Of late the international strategic scenario has been witnessing the evolution of coalition politics at international level and issue based support for international developments. This has put almost all the major powers on a sticky wicket and every power is trying to optimize its national interests with least possible costs. The scenario as of date is such that none of the multilateral organizations both at the international level and even at the regional level are capable of providing /assuring the complete security of the nation. Even more, few of the overenthusiastic strategic experts have negated the possibility of traditional wars among nations. The question is when the interstate conflicts have not diminished how the possibility of war can be discounted. The surge in enhancing defence capabilities is also dependent of the economic growth and allocation for defence. The economic growth depends largely on trade and investment. There is increasing interdependence among the economies and also there is need for recovery from recession.

In such a context Southeast Asia as a region comprising of 11 countries has been trying to stay relevant in terms of multilateral institutions, cater to the domestic constituencies, enhance inter and intra regional trade, discuss contentional issues and present a cohesive posture to the international community. While major powers have also been giving intermittent attention to the region but Southeast Asia a geographical entity has been and will remain relevant in terms of piracy, Sea lanes of Communication, ethnic strife, religious radicalization, secessionist movements and the slow process of nation building. The alliance mentality has faded but affiliation remains. Countries like Singapore, Thailand and Philippines are reconfiguring their relations with the powerful neighbour China while other countries like Malaysia, Indonesia and Brunei are looking for advantages and benefits from economic engagement with China. The countries like Myanmar, Laos and Cambodia are increasingly getting swarmed by Chinese economic investment and trade incentives while at the same time catering to Chinese defence diplomacy. Within Southeast Asia, newly independent countries like Timor Leste are seeking resources for economic sustenance while countries like Vietnam are exploiting resources for sustaining the economic momentum. The strategic and economic priorities are getting diverse and so is the issue of deciphering the likely scenario in the region in the next two decades.

Southeast Asia is transiting a period of flux and uncertainty which has been brought about because of the Global recession as well as domestic instability. Taking the status in each of the countries one by one the conditions are not very optimistic barring few which are enjoying the fruits of globalization. In the Southeast Asian context democracy is fragile and authoritarian rule is the order of the day, though there are exceptions on both counts. In the case of Myanmar, the last two decades have seen the consolidation of the military junta and the democracy movement losing sheen but not international attention. The lone identified face of the democracy movement, Aung San Suu Kyi is under house arrest and there have been lack of coordination among the junior leaders owing to their personal ambitions. Few of the leaders have been shown leniency and were released by the Junta prior to the elections which are supposed to be held in November 2010. The generals have been trying to project their soft image and there are signs of rapprochement between US,EU and Myanmarese governing body better known as SPDC. It is also very much possible that Myanmar might adopt the guided democracy model adopted by Indonesia during Suharto's regime but uncertainty about the political future and economic sanctions prevails. Also there have been unconfirmed reports of Myanmar trying to assemble a nuclear bomb. Whether this was a brainchild of a fictional strategic writer or it does have an iota of truth would be only apparent in future. In the case of Thailand, the King is getting frail and old and the last three years have seen the most violent and erratic political stability. While military still has a say in the governance of Thailand but the clash of interests and the fragile governance structures and judiciary forecasts more instability and unrest in coming years. Malaysia is sliding towards a two party system in future but the ethnic cleavages would determine the future of the nation as well as politics. Singapore is sustaining its economic momentum but it seems that it has reached the development threshold because of stagnant economic growth. Indonesia has been showing signs of growth and is seen as the next happening thing in southeast Asia. Indonesia with the economic growth of 5-6 years in the last couple of years is trying to regain it status as the leader of multilateral organization like ASEAN but is fraught with internal rumblings about the religious radicalism as well as reorganization of bureaucracy and judiciary not to talk about the ever increasing corruption and the nexus between police, bureaucracy and judiciary. Brunei is seeking the alternate way of economic sustenance apart from oil and the efforts are on. Laos and Cambodia are trying to bargain between the powers. While Laos has yet to come to the regional stage as an important voice, Cambodia is trying to get the US investment and Chinese assistance. Vietnam has been slowly emerging as the major fulcrum of the economic growth with the terminology like VISTA which stands for Vietnam, Indonesia, South Africa, Turkey and Argentina being declared as the second rung major economic players at global stage. This cannot be denied at this stage. Philippines is seeing optimistic signals with the coming of the Former president Aquino's son Benigno Aquino as the next president but the recurring coups and public movements have crippled the nation in terms of sustained economic growth as well as investment destination. Though in terms of countering terrorism and communist guerillas it has to be given due credit. Timor has been raising issues about sustaining its nation through Oil and Gas revenues and royalty from exploration rights in the Timor sea but Australia is having its own convictions on the issue. There are a number of secessionist movements exiting in the region which include southern Thailand, Southern Philippines, Papua, Chin and Kachin regions in Myanmar to name few prominent ones. Though Aceh has been given the stature of autonomous region of Indonesia but increasing radicalization is a matter of concern in the region.

The competitiveness of Southeast Asia's trade—and of its increasingly sophisticated production networks in particular—depends on efficient, fast, reliable, and seamless infrastructure connections. Vast parts of Southeast Asia—inland and remote areas, landlocked countries, and distant islands—are isolated economically as well as geographically; so much of the region's huge potential remains untapped. While some of the existing infrastructure in the region is world class, most of it is below average. Rapid economic growth in recent years has put enormous pressure on Southeast Asia's infrastructure, particularly in transport and energy, but also in communications. Unless it can be significantly improved, infrastructure will continue to be a bottleneck to growth, a threat to competitiveness, and an obstacle to poverty reduction. Better connectivity with inland areas, for instance, would boost trade and economic growth in coastal areas, as well as inland ones. These issues present an opportunity for the region to take collective action to further enhance regional cooperation, particularly in environmentally sustainable and greener infrastructure development. The challenge is to build better and seamless connections across Asia and thus to the rest of the world[a]. But apart from trade and defence issues the one major challenge would be to manage population as well as ensuing struggle for resources.

Taking these issues in the background one can try to decipher the scenario in Southeast Asia which comprises of eleven nations including ASEAN Member states and Timor leste. As it is well known that the nation building process in Southeast Asia has not reached a period of stability with regard to nation formation and consolidation. Even when we have entered the year 2010, the secession and the issues of insurgency leading to greater autonomy have been lingering in the backdrop in this region. Even if we take general trends which have an impact on the developments in Southeast Asia one can see as depicted in figure 1.1 that Southeast Asian region would be home to 750 million strong population by 2030, which would be fighting for resources.

Figure 1.1 Population Growth Trends in Southeast Asia

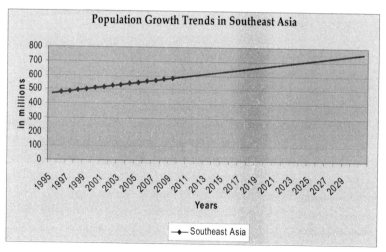

Source: ADB Key Development Indicators 2009

As most of the countries are export led economies so for providing employment and growth the economies of the region also have to proportionally grow so as to thwart any possible domestic instability which might arise in case of low economic growth and increasing population bulge. Even if we take the GDP growth (as given in Fig. 1.2) Indonesia would surge ahead.

Figure 1.2-GDP Growth at Purchasing Power Parity (in million US dollars)

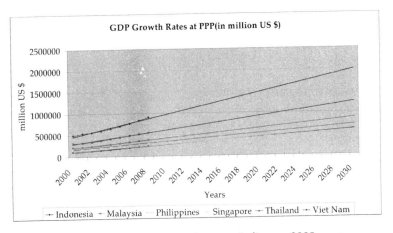

GDP Growth Rates at PPP(in million US $)

Source: ADB Key Development Indicators 2009

This shows that Indonesia would emerge as a two trillion dollar economy followed by Thailand, Malaysia, Philippines, Vietnam and Singapore. In all cases it would be the exports which would determine or influence the course of their economies. There would be other factors like urbanization, fertility, savings, stock markets and capitalization of economies. But there would be few important drivers which would determine the course of events as well as the future of Southeast Asia.

Even if one takes account of the twelve most important drivers that would decipher the scenario in Southeast Asia in 2030, the following would be worth a mention:

1. *Export led economic growth*
2. *Security-Regional and National*
3. *Religious Issues*
4. *Regional Multilateralism*
5. *Governance*
6. *Role of Major Powers*

7. *Secession/Emergence of New Nations*
8. *Ethnic issues*
9. *Terrorism*
10. *Interstate Conflicts*
11. *Refugees*
12. *Population*

With half a billion population Southeast Asia is one of the most growing areas of the Asia. The manufacturing as well as export led growth have led to the economic sustenance and maintaining harmony and peace in the region. Even if one tries to weave all the elements in one framework and tries to look at the possible scenarios then it would be very difficult for any layman to see what could be the scenarios in 2030. Though the wish list might get very long in the next two decades but the important element is how far the national governments would be catering to the demands and requirement of the regional cohesions. Among these twelve the ethnic issues, refugees and population are left out because these do not have very large impact in the region.

Going by the international discourse on the longevity of the multilateral organization both in the realm of security and economic relations, one can prudently say that there would be either evolution or meiosis of the regional organizations. The seeds for departure from the multilateral frameworks have been sown in the current context. Going by the cyclic pattern of regional organizations, it can be stated that with the rather casual approach towards the multilateral structures there would be renewed efforts to put things in right perspective and create pockets of cooperation which would be more rational and pragmatic steps in next two decades. The proliferation of nuclear weapons would coax the nuclear 'elites 'to shed their nuclear flab so as to get leaner and meaner look which should be more aimed towards enhancing the regional clout and seeking cooperation from the not so affluent states. Military would become a secondary element because war would have graduated to the level of cyber wars and space. The shortage and scarcity of water and energy due to rising population as well as depleting resources, would have dictated terms of international and regional engagement among the nations, including Southeast Asian nations.

In such a context if one takes a crystal gazing of the facts and figures as well as a rather conservative skepticism about the situation that would be prevalent during that time, one could make few predictions about the region as a whole but there would be still few important events and irritants which would be guiding the relations between the states in southeast Asia.

SOUTHEAST ASIA-DETERMINANTS/DRIVERS

The Southeast Asia geographical set up might be divided into two; one comprising the mainland Southeast Asia and the other comprising of the peripheral or archipelagic Southeast Asia. Mainland Southeast Asia comprises of Myanmar, Vietnam, Thailand, Malaysia, Singapore, Laos and Cambodia while archipelagic Southeast Asia is constituted by Indonesia, Brunei, Philippines and Timor Leste. Among the countries which have been playing a major role in deciding and have a major influence in the developments in Southeast Asia include Thailand, Vietnam, Malaysia, Singapore, Indonesia and Philippines. The fringe players include Myanmar, Cambodia, Burnei and Laos. The new player which has dominated the scenario in southeast Asian its Timor Leste and is witnessing new tug of war among the major players like Australia, China and Indonesia. In Southeast Asian region majority of countries are export driven economies which have provided sufficient incentives of the foreign institutional investors as well as large fund managers for inviting investment in the region. The export led economy has give n the region the necessary impetus for the economic growth as well as rise in per capita income. This has a large extent subdued the issues of governance and democracy and empowerment of the population has been related to the backstage. But in the southeast Asian context the major drivers would be it the rise of China, interstate conflicts, multi lateral structures, authoritarian rule, status of economic growth, secessionist movements and rise of religious radicalism. Taking the major drivers into account the following are worth a mention.

1. *Rise of China-Peaceful or Revisionist-*(High Uncertainty, High Impact)

While taking into account the recent developments in terms of U.S. engaging China as well as Japan and Australia in getting their military preparedness to counter Chinese military modernization, the stage is set for the emergence of new international order. While China is clamouring for recognition as a player of consequence in the global economy national recognition of its economic power and the military capabilities that it has been building over years. From at least the mid 1990s, China's economic numbers –trade, investment, and raw materials demand-have assumed proportions that have made it an applier of consequence in the global economy and a decisive force naturally in East Asia. It is now commonplace to observe that there is nothing new about this; China has been the dominant economic power in Asia for most of recorded history. This historical norm, however, was interrupted early in the nineteenth century-too far into the past to be recognisable and readily accommodated by the actors today in today's international arena. A powerful China therefore feels new and unfamiliar[b]. The rise of China and its possible unpredictable behaviour in future is creating apprehensions about the Southeast Asian nations.

The net effect of these factors is a considerable dissonance in the international arena in respect of China's rise. China burgeoning power threatens to outrun its strenuous efforts at reassurance. China's government evidently feels that it should be taken at the face value while many of its states that it impinges on are disposed to be cautious, watchful and attracted to hedging strategies if they are available. Though China's intentions are notoriously difficult to define, China's long and uniquely well-documented history could be invoked to confirm a deep seated reluctance to use power, even when it was indisputably predominant, for purposes of aggression or expansion. This seems on the surface to be heroic assertion even on factual grounds, let alone serving as a dependable basis for responding to the China in the foreseeable future[c]. This driver can be slotted into high uncertainty and high impact.

2. *Religious Radicalisation*-(Medium Uncertainty, Medium Impact)

Along the Southeast Asian nations countries like Indonesia and Malaysia are facing the predicament of assuaging the demands of the radical elements in the society or complying by the tolerant format of religious freedom. In the case Malaysia, but religious parties like PAS has somewhat diluted there are stances with regard to imposition of Shariah law in all provinces of Malaysia. Even in Indonesia voices are rising with the imposition of Sharia in Aceh and the Islamic parties buttressing the need for the imposition of shariah law in different provinces of Indonesia. This might undermine the secular courts in Indonesia while erosion has already happened in Malaysia where Shariah courts have dominated the issues related to religion. This can be slotted into Medium Uncertainty, Medium Impact which would have influence in the Southeast Asian region as a number of countries are Muslim majority countries while others have different religious majority like Myanmar-Buddhism, Philippines–Christianity, Vietnam-Buddhism, Thailand – Buddhism and Cambodia and Laos also having Buddhist majority. The demolition of Bamiyan Buddha in Afghanistan has angered the Buddhist majority in Myanmar and thereby led to human rights violations of the minority groups in the past.

3. *Politicisation of Military and Authoritarian rule* –
(Medium Uncertainty, Low Impact)

Military and its role in politics has been eroding in southeast Asia though it has still has its say in Myanmar, Thailand and Philippines while in the case of Indonesia the role of military is eroding. In the case of Malaysia and Singapore there is professionalization of military which has taken place right since the formation of the state. The uncertainty of military usurping power at least in countries like Thailand and Philippines is still high while in the case of Indonesia the military is returning back to barracks and the military farms and other businesses are being taken over by the government. In the case of Myanmar it is very much likely that after the general elections in 2010, the military junta might give way to some sort of a compromise with the civilian opposition and might replicate the Indonesian example of 'guided democracy', this would mean that it would be power-sharing arrangement between the military and the civilian government. But in any case the authoritarian rule has not been a new experience for the fragile nation states in southeast Asia and so this driver would be a high uncertainty but low impact category.

4. *India-China-Japan Power configuration* – Medium Uncertainty, High Impact)

While US has been claimed as the declining power, the recent visits of Obama to China has been seen as US conceding sphere of influence as well as international recognition to the economic growth of China. The interregnum period might be seen as a transfer of power between the existing power and the rising challenger. But with the rise of India and the increasing military might of Japan the power configuration not only in Asia but also in Southeast Asia would need to be rewritten. If somehow China convinces its neighbours with regard to its peaceful rise, the security and strategic scenario in Asia especially in Southeast Asia would undergo a huge transformation. This would mean that US existence would be threatened by the rise of Asian hegemony. US would be the pre-eminent power in the region but it is possible that the regional security contours would be determined increasingly by India, China and Japan. But the question is how far the nations like India and Japan would cater to the demands of security of these southeast Asian nations would determine the relevance of US at the regional stage. In this regard the economic interdependence as well as the growing international trade would undermine the contours of the relationship between the two major powers.

5. *Secession and Formation of New Nations* – (Low Uncertainty, High Impact)

With the resolution of Aceh issue through the Helsinki Accord in 2005 the issue of secession has somehow got undermined.

But the issue which is looming large in the future of newly instituted and created states in Southeast Asia has been the question of viability as well as sustenance and stability in the long run. Timor Leste is facing political instability as well as economic vulnerability about its future. Even though there have been secessionist movements which have been going on in Mindanao, Papua and Southern Thailand with each having different intensities for secession. While southern Philippines issue was nearing resolution but it was stalled because of mistrust between the government and the Moro Islamic liberation front negotiators. The offensive undertaken by the Philippine army have aggravated tensions between the two parties. But it cannot be denied that the issue might not be resolved in future. Also in Papua the willingness to secede is more to do with extensive commercial exploitation and least payback to the locals. The Papuan people have been raising their voice but have not gone all-out for secession. In the case of southern Thailand there is extensive and intense international attention which is given to the region because of the alleged involvement of Al Qaeda in the conflict theatre. In the case of southern Thailand regional Islamic organizations have shown interest in resolving the issue and also there is interest on the part of the government to initiate talks with the recalcitrant groups. So in this context the secession and formation of new nations can be stated to be a low Uncertainty but high impact issue.

6. *Interstate Conflicts* – (High Uncertainty, Low Impact)

Even though a number of people in Southeast Asia have professed in that the ASEAN way of consensus as well as the development of regional identity has subdued the inherent historical tensions among the countries of Southeast Asia. But this notion has been dispelled by the skirmishes between Thailand and Cambodian troops on the issue of sovereignty of perimeter of Preah Vihar temple complex which is a contentious issue between the two countries. Also the diplomatic tensions between Indonesia and Malaysia on the issue of Balinese dance, Patek, have shown that the fissures are still existent among the countries of Southeast Asia. Even though a number of conflicts involving the states of Southeast Asia have been resolved by International Court of Justice like between Singapore and Malaysia as well as between Brunei, Indonesia and Malaysia but the interstate conflicts have not aggravated to the extent of a war. But this cannot be in denied that these issues, a number of which are still to be resolved might become a source of tensions among nations but the uncertainty is low and so is the impact.

7. *Regional Multilateral Organisations* – (High Uncertainty, Medium Impact)

New multilateral structures as well as reconfiguration of the charter of ASEAN have led to issues like human rights and interference into domestic matters which impinge on regional security. Also the evolution of East Asia summit as well as newly propounded Asia-Pacific community by Kevin Rudd and the East Asia community professed by Japanese Prime Minister Hatoyama shows erosion of the old multilateral structures and transformation of the exiting ones. Owing to inherent mistrust and lack of credibility of the organizations like ARF, there would be differences among the nations. These developments have created apprehensions about the enforcing power of those multilateral structures which profess consensus. It is for sure that the evolution and transformation of multilateral structures would jeopardize or even construct a new multilateral order in East Asia in general and Southeast Asia in particular. In recent times the expansion of the existing structures has been mooted and the appraisal of the new alternatives is also proposed. But these multilateral structures would be an important driver but not the most vital one.

8. *Terrorism*–(Low Uncertainty, Medium Impact)

With the death of the iconic terror figures as well as arrest of the top brass of the regional terror groups like Jemaah Islamiyah and Abu Sayyaf, the terrorism in Southeast Asia can be placed into low Uncertainty but medium Impact group because of the lack of cadre strength among the various terror groups and the intense efforts both at the regional and national level show that it would take a while for the terrorism to raise its head in the regional context. But this element has high uncertainty for future but the probabilities are low. Also with regard to the regional apprehensions and the domestic compulsions many terror figures can be catalyst in fomenting trouble between the two nations. For example, Noordin Top was seen as the Malaysian trying to destabilize Indonesia through terror attacks. It needs to be seen how far terrorism can be contained in the next decade and whether any new groups would emerge in the regional theatre.

9. *Economic Growth*–(Low Uncertainty, Low Impact)

Among the Southeast Asian nations, economic growth has been major harbinger of prosperity as well as cohesiveness between nations. Though it is one of the important drivers in the Southeast Asian context but going by the way the region has suffered and recovered from the financial crisis in 1997/98 and thereafter has retained a better than average economic growth shows that it is a driver of low uncertainty and low impact. Even in the Asian Economic Outlook it has been stated that the region would recover much faster than its other Asian counterparts and would sustain the economic growth in the long run. Also going by the integrating production networks as well as 'spaghetti bowl' of bilateral trade agreements it seems that economic growth would be maintained in the next two decades barring the few phases of recession and economic crisis.

Figure-1: The Scenario and Impact Matrix

Low Uncertainty, High Impact (Secession and Formation of New Nations)	Medium Uncertainty, High Impact (India-China-Japan power configuration)	High Uncertainty, High Impact (China's Rise and Assertion)
Low Uncertainty, Medium Impact (Terrorism)	Medium Uncertainty, Medium Impact (Religious Radicalisation)	High Uncertainty, Medium Impact (New Multilateral Structures)
Low Uncertainty, Low Impact (Economic Growth)	Medium Uncertainty, Low Impact (Military/Authoritarian Rule)	High Uncertainty, Low Impact (Interstate Conflicts)

Looking into the matrix, though there are nine possible drivers of change but the three major drivers which would have along term impact on the region would be the secessionist movements, role and power configuration between China- Japan and India and last but most importantly the perceptions and acceptance about the rise of China. Though economic rise and cooperation would be widely accepted but military modernisation and Chinese assertion in South China Sea as well as on the issue of demarcation of the maritime borders would have a long term impact on the region.

POSSIBLE SCENARIOS

The possible scenarios can be deciphered into three major zones of cooperation, chaos and compromise. In case the scenarios are taken into account there are three major impact scenarios which would be as follows

FIRST SCENARIO-RISE OF CHINA AND UNCERTAINTY ABOUT ITS BEHAVIOUR DRIVE THREAT PERCEPTION

With rise of China and the resolution of conflicts on maritime borders through use of power, coercion or aid, the countries of

Southeast Asia might be accommodating China. But countries which have higher stakes like Vietnam and Philippines would start looking for alliances and new strategic partners. China has been facing problems with regard to South China Sea, Taiwan and demarcating maritime borders with the countries of Southeast Asia, though few of them have been resolved bilaterally. China's economic growth has been a lucrative incentive for the countries of Southeast Asia which would be an engaging factor for the Southeast Asian countries. But the negative balance of trade in favour of China might not augur well for the Southeast Asian economies in the long run and so they might seek concession from China. It is yet to be seen that after the China-ASEAN Free Trade Agreement becomes fully operational in 2010 what would be the costs benefits analysis for the Southeast Asian nations. Almost all countries would need China for their export led growth but would like to cooperate with China. So in the current context China's economic clout is increasing and even US is accommodating China to protect its economic and commercial interests. So at the current context the first scenario is that of cooperation with China. Taiwan issue gaining momentum in international sphere and China itself has to counter the secessionist movements in Tibet and Xinjiang. It is likely that there might be conflict between US and China on the issue of Taiwan but it is also a matter of skepticism that China would use military power to assert its sovereignty on Taiwan. It is also to be seen how Tibet and Xingjiang issues are handled by China. Also if in case status quo is disturbed it would be interesting to see US response to the issue whether it would take a constrained position or would stamp its authority in terms of preeminent power. As of date China is in position to counter US but by 2030 it would have naval capabilities to counter US for the duration so as to capture Taiwan. In case, China reclaims Taiwan then the spate of sanctions, which would be subsequently lifted, as it happened after Tiannamen square incident, and the resultant power shifts would make China a stronger power and the loss of face for US. But there is a flip side to it also that in case internal issues get more dominant in Chinese polity and there are secessionist movements which though might not counter Chinese military might but would create fissures within China. In order to curb such internal security issue it might take up issue of Taiwan or countering US so as to whip up Chinese nationalism As nationalism becomes stronger, the scenario of conflict would grow stronger.

Second Scenario-Emerging Power Configuration Between Asian Powers Namely India-China and Japan and Impact in Southeast Asia.

This would drive the areas of conflict and compromise in the Southeast Asian region. This would depend on the economic might and military capabilities of each major player to cede certain concession so as to accommodate rising China and thereby creating a space for negotiations or encroaching in the supposedly China's sphere of influence and thereby creating conflicting strategic spaces. This is witnessed in the case of Indian Ocean, South China Sea but there is a flip side to it also that in the event of India and Japan joining hands to contain China then there would be struggle for power in the region and the divisions of the region along the pro-China and anti- China blocs (as had happened in 1970s). India and Japan would be raising their stakes and would be luring countries to form a containment strategy vis- a-vis China. Also there are apprehensions cast over the continued economic growth of China and so in due course of time China would also face the slowing down phase due to aging population, stagnant productivity and decreasing exports, as it has been happening in the case of Japan. Due to these factors there would be a general understanding which would have developed among the nation sand there would be a sort of compromise or the tug of influence in the region. This would in a major way decide the future of the region in 2030. It is very likely that this might happen if there is no balkanization of the Southeast Asia. This scenario seems most likely because the countries might not want to stall the economic growth and thus would seek negotiations with China.

Third Scenario-Balkanization of Southeast Asia

With the rise in the secessionist movements and the weakening of the governance structures in the fragile states there might be emergence of new nations which would be seeking affiliation to keep themselves afloat. The current example is that of Timor Leste which is advocating greater royalty on explorations rights in Timor Sea and a just and equitable distribution of maritime resources. Also, with the secessionist movements still existent in areas like Southern Thailand and Southern Philippines, both strategically located the nations like US and China would like to exploit the circumstances to create favorable nation states heavily dependent on their aid and investment. This would lead to pockets of influence as well as utter chaos in the new nations. This would also depend on how economies fare in the long run and how the ethnic and religious fissures are contained by the existing government. While China is now investing in Timor, US is reconstructing temporary structures to offset the lack of US bases in the Southeast Asian region.

In all the three scenarios, Southeast Asian countries would be divided on the issue of percentage of support for China, accommodation to India and Japan in power configuration and keeping the nation state in unison on the issue of secessionist movements. While Philippines would retain the support of US but at certain instances enjoying Chinese attention. Indonesia would keep an arms length from Chinese because of domestic sensitivities and would clearly segregate the issues of economic cooperation and strategic priorities. Malaysia would cede and might succumb to Chinese influence. Thailand would try to maintain a balance between US and China and thereby enjoying the support of the two powers. Brunei would like to host Chinese investments and economic support for alternate non oil economy. Vietnam would be skeptically engaged with China but would not like to antagonize China as well as US. Laos and Cambodia would remain heavily under Chinese influence. In such a context the Southeast Asia would be divided into pro China and anti- China Camps. This would manifest in the case of resolution of Spratlys islands dispute as well as demarcation of maritime borders. The radicalization and the inherent historical mistrust would again come to the fore. Though radicalization would have an impact on regional politics but it would impinge more of domestic governance and polity. The interstate disputes on contentious issues would evaporate because a number of countries have resorted to resolution of contentious border and territorial issues by referring it to international court of justice. Other major powers like Japan, India and Russia would try to gain influence in the southwest, northeastern parts of Southeast Asian region and there would be power struggle within Southeast Asia. There would be gradual retreat of US from the bases of Korea and Japan and the two countries would have started building their own defence capabilities. There would be a concert of anti-China countries which would be trying to contain China through unified resistance and coaxing China to adhere to multilateral and regional obligations. This has been witnessed during the Second World war against the axis powers and also China, Brazil, South Africa and India ganging up to protect their interests against European and US coercion during climate Change Summit in Copenhagen in December 2009.

ALTERNATIVES

In fact the medium scenarios act as a buffer to counter the extreme problem of rise of China. The rise of multilateral structures which should be able to engage China would buttress the fact that rise of China would be peaceful. The rise of religious radicalism would also divide the southeast Asian nations on the religious lines, if in case there are inter religious conflicts in countries like Malaysia, Indonesia and Philippines, which are still continuing. Also it would be important that the countries stick to authoritarian regime especially in the case of Myanmar, Singapore and Laos because any change of governance would create problems with regard to accommodation of religious minorities or refugees be it the case of Rohingya in Myanmar or non-Muslims in Malaysia and Indonesia. The problems were manifested during demolition of Bamiyan and the Israel Lebanon war having mirrored anguish in Indonesia and Malaysia. But on the other hand, Southeast Asia has also attached weightage to cultural history and the issue has been the skirmishes between Thailand and Cambodia as well as diplomatic tensions between Indonesia and Malaysia on the Patek dance. This clearly shows whipped nationalism with regard to culture. The other alternative is the peaceful rise of China which is going to reconfigure the affiliations of the countries of Southeast Asia and thereafter there is possibility of peaceful resolution of issues like South China Sea. Also southeast Asian countries due to the increasing connectivity and somehow changing balance of trade which become positive for majority of southeast Asian countries it is likely that US sphere of influence recedes and there is increasing Chinese influence. This might create problems with US allies like South Korea and Japan which be creating opportunities for economic cooperation with China.

The emerging alternative is what has been termed as the surrender of Southeast Asia by US administration to China and the emergence of India and Japan as new guardians of Southeast Asia. This means that China has been accorded status in international sphere and there is convergence between China and US which means the transfer to the second rung of probabilities. In that case the scenario in 2030 would be very similar to that which is existent today. Also it would be important to see how to Japan and India as well as Australia configure their defence to counter the China threat. As already the changes are visible in the defense white papers of countries like Japan, Australia and Vietnam. Japan is also trying to gear up its defence through instituting Ministry of Defence as well as consolidating its navy. India also is gearing up to build its defenses as well as modernize its defense forces.

CONCLUSION

Taking into account all these different aspects as well as scenarios it seems that China would be accorded the status of the rising power and a major determinant in the affairs of Asia. But this would also mean that Japan would try to regain its status like that it had in Second World War and India would be pushing its status in international and regional power structures especially in Southeast Asia and Indian Ocean. So in a way that US hegemony would be on the decline while major power conflict would be instrumental in determining the future of Southeast Asia. India would play a major role but it would be determined by the equation that it has with the US and China as well as its own strategic periphery in Southeast Asia. It is very much possible in the next two decades time that Japan and India can become powerful balancers to the Chinese assertion or encroachments in Southeast Asia but it would be an issue of introspection that the economies of the region would have subdued themselves into Chinese influence or start looking for alternatives. The major headache would be the Balkanisation of Southeast Asia and emergence of fragile states because then the chaos would prevail and the scramble for resources would create major power conflicts and struggle for influence. Southeast Asia would again mirror the events of history which was prevalent during the post colonial period but the major departure would be the trade imperialism and the compulsion to address problems like pandemics, climate change and increasing population. These issues along with religious radicalisation would be creating diversion in the course of future but it is sure that the unity among southeast Asian nations would be responsible for the major power disposition towards this region. But the final prognosis is that China would be accommodated and a compromise strategy would be adopted by all nations if China continues the same growth trajectory as it is now.

NOTES

i   Infrastructure for a Seamless Asia, Asian Development Bank and Asian Development Bank Institute, 2009, p. iii

ii   Ron Huisken ed. Rising China: Power and Reassurance, Strategic and Defence Studies Centre Australian National University E Press, 2009, p. 1

iii   Ron Huisken ed. Rising China: Power and Reassurance, Strategic and Defence Studies Centre Australian National University E Press, 2009, pp. 2-3

15

Japan as A Normal State: Changing Trends and Future Projection

—Pranamita Baruah

INTRODUCTION

In the wake of perceptible changes that are taking place in global affairs, many countries have started redefining their foreign policy priorities in tune with the changed world situation. The impact of this change is much more on Japan than probably any other country in the East Asian region. This has triggered a debate in Japan to rethink on the continuance of its pacifist policy. The debate is further precipitated by the developments in its neighbourhood, such as North Korea's nuclear development programme and China's rise both economically and militarily. At the same time, questions are also being asked about the relevance of Japan's security alliance with the US. The recent defence agreements that Japan signed with India and Australia make analysts suspect that Japan is no longer prepared to rely solely on the US for its security. Japan's recent engagements in war on terror and anti-piracy activities in the Gulf of Aden are indications that Japan is prepared for a more pro-active foreign and defence policy.

Are these indications that Japan is poised to become a normal state? Does this also mean that Japan is likely to revise soon its pacifist Constitution, particularly Article 9? Will a nuclear North Korea precipitate a quick response from Japan to opt for a nuclear path? Since the public approval for Japan opting for a nuclear path seems unlikely in the short term (next five years), external developments might hasten the path for Japan to become a normal state by 2030, by which time the government would have obtained the peoples' mandate for change. This would entail a full nuclear status for Japan, collapse of the Japan- US security alliance and abandonment of the pacifist element in the Constitution, facilitating Japan's strive for normal statehood.

While discussing Japan as a normal state, this paper will be basically divided into three main sections. In the first section, an attempt will be made to define the 'normal' statehood. The definition will be followed by a brief explanation of why Japan is at present not considered a normal state, how 'normalcy' has been denied to Japan since the end of the World War II and the persistent ambivalence within Japan around that issue. In the second section, effort will be made to identify the key indicators and drivers which seem to propel Japan to seek normal statehood. In the next section, based on the key indicators and drivers, a few key assumptions will be made to predict Japan's plausible future in the next two decades. In the fourth and final section, certain scenarios will be drawn to indicate Japan's pursuit for normal statehood in 2030, followed by an appraisal of those scenarios. Finally a conclusion will be drawn on the issue in question.

DEFINITION

In the international system, states have varying degrees of sovereign powers and sovereignty has many dimensions. Kenneth Waltz defines sovereignty as the ability to retain autonomy over the fate of one's state. He also singles out the possession of strategic nuclear forces as a means to achieve sovereignty.[1] However, if analysed from

1   Alker, Hayward R Jr., Thomas J. Biersterker and Takashi Inoguchi, "The Decline of the Superstates: The Rise of New World Order?" Presented at the World Congress of Political Science, International Political Science Association, Paris, July 15-20, 1985. Quoted in Takashi Inoguchi, "Japan's Ambition for Normal Statehood: An Abridged Version", an Abridged of the paper presented at the International Conference on East Asia, Latin America, and the "New" Pax Americana, Weatherhead Center for International Affairs, Harvard University and East Asia Institute, Korea, February 14-15, 2003. It is available on http://unpan1.un.org/intradoc/groups/public/documents/APCITY/UNPAN011419.pdf. (accessed on September 30, 2009).

that perspective, the European states, which have lost their sovereign power to issue currency and exercise exclusive management of their national economies with the creation of the European Union, could not possibly be treated as 'normal' entities.[2]

Over the years, 'normal statehood' has been defined in a variety of ways. States possessing adequate military capability to defend their sovereignty are considered to be 'normal'. Normal states pursue their national interests by projecting their military power as well as exercising diplomatic influence. Experts on international relations often take this interpretation to understand and define a normal state.[3] However, in this paper, 'normal statehood' would be defined in a conventional Westphalian manner, in which the term is basically linked with a state's basic authority and the extent to which it can exercise autonomy in the management of its economic and security affairs.

In simpler terms, normal statehood basically refers to a situation in which a state possesses political and military power commensurate with its economic power. While trying to assume responsibility in international affairs, a normal state takes responsibility for its own defence. It also has the right to use force to resolve international disputes.[4] Instead of taking cues from other states, a normal state pursues a foreign policy that serves its own national interest.

Is Japan a Normal State?

Currently, Japan is not considered normal, basically because, its post-war constitution, coupled with the Japan-US security alliance, deprive it of a key right of a modern sovereign state, i.e., the right to use force to resolve international disputes. This 'abnormality' led to the generation of two characteristics-pacifism and passivism-that remained dominant in the post-war Japanese foreign and security

2   *Ibid.*

3   Noel M. Morada, "Japan as a Normal State: Implications for regional Security", at http://www.isis.org.my/files/apr/NOEL_M_MORADA. pdf. (accessed on November 30, 2009).

4   Yongwook Ryu, "The Road to Japan's 'normalization'?, *The Korean Journal of Defense Analysis*, Vol. XIX, No. 2, Summer 2007, p. 66.

policy orientation. Pacifism was institutionalized in the form of Article 9[5] of the constitution. It had a great impact on Japan's post-war defence profile that included: i) a ban on the export of arms and military technology (announced by Prime Minister Sato in 1986)[6] and the three non-nuclear principles (not to possess, produce or introduce nuclear weapons into Japanese territory). These institutionalized norms of non-military behaviour, along with the famous 'Yoshida doctrine' that argued for Japan's alliance with the US for national security, basically set the tone of post-war Japanese security policy.

Passivism in Japanese foreign policy can be traced back to the formation of the Japan-US security alliance (1951) which not only made Japan dependent on the US for its own security but also set the outer parameters of Japan's foreign policy, largely within the confines of economic roles. Till the end of the Cold War, Japanese foreign policy remained passive and reactive, taking cues from the US' regional policy rather than formulating its own direction. In the early 1990s, although legislation was passed that permitted Japanese Self Defense Force (SDF) to participate in the UN-sanctioned peace keeping operations, this role was largely restricted as the SDF could only join operations only after all fighting had come to an end in the region concerned. In the event of violence, the SDF could defend themselves-not even civilians-and only after being fired upon by the opponent forces. Over the years, those strictures have loosened. Still, due to the large institutional constraints, Japan has not yet been able to achieve normalcy in the strict sense of the term. In other words, Japan has not been able to acquire political and military clout commensurate with its almost universally acknowledged great economic power.

---

5 Article 9 of the Japanese Constitution provides: "Aspiring sincerely to an international peace based on justice and order, the Japanese people forever renounce war as a sovereign right of the nation and the threat or use of force as a means of settling international disputes. In order to accomplish the aim of the preceding paragraph land, sea, and air forces, as well as other war potential, will never be maintained. The right of belligerency of the state will not be recognized."

6 This feature was later modified by Prime Minister Nakasone to make the US the sole exception.

In the 2000s, however, scholars, commentators, and journalists began to report signs that Japanese foreign and security policy is gradually 'normalizing'. The following events and processes were adduced as evidence in this context: i) the passing of cluster of national emergency bills that establish comprehensively-for the first time in the post war period- how to respond to a direct attack; ii) the dispatch of troops to the Indian Ocean in 2001 and Iraq in 2003, entering hostile territory for the first time in the post-war era; iii) the transformation of the Defence Agency into a full fledged Ministry of Defence in January 2007; iv) increasing debates over the revision of the pacifist Constitution and whether to permit the SDF to take part in collective self-defence; and v) growing debate over the possibility of Japan becoming nuclear; etc.[7] In the latter part of this article, an effort will be made to analyse if any of these actually facilitating Japan's so called strive for normal statehood.

AMBIVALENCE ON JAPAN'S 'NORMAL' STATEHOOD

Japan was denied 'normal' statehood by the Occupation forces after Japan's defeat in World War II. The US signed a security treaty with Japan in 1951 based on which the US maintains a military presence in Japan and provides Japan with nuclear and long-term protection. Tokyo only pursues a defence-only posture, as the SCAP[8]-imposed Article 9 of the Constitution not only prohibits Japan from maintaining land, sea and air forces, as well as other war potentials, but also abrogates the use of force in settling international disputes. In fact, the preamble of the Japanese Constitution also contains a passage on an aspiration to eradicate the use of force.[9] Due to these

---

7   Linus Hagstrom, "Normalizing Japan: Supporter, Nuisance, or Wielder of power in the North Korean Nuclear Talk?" *Asian Survey*, Vol. XLIX, No. 5, September/October 2009, p. 832.

8   Supreme commander of Allied Powers (SCAP).

9   The initial part of the Preamble of Japanese Constitution states: "We, the Japanese people, acting through our duly elected representatives in the National Diet, determined that we shall secure for ourselves and our posterity the fruits of peaceful cooperation with all nations and the blessings of liberty throughout this land, and resolved that never again shall we be visited with the horrors of war through the action of government, do proclaim that sovereign power resides with the people and do firmly establish this Constitution---"

initial institutional constraints, Japan has not yet been able to achieve normalcy in the strict sense of the term.

However, for the Japanese people, the term 'normal' remains unclear. The use of the word 'normal' in varying contexts by Japanese leadership has compounded the confusions. Former Japanese Prime Minister Shinzo Abe's aspiration to create 'a beautiful nation' and his foreign minister Taro Aso's desire to see Japan as 'a thought leader' further added to the confusion to the debate on Japan's 'normal' statehood and its foreign policy agenda.[10] This debate injects a bit of uncertainty in Japan in defining its appropriate role in the global affairs. Though Japanese leaders have their own visions about the future of Japan, the people of Japan have not coalesced to a single view. Despite profound changes at home and abroad in recent years, the ambivalence around 'normal' statehood issue persists.

KEY INDICATORS

It has been increasingly argued that over the years, in its pursuit of being a normal state, Japan is steadily loosening its restraints on the post-war pacifist foreign and defence policies. In this context, factors like the dispatch of the Japanese Self Defense Forces (SDF) to overseas destinations for peace support operations; broadening of the interpretations of the Constitution to allow Japanese forces to assist the US war on terror in Iraq and Afghanistan; etc. are often cited as plausible indicators of Japan's march towards 'normal statehood'. However, some additional factors like Japan's militarization of space; easing of the military export restrictions; more pro-active foreign policy; etc. can also be considered as facilitators in Japan's strive for normal statehood.

Throughout the Cold War period, Japan was cocooned from all kinds of external threats with its alliance with the US. The situation underwent change when under pressure from the US and international

---

10 Brad Glosserman, "Japan as a 'Normal' State: Implications for the Region", Asia Pacific Roundtable, Kuala Lumpur, June 6, 2007, at http://www.isis.org.my/files/apr/BRAD_GLOSSERMAN.pdf. (accessed on November 30, 2009).

community for 'humanitarian contribution', Japan eventually dispatched minesweepers to the Gulf after the cessation of hostilities. With the subsequent passage of the International Peacekeeping Cooperation Law (June 1992), Japan earmarked upon several peace support operations abroad. Since then, Japan has participated in such activities undertaken by the UN in Cambodia, east Timor, Haiti, and the Golan Heights.[11] Following 9/11, Japan has also passed an amendment to the International Peace Cooperation Law to permit the SDF engaged in international peace cooperation assignments to use weapons beyond purposes of protecting themselves-to that of protecting the lives of peace cooperation personnel with them on the scene or those who have come under their control while conducting their duties. Subsequently, Japanese Maritime Self Defense Forces (MSDF) has also been engaged in anti-piracy missions in the Gulf of Aden.[12] Thus, a definite gradual shift can be seen in Japan's pacifist policy.

The spirit of Article 9 of the Constitution has been also violated by the passage of the Anti-terrorism Special Measures Law (ATSML) in November 2001, which has allowed the JSDF to provide 'non-combat support' to US-led forces engaged in the war on terror. The law also widened the geographical scope of operations beyond the areas surrounding the SDF by including the Japanese territory, Indian Ocean and related airspace, Diego Garcia and Australian territory. The ATSML enabled Japan to dispatch of JSDF to support the US-led campaign in Afghanistan. From 2004, it also deployed ground and air forces in Iraq and Kuwait under the Iraqi Reconstruction Law on non-combat reconstruction missions. These two missions represented for the first time in Japan's post-war history that its military was officially dispatched overseas during an ongoing conflict. Japan also took the decision to deploy ground SDF for the first time in a conflict situation,

---

11 Arpita Mathur, "Japan's Self-Defence Forces; Towards a Normal Country", Strategic analysis, Vol. 31, issue 5, September 2007, p. 728.

12 See for details, Pranamita Baruah, "Japan's Response to sea Piracy", March 30, 2009, http://www.idsa.in/idsastrategiccomments/ JapansResponsetoSeaPiracy_PBaruah_300309.

beginning with Iraq.[13] All these developments clearly indicate Japan's growing role in the resolution of international disputes

The increasing role of the Japanese SDF was also reflected in the Japan Coast Guard's (JCG) sinking of one of North Korea's alleged 'spy ships' in East China Sea in December 2001; intimations from government officials that they were prepared to consider long-range air strikes against North Korea's ballistic missile sites if it were to repeat its August 1998 Taepodong-1 launch over Japan; and the government's commitment in December 2003 to procure a Ballistic Missile Defense (BMD) system.[14]

During the Cold War, there was standoff between conservative and progressive forces in Japan, and debate over revising the Constitution was considered taboo. The turning point was the debate in the Diet over the 1991 Gulf war regarding how to reconcile making an international contribution using the SDF with the spirit of the constitution. Over the years, with more and more deployments of Japanese troops overseas, without much change in the government's interpretation of the Constitution, there is a growing chorus of voices within both the ruling and opposition parties noting that there is discordance between the Constitution and reality. These voices have spurred the debate over the revision of the pacifist Constitution.[15] This kind of thinking seems to be a long term strategy of Japan to raise the country's consciousness for a move towards amending the pacifist Constitution.

Japan's changing military doctrines is often considered by many an indicative of its aspiration to achieve 'normal' statehood. The emphasis

---

13 Christopher W. Hughes, "Japan's security policy, the US-Japan Alliance, and the 'war on terror': incrementalism confirmed or radical leap?" *Australian Journal of International Affairs*, Vol. 58, No. 4, (December 2004), pp. 428-429.

14 Christopher W. Hughes, "Japan's Reemergence as a 'Normal' Military Power", Adelphi Paper, 2005, International Institute of Strategic studies, London, p. 10.

15 Odawa Atsushi, "The Dawn of Constitutional Debate", *Japan Quarterly*, Vol. 47, Issue 1, January-March, 2000, p. 19.

of 2004 National Defence Programme Guideline (NDPG) on the necessity of Japan to play a more active role both within the context of the Japan-US alliance and the international community, and the emphasis of the 2009 Defence White Paper on the necessity of Japan to strengthen its defence preparedness in view of the deteriorating security environment in the neighbourhood, are some of the examples of the changing nature of Japanese military doctrines.

Despite Japan's defence alone posture, in recent years, Japan has introduced certain highly developed weapon systems, such as the 50-tonne M-90 MBT, lighter 44 tonne TK-X MBT (for counter insurgency operations)[16], the F-2 fighter bomber, KC-767 tanker aircraft with an in-flight refueling capability, *Osumi*-class transport ships for the landing of transport helicopters, etc. This has led many security analysts to believe that Japan is trying to normalize its military force which can not only participate in combat operations but also possess offensive capabilities and play a role in collective security operations.

Besides these, some other factors (militarization of space, easing of the military export restrictions; more pro-active foreign policy; etc.) are also being considered as facilitators of Japan's strive towards normal statehood. For decades, Japan has adhered to the principle of peaceful use of space, which was introduced in 1969.[17] Japan's deployment of spy satellites and BMD in the wake of North Korea's nuclear test in 1998 altered that principle. Since then, the original interpretation of the 1969 principle has been reinterpreted time and again to refer to 'peaceful' as 'non-military', so that the 'defensive'

---

16   Christopher W. Hughes, "Japan Remilitarization", The International Institute for Strategic Studies, London, 2009, p. 40.

17   In May 1969, Japan's lower house of parliament passed a resolution limiting the scope of Japan's space practices. The resolution states: "Japan's launching of objects into outer space...as well as its development and use of rockets to launch such objects should be limited for peaceful purposes only." In addition, the resolution limits the use of space to "non-military" applications, which effectively excludes the SDF from directly controlling satellites whether they are for communications, global positioning or reconnaissance.

military use of space can be legitimized. The Basic Space Law, enacted in May 2008, stipulates that the Japanese government shall take necessary measures to promote the development and use of space that contributes to ensuring the peace and security of the international community, as well as to the security of Japan. The Basic Policy for Space Development and Utilization (January, 2009) published by the Ministry of Defence stipulates that Japan should investigate the acquisition of infrared early-warning satellites to improve effectiveness of the BMD. The Basic Plan on Space Security published in June 2009 also emphasizes on realizing a safe, secure and affluent society as well as strengthening national security through the development of space.[18] In recent times, such developments towards the militarization of space have been increasingly considered as an indicator of Japan's progress towards 'normal' statehood.

Since 1976, Japan has basically adhered to the policy of abstaining from selling arms and sharing of technologies in the international market. However, in recent years, while opining that the arms ban would leave Japan's military industry behind in settling international technological trends and standards"[19], Japan has begun to export 'demilitarized' ex-JCG patrol craft to Indonesia for anti-piracy activities. It has also embarked on new, although small-scale, international defence-technology cooperation. Besides that, the Technical Research and Development Institute (TRDI) in Japan sent observers to Sweden's NBC-warfare research facilities, and has used French facilities for stealth fighter technologies. Thus, the easing of the military export restrictions is being considered as another indicator of a basic shift in Japan's pacifist policy and aspiration to achieve 'normal' statehood.

18   "The Basic of Japan's Defence Policy and Build-up of Defence Capability", *Defence of Japan*, 2009, Part II, Chapter I, p. 123, available on http://www.mod.go.jp/e/publ/w_paper/pdf/2009/20Part2_Chapter1_Sec4.pdf. (accessed on December 4, 2009).

19   Maidhc O Cathail, "The Land of the Rising Military-Industrial Complex: Peace-loving Japan's endangered arms export ban", available online http://world.mediamonitors.net/layout/set/print/Headlines/The-Land-of-the-Rising-Military-Industrial-Complex-Peace-loving-Japan-s-endangered-arms-export-ban. (accessed on November 13, 2009).

The changing trends in Japan's foreign policy are also considered as an indicative of its aspiration for 'normal' statehood. During the Cold War period, Japan's foreign policy had been based on the well known *Yoshida Doctrine* that contains three basic elements: continued reliance on the Japan-US alliance, emphasis on economic relations overseas to assist in the reconstruction of the domestic economy, and the maintenance of low profile in international politics. In recent years, however, the Doctrine seems to have lost its relevance due to growing opposition against the security alliance with the US, and demand within Japan for a more pro-active foreign policy. In the wake of 9/11, through its support in the US war on terror, Japan clearly indicated the arrival of a new era in Japanese foreign policy. By becoming the second largest contributor (next to the US) to the UN General Assembly budget and providing financial support for the expansion of the UN peacekeeping operations, Japan is increasingly trying to gain recognition for its contributions to the international community. Tokyo has also championed UN reform as a vehicle to claim its right to a permanent membership in the international body.

Since the time of Shinzo Abe's administration, Japan has also started to shed its US-centric foreign policy and adopt an Asia-centric policy.[20] Indicative of Japan's 'eastward' move in foreign policy are the forging of defence agreements with Australia and India[21] along with the US; Japan's earlier proposal for the development of an Asian Monetary fund (AMF) in the style of the IMF, and the proposal by former Prime Minister Yukio Hatoyama to establish a East Asian Community (EAC) with Japan,[22] China and South Korea as the major players.

---

20 Rajaram Panda, "An Asia-Centric Foreign Policy for Japan", September 4, 2009, Article No. #2963, http://www.ipcs.org/print_article-details.php?recNo=2985. (accessed on December 8, 2009).

21 *East Asian Strategic Review, 2008*, The National Institute for Defense Studies, Tokyo, p. 216-222.

22 Rajaram Panda, "East Asian Regionalism Vs Asian Regionalism", October 31, 2009, http://www.idsa.in/idsastrategiccomments/EastAsianRegionalismVsAsianRegionalism_RPanda_311009

All these factors mentioned above can be considered as the basic indicators for Japan's growing strive for normal statehood. What are then the key drivers that are pushing Japan to adopt such steps to be 'normal' state? The next section of this paper will identify those drivers.

KEY DRIVERS

Broadly classified, the major factors propelling Japan to seek normal statehood are: the domestic political change in Japan[23], emerging security concerns of Japan, the failure of national security apparatus to deal with Japanese vulnerabilities, change in the mindset of the Japanese leadership, rising nationalism, and changing economic dynamics within Japan.

As regards domestic political change in Japan, two developments deserve mention here: the discrediting of the left after the Cold War, which shifted the center of the political spectrum in Japan to the right, and the rise of power of a younger generation of politicians with different thinking about Japan's appropriate international role. Both expanded the boundaries of the national security debate within Japan. It is often argued that the collapse of the Japan Socialist Party (JCP) has muted a consistent voice against militarism. As a result, many issues which were considered taboo in Japan earlier are now openly debated by Japanese policy makers. One such issue is increasing debate within Japan regarding the possibility of Japan to go nuclear in the event of withdrawal of the US nuclear umbrella in the near future. Since Japan possessed a considerable amount of weapons-grade atomic material,[24] after North Korea's nuclear tests, Japan too going nuclear way was considered by many at that time a real possibility.

Related to the changing domestic political change within Japan is the changing mindset of the Japanese leadership. At present,

---

23 Yuki Tatsumi and Andrew Oros (ed.), "Japan's New Defence Establishment: Institutions, Capabilities and Implications", The Henry L. Stimson Center, 2007.

24 Martin Fackler, "Test puts pressure on Japan's Pacifism", *International Herald Tribune*, October 10, 2006, http://www.boston.com/news/world/asia/articles/2006/10/10/test_puts_pressure_on_japans_pacifism/

Japanese political spectrum is basically dominated by leadership who is comparatively young and is generally unencumbered by war guilt. Unlike the earlier generation of 'pacifist' leadership, the present leadership in Japan tends to look at the world in a more realistic way and think about some 'militaristic' solutions to the growing security threats, particularly from its neighbourhood. Former Prime Minister Shinzo Abe's example can be cited in this context. Being the first Japanese Prime Minister born after World War II, Abe embarked on an ambitious effort to shore up the nation's military, its independence and national pride.

Another significant drivers of Japan's aspiration for 'normal' statehood is the changing international environment. After the end of the Cold War, most Japanese were of the view that international law was ascendant and the international institutions would serve as arbitrators of international disputes. The international community's response to Iraq's invasion of Kuwait largely proved them right. However, in recent years, growing security uncertainty and concerns due to factors like North Korean nuclear crises, rising China, modernization of Chinese military, unresolved territorial disputes among the East Asian countries,[25] have led to the erosion of pillars of the Japanese security. The failure of the Nuclear Proliferation Treaty (NPT) to deal with North Korea and the UN's failure to deal adequately with international crises have damaged Japanese faith in international institutions. All these factors have led many Japanese to argue for more autonomy in finding out solutions to the growing international security threats to serve the country's own national interests.

The failure of the national security apparatus in dealing with Japanese vulnerabilities is another driver in this context. The sarin gas attack on Tokyo subways in 1995 and the Great Hanshin Earthquake of the same year clearly underscored vulnerabilities in Japan's response to emergencies and indicated that Japan was inadequately equipped to deal with crises on its own, a situation that needed to be redressed.

---

25 Arpita Mathur, "Japan's Self-Defence Forces; Towards a Normal Country", Strategic analysis, Vol. 31, issue 5, September 2007, p. 726.

Rising nationalism in Japan is also identified as another driver towards 'normal' statehood. International environment that have put the Japanese public on edge, including the end of Cold War, the rise of China as a military power, North Korea's nuclear programme etc., are often offered as the primary factors that led to the rise of nationalism within Japan. Japan's Asian neighbours cite the following indicators of rising Japanese nationalism-Japanese textbook revisionism, former Prime Minister Junichiro Koizumi's state visits to the Yasukuni war shrine and growing popular support for revising the pacifist Constitution.[26] It has been argued that rising nationalism may compel Japan to seek more autonomy in decision making of its own security affairs and aspire for normal statehood.

Certain economic considerations also may trigger Japan's drive towards normal statehood. At present, China's rapid economic progress and Japan's lengthy inability to recover fully from the collapse of the 'bubble economy' has become a matter of great concern to Japanese decision-makers. They have come to realize that Japan's pre-eminence in Asia is being questioned. This, to some extent, has led them to seek an enhancement in Japan's defence cooperation with the US and consider more independent military capabilities. Such a development also may propel Japan to become a normal state in the future.

KEY ASSUMPTIONS:

Taking into account the key indicators and drivers of Japan's pursuit for 'normal' statehood, a few baseline assumptions can be drawn to predict Japan's plausible future, at least for the next two decades.

Assumption 1: In the coming decades, constitution revision is likely to emerge as a matter of great debate within the country. In order to cope with the changing security environment, the Japanese government will broaden its interpretations of the pacifist

---

26 Frances Rosenbluth, Jun Saito and Annalisa Zinn, "Japan's New Nationalism: The International and Domestic Politics of an Assertive Foreign Policy", January 2007, available on http://eastasianstudies. research.yale.edu/japanworld/rosenbluth.pdf. (accessed on November 3, 2009).

Constitution. However, formal revision of the Constitution will remain an irritant as Japanese people are predicted to largely remain pacifist for some years to come.

Assumption 2: In its pursuit for 'normal' statehood, the Japanese government continues to expand the functions of the SDF. Simultaneously it is also likely to embark upon successive revisions of its national defence doctrines, making them all the more assertive. To deal with the growing security threats from the neighbouring states in particular and the world at large, Japan is to increase its power projection capability further.

Assumption 3: In pursuit of 'normal' statehood, Japan is to adopt a more assertive foreign policy, particularly in relation to Asia. Tokyo is also likely to try to strengthen its profile within the international organizations. As a result, some adjustment in the Japan-US security alliance may occur to make it more 'equal' so that instead of continuing its alleged 'free riding', Japan can assume greater responsibility for its own security as well as an expanded regional and global role.

Assumption 4: In the coming years, the economic interdependence between Tokyo and Beijing will continue to grow although they will still be at odds over the territorial disputes over the Senkaku/Diaoyu Islands. Energy security will particularly be a driving force as far as economic relations between the two countries are concerned. The US will continue playing a crucial role in their bilateral relations.

SCENARIO BUILDING-JAPAN IN 2030

On the basis of the baseline assumptions mentioned above, three scenarios can be drawn to indicate which way Japan might go in 2030 in its strive for 'normal' statehood. While the Japan-US security alliance losing its relevance can be treated as a baseline scenario, Japan shedding away its pacifist policy can be identified as the plausible scenario. Japan going nuclear way, however, can be identified as the wildcard scenario. In this section, an effort will be made to offer a brief overview of each of the three scenarios.

Scenario 1:

Baseline Scenario: Japan-US bilateral alliance will remain relevant for the East Asian security architecture.

For decades, The Japan-US bilateral alliance has been considered critical to maintaining peace, stability and prosperity in Asia as well as to promoting liberty, democracy and free-market principles. During the past ten years, the bilateral security ties between the two states have expanded significantly, resulting in more closely integrated military operations and a broader international role for the SDF. While Japan continues to host the largest contingent of US military forces in Asia, the BMD integration remains bright spot in the relationship and joint operations are becoming more and more coordinated.

Despite periodic hiccups in the relationship, the contours and spirit of the Japan-US security alliance have never been diluted. Although recently, former Prime Minister Yukio Hatoyama's call for a fundamental review of the alliance and then friction over the relocation of the US air Station Futenma almost chilled the bilateral relationship, Japan's subsequent decision to keep intact the 2006 Japan-US pact on the relocation issue reaffirmed the continued relevance of the alliance. Newly appointed Japanese Prime Minister Naoto Kan has continued to stress the importance of the alliance and has agreed with the US President Barrack Obama to "work very closely together to address the many issues facing both nations and the global community, including the challenges posed by North Korea and Iran."[27]

Still, it has increasingly been pointed out these days that due to the US government's growing cooperation with China in dealing with global issues, the relevance of the Japan-US alliance has been marginalized. Meanwhile, the normalization of the bilateral relationship between Japan and China continues to be hindered by the historical animosity and mutual distrust. Factors like Japan's lack

---

27 "Kan, Obama make base accord high priority in first talks", *The Japan Times*, June 7, 2010, at http://search.japantimes.co.jp/print/nn20100607a4.html

of remorse for its remorse for its violent past,[28] territorial disputes over Senkaku islands, frictions over energy resources in the East China Sea region, Japan's concern over China's military rise, China's worries over the Japan-US alliance coming together to constrain its great power aspirations, the inclusion of the peaceful resolution of the Taiwan issue as one of the joint security concerns of the Japan-US alliance in 2005, etc. continue to have adverse impact on Japan-China relations.

Even then, the strategic and political concerns about each other have not jeopardized stable and mutually beneficial economic relations between Japan and China. Japan's economic recovery of 2003-07 was largely made possible due to its economic exchange with China. During that time, China too was benefitted by Japanese investment, technology transfers. Since 2004, the two have deepened their economic interdependence when China (along with Hong Kong) overtook the US Japan's leading trading partner, while Japan ranks as China's second most important country in terms of the value of trade.[29] Today, China cannot afford to damage the economic relations with Japan without putting at risk its economic strategy of close engagement with the economies of East Asia that has so far contributed much to the fuelling of its economic growth.[30] On its part, Japan also realizes that if China's drive to modernization fails, it will cause the country to descend into chaos with calamitous results for both the region as well as for Japan.

However, the mutual distrust between the two countries continues to persist. Under the circumstance, the role played by the US as the provider of security in the remains relevant and will remain so in the next few decades, especially in moderating the hostility between China and Japan. Both Japan and China seem to be aware that Washington can still either mitigate or heighten existing tensions

28   Ralf Emmers, "Geopolitics and Maritime Disputes in East Asia", Routledge, London, 2010, p. 24.
29   Michael Yahuda, "Sino-Japanese relations: partners and rivals?", *The Korean Journal of Defense Analysis*, Vo. 21, No. 4, December 2009, p. 365.
30   Ibid., p. 373.

due to its very presence and network of security cooperation in the region. As for the US, the alliance with Japan remains crucial to its force projection in the region and beyond. For Japan, the alliance has so far obviated its need to develop the full panoply of military power commensurate with its economic power. As far as China is concerned, it requires cooperative relations with the US if it is to enjoy the stable international environment that it deems vital for its own economic development. In the coming decades, such interdependence among the three states will not only keep the Japan-US alliance relevant, but also be instrumental in ensuring peace and stability in the region.

Scenario 2:

Plausible Scenario: Gradual withering away of pacifism in Japan

As mentioned earlier, the pacifist Constitution renounces the possession of any military potential. But in recent past, when Japan has begun a debate on possible constitutional reform, one wonders if the Land of the Rising Sun still remains 'pacifist'. Instances have already been provided on how in order to offer support to the US-led war on terror, Japan has reinterpreted the pacifist principles of the Constitution. Japan's neighbours have seen such steps as a move on Japan's part towards military assertiveness and 'normal' statehood.

Today, Japan has emerged as the fifth largest producer of military weapons for a market value of about $5 billion. Researches conducted so far on the issue indicate prospects of Japan in the military industry for international cooperation. In the areas of miniaturization, mixers and digital optics, Japan already offers an excellent service. Japan might soon follow the example of the US, which is using in Iraq around 12,000 robots equipped with missiles and machine guns.[31] If that is the case, then Japan can no longer be treated as pacifist nation just because its fundamental charter prevents it from owing military weapons. Already over burdened with its defense commitments all

---

31 Pino Cazzaniga, "Growing War Industry in pacifist Japan", July 24, 2009, at http://www.asianews.it/index.php?l=en&art=15869#. (accessed on November 3, 2009).

over the world, the US itself may encourage Japan to rearm itself and shoulder greater defence responsibilities.

The role of Japanese leadership in this context cannot be overlooked. Some right wing political leaders have already begun to defend Japan's imperialistic conquest of Asia during the War. Japan has also begun to be vocal to claim its control of disputed islands and territorial waters. Nationalistic propaganda on all sides has generated an air of hostility in Asia and played into the hands of Japanese conservatives who long Japan to become a 'normal' state and marginalize the influence of pacifism.

Scenario 3:
   Wildcard Scenario: Japan goes nuclear

It has often been argued that for the establishment of a stable new Asian order that accommodates a rising China, Japan will need to become strategically more independent of the US, and will ultimately become nuclear. Japan is at present facing a dilemma. Though it has benefitted from its alliance relationship with the US, it also has entailed some costs and risks. The risks had been acceptable to Japan as long as Japan felt prudent to maintain the relationship for its own security. Currently, however, it feels insecure in the wake of increasing bonhomie between the US and China. At the same time, Japan also does not want the US to disengage from China since an adversarial relationship between the two will not be in Japan's interest.

The only way out of the dilemma would be for Japan to become self dependent for its own security. To achieve that goal, Japan will need to go nuclear, as the heart of Japan's strategic dependence on the US is its reliance on US extended deterrence against nuclear threats. Once Japan comes out of the US nuclear umbrella, the nuclear threats from its neighbours will compel Japan to go nuclear. Japan's high technological capability and efficient civil nuclear programme will only facilitate Japan's progress towards nuclearization.

APPRAISAL OF THE THREE SCENARIOS
Of the three scenarios, both the first and second scenarios seem

to be credible. Despite the recent hiccups in the Japan-US security alliance, most Japanese would still support it not only because the Japanese people still remain largely pacifist, but also because the dissolution of the alliance will heighten Japan's vulnerability vis-à-vis its nuclear neighbours. As regards the US, it will like to remain a resident power of Asia through its alliance with Japan, due to its economic, political and military interests in the region. Even though in the coming years, US relations with China will increase manifold, due to common values shared with Japan (democracy, human rights, etc), the US will continue to emphasize on its alliance with Japan.

In the meantime, due to the increasing economic interdependence among Japan, China and the US, the US will also encourage Japan to engage China either singly or through the alliance. This will help in maintaining peace and stability in the East Asian region in the coming years.

As regards the US, it will like to remain a resident power of Asia through its alliance with Japan, due to its economic, political and military interests in the region. Even though in the coming years, US relations with China will increase manifold, due to common values shared with Japan (democracy, human rights, etc), the US will continue to emphasize on its alliance with Japan.

Over the years, Japan has repeatedly compromised the spirit of the pacifist Constitution while defending its stances in sending the SDF for peace support activities and aiding the US in its war on terror. If the security environment in Asia deteriorates further, Japan will feel increasing pressure to pursue a more independent stance in its security affairs. The pacifist principles would be substantially marginalized as a result.

As far as the wildcard scenario is concerned, the possibility of Japan going nuclear seems to be less likely at the moment, but there can be sudden reversal in Japan's stance should North Korea compels Japan to do so. In the event of a decision in Japan adopting the nuclear path, the existing technological base, including a large civilian nuclear programme with reprocessing facilities,[32] will facilitate a quick transition for a nuclear posture. Japan's continued adherence to the three non-nuclear principles[33] and the Basic Law on Atomic Energy[34] will be compromised.

CONCLUSION

In the near term, Japan's ambition to be a 'normal' state is unlikely to materialize. The Japan-US security alliance will continue to be the linchpin for the stable Asian order for some time. However, should the security environment suddenly deteriorates triggered by North Korea's nuclear development programme and accentuated by declining US interest in Japan and increasing US interest in China, Japan opting for nuclear path would seem more real. In such a scenario, Japan's ambition for 'normal' statehood will not trigger a dramatic systemic change as the Japan-US security alliance would be weakened but not dissolved. As a result, the pacifist Constitution would be substantially revised and Japan would adopt a more proactive and independent foreign and security policy. It is however premature to hazard a conclusion if a 'normal' Japan will be benign or pregnant with disturbing ripple effects for the Asian security order. This dilemma will continue to persist for quite some time for security analysts and Japan watchers.

---

32 Kenneth N. Waltz, "The Emerging Structure of International Politics", *International Security*, Vol. 18, No. 2, (Fall 1993), pp. 44-79.

33 The three Non-nuclear principles- non possession, nonproduction, and non introduction of nuclear weapons-were introduced by Japanese Prime Minister Eisaku Sato in 1967 and adopted in 1971.

34 Article 2 of the Basic Law on Atomic Energy establishes that research, development, and utilization of atomic energy must be limited to peaceful purposes and carried out independently under the democratic management. See, Llewelyn Hughes, "Why Japan will not go nuclear (yet): International and Domestic Constraints on the Nuclearization of Japan", *International Security*, Vol. 31, No. 4 (Spring 2007), pp. 67-96.

16
China 2030: Drivers and Scenarios
—Gunjan Singh

The rise of China has become the buzzword for the last few decades. The way China has transformed itself, both internally as well as externally, has become a benchmark. China has successfully managed to provide an alternate model of economic growth to the world. The prediction that the future of the international world order is based in Asia appears to be quite true. From an isolated nation, China has come to play a very important role in international organisations and has become an integral part of the international system. Even the United States today is extending greater role to Beijing and trying to make China more ingrained in the system. The significance of China rise has been such that it has become a timeline in the modern world history. So much has changed that today scholars are coming up with terms like AC (After China) and BC (Before China).[1] Economic crisis of 2008-09 has increased China's clout further.

China is also playing a very important role in the regional architecture and working on a number of multi-lateral structures. The most prominent example here is the Shanghai Cooperation Organisation (SCO). China has successfully utilised this platform to better its relations with states at its western border. Beijing has come to make a number of concessions and has given a large amount of aid to a various countries. The major argument about this is that China is working towards safeguarding its energy requirements. China

---

1   "When China Rules the World: The Rise of the Middle Kingdom and the End of the Western World" by Martin Jacques, p 185, Allen Lane, 2009.

cancelled a loan of about $ 1.3 billion to the African Countries and extended a loan of $ 3 billion in the year 2009.[2] These actions have been perceived cautiously by the rest of the world.

China is extending its role in the South Asian region. It has been extending assistance to countries like Nepal, Sri Lanka and Bangladesh. This has become a cause of concern for India. New Delhi has been quite apprehensive regarding these overtures by Beijing.[3] But not all countries perceive China's regional role with the same degree of apprehension. During his November 2009 visit to Beijing, Obama extended his approval for an increasing Chinese role in the South Asian region. This has not been viewed favourably by New Delhi. Washington has also asked for an increasing role by Beijing in the ongoing Afghan war.

As the first decade of the 21st century comes to an end China is the third largest economy in the world. It grew at 8.7% for the year 2009.[4] It's high rate of development even during the ongoing financial crisis clearly shows that China is gradually becoming the centre of the world economy. The more China participates in the world economy the more the world seems to be dependent on it.

It is not only the economy making the world sit back and take note of China but also its military modernisation. The Anti-Satellite Test of 2007 and the successful Space Walk which followed are just a few examples. The 60th Anniversary celebrations in 2009 have even brought to light the question of weather modifications which China is undertaking.[5] China is modernising its army in almost all the spheres.

2   China's Global Strategy: Towards a Multipolar World" by Jenny Clegg, p 211, Pluto Press, 2009.

3   "India summit sneak preview", Posted By Josh Rogin,, November 20, 2009 at http://thecable.foreignpolicy.com/category/region/south_asia, Accessed on January 1, 2010

4   "China's GDP grows at 8.7% in 2009", *China Daily*, January 21, 2010 at http://www.chinadaily.com.cn/bizchina/2010-01/21/content_9354887. htm, Accessed on February 01, 2010.

5   "China's 'weather modification' works like magic", *The Guardian*, October 1, 2009 at http://www.guardian.co.uk/environment/blog/2009/ oct/01/china-cloud-seeding-parade Accessed on December 25, 2009

The policy of modernisation is also primarily indigenous. The 2008 Defence White Paper has stated that China was working to "develop new and high-tech weaponry and equipment, conduct military training in conditions of information technology and build a modern logistics system in an all-round way".[6] The 2009 Chinese defence budget was around $ 70.2 billion, though this figure has been highly questioned by the other countries, especially the United States. Li Zhaoxing, who is the 11th National People's Congress spokesperson has said that "Defense spending accounts for 6.3 percent of the country's total fiscal expenditure in 2009."[7] There is also a perceived feeling that the actual allocation could be much higher than what is generally quoted by the Chinese government.

Considering these developments the questions that arises is that what is in store for the future of China and future of the international system. There are predictions, which suggest that China may become the next superpower.[8] If this happens then there will be a multi polar world order as the United States will continue to be a key player. In contrast to this, it would not be wrong to suggest that there might be a situation where China may not be able to sustain the current level of economic growth which in turn will cause the ultimate breakdown of the present system.

For either of these expectations to come true, the following would be the key drivers. The most prominent drivers which will be crucial in bringing about any change are, Economy, Environment, Ethnic Issues and Nationalism. The following section studies these drivers.

6   "China issues white paper on military modernisation", January 20, 2009 at http://www.thaindian.com/newsportal/world-news/china-issues-white-paper-on-military-modernisation_100144894.html Accessed on January 7, 2010

7   "China Increases Defense Budget", DefenseNews, March 4, 2010 at http://www.defensenews.com/story.php?i=3973307 accessed on June 27, 2010

8   "China: the Emerging Superpower", By Major H.A. Hynes at http://www.fas.org/nuke/guide/china/doctrine/0046.htm Accessed on January 1, 2010

1. Economic Transition

The Chinese economy is the third largest economy in the world today, but keeping in view the level of growth in 2009 it is accepted that it is on its way to become the second largest economy replacing Japan. A major component of this is the Chinese demographic profile. It is expected that by the year 2030 the Chinese population will reach 1.6 billion.[9] By the same time frame about 700 million Chinese would have joined the "consumer class," or the middle class. This is approximately ten-fold the number of middle class in the U.S. as of 2009.[10]The Chinese government has maintained that approximately 300 to 500 million more people would be shifted out from subsistence agriculture by 2030.[11] China is considered the factory of the world today. Since China opened up in the late 1980s the Chinese Communist Party (CCP) has managed to sustain a yearly growth rate of almost 9%. This has brought a lot of people out of poverty and has created a new rich in the Chinese society. The famous saying by Deng Xiaoping that 'it does not matter whether a cat is black or white if it catches mice' implied a break from Mao's policy of egalitarianism. Based on this dictum China has religiously followed a growth oriented economic strategy. Getting rich is not a taboo in China anymore. This has created a lot of disproportionate development. The development has taken place primarily in the coastal and the urban areas. The rural areas have been left underdeveloped.[12] Due to this the urban population is richer compared to the rural population. The rural population does feel left out from the mainstream development. This pace of development has also resulted in the increase in the number

9   "The Urban-Rural Income Gap in China: Implications for Global Food Markets" By Colin A. Carter, American Journal of Agricultural Economics, Vol. 79, No. 5, Proceedings Issue (Dec., 1997), pp. 141

10 "What Happens When 700 Million Chinese Want their Equivalent of Santa Shoppe?" Kudzu Telegraph, November 25, 2009 at http://www.kudzutelegraph.com/node/320, Accessed on December 30, 2009

11 China's Global Strategy: Towards a Multipolar World" by Jenny Clegg, p 151, Pluto Press, 2009.

12 W. China Development Strategy Bears Fruit Xinhua, August 31, 2006 at http://www.china.org.cn/english/features/poverty/179749.htm

of floating population in the urban areas.[13] This is the unintended outcome of the weakening of the 'iron rice bowl' system in China.[14] CCP has also withdrawn in a large way from the social security system. There has been a massive rise in the medical as well as the educational costs in China. Though the current leadership under Hu Jintao and Wen Jiabao is working towards bridging the gap between rich and the poor it is not achievable in a short period.

It was reported that at the end of 2008, China had 40 million people living below the poverty line which was about 4.2 percent of the total rural population.[15] This is based on 1,196 yuan ($175) per capita net income a year. This threshold is pretty low when compared to 1$ per day level and it is too low when one compares this with the level Chinese economic development and living standard. If we calculate from today's standard China's poor actually totals 150 million.[16]

The recent economic slowdown showed an economically resilient China. But the slowdown has highlighted that the Chinese government needs to re-frame the export model which it was depended on till now.

---

13 "A recent report indicated that China's floating population of migrant workers reached a record 211 million in 2009 and will hit 350 million by 2050 if government policies remain unchanged." Reported in China Daily, June 27, 2010 (China's 'floating population' exceeds 210m) at http://www.chinadaily.com.cn/china/2010-06/27/content_10024861. htm Accessed on June 28, 2010

14 "The Iron Rice Bowl is a Chinese idiom referring to the system of guaranteed lifetime employment in state enterprises. Job security and level of wages were not related to job performance - but adherence to Party doctrine played a very important role." For more information read Iron Rice Bowl" BBC News September 1999, at http://news.bbc. co.uk/hi/english/static/special_report/1999/09/99/china_50/iron.htm Accessed on December 31, 2009

15 "Getting the lowdown on development" By Alexis Hooi in China Daily, at May 7, 2010 at http://www.chinadaily.com.cn/opinion/2010-05/07/ content_9820373.htm, Accessed on July 01, 2010.

16 "Country's poverty line misleading, expert says" People's Daily Online, December 29, 2009 at http://english.people.com.cn/90001/90776/908 82/6854451.html Accessed on December 29, 2009

The major exports markets of China have been hit badly and in order to sustain the level of development the government needs to expand its domestic market. In order to do this it needs to encourage domestic consumption but this may take years to happen. The current levels of huge stimulus spending cannot be sustained for longer period.[17]

There are also predictions regarding China's GDP. Most of the experts from China conclude that the Chinese GDP is expected to grow to about US $5.9 trillion in 2030 and reach $ 6.7 trillion in 2035. By the 2030-2035, rate of economic growth is expected to get to the level of about 2% to 5% per annum.[18]

2. Environmental Degradation

The Chinese government has been under pressure to maintain the level of economic development in order to maintain its legitimacy. In order to do this the government has been making a lot of compromises in the field of environment. China today has a major problem with the water and air pollution; land degradation, desertification and so on. With its obsession on the pace of growth, the government has compromised with the environment. Environmental degradation became a matter of concern by the end of 1980s and its seriousness has continued to increase. As of 2005, an estimated 400 of the mainland's 669 largest cities had water shortage. By the year 2030 when the population is expected to be 1.6 billion, the level of per capita water sources available will be approximately 1760 m³ which is slightly above the critical limit of 1700 m³.[19] In a recent disclosure the Chinese government has claimed that the 2007 water pollution levels were actually double than the government had declared as agricultural

---

17 "The cautious leap forward" The Economists, November 13, 2009 at http://www.economist.com/displayStory.cfm?story_id=14742402&fsrc=nwl Accessed on December 25, 2009

18 "What Will China Look Like in 2035?" By Robert Lawrence Kuhn, Business Week, October 16, 2007 at http://www.businessweek.com/globalbiz/content/oct2007/gb20071016_143714.htm, Accessed on December 28, 2009

19 "China's Political System: Modernization and Tradition", June Teufel Dreyer, Pearson Longman, 2006, p 251.

waste was not taken into consideration.[20] Meanwhile between 2001 and 2005, it is concluded that approximately 54 percent of the seven main rivers in China contained water which was declared unsafe for human consumption.[21]

There has also been an increase in the level of air pollution in China. The number of people who own cars in China is growing. It is assumed that China will be choked by the level of air pollution caused by its own cars. According to the World Health Organization data, 9 out of the 10 most polluted cities in the world are in China.[22] Soil erosion and deforestation are added problems.

3. Ethnicity

Mao Zedong's (1949-1976) policies towards the ethnic minorities shifted between accommodation and assimilation of minorities' languages, traditions, and other characteristics. As a result of this, the policies formulated by Beijing were obeyed even in the remotest areas. Deng Xiaoping reversed many of these policies. In an effort to modernize China, Deng successfully decentralized economic power which was necessary. In addition he also changed Mao Zedong's policies which lead to investment in the coastal regions of China.

When Deng Xiaoping came to power he introduced the new economic reforms. These policies worked. Chinese economy took to an upward trend but it did not include the inland provinces. It also left the areas inhabited by ethnic minorities underdeveloped. Due to this, the ethnic population has had a general feeling of being exploited. Another important factor has been that most of these ethnic areas like Xinjiang, Tibet are resource rich. Due to this, the ethnic population believes that they are being exploited for these very resources. Secondly the policy adopted by the government of sending people from the Han ethnic group to this areas has lead to

---

20 "China says water pollution double official figure" Reuters, February 9, 2010 at http://uk.reuters.com/article/idUKTRE6180U320100209

21 "Cost of Pollution in China: Economic Estimates of Physical Damages" Conference Edition, World Bank and People's Republic of China, pp xi at www.worldbank.org/eapenvironment

22 Ibid 10.

demographic changes. The original inhabitants of these regions feel they are turning into minority in their own regions.

After the collapse of the Soviet Union, the western border of China has witnessed an increasing level of protests. The Uyghur have had support from the newly formed countries of the Central Asia. The people here also feel that they have more in common with the people across the border than with the Han Chinese. The 2009 unrest in the Xinjiang region clearly highlights the level of grievance which this area have against the Party. More than hundred people were killed in this clash. In this region also the Party is deliberately diluting the ethnic demography by sending people from Han ethnic group.[23]

Similar unrests have been seen in the Tibetan region as well. The more the CCP denies to talk with the Dalai Lama the more it is pushing the Tibetans away from its control. The Tibetan youth today is fighting for independence and not happy to be under the control of the central government. The Chinese government has deployed a large number of armed personnel to the Tibetan region in order to curb the 2008 pre-Olympics Uprising. But though the situation is under control CCP is not comfortable with the idea of withdrawing these forces.[24]

At present the party has been able to control the discontent from getting out of control, but there has been an increase in the number of incidences occurring. The government is still working towards formulating a policy which will be helpful in preventing them.

4. Nationalism

Another essential driver is nationalism. The CCP has used the Chinese nationalist feelings as and when it has deemed necessary. With the erosion of ideology, the Party as always resorted to the

---

23 "Why the Xinkiang uprising was so serious Hu Jintao had to lose face at the G-8" The world Tribune, July 10, 2009 at http://www.worldtribune. com/worldtribune/WTARC/2009/mz0549_07_03.asp Accessed on December 25, 2009

24 Ibid 9.

feeling of nationalism when it wanted Chinese people to stand by its side against any one specific enemy. Today it is widely accepted that the economic development is providing the CCP with the legitimacy to rule over the Chinese people. The day the Party is not able to deliver what the people want, it might be difficult for it to sustain itself in the command position. Today whenever Party needs the support of the people for its foreign policy; it ignites the fervour of nationalism. If one day the people direct their nationalism towards the Party, this could lead to it's downfall.

In the past decade, whenever the Party required the support of the people vis-à-vis the United States, as in the case of Yugoslavia Embassy Bombing or the spy plane incident the Party has used nationalism to buttress its stand. It has attempted to portray to its citizens that it is trying to fight for the Chinese nationalism vis-à-vis international imperialist forces like the United States. Even in the case of Japan the CCP has always flared up the feelings of nationalism to support its stance against it. But it has continued to accept Foreign Direct Investment (FDI) from Tokyo. Historical issued are regularly used by Beijing to get popular support for various foreign policy issues. The textbook row in the year 2005 is one such example.[25]

While on the one hand, it provides space for such feelings to be expressed when it is beneficial; it has also been trying to curb such expression when it does not deem it fruitful. It has been using public sentiment to justify some of its foreign policy objectives and convince the Chinese people that it is working towards establishing their just position in the international world order. Even the Chinese media which is generally highly controlled is now being given some amount of freedom to get the opinions of the people and provide them an outlet. The proliferation of the telephone and internet has further complicated things for the PRC because it is getting difficult for the Chinese government to trace who is writing what on the internet

---

25 "Japan history texts anger E Asia" BBC News, April 5, 2005 at http://news.bbc.co.uk/2/hi/asia-pacific/4411771.stm Accessed on December 26, 2009

sites and blogs, despite the highly efficient system to monitor such activities.[26]

This might prove to be a two edged sword for the Party to handle effectively. If it is used more often by the Party, the people might start questioning the legitimacy of the Party to rule. The CCP definitely realizes this duality in its policy, but is unsure about what needs to be done. Today the Party easily passes the responsibility on someone else for things that go wrong and exaggerates the success in the name of strengthening the Chinese nation. The successful completion of the Olympics and the Space Walk are some cases. The Chinese government had blamed the international community for the Tibetan uprising of 2008, which occurred prior to the Olympics.

SCENARIO BUILDING

Based on the drivers mentioned above, one can design the scenarios based on the combination of different variables to get a sense of the future. The future of the China can be assessed by developing scenarios the following scenarios.

1) Scenario I: China becomes stronger:

In this scenario, China successfully manages to sustain its current level of economic development. The problem of inequality between the urban and the rural populations is managed by the government. Even the ethnic issues are sorted out by extending greater autonomy to the ethnic regions. They come to play more incorporative role in the functioning of the Party. As a result the Party has less internal discontent to handle and can thus concentrate on strengthening the domestic environment. There is more all round development and China becomes the number one economy in the world. As the economy develops, the government invests more and more on greener technology and thus there is reduction in the level of environmental degradation.

China invests more and more on its military development and

---

26 "China At 60 – Nationalism" By Gunjan Singh, October 30, 2009 at http://ipcs.org/article/china/china-at-60-nationalism-2994.html Accessed on December 29, 2009

looking at the level of economic benefits and a weakening United States, Taiwan accepts 'one country two systems' policy. After the death of the Dalai Tama, the struggle for an autonomous or independent Tibet withers away.

The Chinese military is modernised and becomes one of the most advanced armies in the world. As China becomes stronger it starts pushing for the solution of the boundary issue with India. Considering that India is sidelined in the international system as the ties between United States and China has increased and China has emerged as the second most important nation in the world, New Delhi has no other option but to accept what Beijing says.

With its successful management Beijing has proved all the predictions of its ultimate downfall as false. With its economic might China has managed to influence countries of Latin America, Africa and the Middle East. As a result, it has successful managed to gain resources and markets to sustain the growth. The world has to fight Beijing in order to gain access to resources.

China also has tapped the water sources in the Tibetan plateau and has caused a concern for the Indian sub continent. Though the United States was one of the premiers in the field, with its weather modification techniques the Chinese army can successful problematise the ecological balance of countries with which it harnesses tensions. Such superior techniques have made the world once again kowtow to Beijing. According to the Chinese world order China has gained its rightful place in the world. As China gained further expertise it is in direct conflict with the US. The Middle Kingdom has re-emerged. It is the only super power which has established itself solely on economic supremacy and not entirely on military might.

Though it appears that China may be able to achieve all this there are a number of probabilities which may not allow this to happen. We are expecting that the Chinese economy will sustain its current level of development. But the most prominent uncertainty in this regard is that Chinese development is export driven. Due to the 2008 financial crisis most of its export destinations have been hit the most. Though achieve growth it has to develop domestic consumption which might prove to be very difficult for Beijing. Secondly, though China may decide to give further autonomy to the troubled regions it may not be such a smooth transformation. It does not appear to be plausible that the demand for independence in Xinjiang and greater autonomy in Tibet will wither away that soon. Thirdly the United States is the sole superpower till date and China trying to come shoulder to shoulder in military might of Washington may not be peacefully accepted by it. Washington may decide to invest more in further military modernisation and prevent China from gaining newer technologies. Finally India's rising global profile will limit China's complete domination in the South Asian region.

2) China Implodes: Alternate Scenario:

The increasing level of economic development proves difficult for the Party to sustain. As there were already ongoing protests based on the disproportionate level of development and an increase in the number of the floating population the number of people affected increases. The reduction in the level of development forces the government to withdraw more and more from the social security measures. Majority of the people lack retirement benefits and other facilities. Cost of living goes up drastically. More number of people are unable to afford medical facilities. Inflation rises and this pushes a large number of people below poverty line. As the economic development slows down more and more people are forced out of job. And they form the section of the people who want to bring change in the system.

There is an increase in the demand for democracy and people show less and less confidence in the CCP and the existing one Party system. Nationalism has an important role to play. Till date the Party had used the upsurge in the nationalists feelings in order to sustain it self. But now these very sentiments are being directed against the Party. The Party is being criticised both politically as well as socially. The people get more agitated as they realise that the Party members are corrupt and they are just concerned about their interest.

As China becomes weaker the Taiwan crisis intensifies. United States is no more interested in the stability of the Mainland as it is not economically intertwined. Due to this, the United States supports the Taiwan independence movement. In this backdrop the Tibetan and Uyghur independence movements also intensifies. The People's Liberation Army (PLA) is not capable of handling crisis on multiple fronts. These outcomes have impact on the region as well. The Central Asian countries have a disturbed boundary. A stable and united China was beneficial for them. They were gaining with respect to trade and other aspects as well. Now they have people from China moving into their territories and this places constraints on their already stretched resources.

The Tibetan independence movement intensifies the situation in India considering the fact that a large Tibetan exile population resides there. The last intensive struggle was after the death of the Dalai Lama but China had successfully managed to curb this. As China faces more such problems India finds opportunity to solve the ongoing boundary issue. Both sides had been trying to work to solve this issue. But there was no solution found. Now New Delhi sensing that Beijing is already weakened pushes for settlement. But in return there are a large number of Tibetan people who refuse to go back to Tibet sensing that there are no more economic gains if one stays with Beijing. India is again placed next to a weak country and the refugee problem intensifies. Tibetans, and even Chinese start moving into the Indian Territory in search of work through Nepal.

There are a number of factors which may prevent this situation. First and foremost the economic meltdown of 2008 clearly showed that the United States economy is completely intertwined with the Chinese economy today. If the US has to survive and be stable it needs the support of Beijing. Secondly the Chinese are investing heavily in their military modernisation. They know and have learnt it that in order to maintain internal stability they have to have resources in both military and economic sense. Third and the most important reason is that it is in the interest of the other countries of the region to have a stable China. Even though China may start getting a little weak the United States will not let it implode. It has a lot at stake and will work towards maintaining a stable China. Though it can be argued that United States will be happy to see China implode, one has to accept that the way China is conducting itself in the international system it is becoming more and more indispensable. China is successfully working towards becoming a 'responsible stake holder' in the international system.

3) Status Quo Continues:

With the passage of time, the Chinese economy reaches its limits and is exhausted. There are no new markets to be exploited and the demands reach the optimum level. In spite of the fact that the government has worked towards increasing the level of domestic demand, there are no more avenues for growth left.

The Chinese economy also has to bear the burden of environmental degradation. Though the government has invested some resources towards development of greener technologies, it has not proved to be quite useful. The level of pollution continues to grow.

Another aspect is the gap between the rich and the poor. China today describes the most blatant example of a developing third world economy. The job market is saturated and though the government tried to encourage domestic consumption, it has not proved to be quite helpful in sustaining the level of growth.

The degree of discontent against the government has risen and there are daily protests against the government policies and the people are lobbying everyday for a more democratic set up. The CCP has to struggle everyday to sustain itself in power. It is viewed as autocratic and the people want more freedom. The media is also freer as the Party has no ways and means to control it any more. The second channel publications have become more and more prominent.

The ethnic problems have also intensified and the government has decided to give more autonomy to the concerned regions. Tibet and Xinjiang have more autonomy and have higher number of representatives in the Central government. As a result there is greater attention being paid to these regions.

Considering the restraint on the resources the government is not able to invest heavily in military modernization and one witnesses a stunting of level of modernization of the Chinese military. The other armies in the region have become more modernised (India). As a result, the ongoing border crisis is not on a verge of being solved. On the other hand, India has managed to sustain its rise and thus is more stable both economically as well as militarily. India is also lobbying to send the Tibetan origin people back to Tibet and the negotiations are continuing.

In the resource market, China is now facing major competition as it does not have money to give in grant and long term loans. African and Latin American countries are giving access to their resources to the highest bidder. One can clearly see that the resource rich areas have become the battleground for the developing countries and China is losing its initial success.

The major predictions are about the ultimate downfall of the Chinese system if something major is not undertaken to change the situation. This is what is expected to be the outcome if the Chinese continue to grow with the same approach which they have now. But there are factors which may not let this be the situation. The more the Chinese economy grows it has managed to get access to more economies. Today there is no region which is not deeply connected with the Chinese economy. Secondly the Chinese also understand that they need to look for alternate options if they have to sustain this level of growth. China has been investing heavily in its military modernisation knowing that it is an essential component for stable growth. In the next two decades it is not likely that China will not be able to sustain its level of growth. 'Hide your strength and bide your time' is what Chinese believe in following.

Conclusion

Considering the above scenarios the most probable one appears to be the third one. The United States is the sole superpower not only due to its economic might but also due to its military might. To expect that any other country will reach that level in the next two decades is quite optimistic. China is also investing greatly in its military modernization but it has to battle its way through the huge number of organizations which the United States has created in order to keep a check on other countries. Even in the field of technological innovation China will have to invest huge amounts in order to get to the level of United States.

Secondly, China is highly dependent on the United States as it is Beijing's largest market. After the economic slowdown there have been efforts being undertaken by China to encourage domestic consumption but it appears to be a far fetched goal. What appears likely is that China will continue to look for more export markets in order to sustain its economic growth. And due to this factor the United States will continue to be an essential player. Some scholars predict that, the progress which the American economy achieved in the period of 85 years from (1945 to 2030), China would have to achieve in a time span of 25 years from 2005 to 2030 for it approach the American level of economic growth.[27]

Thirdly, considering the fact that the United States shares good relations with Japan as well as Taiwan it will be not possible for China to push its way through in the region that easily. Both economically and militarily the United States has wowed to help these allies. Both Taipei and Tokyo are not very comfortable with a strong Beijing and they will continue to cooperate with Washington in order to keep Chinese influence out of the region.

Keeping in view the above points it is highly likely that China and United States will be two of the most key players in the international arena by the year 2030. Though it is not clear as to which one of these would be 'the' most important player. What appears from the given situation today is that the United States

27 "Why the US Will Still be the Only Superpower in 2030" The Futurist, May 2006 at http://futurist.typepad.com/my_weblog/2006/05/why_ the_us_will.html Accessed on December 29, 2009

will manage its super power status but definitely with the support of Beijing.

On the regional front there are assumptions that India would also witness a high level of growth and come to be an important player. But the Chinese today are not that concerned about New Delhi's rise and it will be apparent in 2030 as well. China is more focussed towards its status vis-à-vis the United States rather than India. But any drastic transformation in China will definitely affect India directly.

17
Strategic Trends and Challenges in East Asia in 2030
—Ishida Yasuyuki

INTRODUCTION

East Asia has been undergoing unprecedented rapid economic development and changes.[1] The East Asian economies are growing amidst the financial and economic crises world-wide. Multiple multilateral cooperation is developing in the region, such as the East Asian Summit (EAS), ASEAN Plus Three, and Japan-China-ROK Trilateral Meeting. After the Cold War, the balance-of-power equations and the great powers' policies are changing. China and India are rising extraordinarily. Japan's security policy is "normalizing". The United States' Asia policy is also changing. The East Asian region faces new security challenges, such as the intense rivalry between Japan and China, North Korean missile/nuclear challenges, fundamentalist terrorism, pandemics, natural disasters, and financial crises.

Probably, no region is more important than East Asia to the

---

1   In this paper, "East Asia" means the region of Far East Asia, Eastern Eurasia and Western Pacific centred on continental China and maritime Japan. The main states of East Asia are China, Japan, South Korea, ASEAN 10 (Brunei, Burma, Cambodia, Indonesia, Laos, Malaysia, the Philippines, Singapore, Thailand, and Vietnam) and the key Pacific states of Australia and New Zealand. These states are participants of the East Asian Summit (EAS). The East Asian region also includes Mongolia, North Korea, and Taiwan. Key great powers in East Asia are China and Japan. The US and Russia engaged deeply in East Asia throughout the twentieth century. India is increasing its presence in the region in recent years.

course of global geo-political economy in the current century. The centre of gravity is shifting from West to East. Kishore Mahbubani argues about the "irresistible shift of global power to the east": "Asia is returning to the centre stage it occupied for eighteen centuries before the rise of the West."[2] According to G.V.C. Naidu,

By all indications, the focus is shifting away from Europe to Eastern Asia. The current century will be dominated by events in this region in terms of the emergence of new power centres, proliferation of WMD technologies, terrorism, and economic vibrancy ... With the locus of the international political economy moving inexorably towards the Asia-Pacific, Eastern Asia is likely to emerge as the new cockpit of the 21st century.[3]

For the first time in modern history, East Asia is regaining its own dynamics of power, influence and autonomy.[4]

With East Asia's remarkable resurgence, many debate the future. Goldman Sachs in its report "Dreaming with the BRICs" predicts that "Over the next 50 years, Brazil, Russia, India and China—the BRICs economies—could become a much larger force in the world economy." Project 2020 of the National Intelligence Council (NIC), *Mapping the Global Future*, predicts that

The likely emergence of China and India as new major global players (similar to the rise of Germany in the 19th century and the United States in the early 20th century) will transform the geopolitical landscape, with impacts potentially as dramatic as those of the previous two centuries.[5]

2   Kishore Mahbubani, *The New Asian Hemisphere: The Irresistible Shift of Global Power to the East* (New York: Public Affairs, 2008).

3   N.S. Sisodia and G.V.C. Naidu (eds.) (2005), *Changing Security Dynamic in Eastern Asia: Focus on Japan.*

4   For an insightful review of the "resurgence" of Asia, see John McKay, "A resurgent Asia in the new global order", *Australian Journal of International Affairs*, 63(1) (March 2009): 121–32.

5   Dominic Wilson and Roopa Purushothaman, *Dreaming with BRICs: The Path to 2050*, Goldman Sachs, Global Economics Paper No. 99 (2003); NIC, *Mapping the Global Future, Report of the National Intelligence Council's 2020 Project* (2004).

Considering the rapid development and changes in the region in recent years, it is difficult to predict the region's course even in the short - and mid-term future. A Chinese-Japanese maxim says, "Policymaking needs planning a hundred years ahead." In this fast changing world, however, it is difficult to foresee even ten years ahead.[6]

History is our guide to the future; it makes sense by our dialogue between past, present and future.[7] The course of history, however, abounds with accidents, surprises, and mysteries. The NIC report, *Global Trends 2025,* emphasizes change rather than continuity:

> The rapidly changing international order at a time of growing geopolitical challenges increases the likelihood of discontinuities, shocks, and surprises. No single outcome seems preordained ... In the 20th century, experts forecasting the next 20 years ... often missed major geopolitical events, basing their predictions largely on linear projections without exploring possibilities that could cause discontinuities.[8]

This paper aims to prescribe a broad range of future scenarios "based not on predictions but on alternative possibilities".[9] It adopts

---

6   For the difficulties of prediction in international relations see, for example, Stanley Hoffmann, *World Disorders: Troubles Peace in the Post-Cold War Era* (Lanham: Rowman & Littlefield, 1998); Stanley Hoffmann, "The Future of the International Political System: A Sketch", in *Janus and Minerva: Essays in the Theory and Practice of International Politics* (Boulder: Westview Press, 1987); Robert Jervis, "The Future of World Politics: Will it Resemble the Past?", *International Security*, 16(3) (Winter 1991–1992): 39–73; John Lewis Gaddis, "International Relations Theory and the End of the Cold War", *International Security*, 17(3) (Winter 1992–1993): 5–58.

7   Edward Hallett Carr, *What is History?* (40th anniversary edition) (Basingstoke: Palgrave, 2001). Although Carr insightfully analyses the problem of the interwar period for twenty years in his enduring classic *The Twenty Years' Crisis*, his later works overestimated Great Britain's role as a great power in the post-World War II world and the future of socialist economic planning.

8   <http://www.dni.gov/nic/PDF_2025/2025_Global_Trends_Final_Report.pdf>.

9   For futuristic works of prediction after the Cold War see, for example,

the Strategic Trends approach used by the Development, Concepts and Doctrine Centre (DCDC), Ministry of Defence, UK. "The benefit of strategic futures work is not that it predicts the future, which is unpredictable, or enables organizations to control it. It is about rehearsing possibilities, so one is better able to respond if they happen."[10] This approach starts by "identifying the major trends in each of these dimensions and analyses ways in which these trends are likely to develop and interact" in order to explore a range of probable outcomes. The approach identifies important security implications associated with the outcomes.[11]

> One of the strengths of the Strategic Trends assessment is its independence from routine staffing and wider Defence decision-making ... Strategic Trends is able to inform Defence decisions, without being constrained by the latest good idea, fashionable trend or received wisdom. Some of the findings in Strategic Trends will, therefore, challenge views which derive from existing or transient circumstances, rather than from long-wave trends and from the enduring features of the strategic context.[12]

The roadmap of this paper, dealing with East Asia, is as follows. First, it explains the regional characteristics and historical background. Next, it analyses contemporary trends, key issues and

Francis Fukuyama, *The End of History and the Last Man* (London: Hamish Hamilton, 1992); Samuel Huntington, *The Clash of Civilizations and the Remaking of the World Order* (New York: Simon & Schuster, 1996); John J. Mearsheimer, "Back to the Future", *International Security*, 15(1) (Summer 1990); Robert D. Kaplan. *The Coming Anarchy: Shattering the Dreams of the Post Cold War* (Vintage, 2001).

10 *Benchmarking UK Strategic Futures Work*, Government Performance and Innovation Unit.

11 Development, Concepts and Doctrine Centre, Ministry of Defence (UK), *The DCDC Global Strategic Trends Programme: 2007–2036*, 3rd edition (Swindon, January 2007) (henceforth, *DCDC 2007–2036*): x–xiv. For a critical understanding of strategic simulations and scenario planning, see Ken Jimbo (2008), "Kaiho to Kyousei ni Mukatte – Kokusai Seiji no Kouzou Hendou to Nihon Gaiko (Toward Opening and Coexistence: Structural Changes in International Politics and Japanese Diplomacy)", *Gaiko Forum*.

12 *DCDC 2007–2036*, ibid., p. x.

debates. Third, main drivers in the region are identified to prescribe a set of future scenarios in 2030. Fourth, various future scenarios are depicted in a broad spectrum. Fifth, the risks and challenges that the region will face are discussed. The paper concludes to summarize the argument, consider the implications, and prescribe some policy recommendations.

BACKGROUND

GEO-POLITICAL CHARACTERISTICS OF EAST ASIA

Diversity is the most salient feature of East Asia. Geo-politically, the region consists of continental Eastern Eurasia and oceanic Western Pacific. According to Robyn Lim,

> East Asia's strategic geography will be defined as those parts of the Eurasian landmass adjoining the Pacific Ocean, their hinterlands, and the offshore islands. Large landmasses further afield, notably the Indian subcontinent and the island continent of Australia ... are also relevant to East Asia's strategic geography because they affect the regional balance. East Asia possesses two "core areas", China and Japan. China is a mostly self-sufficient continent-sized land power which occupies the central geographical position on the eastern edge of the Eurasian landmass. For its part, Japan is a resource-poor but populous archipelago barely off the littoral.[13]

Geo-politics among the great powers remains crucial in East Asia. Henry Kissinger notes:

> The great powers of Asia—larger in size and far more populous than the nations of nineteenth-century Europe—treat one another as strategic rivals. India, China, Japan, Russia—with Korea and the states of Southeast Asia not lagging far behind—consider that some of the others, and certainly a combination of them, are indeed capable of threatening their national security. Wars among these powers are not imminent, but they are not inconceivable either. Asian military expenditures are rising, and

---

13 Robyn Lim, *The Geopolitics of East Asia: The search for equilibrium* (London: Routledge, 2003), p. 3.

they are designed principally as protection against other Asian nations (though some of China's military effort includes as well the contingency of a war with the United States over Taiwan). As in nineteenth-century Europe, a long period of peace is possible— even likely—but a balance of power will necessarily play a key role in preserving it.[14]

The East Asian region includes two relatively separated sub-regions, that is, North-East and South-East Asia. To quote Kissinger again:

> In contrast to nineteenth-century Europe, there exists no single homogeneous equilibrium in Asia; the vastness of the region and the differences in culture and history have combined to produce two strategic balances: in Northeast Asia, China, Japan, Russia, and the United States interact with a potential flashpoint on the volatile Korean peninsula; in Southeast Asia, China, India, Japan, the United States, and Indonesia are the principal actors whose interests must be reconciled with those of Vietnam, Thailand, Australia, and the Philippines.[15]

Broadening regionalism and economic dynamics have been encouraging East Asia to be more open and inclusive. India, Australia, and New Zealand were not traditionally closely integrated in the East Asian geopolitics. In recent years, however, they are joining East Asian economic dynamics and various regional multilateral frameworks more inseparably. India, Australia, and New Zealand are original members of the EAS.

RISE AND FALL OF EAST ASIAN REGIONAL ORDER IN FLUX

East Asia has undergone rapid and dramatic changes. The regional order has risen or fallen due to geo-political competitions

---

14 Henry Kissinger, *Does America Need Foreign Policy?* (New York: Simon & Schuster, 2001).

15 Ibid., pp. 113–14. See also Byung-Kook Kim and Anthony Jones (eds.), *Power and Security in Northeast Asia* (2008); Raghavan (ed.), *Asian Security Dynamic: US, Japan and the Rising Powers* (2008); Kokubun Ryousei (ed.), *Challenges for China-Japan-U.S. Cooperation* (Tokyo: Japan Center for International Exchange, 1998); Derek McDougall, *Asia Pacific in World Politics* (2008).

and rivalries. After the Western impact in the nineteenth century, East Asia became the region of constant power struggle among the great powers; until the end of the Cold War, it was the region of great-power wars and conflicts. Even today, East Asia continues to be the arena of geo-strategic rivalry among external and internal great powers.[16]

Though the Chinese "Middle Kingdom" was literally the centre of the East Asian regional order in pre-modern times, this order was broken by the Western imperial powers and modernizing Japan. Modern Japan rose to be a regional power by defeating China and Russia by the beginning of the twentieth century. After World War I, the American-led Washington system brought stability to East Asia in the 1920s. With the world economic crisis in the 1930s, Japan's attempt to revise the Western-dominated East Asian order ended in disastrous defeat. The latter half of the twentieth century was dominated by the Cold War among the US, China and Russia (the former Soviet Union) though East Asia experienced regional wars, including the Korean War and the Vietnam War. Throughout the twentieth century, the United States increased its power, engagement and influence in East Asia by defeating Japan in the Pacific War and Russia (the former Soviet Union) in the Cold War. Pyle depicts this flux of changes of the rise and fall of the East Asian order as follows:

(1)   the collapse of the Sino-centric system and the establishment of the Western imperialist order in the mid-nineteenth century;

(2)   the end of the imperialist system after World War I and

16   Robyn Lim, *Geopolitics of East Asia*; Suisheng Zhao, *Power Competition in East Asia: From the Old Chinese World Order to Post-Cold War Regional Multipolarity* (Basingstoke: Macmillan, 1997); Michael Yahda, *The International Politics of the Asia-Pacific, 1945–1995* (London: Routledge, 1996); Derek Mcdougall, *Asia Pacific in World Politics* (2008). See also Barry Buzan, "The Asia-Pacific: what sort of region in what sort of world?", Joon Num Mak, "The Asia-Pacific security order", Colin Mackerras, "From imperialism to the end of the Cold War", all in Anthony McGrew and Christopher Brook (eds.), *Asia-Pacific in the New World Order* (London: Routledge in association with the Open University, 1998).

the beginning of a new American-inspired system based on several treaties negotiated at the Washington Conference in 1921-1922;

(3) the disintegration of this U.S.-led system and the anarchy of the 1930s, which enticed Japan into attempting to create its own East Asian order;

(4) the crushing defeat of Japan's new order and the establishment of a new U.S.-dominated liberal order after 1945 and the beginning of the Cold War;

(5) the end of this Cold War bipolar system with the collapse of the Soviet Union in 1989.[17]

East Asian Resurgence Throughout the Twentieth Century

In this highly fluid geo-political region, the resurgence of Asia has been a long historical process. Japan joined the group of great powers by developing "rich nation, strong army" and by defeating Chinese and Russian imperialism by the early twentieth century. Despite the disastrous defeat of the Pacific War, Japan revived as an economic power by the 1960s. In the post-Cold War era Tokyo plays a more active international and regional role as a peace-fostering civilian power.

The Asian nations got political independence from colonialism in the second half of the twentieth century. Nationalism is a strong trend of modern international relations. After the Pacific War and struggles for independence, the Asian nations were liberated from Western colonialism. It was symbolic that China and India took the leadership at the Asian-African (Bandung) Conference of 1955.

The regional Cold War between the US and China (PRC) ended by the rapprochement between the two countries in the 1970s. Despite the legacy of the divisions on the Korean Peninsula and in the Taiwan Strait remaining unresolved, the decline and end of the Cold War greatly enhanced peace and stability in East Asia.

After achieving a sort of regional political stability, the East Asian

---

17   Pyle, *Japan Rising*, p. 28.

economies began dynamic economic development. Japan revived as an economic power by the 1960s, followed by the newly industrializing economies (NIEs) or "Four Asian Little Dragons" (South Korea, Hong Kong, Taiwan, Singapore), and the ASEAN-4 (Indonesia, Malaysia, the Philippines, Thailand), China and Vietnam. The 1993 World Bank Report named this dynamic economic development as the "East Asian Economic Miracles". India followed this Asian economic development by the 1990s.[18]

TRANSFORMING EAST ASIAN DYNAMICS AFTER THE COLD WAR[19]

With remarkable economic development, democratization seems to be a major trend in Asia-Pacific. The liberal democratic system and values of human rights are deeply embedded not only in Western-originated Australia and New Zealand in the Pacific but also in Japan, South Korea, Taiwan, the Philippines and India, which have historically been influenced by Anglo-Saxon liberalism. With economic development, the South-East Asian countries are undergoing democratization. As "republican peace" or "democratic peace" theorists argue, it is widely observed that liberal democratic

18   World Bank, *The East Asian Miracle: Economic Growth and Public Policy*, A World Bank Policy Research Report (New York: Oxford University Press, 1993). See also Taizo Miyagi, Shin Kawashima and Hirotsugu Tamura, "Nihon ga Motomeru Ajia, Ajia ga Motomeru Nihon (Japan expects Asia, and Asia expects Japan), *Gaiko Forum*, No. 245 (December 2008); Colin Mackerras, "From imperialism to the end of the Cold War", in Anthony McGrew and Christopher Brook (eds.), *Asia-Pacific in the New World Order* (London: Routledge, 1998); Mark T. Berger, *The Battle for Asia: From decolonization to globalization* (London: Routledge Curzon, 2004).

19   For the work in the 1990s, see Michael Mandelbaum (ed.), *The Strategic Quadrangle: Russia, China, Japan and the U.S. in East Asia* (New York: Council on Foreign Relations Press, 1995); Gerald Segal, "The Asia-Pacific: what kind of challenge?" in McGrew and Brook (eds.), *Asia-Pacific in the New World Order* (1998); Brzezinski, *The Grand Chessboard: American Primacy and its Geostrategic Imperatives* (1997); Michael Mandelbaum (ed.), *The Strategic Quadrangle – Russia, China, Japan, and the United States in East Asia* (New York: Council on Foreign Relations Press, 1995); Kent Calder, *Asia's Deadly Triangle* (London: Nicholas Brealey, 1996); *A Foreign Affairs Reader, Asia - Rising or Falling?* (New York: Council on Foreign Relations).

republics tend to not fight each other. It is very difficult to imagine that Japan and the United States fight each other in the foreseeable future.[20]

Regional cooperation and gradual integration are remarkable trends today. Economic cooperation started as Asia-Pacific Economic Cooperation (APEC) in the late 1980s. Today, the emerging regional cooperation centred on East Asia is driven by the ASEAN Plus Three (Japan, China and South Korea), but is also attracting neighbouring economics including the US, India, Australia, New Zealand, and possibly Russia. In recent years, the dynamics of regionalism has shifted from broader Asia-Pacific to East Asia, with Asia-Pacific becoming more integrated into the East Asia-centred Asian region. The remarkable characteristics of regionalism in East Asia are open and inclusive cooperation based on common interests and opportunities.[21]

A sense of commonality and regional identity is gradually emerging due to regional cooperation, economic development and interdependence, common interests and agendas. The region is sharing opportunities, challenges, interests and identities, leading to "Asianization of Asia".[22] Although some Asian leaders in the 1990s loudly asserted the "Asian values" to protest American intervention, Asian leaders today are more confident of their economic

---

20 For Kantian liberal republican peace, see Michael Doyle, *Ways of War and Peace* (New York: W.W. Norton, 1997); Seizaburo Sato, "Why the shift from kokubo (national defense) to anzen hosho (security)?: A study of the basic issues surrounding Japan's security", *Asia-Pacific Review*, 7(2) (2000).

21 Robert Ayson, "Multilateral Institutions and Major-Power Cooperation: A Framework for Analysis", in Sisodia and Krishnappa (eds.), *Global Power Shifts and Strategic Transition in Asia* (2009); Amitav Acharya, "Why Asia's Past Be Its Future?", *International Security*, 28(3) (Winter 2003–04).

22 Yoichi Funabashi, "The Asianization of Asia", *Foreign Affairs*, 72(5) (November/December 1993). See also Kishore Mahbubani, *Can Asians Think? Understanding the Divide between East and West*, 3rd edn. (New Delhi: Penguin, 2004).

development and modernization. Asia has become the region truly for Asian people, which are centred on ASEAN Plus Three. The East Asia Summit (ASEAN+3, India, Australia, New Zealand) has been evolving to create an East Asian Community (EAC) as a long-term objective.[23]

According to Japan's *Diplomatic Bluebook 2009*,

Having overcome the economic crisis of 1997, Asia has ridden the wave of globalization to attain continuous high economic growth, with its intra-regional mutual economic interdependence deepening through the expansion of its manufacturing industries' production networks. The creation of a sense of community within the region is also emerging through the permeation of shared lifestyles, increasingly dynamic people-to-people exchanges, and the expansion of pop culture. Against such a backdrop, there have been increasingly intense discussions in recent years regarding the formation of an East Asian community.[24]

Contemporary Trends, Key Issues and Debates

In assessing the possible future of East Asia in the next two decades, the aspects presented in Table 1 need to be kept in perspective.

---

23 For regional cooperation and multilateralism in East Asia and the Pacific, see "Ajia wa hitotsu ka (Is Asia One?)", *Gaiko Forum*, No. 245 (December 2008); Takeshi Yuzawa, "Asian Security Institutions in Great Power Dynamics: Adjuncts to Balance of Power or Forces for Regional Stability?" and Zhu Feng, "Regionalism, Multilateralism and Institutional Building in East Asia", both in Raghavan (ed.), *Asian Security Dynamic: US, Japan and the Rising Powers* (2008); Amitav Acharya, "Regional Institutions and Asian Security Order: Norms, Power, and Prospects for Peaceful Change", in Muthaih Alagappa (ed.), *Asian Security Order* (2003).

24 Ministry of Foreign Affairs, Japan, *Diplomatic Bluebook 2009*. See also Shigekatsu Kondo, "Japan and the East Asian Security in the Twenty-first Century", in Sisodia and Krishnappa (eds.), *Global Power Shifts and Strategic Transition in Asia* (2009).

Table 1. Asia's geo-political architecture in the current century
• No country is seeking to transform US politics or assert hegemony over countries of vital interest to the United States.
• Threats to US security are increasingly from terrorism, guerrilla warfare, and proliferation of WMDs, not traditional security threats.
• China is joining the system; not subverting it.
• Asia's architecture is determined by the United States, China, and Japan.
• India is rising, but the gap with China continues to widen.
» Vietnam is rising but is not yet a regional geopolitical force.   » Russia is a Central Asian power, not a Pacific or South Asian power.
• Korea is torn between consensus needed for alliance with the United States and rising concern about excessive confrontation with North Korea (DPRK) or the US-Japan alliance dragging it into a confrontation with China.
• China is the principal sponsor of development through multilateral economic liberalization in South-East Asia; South-East Asia is no longer dependent on US largesse.
• Sino-Japanese rivalries are reviving.
• Interest alignments are increasingly blurred.
» The US-Japan military/ideological alliance continues to strengthen.   » US-Chinese political-economic cooperation grows as well.
• Asia is increasingly multipolar.
• An economically dynamic, militarily weak (for now) China is replacing Japan as the regional leader.

> - Vietnam is joining the Asian-miracle system and eschewing further geopolitical expansion.
> - US priorities have shifted from economy-and institution-building to more exclusive military-and democracy-building.
>
> Source: Overholt, *Asia, America, and the Transformation of Geopolitics*: 29.

Future of East Asia: Militarist or Pacific?

With the remarkable resurgence of Asian economic, political and military power, Asia has become the centre of attention and debate in international relations. Many questions are being asked on the status, implications and future of Asia. How and why are Asian political economies rising so remarkably? Will China's rise be peaceful or provocative? Will the rise of Asia bring promises or problems? Will China's future be promising or problematic? Are the US and Japan, the advanced powers, declining? What are the likely consequences of these rapid and drastic changes of powers in Asia? Can cooperation be promoted in the EAS to create an EAC? Broadly, there are two theoretical opposite views on East Asia. Whereas the liberals are optimistic to seize the opportunities, the realists are pessimistic about coping with uncertainties and challenges in the region.[25] The liberals,

---

25 For comprehensive theoretical assessments of Asia, see Muthiah Alagappa (ed.), *Asian Security Practice: Material and Ideational Influences* (Stanford: Stanford University Press, 1998); Muthiah Alagappa (ed.), *Asian Security Order: Instrumental and Normative Features* (Stanford: Stanford University Press, 2003); G. John Ikenberry and Michael Mastanduno (eds.), *International Relations Theory and the Asia-Pacific* (New York: Columbia University Press, 2003); and J. Shu, Peter Katzenstein and Allen Carlson (eds.), *Rethinking Security in East Asia: Identity, Power, and Efficiency* (Stanford: Stanford University Press, 2004). For articles, see David C. Kang, "Getting Asia Wrong: The Need for New Analytical Frameworks," *International Security*, 27(4) (Spring 2003); Amitav Acharya, "Will Asia's Past Be Its Future?", *International Security*, 28(3) (Winter 2003/04): 149–64; Aaron L. Friedberg, "Europe's Past, Asia's Future", SAIS Policy Forum Series, No. 3 (October 1998). For constructivist arguments, see Thomas Berger, "Set for stability?: Prospects for conflict and cooperation in East Asia", *Review of International Studies*, Vol. 26 (2000): 405–28.

suggesting optimism, point out that East Asia's peace, prosperity and progress are enhanced by various forums of politico-economic multilateral cooperation and regionalism, liberal globalization and interdependence, and democratization. Major wars among the great powers are unlikely, being too costly and devastating. Asians will be able to create an EAC just as the Europeans are developing the European Union (EU).[26] On the other hand, the realists are cautious. The region is facing negative trends of rising nationalism, uneven economic growth and changing balance of power and transition, arms build-up, and unresolved territorial and sovereignty disputes. The legacies of the Cold War, Taiwan and the Korean Peninsula, remain the most dangerous spots in global security. Furthermore, nuclear and missile proliferation, terrorism, piracy, environmental problems, energy security, and epidemic diseases pose challenges to Asian security.[27]

With its dynamic and irreversible resurgence, the East Asian region poses challenges, uncertainties, and opportunities. The touchstone of ongoing unsolved theoretical debates on East Asia is the course of history for years to come.[28]

---

26 For liberal arguments on East Asia, see Ralph A. Cossa and Jane Khanna, "East Asia: economic interdependence and regional security", *International Affairs*, 73(2) (1997): 219–34.

27 For realists arguments of Asian security in the 1990s, see Paul Dibb, David D. Hale, and Peter Prince, "Asia's Insecurity," *Survival* (Autumn 1999); Matake Kamiya, "Hopeful Uncertainty: Asia-Pacific Security in Transition", *Asia-Pacific Review*, 3(1) (Spring/Summer 1996); Thomas J. Christensen, "China, the U.S.-Japan Alliance, and the Security Dilemma in East Asia," *International Security*, 23(4) (Spring 1999); Richard Betts, "Wealth, power and instability: East Asia and the United States after the Cold War", *International Security*, 18(3) (1993-94); Aaron Friedberg, "Ripe for rivalry: prospects for peace in a multipolar Asia", *International Security*, 1994; Barry Buzan and Gerald Segal "Rethinking East Asian security", *Survival*, 36(2) (1994).

28 For recent theoretical works, see Namrata Goswami (2009), "Theorising the Rise of Asia: Global Power Shifts and State Responses", in Sisodia and Krishnappa (eds.), *Global Power Shifts and Strategic Transition in Asia*.

Key Drivers of Strategic Trends in East Asia toward 2030

By identifying the major trends and driving factors, the Strategic Trends approach analyses ways in which these trends are likely to develop and interact. The key drivers largely influence the major strategic trends and future scenarios. What are the key drivers of East Asia in the foreseeable future?

In the twentieth century East Asia was decisively influenced by the West-originated forces of modernization, particularly nationalism, economic industrialization (with applications of science and technology), political democratization and social equalization. These modernization processes were examined by social scientists since the birth of social science. As these classical thinkers foresaw, these forces prompted Asian resurgence and decisively changed the face and feature of our world, including the East Asian region.[29]

American hegemony has been the driver of global forces such as globalization, liberal and economic liberalization, modernization, and geopolitics. Throughout the twentieth century, the United States rose to a global power, especially by winning World War II and the Cold War. In the early twenty-first century, however, US primacy has been declining due to the rise of the rest, the global power shift from West to East, and the remarkable Asian resurgence, particularly of China and India. Despite its relative decline, the United States has been the leading state with vigorous "hard and

---

29   These modernization forces were analysed by the founding fathers of modern social and political science, notably Max Weber, Karl Marx, John Stuart Mill, and Alex de Tocqueville. For distinguished Japanese works on international political economy and modernization, see Yasusuke Murakami, *An Anticlassical Political-economic Analysis: A Vision for the Next Century*, trans. by Kozo Yamamura (California: Stanford University Press, 1996); Seizaburo Sato, "Three Major Twentieth Century Trends and Japan's Future Role", *Asia-Pacific Review*, 3(1) (1996). Akihiko Tanaka's major work, *Atarashii Chusei (A New Medieval Age)* analyses three basic models of international relations by identifying key drivers in the post-Cold War international system such as economic interdependence, liberal democracy, the future of American hegemony and nation-states.

soft power", thus becoming the main force of globalization and liberalization.[30]

This project identifies four key drivers and dynamics, that is, the major strategic trends in East Asia: (1) great powers' geopolitics; (2) globalization and liberalization; (3) regionalism and regionalization; and (4) energy, resource, and environment.[31]

GREAT POWERS' GEO-POLITICS[32]

Since the Western impact, East Asia has been the region of geo-politics among the great powers. Regional geo-political dynamics means the geo-political structure and process among the major powers in East Asia. The salience of geo-politics among the great powers is a fact of life. Recent debates on Asian resurgence include various geo-political issues such as the rise of China and India, the "normalization" of Japan's security policy, the future of American hegemony and its Asia policy, diversifying strategic partnership such as Indo-US strategic partnership and Japan-India global strategic partnership, and intensifying rivalry and competition including Japan-China or India-China relations.

From a geo-strategic perspective, "genuinely tectonic shifts are occurring in East Asia's geopolitical landscape." Zbigniew Brzezinski insightfully notes:

---

30 For various assessments of American hegemony today, see Melvyn P. Leffler and Jeffrey W. Legro (eds.), *To Lead the World: American Strategy after the Bush Doctrine* (Oxford: Oxford University Press, 2008); Eric Hobsbawn, *Globalisation, Democracy and Terrorism* (London: Little Brown, 2007); Fareed Zakaria, *The Post-American World* (New Delhi: Penguin, 2008).

31 Many studies examine these key factors for the future. See NIC, *Global Trends 2025* and *Mapping the Global Future*; *DCDC 2007–2036*.

32 Geo-politics means an "approach to politics ... that stressed the constraints imposed on foreign policy by location and environment". This approach originated in late-nineteenth-century Germany, and mediated to policymakers by Karl Haushofer and Halford Mackinder. The idea contributed to modern political realism, notably by N. Spykman, S.B. Cohen, Henry Kissinger, and Zbigniew Brzezinski in US foreign policy. Ian McLean and Alistair McMillan (eds.), *Oxford Concise Dictionary of Politics, Indian Edition* (New Delhi: Oxford University Press, 2004).

- China, whatever its specific prospects, is a rising and potentially dominant power.

- America's security role is becoming increasingly dependent on collaboration with Japan.

- Japan is groping for a more defined and autonomous political role.

- Russia's role has greatly diminished, while the formerly Russian-dominated Central Asia has become an object of international rivalry.

- The division of Korea is becoming less tenable, making Korea's future orientation a matter of increasing geostrategic interest to its major neighbors.[33]

In East Asian geo-politics, the main players are the US, Japan, China, but also increasingly emerging India and resurgent Russia.[34] The US and Japan have both "hard power" and "soft power" despite their relative decline of power and influence. Chinese and Indian political and military powers are increasing with economic growth. Russia is gradually recovering its political power and economy. In recent years, the regional balance of power has been shifting to East Asia due to the remarkable rise of China and India and Japan's steady resurgence.[35]

---

33 Zbigniew Brzezinski, *The Grand Chessboard* (New York: Basic Books, 1997), p. 157.

34 ASEAN is an important regional organization economically and politically as a driver of multilateral cooperation, but its geo-political power and influence remain considerably limited as a middle power for the foreseeable future. However, further ASEAN integration and economic growth will considerably contribute to regional stability and economic growth and the promotion of multilateral cooperation in East Asia and the Pacific.

35 For recent works on geo-politics of East Asia, see William H. Overholt, *Asia, America and the Transformation of Geopolitics* (Cambridge: Cambridge University Press and Rand Corp.); Byung-Kook Kim and Anthony Jones (eds.), *Power and Security in Northeast Asia: Shifting Strategies* (New Delhi: Viva Books, 2008); Bill Emmott, *Rivals – How the Power Struggle between China, India and Japan Will Shape Our Next Decade* (London: Penguin, 2008); Samuel Kim (ed.), *The International Relations of North East Asia*

Since the decline of the Cold War, the great powers' relations in East Asia have largely been cooperative without direct military conflicts. First, the great powers' imperialistic intervention lost legitimacy. Second, security communities among liberal democracies with advanced economies are developing, and they are unlikely to fight each other using military force. Third, both developed and developing countries are focusing more on economic growth than on military power. Due to the nuclear revolution, economic interdependence, and liberal democratic regimes, major wars among the great powers are too costly and unlikely today, if not unthinkable.

GLOBALIZATION AND POLITICO-ECONOMIC LIBERALIZATION[36]

After the end of the Cold War, globalization and economic and political liberalization are widening and deepening all over the world. Liberal economy and liberal democracy are closely interrelated. In the 1930s, economic stagnation and bloc economy caused political and social instability in East Asia and for the Japanese adventurous policy to revise the status quo. Since the 1970s and '80s, remarkable economic growth and development have prompted political liberalization, that is, democratization in East Asia.

Globalization and liberalization are prompted by science and technology such as Information Technology (IT), communication system, and the Internet. With accelerated globalization, new security challenges are emerging: financial/currency instability, infectious diseases, low-intensity conflicts, civil wars, energy, resource, and environment security including climate change, and natural disasters.

(London: Rowman & Littlefield); Emmott, *Rivals*; Raghavan (ed.), *Asian Security Dynamic: US, Japan and the Rising Powers*; Maharajakrishna Rasgotra, *The New Asian Power Dynamic* (New Delhi: Sage, 2007).

36 Globalization is "a historical process involving a fundamental shift or transformation in the spatial scale of human social organization that links distant communities and expands the reach of power relations across regions and continents. It is also ... often used to describe a single world-economy after the collapse of communism, though sometimes employed to define the growing integration of international capitalist system in the post-war period." Baylis, Smith and Owens, *The Globalization of World Politics*, 4th edition, pp. 580 and 582.

Terrorism and the proliferation of WMDs are the most important security agenda for the US and the global security discourse.[37]

The DCDC Global Strategic Trends Programme 2007–2036 (UK) regards globalization as the top priority, as follows:

> *A defining feature during the next 30 years will be the constant tension between greater interdependence and intensifying competition...* During the next 30 years, the volume of transactions, conducted irrespective of the physical distance between those engaged, *will* continue to expand, shaping and improving everyday life for millions of people. A key feature of globalization *will* be the continuing internationalization of markets for goods, services and labour, which *will* integrate geographically dispersed sets of customers and suppliers. This *will* be an engine for accelerating economic growth, but *will* also be a source of risk, as local markets become increasingly exposed to destailizing fluctuations in the wider global economy... Life will, as a result, be competitive, dynamic and fluid... Politically, globalization will raise levels of interdependence between states that are increasingly integrated within the globalized economy.[38]

REGIONALISM AND REGIONALIZATION[39]

Regionalism and regionalization have been a major trend in East Asia and the Pacific. In the 1970s–'90s, regional cooperation developed in the Asia-Pacific region such as ASEAN, APEC in economy, trade, and investment, and the ASEAN Regional Forum (ARF) in security. In 1993 US President Bill Clinton proposed to build up a "Pacific Community".[40]

---

37   William T. Tow (ed.), *Security Politics in the Asia-Pacific: A Regional-Global Nexus?* (New York: Cambridge University Press, 2009).

38   *DCDC 2007–2036:* 3. See also NIC, *Global Trends 2025: A Transformed World* (2008).

39   Regionalism means "development of institutionalized cooperation among states and other actors on the basis of regional contiguity as a feature of the international system." Regionalization is defined as "growing interdependence between geographically contiguous states." Baylis, Smith and Owens, *The Globalization of World Politics*, 4th edition, p. 586.

40   Christopher Brook, "Regionalism and globalism"; John Ravenhill, "The growth of intergovernmental collaboration in the Asia-Pacific region"; and

With increasing interdependence, regionalization and globalization, regional cooperation is required even more to deal with various problems and challenges. East Asia experienced a financial and currency crisis in 1997-8, natural disasters, new influenza, infectious diseases, terrorism, and piracy. Such variety of problems, risks and challenges are enhancing regional multilateralism. In recent years, East Asian regionalism is developing from functional cooperation to institution building. Furthermore, the EAS aims to foster community building, that is, an EAC as a long-term goal.

According to the NIC report *Global Trends 2025*, "Greater Asian regionalism—possible by 2025—would have global implications, sparking or reinforcing a trend toward three trade and financial clusters that could become quasi-blocs: North America, Europe, and East Asia."[41]

ENERGY, RESOURCES, AND ENVIRONMENT[42]

Our life depends entirely on air, water, food, environment and the eco-system on planet Earth. The common environmentalist slogan "Save Our Planet" is nonsense because planet Earth does not need human beings; but we depend on it entirely! Our civilization, particularly modern industrial civilization based on anthropocentrism, not only heavily depends on energy and resources but also destroys the environment and eco-system, leading to phenomena such as climate changes and global warming in recent years. As the number of population and industrializing states is rapidly increasing,

---

Lawrence T. Woods, "Regional co-operation: the transnational dimension", all in McGrew and Brook, *Asia-Pacific in the New World Order*.

41 NIC, *Global Trends 2025*, p. xi.

42 According to *New Pocket Oxford Dictionary*, 9th edition (2001), "energy" is defined as "power derived from physical and chemical resources to provide light and heat or to work machines", originated from Greek *energeia;* "resources" means "a country's means of supporting itself, as represented in its minerals, land, and other assets", originated Old French dialect *resourdre* "rise again". According to McLean and McMillan (eds.), *Oxford Concise Dictionary of Politics*, "environment" is derived simply from the French verb *environner*, to surround. Our environment is our surroundings.

energy and resources, such as oil and gas, are being irreversibly consumed. It is widely acknowledged that competition for limited energy and resources is likely to intensify (although technological breakthroughs may mitigate the problem). With rapid economic growth, the environment and the availability of basic resources are rapidly worsening. The most visible case in recent years is China and potentially India.[43]

The DCDC Global Strategic Trends Programme 2007–2036 sees energy and resources as the top theme, as follows:

> Sustained population growth, aggressive economic competition and increased consumption, together with rapid modernization and urbanization, *will* result in intensive exploitation and pressure on resources of all kinds. These tendencies *will* be aggravated by the consequences of climate change, environmental changes and an increased human footprint. Consequently, the availability and flow of energy, food and water *will* be critical issues, with the potential for fluctuations and imbalances in both production and distribution, at global, regional and local levels. Resource challenges *will* intensify in those areas already badly affected, typically in low and lower-middle income regions where population expansion has the greatest impact relative to local resources and economic growth…. This is *likely* to lead to populism, human crises and confrontations, typified by inter-communal and inter-ethnic conflicts at local level, but, when related to access to strategic resources necessary to sustain developed or developing economies, *may* increase the incidence and risk of international confrontation.
>
> [Energy and resource competition:] Economic growth and increased consumption *will* result in greater demand and competition for essential resources. Demand for energy is *likely* to grow by more than half again by 2035 and fossil fuels *will* have to meet more than 80% of this increase. Major reserves are in politically unstable regions and primary consumer nations are

43   For environmental problems see, for example, John Vogler, "Environmental issues", in Baylis, Smith and Owens (eds.), *The Globalization of World Politics* (2008).

likely to be increasingly reluctant to trust security of supply to market forces and the integrity of the international system.

[Environmental Impacts:] By the end of the period, nearly two-thirds of the world's population *will* live in areas of water stress, while environmental degradation, the intensification of agriculture, and pace of urbanization *may* reduce the fertility of, and access to, arable land. There *will* be a constant heavy pressure on fish stocks, which are *likely* to require careful husbanding if major species are not to become depleted or extinct. Food and water insecurity *will* drive mass migration from some worst affected areas and the effects *may* be felt in more affluent regions through distribution problems, specialized agriculture and aggressive food-pricing.[44]

EAST ASIA TOWARD 2030: MILITARISTIC OR PACIFIC?

This research proposes not "prediction" but a wide range of "scenarios", both optimistic and pessimistic. Extreme alternatives of highly optimistic and pessimistic scenarios are less likely to happen; the future course will be somewhere in between. "Nothing in the future is guaranteed, of course, and Strategic Trends varies the strength of its assessments to highlight sets of Alternative Outcomes that, while less probable, are nonetheless highly plausible".[45] The aim of scenario building is not prediction with high plausibility, rather to open and prepare our mind-sets for a broader range of future possibilities. In Overholt's words, "Our vision of the future is not like a laser beam, which could pinpoint one exact outcome; rather, it is like a wide-angle flashlight illuminating a range of different possibilities."[46]

This section will examine a broad range of scenarios by changing the main drivers of East Asia.

44 *DCDC 2007–2036:* 6–8.
45 Ibid., p. xi.
46 Overholt, *Asia, America, and the Transformation of Geopolitics.* Most of these future scenarios of East Asia are proposed and critically examined by Overholt and others, including Shambaugh, *Power Shift* (2005); Shambaugh, "China Engages Asia: Reshaping the Regional Order", *International Security*, 29(3) (Winter (2004/2005): 64–99; Robyn Lim, *The Geopolitics of East Asia*, pp. 161–71.

SCENARIOS OF EAST ASIA TOWARD 2030

Polarity of Region	Order And Stability	Rivalry and Instability
Non-polarity	(1) Pacific East Asia	(2) Panic of Anarchy
Multipolarity	(3) Concert of East Asia	(4) Great Powers' Rivalry
Bipolarity	(5) US-Japan Liberal Pacific Union (6) US-China Condominium	(7) Cold War II
Unipolarity	(8) US Hegemony Die-hard (1990s) (9) Chinese Middle Kingdom	—

NON-POLAR STRUCTURE

(1) Pacific East Asia

- *Scenario*: This is an optimistic and progressive scenario from open and transparent regional cooperation to institution and community building in East Asia. ASEAN plays a leading role in regional multilateralism to foster an EAC as a normative regional order.[47] The region enjoys peace, prosperity and progress at all levels with equal partnership.

- *Assumptions*: This scenario is based on optimistic assumptions of major trends. These include: the great powers maintaining cooperation and the middle powers and other non-state actors playing more significant and constructive roles; peaceful and harmonious globalization, liberalization and economic interdependence; deepening and broadening open and transparent regional cooperation and integration; adequate energy, resource and environment to be sustainable. Historical mistrust and geo-political rivalry

---

47 For the vision of an EAC, see East Asian Vision Group (2001), *Toward an East Asian Community: region of peace, prosperity and progress*, East Asia Vision Group Report, <www.mofa.go.jp/region/asia-paci/report2001.pdf>.

are considerably mitigated or solved. The legacy problems of Korea and Taiwan are resolved with consensus of the parties concerned.

- *Proponents*: Liberal and normative scholars such as Amitav Acharya, Muthiah Alagappa, and Akihiko Tanaka.[48]

(2) Panic of Anarchy

- *Scenario*: This very pessimistic scenario is characterized by Hobbesian anarchy and disorder. The region confronts chaotic anarchy at all levels to confront all kinds of problems, risks and dangers: economic and political turmoil, arms race, WMD proliferation, military conflicts, fundamentalist terrorism, massive immigration, epidemics, environmental disasters. This scenario may include the possibilities of major wars among the great powers, nuclear wars and WMD weapon terrorism.[49]

- *Assumptions*: This scenario assumes extremely negative assumptions, including shocks and surprises. These include intensifying confrontation and military conflicts among the great and other powers; the collapse of harmonious globalization and liberalization; the collapse of regionalism and regionalization; severe shortage of energy and resources, and deteriorating environment and non-traditional security issues. With the clash of economic development, China and India severely suffer from internal problems, which negatively impacts on regional stability. States and non-state actors resort to military measures in this anarchy and chaos.

---

48 Muthiah Alagappa (ed.), *Asian Security Order* (2003); Amitav Acharya, "Will Asia's Past Be Its Future?" (2003/2004); Akihiko Tanaka, *Atarashii Cyusei (A New Middle Age)*.

49 The worst possibilities of nuclear wars are seriously debated by realists, including Hans Morgenthau, John Harts, Raymond Aron, George Kennan and Colin Gray. For contemporary assessment, see NIC, *Global Trends 2025*.

- *Proponents*: Realist scholars such as Robert Kaplan and John Gray.[50]

MULTIPOLAR STRUCTURE

(3) Concert of East Asia

- *Scenario*: This is an optimistic scenario based on the classical balance of power close to Kissinger's ideal type of the Concert of Europe in the nineteenth century. All great powers concerned are comparatively equal and manage to sustain regional stability and status quo via regular diplomatic consultation. This Concert of East Asia develops existing multiple multilateralism such as the Six Party Talks, EAS, ARF, and APEC to maintain the status quo-oriented regional order.

- *Assumptions*: This scenario assumes relatively positive strategic trends, such as: all great powers concerned develop security partnership and coordination; relatively peaceful and harmonious globalization and liberalization; widening and institutionalized regional cooperation; relatively manageable energy, resource and environment. In this scenario, "rivalry is not inherent, but rather the maintenance of stability is shared among several major nations or alliances of nations."[51] China, Japan, and the US are the main players, possibly together with resurgent Russia and emerging India. China's rise is cooperative to existing multilateralism. All powers concerned deal with key security issues such as the Korean Peninsula, the Taiwan Strait, and South and East China Sea by diplomatic measures of all great powers concerned.

- *Proponents*: Henry Kissinger and Douglas Stuart.[52]

---

50   Robert Kaplan, *Coming Anarchy*.
51   Shambaugh, *Power Shift*, pp. 14–15.
52   Stephen Van Evera, "A Farewell to Geopolitics", in Leffler and Legro (eds.), *To Lead the World* (2008); Amitav Acharya, "A Concert of Asia?", *Survival*, 41(3) (Autumn 1999): 84–101; Douglas T. Stuart, "Toward Concert in Asia", *Asian Survey*, 37(3) (March 1997). See also Henry

(4) Great Powers' Rivalry[53]

- *Scenario*: This relatively pessimistic scenario is featured by the Machiavellian zero-sum game of power politics. The regional geo-politics is dominated by intensifying rivalry, competition, and confrontation among the great powers concerned, posing risks and dangers of arms race and conflicts. The US-Japan alliance is weakened or ended and Japan becomes a comprehensive great power, possibly with nuclear weapons. Russia and India are fully developing economic and military power to engage in East Asian geo-politics centred on China.

- *Assumptions*: This scenario presumes a set of negative trends and assumptions, such as: the great powers' geo-political relations getting intensified; globalization going bankrupt or getting considerably strained; regional cooperation not proceeding well; energy, resource and environment being severely in shortage to sustain economic growth and prosperity for all.

- *Proponents*: Realists such as Aaron Friedberg, John Mearsheimer, Robert Kagan, Robyn Lim.[54]

BIPOLAR STRUCTURE

(5) US-Japan Liberal Pacific Union

- *Scenario*: Optimistically characterized by international liberalism: Kantian republican peace or Wilsonian internationalism. The region is dominated by stable liberal democracy and economy, and enjoys peace, prosperity and progress at all levels and in all areas.

- *Assumptions*: This scenario is based on the optimistic assumptions of major trends: peaceful and harmonious globalization; stable liberal economy and democratization;

Kissinger, *Diplomacy* (New York: Simon & Schuster, 1994).

53 See *DCDC 2007–2036*: 49.

54 See John Mearsheimer, *The Tragedy of Great Power Politics*; Robyn Lim, *The Geopolitics of East Asia*; Robert Kagan, "End of Dreams. Return of History", in Leffler and Legro (eds.), *To Lead the World* (2008).

great powers' cooperation; deepening regional cooperation and integration; and fully sustainable energy, resource and environment. The strong US-Japan Security Community is the basis of this liberal pacific union together with emerging India, liberalized and democratized Russia and China. The legacy problems of Korea and Taiwan are resolved with the parties concerned. This scenario is currently challenged by the global financial and economic crisis caused by the US economy and the intensifying tensions between the US and Japan.

- *Proponents*: Mainstream scholars in the US and Japan, including John Ikenberry, Mick Mochizuki, Seizaburo Sato, Akio Watanabe, Masashi Nishihara, Satoshi Morimoto.[55]

(6) US-China Strategic Condominium
- *Scenario*: This scenario is an East Asian region characterized by growing strategic coordination between the US and rising China. Most of the critical regional issues need close US-China coordination such as security, economy, trade, environment and energy, and most importantly North Korean nuclear/missile challenge and the Taiwan Strait.

- *Assumptions*: This scenario assumes rising Chinese economic,

---

55 John Ikenberry (2008), "Liberal Order Building", in Leffler and Legro (eds.), *To Lead the World* (2008); Akio Watanabe, "A Continuum of Change", *The Washington Quarterly*, 27(4) (Autumn 2004); Seizaburo Sato, "Asia-Pacific and Japan-US-China Relations"; Seizaburo Sato, "The U.S.-Japan Alliance under Changing International Relations", *The Washington Quarterly* (Summer 1990). For US-Japan relations in the Asia-Pacific region, see Ellis S. Krauss and T.J. Pempel (eds.), *Beyond Bilateralism: U.S.-Japan Relations in the New Asia-Pacific* (California: Stanford University Press, 2004); G. John Ikenberry and Takashi Inoguchi (eds.), *Reinventing the Alliance: U.S.-Japan Security Partnership in an Era of Change* (New York: Palgrave Macmillan, 2003); Nishihara Masashi (ed.), *The Japan-US Alliance: New Challenges for the 21st Century* (Tokyo: Japan Center for International Exchange, 2000)); Mike M Mochizuki (ed.), *Toward a True Alliance: Restructuring U.S.-Japan Security Relations* (Washington D.C.: Brokings Institution Press, 1997).

political and military power to match the US and drastic decline of Japanese power, influence and status in East Asia. The US and China come close to becoming strategic allies to leave Japan aside. Despite impressive current trends, many scholars conclude that this scenario is unlikely in the foreseeable future.

- *Proponents*: This scenario is contended by Robert Ross.[56]

(7) Renewed Cold War
- *Scenario*: This is a bipolar balance-of-power model, in which "two major competitive powers possess roughly equal distribution of power, thus offsetting each other and maintaining the balance." The scenario assumes increasing intense confrontation between the US and China. The rivalry may expand into politico-ideological strategic competition between liberal democracies and autocratic powers and rigid bipolar alliance system centred on the US (NATO, Japan, India) and China-Russia (SCO). The vicious circle prompts political confrontation, arms race, and security dilemma at both regional and global levels.[57]

- *Assumptions*: This scenario anticipates

an inevitable clash between the existing dominant power (the United States) and the rising power (China), owing to the asymmetric structural properties of the regional system … rising powers inevitably challenge dominant powers, and that this zero-sum competition for dominance…the period of "power transition" is particularly unstable and conflict-prone.

It is enhanced by the US tendency to confront rising powers and the Chinese inclination to regain national greatness. Increasing arms race and nationalism on both sides of the Taiwan Strait

---

56 Robert S. Ross, "The Geography of the Peace: East Asia in the Twenty-first Century", *International Security*, 23(4) (Spring 1999): 81–118.

57 Shambaugh, *Power Shift*, p. 13. Tow, *Security and Politics in the Asia-Pacific*.

and two Koreas can cause this dangerous confrontation between China and US-Japan.

- *Proponents*: John Mearsheimer.[58]

UNIPOLAR STRUCTURE

(8) American Hegemony Die-hard
- *Scenario*: This is a continuation of US primacy based on American military superiority supported by technological advance, the revolution in military affairs, and the hub-and-spoke alliance system centred on the strengthened US alliance with Japan.

- *Assumptions*: This scenario assumes continuity of US leadership and influence supported by both hard and soft power. The US keeps benefiting from the advantages of globalization and politico-economic liberalization, open Asia-Pacific regionalism, and sufficiently abundant energy and resources.

- *Proponents*: Both realist and liberal scholars such as Bruce Cumings, Michael Mastanduno, Jonathan D. Pollack.[59]

(9) Return to the Chinese Middle Kingdom and Tributary System[60]
- *Scenario*: China is dominating East Asia to establish its hierarchical regional order similar to the pre-modern "Chinese Middle Kingdom" and its tributary system. This is a hegemonic system, either coercive (badao) or benign (wangdao). Other nations are subsumed by a domineering China or "bandwagon" with China. China as the major

---

58 John Mearsheimer, *The Tragedy of Great Power Politics* (New York: W.W. Norton, 2001).

59 Bruce Cumings, "On the History and Practice of Unilateralism in East Asia", in Sisodia and Krishnappa (eds.), *Global Power Shift* (2009); Michael Mastanduno, "Incomplete Hegemony: The United States and security order in Asia" (2003); Jonathan Pollack, "US Strategies in Northeast Asia: A Revisionist Hegemon", in Kim and Jones (eds.), *Power and Security in Northeast Asia* (2008).

60 *DCDC 2007–2036:* 50.

power in the region is at the apex of the regional hierarchical pyramid, thus the revival of the ancient tribute system.

- *Assumptions*: For this to happen, China continues its economic growth and its growing comprehensive power overwhelms all other Asia including Japan. US military presence and influence needs to be excluded from East Asia. Unless the Japan-US alliance is considerably weakened or collapses, this scenario is unlikely in the foreseeable future.

- *Proponents*: David Kang, David Shambaugh, Martin Jacques.[61]

Strategic Risks and Challenges in East Asia toward 2030[62]

Since history often deceives our common sense, this scenario building cannot neglect possibilities of unexpected shocks and surprises. Contingent strategic shocks and surprises mean that "the world might develop in ways that are radically and intuitively different from outcomes derived from linear analysis." The future course of East Asia may largely be influenced by strategic risks and challenges, some of which are given below.

FUTURE OF CHINA[63]

The future of China is quite important for East Asia as a whole. On the one hand, China has been facing increasingly serious internal problems in recent years. Rapid economic development brings not only prosperity but also massive problems such as large and growing disparities

---

61 Shambaugh, *Power Shift*, pp. 12–13. David Kang, "Getting Asia wrong: the need for new analytical frameworks", *International Security*, 27(4) (2003): 57–85; David Kang, "Hierarchy and stability in Asian international relations", in Ikenberry and Mastanduno (eds.), *International Relations Theory and the Asia-Pacific* (2003). See also Martin Jacques, *When China Rules the World: The Rise of the Middle Kingdom and the End of the Western World* (London: Allen Lane and Penguin, 2009).

62 NIDS, *East Asian Strategic Review 2008*; Douglas H. Paal, Asia Shaping the Future, Policy Brief No. 62, June 2008, at <http://www.carnegieendowment.org/files/pb62_paal_final.pdf>; Gerald Segal, "The Asia-Pacific: what kind of challenge?", in McGrew and Brook (eds.), *Asia-Pacific in the New World Order*.

63 *DCDC 2007–2036*: 81, 84.

in development, growing labour unrest, and environmental problems. The current government needs to deal with a weak social safety net, an ageing community, systemic corruption, a weak banking and financial system, lingering ethnic disputes, and vulnerability to epidemic diseases. The Chinese Communist Party regards liberal democratic movements as illegitimate internal political disturbance and illegitimate interference of foreign countries. Beijing has been finding difficulty in dealing with mass political movements caused by increasing political, economic and social problems in recent years. The future of China's "harmonious society" is of importance to East Asia and Japan.[64]

On the other hand, the rise of China, especially China's modernizing military power and underdeveloped transparency, are serious concerns for most of the East Asian neighbours. With China's defence budget rapidly growing in the last two decades, the current military modernization and developing power projection capability may cause an arms race and security dilemma. As China's defence expenditure and military build-up are not transparent, Japan and the US demand from China considerable progress in the confidence-building measures (CBMs).[65]

---

64   Kondo, "Japan and the East Asian Security" (2009), p. 97. For the domestic instability of China see Susan l. Shirk, *China: Fragile Superpower* (New York: Oxford University Press, 2007). For insightful analyses of China's future in Asian security, see Joseph S. Nye Jr., "China's Re-emergence and the Future of the Asia-Pacific", in Guoli Liu (ed.), *Chinese Foreign Policy in Transition* (New York: Aldine de Gruyter, 2004); Seizaburo Sato, "Asia-Pacific and Japan-US-China relations", at <http://nippon.zaidan.info/seikabutsu/1996/00186/mokuji.htm>.

65   For the rise of China and East Asian security see, for example, NIDS, *China's Rise and its Limitations: China at the Crossroads* (Tokyo: National Institute for Defense Studies, 2007); David Shambaugh (ed.), *Power Shift: China and Asia's New Dynamics* (Berkeley: University of California Press, 2005); Guoli Liu (ed.), *Chinese Foreign Policy in Transition* (New York: Aldine de Gruyter, 2004); Kokubun Ryosei and Wang Jisi (eds.), *The Rise of China and a Changing East Asian Order* (Tokyo: Japan Center for International Exchange, 2004); Avery Goldstein, "Balance-of-Power Politics: Consequences for Asian Security Order", in Muthiah Alagappa (ed.), *Asian Security Order* (2003); Robert Gilpin, *War and Change in World Politics* (1999).

JAPAN-US RELATIONS

The Japan-US alliance has been the cornerstone of stable Japan-US bilateral relations and East Asia-Pacific region as a whole. With changing international, bilateral, and domestic circumstances, the future of Japan-US relations remains uncertain. If the alliance is considerably weakened or collapses, international relations in East Asia face drastic and unpredictable changes.

RESURGENT NATIONALISM AND POLITICAL INSTABILITY

Resurgent nationalism is a cause of concern in East Asia. Prime Minister Junichiro Koizumi's visit to the Yasukuni Shrine caused fierce anti-Japanese protest movements and incidents in China. Tokyo's relationship with Beijing got severely strained by the problem of history. With increasing domestic instability and discontent from various grievances, Chinese policy emphasizes the greatness of Chinese civilization to strengthen nationalism. The East Asian nations need to overcome excessive nationalism to enhance any durable reconciliation, mutual understanding and trust.[66]

Political stability is important for regional security, stability and prosperity. With the "Third Wave" of democratization, many East Asian countries peacefully soft-landed to liberal democracy, such as South Korea and Taiwan. However, democratization is not always smooth, for example as in Indonesia. North Korea and Myanmar maintain authoritarian and oppressive political regimes under which human rights, individual liberty and freedom are severely constrained.

TERRITORIAL AND SOVEREIGNTY DISPUTES

Despite its remarkable resurgence, East Asia contains uncertainties, instability, and some serious military flash points such as the Korean Peninsula, the Taiwan Strait, and the South and East

---

66 Arpita Mathur, "Japanese Nationalism: Implications for Asian Security" and Abanti Bhattacharya, "In Defence of Identity: Chinese Nationalism and Asian Security", both in Sisodia and Krishnappa (eds.), *Global Power Shifts and Strategic Transition in Asia* (2009); Takako Hirose, "Japanese Emerging Nationalism and its New Asia Policy", in Raghavan (ed.), *Asian Security Dynamic: US, Japan and the Rising Powers* (2008).

China Seas. East Asian countries have yet to resolve historical mistrust and territorial disputes. According to Michael Oksenberg, since the early 1900s, major powers have geo-strategic interests in a number of locales in North-East Asia such as the Pacific islands, Taiwan, the Indochina peninsula and the South China Sea, the Strait of Malacca, the Himalayas and Tibet, Central Asia and Xinjiang, Mongolia, Siberia, Manchuria, the Sea of Okhotsk and its surrounding territory, Korea. "Most of the wars involving the major powers have arisen over their competition for influence and control of these locals."[67] Zbigniew Brzezinski points out that disputes and potential conflict zones remain unresolved in East Asia as follows:

- The division of Korea and the inherent instability of North Korea—made all the more dangerous by North Korea's quest for nuclear capability—pose the risk that a sudden explosion could engulf the peninsula in warfare, which in turn would engage the United States and indirectly involve Japan.

- China's resentment of Taiwan's separate status is intensifying as China gains in strength and as the increasingly prosperous Taiwan begins to flirt with a formally separate status as a nation-state.

- The Paracel and Spratly Islands in the South China Sea pose the risk of a collision between China and several Southeast Asian states over access to potentially valuable seabed energy sources, with China imperially viewing the South China Sea as its legitimate national patrimony.

- The Senkaku Islands are contested by both Japan and China (with the rivals Taiwan and mainland China ferociously of a single mind on this issue), and the historical rivalry for regional preeminence between Japan and China infuses this issue with symbolic significance as well.

---

67 Michael Oksenberg, "China: A Tortuous Path onto the World's Stage", in Pastor (ed.), *A Century's Journey* (New York: Basic Books, 1999), p. 297.

- The issue of the southernmost Kuril Islands, unilaterally seized in 1945 by the Soviet Union, continues to paralyze and poison Russo-Japanese relations.

- Other latent territorial-ethnic conflicts involve Russo-Chinese-Vietnamese, Japanese-Korean, and Chinese-Indian border issues; ethnic unrest in Xinjiang Province; and Chinese-Indonesian disputes over oceanic boundaries.[68]

Above all, the legacy problems of the Korean Peninsula and the Taiwan Strait remain the most serious source of conflicts. The North Korean nuclear and missile problem poses security threats to the Japanese and other East Asian neighbours. The on-going rounds of China-chaired Six-Party Talks have borne little fruit in disarming North Korea. The abduction of Japanese citizens by North Korea needs to be properly addressed to establish a normal relationship between the two countries. With the increase of anti-American sentiment in South Korea, the future of the Korean Peninsula poses grave challenges to East Asia and Japan. Taiwan Strait remains a grave challenge to East Asian security. Chinese military modernization with its economic growth enhances the arms race and security dilemma between China and Taiwan backed by the US and Japan.[69]

ARMS RACE

With rapid economic growth and resurgent nationalism and rivalry, East Asian nations head toward a slow but steady arms race. Arms race and competition, disputes and conflicts are inseparably interrelated. The arms race will intensify with further nuclear and other WMD weapons proliferation and their delivery systems, ballistic missiles, and development of other power projection capability. The area includes traditional sea, land and air power, and the new frontier area of space.

---

68 Brzezinski, *The Grand Chessboard* (1997), pp. 154–55.

69 For security challenges of Taiwan and Korea, see Kondo, "Japan and East Asian Security" (2009); Nobukatsu Kanehara and James J. Przystup, "Amerika no ajia taiheiyou senryaku to nichibei doumei (American Asia-Pacific Strategy and Japan-US Alliance)", *Gaiko Forum*, No.198 (January 2005); David Kang, "Acute Conflicts in Asia after the Cold War: Kahmir, Taiwan, and Korea", in Muthiah Alagappa (ed.), *Asian Security Order* (2003).

MULTILATERAL SECURITY COOPERATION

Asian multilateral security cooperation has been unable to make notable progress in regional security measures. The Six-Party Talks are stagnating. The ARF is unable to make progress in CBMs and preventive diplomacy because of China's reluctance. ASEAN needs to overcome differences on issues such as human rights and liberal democracy.[70]

NON-TRADITIONAL SECURITY AGENDAS

In recent years, East Asia and the Pacific region face emerging security challenges: international terrorism and piracy, maritime security, energy and resources, environment problems including natural disasters and climate change, illicit drugs, human trafficking and pandemic influenza, AIDS and other infectious diseases. These common regional security agendas, namely "non-traditional" security agendas need adequate regional cooperation and states' policy with multilateral cooperation.[71]

ECONOMIC AND FINANCIAL INSTABILITY

Contemporary East Asia needs to deal with economic and financial instability. The East Asian economies experienced the Asian financial crisis of 1997 and suffer from the global financial and economic crisis in 2008. China is leading economic development in Asia-Pacific and the world, but needs to cope with intensifying internal problems. In East Asia, the level of economic development is quite diverse, with

---

70   Takeshi Yuzawa, "Asian Security Institutions in Great Power Dynamics: Adjuncts to Balance of Power of Forces for Regional Security?", in Raghavan (ed.), *Asian Security Dynamic: US, Japan and the Rising Powers* (2008). For the limit of multilateral security cooperation, see Seizaburo Sato, "Why the shift from kokubo (national defense) to anzen hosho (security)? A study of the basic issues surrounding Japan's security", *Asia-Pacific Review*, 7(2) (2000); John Mearsheimer, "The False Promise of International Institutions".

71   Ministry of Foreign Affairs, Japan, *Diplomatic Bluebook 2009*, p. 14; P.K. Gautam, "Cooperative Framework for Asian Security in the Twenty-first Century: Climate Change and Environment", in Sisodia and Krishnappa (eds.), *Global Power Shifts and Strategic Transition in Asia* (2009); Suchit Bunbongkarn, "Non-Traditional Security Challenges in East Asia", in Sisodia and Naidu (eds.), *Changing Security Dynamic in Eastern Asia* (2005).

advanced economies of Japan, Singapore and South Korea and almost bankrupt North Korea and Myanmar. With widening and deepening globalization and economic interdependence, the regional economy and finance remains fragile to shocks and instability.[72]

CONCLUSION

- *This research aimed to develop a broad range of East Asian scenarios and challenges toward 2030 by identifying the major trends of the region.* Throughout the twentieth century, geo-politics among the great powers was salient and the East Asian regional order was in flux. Since the end of the Cold War, East Asia has enjoyed remarkable economic development in a relatively peaceful security environment.

- This research identified key drivers in East Asia toward 2030 as follows:

  (1) great powers' geo-politics;

  (2) globalization and politico-economic liberalization;

  (3) regionalism and regionalization; and

  (4) energy, resources, and environment.

- Key findings of this research are a broad range of East Asian scenarios as follows:

  (1) PacificEast Asia: East Asia enjoys peace and prosperity with open and equal regional cooperation, institution and community building.

  (2) Concert of Europe: East Asia maintains relative stability, with Kissinger's "classical balance of power" among the great powers.

  (3) Great Powers' Rivalry: East Asia is in peril of instability

---

72 Joseph Stiglitz, "Crises Today and the Future of Capitalism", The 10th D.T. Lakdawala Memorial Lecture, 20 December 2008 (New Delhi: Institute of Social Science); Ashley Tellis, Andrew Marble and Travis Tanner (eds.), *Strategic Asia 2009-10: Economic Meltdown and Geopolitical Stability*, at <http://www.carnegieendowment.org/files/SA09-10_Overview.pdf>; Ming Wan, "Economic Interdependence and Economic Cooperation: Mitigating Conflict and Transforming Security Order in Asia", in Muthiah Alagappa (ed.), *Asian Security Order* (2003).

characterized by Mearsheimer's "tragedy of great powers' politics", rivalry and conflict.

(4) Panic of Anarchy: East Asia declines to a vicious circle of Hobbesian world of insecurity, mistrust, dangers, and conflicts at all levels.

(5) US-Japan Liberal Pacific Union: East Asia maintains stability centred on the US-Japan security community.

(6) US-China Strategic Condominium: East Asia is largely shaped by the US-China strategic condominium as a G-2 partnership.

(7) Renewed Cold War: East Asia faces an intense rivalry between the US and China with resurgent nationalism, deadly arms race and competition.

(8) American Hegemony Die-Hard (1990s): US military primacy continues to be dominant in East Asia with its hub-and-spoke alliance system.

(9) Chinese Middle Kingdom and its Tributary System: East Asia sees the revival of China-centric hierarchical regional order.

- Major strategic risks and challenges in East Asia toward 2030 will be as follows:

  (1) Future of China

  (2) Future of Japan-US relations

  (3) Resurgent nationalism and political instability

  (10) Territorial and sovereign disputes (two Koreas and China-Taiwan)

  (11) Arms race (including WMD, nuclear and missile proliferation)

  (12) Underdeveloped multilateral security system

  (13) Non-traditional security agendas (including terrorism, cyber-terrorism, epidemics, energy, resource and environmental security)

  (14) Financial and economic instability.

Panorama
—Ajey Lele and Namrata Goswami

Featuring feudal and federal systems, communism and capitalism, authoritarianism, republicanism and democracy, Asia is a kaleidoscope of ideas, faiths and systems. Though like any other society in the world, Asian societies are also imperfect and abound in contradictions, the continent has been energized by dynamism in the last couple of decades. Asia houses over 60 per cent of the world's population and has shown remarkable economic progress over the last several decades. While facing new problems like climate change and environmental degradation and battling earlier problems like poverty, disease and poor livelihood, states in this region are learning from history and espouse a strong desire to better themselves than societies of the past.

Every state in the region has its unique geographic and economic circumstances. Some have witnessed sustained economic growth for many years while some others are almost bankrupt, depending mostly on outside help for economic survival. The region has witnessed some of the bloodiest conflicts in the recent past; some areas in the region are also experiencing constant threat from terrorism. Out of the nine nuclear weapon states in the world, the region has five, and four of them (India, Pakistan, Israel and North Korea) are outside the realm of the global nuclear weapons treaty mechanism.

Asia understands that its future depends on Asians. In this era of globalization and greater connectivity, however, no country can keep itself isolated; it can prosper if it makes itself relevant to the rest of the world; it needs the support of outside powers and have access to more developed market systems. Also, given the fragile internal governance mechanisms of most Asian countries, there is an urgent necessity for them to study various successful as well as unsuccessful western models in fields ranging from governance, economy, education, technology advancement, infrastructure development to poverty eradication to draw lessons for themselves.

Asia's future would also depend entirely on how it makes itself relevant in the larger global geopolitical architecture. Chapters in this book have looked at a range of issues generic to the Asian region, and have provided alternative futures on issues critically important to various regions. The attempt has been to analyse and offer certain future possibilities on issues most important to Asia's growth like climate, great-power politics, economy, water resources, regional issues, etc.

The scenarios developed in some of the chapters could be viewed as new visions of possible futures. They also identify the uncertainties these regions are expected to encounter in 2030. No single scenario depicted in this work may, however, be entirely accurate; none of them should also be perceived as the only possible future. Many more alternative scenarios could be developed on Asia's future depending on where an expert's vantage point is. The core issues discussed here are the various security implications of the critical challenges the region is facing. Issues having the potential for future conflicts have been identified and prognosticated.

There are many indices like human security, internal security, food security, environmental security, etc., on the basis of which a state's capacity is critiqued on delivering governance to the people. Various challenges this region is facing or is likely to face both in the near or distant futures are of such vast magnitude that they require comprehensive understanding of regional specificities. This book attempts to peep into the future with an aim that it would allow states to be more aware of the challenges ahead. This may also give them leads to develop an agenda for policy response. There is a need for the world community to undertake a proactive strategy aimed at restoring long-term security. An effort of the kind made in this book allows them to see the possibilities for tomorrow.

As explained in the introductory chapter, this work revolves mainly around two basic themes. One discusses country-specific problems; the other takes itself beyond regional boundaries and discusses issues related to militaries and technology. It may be noted that the twenty-first century is dominated by dual-use technologies, which need to be viewed against the larger strategic relevance than narrow military relevance.

Asia has to chalk out a future for itself based on two competing paradigms of international politics: cooperation and conflict. Most western discourses of international politics warn of a possible flashpoint in four areas of Asia: India–Pakistan nuclear flashpoint; the Indian Ocean Region; a possible nuclear flashpoint in West Asia between Israel and Iran if the latter goes nuclear; and finally, a nuclear peninsula in East Asia if Japan goes nuclear in the face of a more belligerent North Korean nuclear threat. While cooperation through multilateral institutions seems to be the most viable way out of interstate conflict in the twenty-first century, competition over resources like oil and gas and the desire to dominate the sea lines of communication (SLOCs) for purposes of military movement and trade in the Malacca Straits could result in potential conflict between China and India, the rising giants of Asia.[1] The internal problems in these two countries could also precipitate a crisis of a regional and later, global dimension, given the rather strong inter-connectedness of various countries in today's globalized world. China's authoritarian system must be seen by 2030 as reaching out to its minorities and the provinces if it realistically wants to keep internal dissent down to manageable levels. Political reform is an urgent necessity in China if the growing political aspirations of its people have to be met by 2030. India too has to tackle internal conflicts such as Naxalism and insurgencies in its peripheral states, poverty, etc, with better development, infrastructure and law enforcement.

---

1   Robert D. Kaplan, "Centre Stage for the 21st Century", *Foreign Affairs*, March-April 2009, at <http://www.foreignaffairs.com/articles/64832/robert-d-kaplan/center-stage-for-the-21st-century>, accessed 24 December 2009.

While Europe's violent past need not be Asia's future given the difference in the culture of both continents, differences between countries should be tackled at an institutional level and age-old conflicts like that between India and Pakistan should be resolved through the mechanism of dialogue. Also, Asia should take lessons from its historical experiences of prosperity before the advent of colonialism and chalk out for itself a path based on the nature and health of its people. Regional institutions like the Association of South East Asian Nations (ASEAN), South Asian Association for Regional Cooperation (SAARC) and summits like the East Asia Summit could serve a great purpose by enabling countries to come together on a common platform and work towards greater regional cooperation on issues of grave security concern. India's or China's fear of being dominated by the US in the Indian Ocean Region, especially with regard to the Malacca Straits, can be resolved with the formation of an Indian Ocean Region Management Association (IORMA) in which all states of the Indian Ocean region besides China and India should be members, with the US having an observer status. This will greatly help deflect conflicts of the future.

While interstate conflict over resources is the inevitable implication of the realist school of international relations – since, according to this school, states are mostly dictated by the desire for power maximization and selfish national interests – the benefits from cooperation at the systemic level must also be kept in stark focus, especially by the rapidly rising powers of Asia like India and China. The international system as it exists today is open and flexible and has made possible the integration into the global economic network of countries like China despite its inherent authoritarian political structures. While the world has benefited immensely from the Chinese manufacturing industry, China has also benefited no less from being able to trade globally. China's and India's rising status in the forum of the United Nations and in other arrangements like G-20 gives them enough space to put forward their views and offer an alternative viewpoint on world affairs, as was obvious in the UN-sponsored Climate Change summit in Copenhagen in December 2009.

The US has an important role to play as well in ensuring that its behaviour in East Asia takes into account Chinese sensitivities. The rise of China and India is also unique because for the first time in modern world history, there is an apparent transfer of power from West to East without war at the systemic level. This unique phenomenon has mostly been helped by China's and India's own civilizational wisdom and cultural ethos. For centuries the two countries inhabited parallel spaces without breaking out into destructive conflicts. The rise of Asia perhaps foretells a century of hope for humankind after the episodes of devastation in the twentieth century. In a thought-provoking essay in *Foreign Affairs,* Dominique Mousi argues that the US and Europe are dominated by a culture of fear. For Europe the anxieties are about loss of identity, demographic challenges within from the poor South, fundamentalist Islam, economic decline and a Muslim-majority population given the high flow of Muslim population into Europe. "For many Europeans, globalization has come to be equated with destabilization and job cuts. They are haunted by the fear that Europe will become a museum – a larger and more modern version of Venice, a place for tourists and retirees, no longer a center of creativity and influence".[2] For the US, it is an obsession with terrorism after the terrorist attacks of 11 September 2001 on the US home territory. This national security obsession is mostly because the Americans' belief that their homeland was exceptional and could never be vulnerable internally was shattered by 9/11. The US obsession to avert any future terrorist attack categorizes it in the "culture of fear". The Middle East suffers from a "culture of humiliation" based on the creation of the state of Israel, and the winners of the globalization game like the West and East Asia add to the feeling of humiliation. This feeling extends itself to the Muslim diaspora in the West as well.

Significantly, besides the Middle East or West Asia where there is a certain *us versus them* dichotomy ongoing, the rest of Asia is

---

2   Dominique Mousi, "The Clash of Emotions", *Foreign Affairs,* January/ February 2007, at <http://www.foreignaffairs.com/articles/62267/dominique-mo%C3%83%C2%AFsi/the-clash-of-emotions>, accessed 24 December 2009.

categorized by the author as enjoying a "culture of hope".[3] This hope springs from the fact that the structures of progress are shifting east. Both China and India are progressive and brim with confidence to take up more responsibilities at the global level. As regards India:

Cooperating diplomatically with the United States and making economic deals in Europe, the emerging Indian elites are displaying even more pride and optimism than their Chinese counterparts. The world's largest democracy will soon emerge as the most populous country, and it seems to know no limits.[4]

With this buoyant rise of Asia, which is a collective rise with several countries in the region showing growth and enormous confidence, in 2030, the international system will look fundamentally different from the one that was set up after 1945. It is, however, in the larger interest of humankind and its survival that leaders the world over learn from history and devise a future mechanism which not only ensures continued progress and human upliftment but renders interstate wars irrelevant and archaic. In that, Asia has a huge role, given the wisdom of its people and the mature civilizational behaviour of its statesmen for centuries in the game of survival.

---

3   Ibid.
4   Ibid.